50% OFF CSET Multiple Subjects Test Prep Course!

Dear Customer,

We consider it an honor and a privilege that you chose our CSET Multiple Subjects Study Guide. As a way of showing our appreciation and to help us better serve you, we have partnered with Mometrix Test Preparation to offer you **50% off their online CSET Multiple Subjects Prep Course.** Many CSET courses are needlessly expensive and don't deliver enough value. With their course, you get access to the best CSET prep material, and you only pay half price.

Mometrix has structured their online course to perfectly complement your printed study guide. The CSET Multiple Subjects Prep Course contains **in-depth lessons** that cover all the most important topics, over **1,000 practice questions** to ensure you feel prepared, more than **1400 flashcards** for studying on the go, and over **410 instructional videos**.

Online CSET Multiple Subjects Prep Course

Topics Covered:

Reading, Language, and Literature
- Foundations of Grammar
- Style and Form

History and Social Science
- United States History
- U.S. Government and Citizenship

Science
- Physical, Earth, and Space Sciences

Mathematics
- Algebra and Functions
- Measurement and Geometry

Physical Education and Human Development
- Health, Wellness, and Fitness

Visual and Performing Arts
- Elements and Appreciation of Art

And More!

Course Features:

CSET Multiple Subjects Study Guide
- Get access to content from the best reviewed study guide available.

Track Your Progress
- Their customized course allows you to check off content you have studied or feel confident with.

6 Full-Length Practice Tests
- With 1,000+ practice questions and lesson reviews, you can test yourself again and again to build confidence.

CSET Multiple Subjects Flashcards
- Their course includes a flashcard mode consisting of over 1400 content cards to help you study.

To receive this discount, visit them at www.mometrix.com/university/csetms/ or simply scan this QR code with your smartphone. At the checkout page, enter the discount code: **APEXCSETMS50**

If you have any questions or concerns, please contact them at universityhelp@mometrix.com.

Sincerely,

FREE

Free Study Tips Videos/DVD

In addition to this guide, we have created a FREE set of videos with helpful study tips. **These FREE videos provide you with top-notch tips to conquer your exam and reach your goals.**

Our simple request is that you give us feedback about the book in exchange for these strategy-packed videos. We would love to hear what you thought about the book, whether positive, negative, or neutral. It is our #1 goal to provide you with quality products and customer service.

To receive your **FREE Study Tips Videos**, scan the QR code or email freevideos@apexprep.com. Please put "FREE Videos" in the subject line and include the following in the email:

  a. The title of the book

  b. Your rating of the book on a scale of 1-5, with 5 being the highest score

  c. Any thoughts or feedback about the book

Thank you!

CSET Multiple Subject Test Prep

3 Practice Exams and Study Guide for
California Teachers [2nd Edition]

J. M. Lefort

Table of Contents

Welcome

Dear Customer,

Congratulations on taking the next step in your educational journey, and thank you for choosing APEX to help you prepare! We are delighted to be by your side, equipping you with the knowledge and skills needed to make this move forward. Your APEX study guide contains helpful tips and quality study material that will contribute to your success. This study guide has been tailored to assist you in passing your chosen exam, but it also includes strategies to conquer any test with ease. Whether your goal is personal growth or acing that big exam to move up in your career, our goal is to leave you with the confidence and ability to reach the top!

We love to hear success stories, so please let us know how you do on your exam. Since we are continually making improvements to our products, we welcome feedback of any sort. Your achievements as well as criticisms can be emailed to info@apexprep.com.

Sincerely,
APEX Team

FREE Videos/DVD OFFER

Achieving a high score on your exam depends on both understanding the content and applying your knowledge. **Because your success is our primary goal, we offer FREE Study Tips Videos, which provide top-notch test taking strategies to help optimize your testing experience.**

Our simple request is that you email us feedback about our book in exchange for the strategy-packed videos.

To receive your **FREE Study Tips Videos**, scan the QR code or email freevideos@apexprep.com. Please put "FREE Videos" in the subject line and include the following in the email:

    a. The title of the book
    b. Your rating of the book on a scale of 1-5, with 5 being the highest score
    c. Any thoughts or feedback about the book

Thank you!

Test Taking Strategies

1. Reading the Whole Question

A popular assumption in Western culture is the idea that we don't have enough time for anything. We speed while driving to work, we want to read an assignment for class as quickly as possible, or we want the line in the supermarket to dwindle faster. However, speeding through such events robs us from being able to thoroughly appreciate and understand what's happening around us. While taking a timed test, the feeling one might have while reading a question is to find the correct answer as quickly as possible. Although pace is important, don't let it deter you from reading the whole question. Test writers know how to subtly change a test question toward the end in various ways, such as adding a negative or changing focus. If the question has a passage, carefully read the whole passage as well before moving on to the questions. This will help you process the information in the passage rather than worrying about the questions you've just read and where to find them. A thorough understanding of the passage or question is an important way for test takers to be able to succeed on an exam.

2. Examining Every Answer Choice

Let's say we're at the market buying apples. The first apple we see on top of the heap may *look* like the best apple, but if we turn it over we can see bruising on the skin. We must examine several apples before deciding which apple is the best. Finding the correct answer choice is like finding the best apple. Although it's tempting to choose an answer that seems correct at first without reading the others, it's important to read each answer choice thoroughly before making a final decision on the answer. The aim of a test writer might be to get as close as possible to the correct answer, so watch out for subtle words that may indicate an answer is incorrect. Once the correct answer choice is selected, read the question again and the answer in response to make sure all your bases are covered.

3. Eliminating Wrong Answer Choices

Sometimes we become paralyzed when we are confronted with too many choices. Which frozen yogurt flavor is the tastiest? Which pair of shoes look the best with this outfit? What type of car will fill my needs as a consumer? If you are unsure of which answer would be the best to choose, it may help to use process of elimination. We use "filtering" all the time on sites such as eBay® or Craigslist® to eliminate the ads that are not right for us. We can do the same thing on an exam. Process of elimination is crossing out the answer choices we know for sure are wrong and leaving the ones that might be correct. It may help to cover up the incorrect answer choice. Covering incorrect choices is a psychological act that alleviates stress due to the brain being exposed to a smaller amount of information. Choosing between two answer choices is much easier than choosing between all of them, and you have a better chance of selecting the correct answer if you have less to focus on.

4. Sticking to the World of the Question

When we are attempting to answer questions, our minds will often wander away from the question and what it is asking. We begin to see answer choices that are true in the real world instead of true in the world of the question. It may be helpful to think of each test question as its own little world. This world may be different from ours. This world may know as a truth that the chicken came before the egg or may assert that two plus two equals five. Remember that, no matter what hypothetical nonsense may be in the question, assume it to be true. If the question states that the chicken came before the egg, then choose your answer based on that truth. Sticking to the world of the question means placing all of our biases and assumptions aside and relying on the question to guide us to the correct answer. If we are simply looking for answers that are correct based on our own judgment, then we may choose incorrectly. Remember an answer that is true does not necessarily answer the question.

5. Key Words

If you come across a complex test question that you have to read over and over again, try pulling out some key words from the question in order to understand what exactly it is asking. Key words may be words that surround the question, such as *main idea, analogous, parallel, resembles, structured,* or *defines.* The question may be asking for the main idea, or it may be asking you to define something. Deconstructing the sentence may also be helpful in making the question simpler before trying to answer it. This means taking the sentence apart and obtaining meaning in pieces, or separating the question from the foundation of the question. For example, let's look at this question:

> Given the author's description of the content of paleontology in the first paragraph, which of the following is most parallel to what it taught?

The question asks which one of the answers most *parallels* the following information: The *description* of paleontology in the first paragraph. The first step would be to see *how* paleontology is described in the first paragraph. Then, we would find an answer choice that parallels that description. The question seems complex at first, but after we deconstruct it, the answer becomes much more attainable.

6. Subtle Negatives

Negative words in question stems will be words such as *not, but, neither,* or *except.* Test writers often use these words in order to trick unsuspecting test takers into selecting the wrong answer—or, at least, to test their reading comprehension of the question. Many exams will feature the negative words in all caps (*which of the following is NOT an example*), but some questions will add the negative word seamlessly into the sentence. The following is an example of a subtle negative used in a question stem:

> According to the passage, which of the following is *not* considered to be an example of paleontology?

If we rush through the exam, we might skip that tiny word, *not,* inside the question, and choose an answer that is opposite of the correct choice. Again, it's important to read the question fully, and double check for any words that may negate the statement in any way.

7. Spotting the Hedges

The word "hedging" refers to language that remains vague or avoids absolute terminology. Absolute terminology consists of words like *always, never, all, every, just, only, none,* and *must.* Hedging refers to words like *seem, tend, might, most, some, sometimes, perhaps, possibly, probability,* and *often.* In some cases, we want to choose answer choices that use hedging and avoid answer choices that use absolute terminology. It's important to pay attention to what subject you are on and adjust your response accordingly.

8. Restating to Understand

Every now and then we come across questions that we don't understand. The language may be too complex, or the question is structured in a way that is meant to confuse the test taker. When you come across a question like this, it may be worth your time to rewrite or restate the question in your own words in order to understand it better. For example, let's look at the following complicated question:

> Which of the following words, if substituted for the word *parochial* in the first paragraph, would LEAST change the meaning of the sentence?

Let's restate the question in order to understand it better. We know that they want the word *parochial* replaced. We also know that this new word would "least" or "not" change the meaning of the sentence. Now let's try the sentence again:

Which word could we replace with *parochial,* and it would not change the meaning?

Restating it this way, we see that the question is asking for a synonym. Now, let's restate the question so we can answer it better:

Which word is a synonym for the word *parochial?*

Before we even look at the answer choices, we have a simpler, restated version of a complicated question.

9. Predicting the Answer

After you read the question, try predicting the answer *before* reading the answer choices. By formulating an answer in your mind, you will be less likely to be distracted by any wrong answer choices. Using predictions will also help you feel more confident in the answer choice you select. Once you've chosen your answer, go back and reread the question and answer choices to make sure you have the best fit. If you have no idea what the answer may be for a particular question, forego using this strategy.

10. Avoiding Patterns

One popular myth in grade school relating to standardized testing is that test writers will often put multiple-choice answers in patterns. A runoff example of this kind of thinking is that the most common answer choice is "C," with "B" following close behind. Or, some will advocate certain made-up word patterns that simply do not exist. Test writers do not arrange their correct answer choices in any kind of pattern; their choices are randomized. There may even be times where the correct answer choice will be the same letter for two or three questions in a row, but we have no way of knowing when or if this might happen. Instead of trying to figure out what choice the test writer probably set as being correct, focus on what the *best answer choice* would be out of the answers you are presented with. Use the tips above, general knowledge, and reading comprehension skills in order to best answer the question, rather than looking for patterns that do not exist.

Bonus Content

You can access numerous bonus items online, along with all three practice tests for this study guide. Go to the following URL or scan the code below.

apexprep.com/bonus/cset

After you go to the website, you will have to create an account and register as a "new user" and verify your email address before you begin.

If you need any help, please contact us at info@apexprep.com.

Introduction

Function of the Test

The California Subject Examinations for Teachers (CSET) Multiple Subjects Exam was developed by the Commission of Teacher Credentialing (CTC) to test and certify that candidates have the knowledge and skills necessary to teach elementary or special education in the state of California. The exam is separated into three subtests and tests applicants on their knowledge of (1) Reading, Language, Literature, History, and Social Science; (2) Science and Mathematics; and (3) Physical Education, Human Development, and Visual and Performing Arts. During the 2016-2017 time period, 8,838 applicants attempted to pass the test. Of this number, 6,379 passed making the passing rate about 72 percent.

Test Administration

The exam is offered in testing centers across California. There is also an online option to test remotely for Subtest I and Subtest III. Those interested in testing should visit the CSET website, www.ctcexams.nesinc.com/about_CSET.asp, and search for appointments at a testing center nearby or for online proctoring information. The CSET Multiple Subjects Exam is available year-round by appointment, Monday through Saturday except for some holidays. The subtests can be taken at the same time in a single session or separated to be taken one at a time. Registration is required before making an appointment.

If you fail one of the subtests, you can take that subtest again until you pass. To retake the exam, you must complete the registration on the exam's website again. You must wait 45 calendar days from a failed attempt to retake the test or subtest.

Test Format

The CSET Multiple Subjects exam is a computer-based exam divided into three different subtests. Subtest I and II each last three hours, and Subtest III lasts two hours and fifteen minutes. Five hours is allowed when all three subtests are taken together during a single session. In this scenario, the subtests are not timed individually and may be completed, one at a time, in any order. Restroom breaks are allowed but use up a portion of the available testing time.

Test takers are provided with a basic on-screen calculator for the science and mathematics portions of the exam. Personal calculators are not allowed during the exam.

All three subtests include both multiple-choice and constructed-response type questions. The breakdown of the exam is shown below:

Subtest	Domains	Multiple-Choice	Constructed-Response
Subtest I	Reading, Language, and Literature	26	2
	History and Social Science	26	2
Subtest II	Science	26	2
	Mathematics	26	2
Subtest III	Physical Education	13	1
	Human Development	13	1
	Visual and Performing Arts	13	1

Scoring

Scores on the CSET Multiple Subjects Exam are scaled based on the raw score points earned on the sections. A proportion of the score comes from both the multiple choice and the constructed response sections. The raw scores are converted to a 100 to 300 scale. The minimum passing score is 220. Official test scores are generally available between three to six weeks following the examination date. Scores will be sent to the test taker and to any other institutions that the test taker indicated should receive scores.

Study Prep Plan

1 Breathe

Reducing stress is key when preparing for your test.

2 Build

Create a study plan to help you stay on track.

3 Begin

Stick with your study plan. You've got this!

1 Week Study Plan

Day 1	Day 2	Day 3	Day 4	Day 5	Day 6	Day 7
Subtest I: Reading, Language, and Literature	Subtest I: History and Social Science	Subtest II: Mathematics	Subtest III: Physical Education	Practice Test #1	Practice Test #2	Take Your Exam!

2 Week Study Plan

Day 1	Day 2	Day 3	Day 4	Day 5	Day 6	Day 7
Subtest I: Reading, Language, and Literature	Non-Written and Written Communication	Reading Comprehension and Analysis	Subtest I: History and Social Science	California History	Earth and Space Sciences	Subtest II: Mathematics

Day 8	Day 9	Day 10	Day 11	Day 12	Day 13	Day 14
Measurement and Geometry	Statistics, Data Analysis, and Probability	Subtest III: Physical Education	Subtest III: Visual and Performing Arts	Practice Test #1	Practice Test #2	Take Your Exam!

30 Day Study Plan

Day 1	Day 2	Day 3	Day 4	Day 5	Day 6	Day 7
Subtest I: Reading, Language, and Literature	Literacy	Non-Written and Written Communication	Non-Written Communication	Reading Comprehension and Analysis	Reading Informational Text	Subtest I: History and Social Science

Day 8	Day 9	Day 10	Day 11	Day 12	Day 13	Day 14
United States History	California History	Subtest II: Science	Life Sciences	Earth and Space Sciences	Subtest II: Mathematics	Algebra and Functions

Day 15	Day 16	Day 17	Day 18	Day 19	Day 20	Day 21
Linear and Quadratic Equations and Inequalities	Measurement and Geometry	Techniques, Tools, and Formulas for Determining Measurements	Statistics, Data Analysis, and Probability	Basic Notions of Chance and Probability	Subtest III: Physical Education	Subtest III: Human Development

Day 22	Day 23	Day 24	Day 25	Day 26	Day 27	Day 28
Subtest III: Visual and Performing Arts	Contextual Analysis	Practice Test #1	Answer Explanations #1	Practice Test #2	Answer Explanations #2	Practice Test #3

Day 29	Day 30
Answer Explanations #3	Take Your Exam!

As you study for your test, we'd like to take the opportunity to remind you that you are capable of great things! With the right tools and dedication, you truly can do anything you set your mind to. The fact that you are holding this book right now shows how committed you are. In case no one has told you lately, you've got this! Our intention behind including this coloring page is to give you the chance to take some time to engage your creative side when you need a little brain-break from studying. As a company, we want to encourage people like you to achieve their dreams by providing good quality study materials for the tests and certifications that improve careers and change lives. As individuals, many of us have taken such tests in our careers, and we know how challenging this process can be. While we can't come alongside you and cheer you on personally, we can offer you the space to recall your purpose, reconnect with your passion, and refresh your brain through an artistic practice. We wish you every success, and happy studying!

Subtest I: Reading, Language, and Literature

Language and Linguistics

Language Structure and Linguistics

Human language is founded upon the ability to create and comprehend both written and spoken words. Language is a complex neurological process that demands a high level of cognitive processing. Human language is built upon the fundamental concepts of grammar, lexicon, semantics, pragmatics, phonemes, morphemes, lexemes, syntax, and context. Human language is so complex that an entire field – linguistics – is devoted to studying its fundamental concepts and components.

Fundamental Concepts of Human Language

Every type of human language follows combinatory rules that help convey an infinite number of ideas. Combinatory rules change from language to language. For instance, the combinatory rules for Latin are different than the combinatory rules for Spanish or English. Likewise, the rules for Mandarin are different than the rules for Japanese. Collectively, these different sets of combinatory rules are known as **grammar**. Native speakers typically internalize grammar within their speech patterns. However, native speakers do not always internalize grammar when they are writing. Grammar must, therefore, be explicitly taught to both native and non-native speakers.

While grammar serves as the rules of a language, these rules would mean nothing without words. Every human language has a **lexicon**, or a sum total of words that can be applied to a particular grammatical framework. When grammatical combinations are applied to certain words in a particular lexicon, human beings are able to communicate an infinite amount of ideas.

In a global society, one language's lexicon may borrow from another language's lexicon. **Loanwords** are words that appear in two or more lexica. An example of a loanword in the English lexicon is *mosquito*, which means "little fly" in Spanish. Words that sound similar in two different lexica are called **cognates**. The words *domestic* (English) and *doméstico* (Spanish) are cognates that both mean "relating to home." Loanwords and cognates are examples of the ways in which lexica around the world are constantly interacting with one another through human communication.

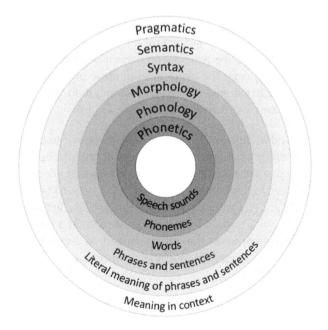

Phonemes are the smallest units of sound in a human language. Phonemes do not have their own meaning within a human language. Rather, they are units of sound that may change cause a change meaning within a human language. The word *bog* has three phonemes: /b/,/o/,/g/. The word *dog* changes only one of these phonemes – /b/ to /d/ – but this one change alters the entire meaning of a word. Sometimes words have more letters than phonemes. The word *kale* has 4 words, but only 3 phonemes: /k/, /long-a/, and /l/. The *e* is silent and therefore not a phoneme.

Phonetics is different than **phonology**. People who study phonetics study individual speech sounds. People who study phonology study phonemes, or the speech sounds of a particular human language. Phonetics cover all sounds that humans can make, while phonology covers all sounds present in a particular language. These overlapping fields study individual units of sounds but in different ways. A phonologist would be able to explain why the English words *god* and *dog* employ the same English phonemes but have different English meanings when rearranged. A phonologist would likely know the 45 phonemes in the English language, but a phonetics expert would be able to describe all sounds that human beings can make.

Morphemes are strings of phonemes that form the smallest *meaningful* units of human languages. The study of morphemes is known as **morphology**. There are two major types of morphemes studied by morphologists: free morphemes and bound morphemes. **Free morphemes** are individual words that can convey meaning without any other morphemes. An example of a free morpheme is *cat*. The word *cat* can convey meaning without any other morphemes. However, prefixes, suffixes, and other linguistic additions can be added to free morphemes to change their meaning. The most commonly used suffix is adding an *-s* at the end of a free morpheme to make it plural. Adding an *-s* to the end of *cat* to make it *cats* is an example of using a **bound morpheme** to alter the meaning of a free morpheme. An *-s* is a bound morpheme because it is *attached*, or bound, to a word.

There are two subcategories of bound morphemes. These subcategories including inflectional morphemes and derivational morphemes. Adding an *-s* to *cat* is an example of an **inflectional morpheme** because it modifies the numerical value or tense of a word. **Derivational morphemes** change the part of speech or the entire meaning of a word. When *mad* is changed to *madness* the part of speech is changed, making *ness* a derivational morpheme.

Lexemes are groups of inflected forms that create entire families of words that stem from one word. As the chart below explains, the words *eat, eats, eating, ate,* and *eaten* are all forms of the lexeme *eat.* The words *jump, jumps, jumping,* and *jumped* are all forms of the lexeme *jump.* And the words *fall, falls, falling, fell,* and *fallen* are all forms of the lexeme *fall.*

Syntax is a subsection of grammar – it is a set of rules for constructing full sentences using phrases and words. All human languages have some sort of syntax, yet the syntactical rules of each human language are unique. Syntax is, therefore, both a universal and hyper-specific linguistic phenomenon. Noun phrases and verb phrases serve as the smallest units of syntax in the English language. The word order of these phrases dictates the syntactical meaning. For example, "The dog licked the bowl" has an extremely different meaning than "The bowl licked the dog." In some languages, word order is not as important, but the rules of syntax in English makes the position of every word matter.

Words carry different connotations within different contexts. These contexts can be historical, cultural, regional, or local in character. Students must be aware of contextual differences in order to be fully fluent in one language or multiple languages. For instance, a word like *pop* has multiple meanings that are dependent upon context. At a fair or carnival, someone might pop a balloon. In this context, the word *pop* means to burst. In a grandfather's household, the word *pop* may serve as a term of endearment or a synonym for grandpa. In the Midwestern United States, the word *pop* may be used as a nickname for a carbonated beverage or soda. At a record label, the word *pop* may be used to refer to a particular genre or style of music that is popularized. At a movie theater, the word *pop* may refer to the sound of popcorn kernels exploding in a popcorn machine. Context matters, not only for a word like *pop*, but for many words in the English language.

Semantics and pragmatics both generally focus on the study of the denotation of words within a sentence. **Semantics** is the study of how words help convey the meaning of real objects or concepts. **Pragmatics** is broadly defined as the meaning of words or sentences within a specific context. The exclamation *Fire!* is a perfect example of the ways in which pragmatics come into play when studying human language. *Fire!* in a burning building means something completely different than *Fire!* on a military battlefield.

The Role of Pragmatics in Using Language to Communicate

Pragmatics is broadly defined as the meaning of words or sentences within a specific context. It is the meaning that emerges from the relationships between linguistic forms and the users of those linguistic forms. These "users" are the speakers and listeners who communicate within a particular context. Pragmatics reflects the identities of these users; it also reflects the choices made by these users. Pragmatics, therefore, inevitably reflects the social factors and constraints that define a context. In order for a person to communicate competently and pragmatically, they must, in theory, have an appropriate comprehension of the identities, choices, factors, and constraints that are expressed within a context.

The role of pragmatics is that it dictates the linguistic action and targeted language of communication. Different contexts demand different pragmatics. The most fluent speakers maintain a relative amount of "pragmatic competence" – they are able to shape their language for a variety of contexts. They might change the style, vocabulary, body language, or inflection of their linguistic action in order to communicate accurately and appropriately within different social and cultural circumstances.

Students move from basic communicative (in)competence to pragmatic competence as they progress through the linguistic process. **Basic communicative (in)competence** is communication that is devoid of grammatical structure. **Enhanced communicative competence** occurs when students begin to increase their grammatical structure and competence by respecting and implementing "the rules of the language." **Pragmatic competence** takes root when students are able to shape their language to meet the norms of the sociocultural context. The highest level of communication can only occur when, not only grammatical structure is mastered, but also social norms.

In order to understand this concept, think about the level of nuance it takes to master both communication skills in a local bar and communication skills in an executive interview. These different contexts create different social norms that demand different linguistic approaches. A speaker with a high-level of pragmatic competence would be able to engage listeners equally in both contexts. Speakers with the highest levels of pragmatic competence can "code switch" in multiple contexts – they have the ability to change from one level or type of language to another according to situational demands. These people have the unique ability to master and change dialects or languages to cater to different contexts.

Differences Among Languages and the Universality of Linguistic Structures

Anthropological research has shown that the **phonemic diversity** of human language – that is, the number of perceptually distinct number of sounds (i.e., consonants, vowels, and tones) – is largely dependent upon sound symbolic patterns that emerged from the geographic dispersion of human cultures beginning around 100,000 years ago in Africa. According to this theory, the potential differences among languages is dependent upon this current worldwide pattern of phonemic diversity, which statistically signals that an array of unique phonemes emerged as a result of geographic migration and isolation. For example, anthropologists believe migration patterns and speech evolution have helped create larger phonemic inventories in Africa than in South America. In other words, there is a greater concentration of speech differences in Africa than in South America. That's because, according to this theory of "phonemic diversity," some phonemic patterns have gone extinct as a result of colonization.

Some scholars have also adopted a "universality of language" theory, which was famously promoted by neuroscientists Noam Chomsky. This theory suggests there are some aspects of phonemic development that occur in all humans, regardless of cultural differences. Scientists like Chomsky believe this has to do with a specific speech-development gene in human beings. According to this theory, humans "speak the same language in a primordial sense."

<u>Applying Knowledge of Phonemic Awareness</u>

The steps of applying phonemic awareness progress from less complex activities to more complex activities in the classroom, as illustrated in the visual below. Implementing these steps should also help teachers evaluate student performance to gain a better understanding if they are at the beginning, developing, or proficient stages for each step.

Spectrum of Phonological Awareness

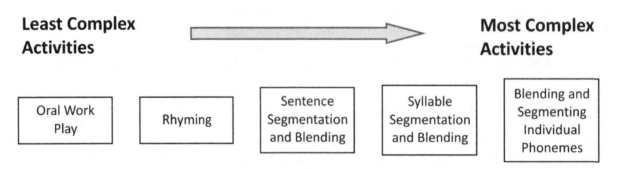

Oral Work Play

Regardless of their backgrounds, many students immersed in a new culture will have gained some background knowledge of the target language through media, digital technologies, and the local environment, which is also known as **incidental learning**. Oral work play – which combines oral recitations and communications with fun, playful activities – can help reinforce student learning by rectifying any confusions and explicitly teaching new skills.

The Process of Rhyming

Rhyming activities encourage students to develop explicit phonemic awareness techniques. Identifying and generating rhymes within an authentic context, such as a song or a poem, can help students master the manipulation of onset and rime. **Onsets** are the beginning sounds or letters of words. **Rimes** are the stems of each word. Take the word "sit" for example. The onset, or beginning sound, of sit is /s/. The rime, or word stem, is /it/. Identifying onsets and rimes will help students generate rhymes; it will provide students with fundamental phonemic awareness techniques that will help students acquire and develop a particular language. Identifying and generating rhymes are strategies that can be used at any point along the progression from less complex activities to more complex activities. However, this fundamental skill should be mastered well before a student moves on to sentence segmentation. Research shows that language learners benefit from explicit rhyming activities.

Sentence Segmentation and Blending

Sometimes referred to as "sentence boundary detection," **sentence segmentation** is the process of hearing individual words in a spoken sentence or dividing up a text into words and deciding where sentences begin and end. When learning a new language, word relations, punctuation, and sentence boundaries can be confusing. Practicing sentence segmentation out loud and visually will help language learners acquire and develop the phonemic awareness skills necessary to succeed in a classroom.

Sentence segmentation can be taught in isolation, or it can be taught in conjunction with **sentence blending.** Sentence blending is the process of understanding the ways the segments blend (or combine together) to form entire statements, questions, declarations, or interjections.

Syllable Segmentation and Blending

Likewise, **syllable segmentation** is the process of cutting up or separating sounds to better understand the overall pronunciation of words. **Syllable blending** is combining these sounds to further understand the overall pronunciation of words.

This graph shows how a gradual progression from "simple syllable segmentation and blending" to "most complex syllable segmentation and blending" can be implemented progressively in the classroom for best results.

Blending and Segmenting Individual Phonemes
The last, most complex, step is getting students to understand individual phonemes in words so that they can begin to understand not only pronunciation, but also meaning. This understanding, once again, can be developed through the blending (combining) and segmenting (separating) of original phonemes.

Similarities and Differences Between Phoneme Awareness and Phonics
In a K-12 classroom, **phonics** focuses on the relationship between written symbols (such as letters) and sounds. Alternatively, **phoneme awareness** focuses on the relationship between spoken words and sounds. Consequently, phoneme awareness strategies tend to be carried out orally in a K-12 classroom. Phonics instruction tends to center more on helping students to understand sound-spelling relationships as exemplified in printed materials and written texts. Nevertheless, in spite of their different nuances, students need to learn to command both phonemes and phonics as children. Phoneme awareness instruction and phonics instruction are both necessary for students to command human language at an early age. For example, students cannot fully grasp sound-spelling relationships for decoding printed texts and written words if they do not fully understand phonemes, the set of sounds associated with written or spoken words. Phoneme awareness allows each student to understand the discrete sounds associated with a string or series of letters or words. Phonics instruction would therefore not be possible without the fundamental skills that are bequeathed to students by phoneme awareness techniques.

The Predictable Patterns of Sound-Symbol and Symbol-Sound Relationships
Understanding the **Alphabetic Principle** is an important component of a student's language acquisition and development. It enables students to identify and apply predictable and systematic patterns between sounds and letters. Mastering the Alphabetic Principle is contingent upon mastering the patterns of sound-symbol and symbol-sound relationships; students need to understand that letters and letter patterns convey certain sounds. The Alphabetic Principle is a cornerstone of phonics instruction because it allows students to make connections between the sounds of spoken language and the letters/symbols of written language. Without mastering the Alphabetic Principle, students cannot fully master the accuracy, rate/automaticity, and prosody that is necessary for reading fluency. In terms of phonics instruction, teachers must consider their plan of instruction and the rate/sequence of instruction in order to help students grasp the Alphabetic Principle.

General guidelines for creating a good plan of instruction:

- Explicitly instruct students about letter-sound relationships
- Teach these relationships in isolation from one another
- Create daily lessons that allow students to practice letter-sound relationships
- Provide explicit practice opportunities for acquiring new sound-letter relationships over time
- Cumulatively review previously taught sound-letter relationships
- Give students opportunities to expand their knowledge of sound-letter relationships
- Allow students to practice using phonetically spelled words that may be familiar

General guidelines for assessing the proper rate/sequence of instruction:

- Accept that no specific rules govern how fast a teacher should introduce letter-sound relationships to each student
- Remind yourself that each student learns sound-letter relations at different rates
- It is strongly encouraged to teach high-utility letter-sound relationships (f, m, n, r, s) first and in isolation from letters that auditorily or visually confusing (b, v, i, e, b, d, p, g)
- Throughout instruction, separate auditorily and visually similar letters and sounds

- Single consonant sounds and consonant clusters should be taught in isolation to avoid student confusion
- Direct, explicit instruction is proven to be more effective than other forms of instruction

Parts of Speech and Their Morphology

There are eight parts of speech: nouns, pronouns, verbs, adjectives, adverbs, prepositions, conjunctions, and interjections.

Morphemes are traditionally separated into two overarching categories: 1) Free Morphemes, and 2) Bound Morphemes. These categories of morphemes affect parts of speech in different ways.

Back, pack, key, board, note, book, worm, fire, green, and *house* are all nouns that can also be considered **free morphemes**. That is, they are all meaningful units in language that do not need other morphemes; they are not bound to other morphemes. However, two free morphemes can combine in the English language to create **compound words**.

Below are some examples of compound words created by two free morphemes:

Free Morpheme 1	+	Free Morpheme 2	=	Compound Word
back	+	pack	=	backpack
key	+	board	=	keyboard
key	+	note	=	keynote
note	+	book	=	notebook
book	+	worm	=	bookworm
fire	+	house	=	firehouse
green	+	house	=	greenhouse

Notice how the meaning of the compound word usually is related to the meaning of the original free morphemes, but creates an entirely new noun. For instance, a greenhouse is a noun referring to a house-like structure (stemming from the free morpheme *house*) that protects plants (stemming from the free morpheme *green*). The word is entirely new but maintains some of the original characteristics/meanings of the free morphemes.

Bound morphemes cannot stand alone like free morphemes – they must be attached or bound to free morphemes in order to gain meaning. Alone, bound morphemes cannot act as words. They only function as parts of other words.

The most common type of bound morpheme is a simple *–s*. Adding *–s* to certain free morphemes that act as nouns can make the nouns plural. An *–s* helps add meaning to an otherwise meaningful free morpheme by indicating plurality.

Some bound morphemes – like *un-*, *dis-*, and *re-* – attach to the beginning of other morphemes, while other bound morphemes – like *-less*, *-ness*, and *-er/-or* – attach to the end of other morphemes. Collectively, these bound morphemes are known as **affixes**. If they occur at the beginning of other morphemes, they are defined as **prefixes**. If they occur at the end of other morphemes, they are defined as **suffixes**.

Take a look at the prefix *dis-* attached to various words, changing their meaning:

Prefix (Bound Morpheme)	+	Original Morpheme	=	New Word (New Meaning)
dis-	+	*content*	=	*discontent* (the opposite of content)
dis-	+	*qualify*	=	*disqualify* (the opposite of qualify)
dis-	+	*agree*	=	*disagree* (the opposite of agree)
dis-	+	*trust*	=	*distrust* (the opposite of trust)
dis-	+	*like*	=	*dislike* (the opposite of like)

Syntactic Components

Syntactic components include phrases and clauses. Understanding syntactics allows for the development of a variety of sentence types.

Clause

A **clause** is the smallest grammatical unit containing a subject and predicate. Two kinds of clauses are the independent clause and the dependent clause.

The **independent clause** can stand by itself as a complete sentence. It must contain a subject and a predicate at minimum, but it must not begin with a subordinating conjunction. The following two sentences are considered independent clauses:

> She swam.

> He ran to the edge of the sea and stuck his toe in.

Both of these are considered independent clauses because they express a complete thought. A **dependent clause** begins with a subordinating conjunction and is not considered a complete sentence, because it needs an independent clause to complete it. Let's add subordinating conjunctions to the sentences above and make dependent clauses:

> *Because* she swam.

> *Although* he ran to the edge of the sea and stuck his toe in.

These two sentences have become dependent on another idea due to the addition of subordinating conjunctions. Let's make these sentences complete by adding an independent clause:

> Lilo was very healthy because she swam.

> Although he ran to the edge of the sea and stuck his toe in, it was too cold to jump in.

Now these sentences consist of an independent clause and a dependent clause, which creates a complete sentence.

Phrase

A **phrase** is two or more words that stand together as a single unit. The difference between a phrase and a clause is that a clause contains the subject/verb pair, while a phrase does not. There are seven types of phrase examples listed below in italics:

- Noun phrase: made up of a noun and its modifiers. "*The astute, aged professor* started teaching again."

- Prepositional phrase: made up of a preposition and its object, and sometimes one or more adjectives. "I headed south *for the warm winters.*"

19

- Participial phrase: begins with a past or present participial. The participial phrase serves as an adjective to the subject of the sentence. *"Having made up her mind to go to college,* Savannah took all the necessary classes for preparation."

- Gerund phrase: can be the subject of a sentence, the sentence's object, or the object of a preposition. Here is a gerund as the subject of a sentence: *"Swimming laps* was Harrison's favorite pastime."

- Infinitive phrase: phrase that begins with an infinitive ("to" + a verb). "My family loves *to vacation at the beach.*"

- Appositive phrase: restates or describes a noun. "Dr. Masie, *the department chair in Chemistry,* is teaching the class."

- Absolute phrase: contains a subject but no acting verb. *"Her hands in the air,* she stared from the roller coaster into the dark tunnel."

Sentence Types

When deconstructing sentences grammatically, there are four types of sentence structures: simple, compound, complex, and compound-complex.

Simple sentences contain a subject and a verb, and may contain additional phrases, indirect objects, or direct objects behind the sentence or verb. A simple sentence contains one independent clause only. Simple sentences can be as simple as saying, "Joanie laughed," or they can contain a compound subject, such as "Joanie and Marisa laughed." Simple sentences can also contain prepositional phrases and compound verbs, such as "Joanie and Marisa laughed at the movie and ate chocolate covered pretzels." Here we have a compound subject "Joanie and Marisa" and a compound verb "laughed and ate," yet we still have a single independent clause.

Compound sentences join two independent clauses together by a conjunction (for, and, nor, but, or, yet, so). An example would be, "Zoe wanted to go to the zoo, but it was closed on Sundays." Here, we have two sentences that can stand on their own: "Zoe wanted to go to the zoo." "It was closed on Sundays." We could turn the simple sentence above into a compound sentence: "Joanie and Marisa laughed at the movie, and they ate chocolate covered pretzels." Adding "they" to the second part of the sentence creates two independent clauses. In a compound sentence, the FANBOYS are always separated by commas.

Complex sentences contain one independent clause and one dependent clause. As stated above, dependent clauses are similar to independent clauses; however, they lack some kind of unit that allows them to be a complete sentence. Dependent clauses may look like the following:

- When it started to rain
- After she bought the furniture for her new house
- Until the neighborhood street has a bike lane

In order to make these into complex sentences, we must attach independent clauses to each, either before or after the dependent clause. Here are some examples of a complex sentence:

- When it started to rain, Mazey shut all the windows except the one in the living room.
- Carolynn was ecstatic after she bought the furniture for her new house.
- Until the neighborhood street has a bike lane, I would prefer to take Charlie to the park.

Notice that the independent clauses are able to stand on their own, while the dependent clauses depend on the independent clause to complete the thought.

Compound-complex sentences occur when a complex sentence is merged with a compound sentence. These sentences have two independent clauses and one dependent clause. In the following examples, the dependent clauses are in bold, while the independent clauses are in italics:

- **When it started to rain**, *Mazey shut all the windows except the one in the living room*, and *her brother got out a board game to play.*

- *Carolynn was ecstatic* **after she bought the furniture for her new house**, but *she returned two pieces a day later.*

- **Until the neighborhood street has a bike lane**, *I would prefer to take Charlie to the park to ride his new bike*, for *this road is too busy to ride on.*

Language Development and Acquisition

Development of First and Subsequent Languages

The development of a first language and the acquisition of subsequent ones usually occurs across five stages or domains: 1) Preproduction, 2) Early Production, 3) Speech Emergence, 4) Intermediate Fluency, 5) Advanced Fluency.

Stage 1: Preproduction

Often known as "the silent period" or "the mute period," **preproduction** is the stage or domain in which language learners understand upward of 500 new vocabulary terms, but they are not quite ready to speak. This stage usually lasts from 0-6 months. Parroting typically occurs at this stage – students repeat everything their teachers say, but they are not actually mastering or producing language. At this stage, language learners can listen attentively and copy written words. They can respond to visuals with "yes" or "no" signals of understanding. Students can also understand and imitate body language to convey understanding at this stage. Teachers should consequently try to incorporate kinesthetic learning activities into the classroom. Additionally, teachers should try to focus on building receptive vocabulary through auditory comprehension activities. Frequent repetition and peer-to-peer tutoring interventions will help language learners acquire the target language at a much faster rate. This stage may also be overwhelming for language learners because they will be exposed to an unfamiliar language for long periods of time in an immersive setting.

During this stage, teachers can help language learners by:

- Reinforcing positive yes/no signals of understanding
- Using kinesthetic learning activities
- Instituting strategic peer-to-peer interventions
- Influencing immersion through listening and memory activities
- Being cognizant of the need for breaks during moments of exhaustion

Stage 2: Early Production

Early production may last anywhere from 6 months to a year, depending on the rate of language acquisition and the quality of instruction. Students receptively and actively master around 1000 words during this stage. Students will progress from parroting to one-to-two-word phrases throughout early production. Students will have language chunks memorized, but they may not have reached the linguistic mastery that allows them to use these language chunks correctly and consistently.

During this stage, teachers can help language learners by:

- Encouraging and accepting one-to-two-word answers
- Facilitating peer-to-peer interventions and whole class inclusion
- Prompting student knowledge with pictures and building vocabulary with visuals

- Scaffolding and differentiating reading content
- Asking simple questions with either/or, yes/no answers
- Incorporating simple books with predictable text levels and patterns
- Nurturing language acquisition with auditory activities
- Teaching explicit use of graphic organizers, such as charts and graphs
- Fostering writing techniques by using frames for scaffolding

Stage 3: Speech Emergence

The approximate time frame of the **speech emergence** stage of language development and acquisition is 1 to 3 years. Students will have developed around 3000 words during this stage of development. Students will also be able to communicate with simple phrases, simple sentences, and simple questions. Grammatical accuracy is not guaranteed at this stage. Language learners, for example, may ask questions like "May I go wash hands?" instead of "May I go wash my hands?" Students will start initiating terse conversations in their target language. Teachers may notice them being more sociable with their native-speaking peers. With teacher assistance and intervention, they will be ready for content-based activities in the classroom.

During this stage, teachers can help language learners by:

- Modifying and introducing new content-based texts at the appropriate Lexile range
- Explicitly teaching students how to sound out stories phonetically
- Implementing content-based flash card activities
- Continuing practice with graphic organizers
- Introducing students to word bank activities
- Instituting matching activities that ask students to match vocabulary terms and definitions
- Teaching students how to use graphs and other text features to answer questions
- Participate in "dialogue journal" activities that allow teachers and students to communicate via written language
- Practicing choral reading
- Helping students use illustrations to tell short graphic stories about personal experiences

Stage 4: Intermediate Fluency

Intermediate fluency usually begins to take hold around 3-5 years. Students will begin utilizing more complex sentences with few grammatical errors.

During this stage, teachers can help language learners by:

- Correct the remaining few grammar errors
- Start preparing students to apply language to new contexts
- Challenge students to write in complex and compound-complex sentences, with a flawless command of grammar

Stage 5: Advanced Fluency

This stage takes 5-7 years to develop. Students with **advanced fluency** would have a near-native command of the new language. Teachers can support these students by explicitly teaching them how to apply their new language skills to unique socio-cultural contexts.

Major Theories that Explain the Processes of Development and Acquisition

Noam Chomsky – the American linguist, philosopher, and cognitive scientist – put forward the well-known **nativist theory** to explain the processes of language development and acquisition, establishing a biological and neurological explanation for language development. Chomsky argues that every child's brain plays host to a theoretical Language Acquisition Device (LAD) that allows them to understand grammar universals without any formal teaching. Although

22

there is not a "language organ" in the brain, children are able to subconsciously map new lexical items to universal rules of grammar and syntax. According to Chomsky, children's brains have building blocks that allow them to pick up grammar and syntax without formal training. These building blocks help children decipher the linguistic inputs around them. Although brain imaging studies have not discovered Chomsky's alleged Learning Acquisition Device (LAD), the nativist theory of language development and acquisition is still held in high regard by many linguistic experts.

The **learning theory** of language development and acquisition assumes that children develop linguistic skills from stimuli and stimuli response. According to this theory, children develop and acquire language through explicit lessons much like they learn how to develop other skills, such as tying their shoes. Children initially babble words but are positively or negatively reinforced through the teachings of their parents.

According to the **sociocultural/interactionist theory**, children acquire and develop language through a blend of biological and sociological factors. Part of the development and acquisition results from the innate human desire to communicate with the rest of the world. According to this theory, while biological factors can affect development and acquisition, social interactions – which stem from cultural contexts – serve as the primary catalyst to language development and acquisition. According to this theory, the environment that students grow up in heavily influences their personal lexicon and fluency.

Most educators draw from all three theories since a proven theory of language development and acquisition has not yet been identified. Language development and acquisition is a complicated phenomenon that brings together the fields of neuroscience, biology, sociology, and education. Educators must take "best practices" from multiple fields and apply these practices to their work in classrooms in order to help students mature in their speech, reading, and writing.

Issues Related to the Interaction of First Languages and Other Languages

The following concepts can help guide educators as they respond to a range of issues related to the interaction of first languages and other languages.

The impact of language acquisition on all languages – native and new – is a multilateral, rather than unilateral, phenomenon. When instructing language learners in a K-12 setting, educators should, first and foremost, be aware that first-language, or native-language, skills can impact second-language acquisition. Likewise, research has also indicated that subsequent acquisition of new languages can also affect the ways language learners manage information in their first language. This means that language acquisition is a multilateral, rather than unilateral, in terms of its impact: all languages involved are inevitably affected by the collision of disparate linguistic sources and traditions.

Language learners acquire a range of issues from a variety of sources, and educators must, therefore, acquaint themselves with a variety of disciplines. Understanding the impact of each language on the other is not yet a "hard science." Instead, in order to understand this multilateral impact, which manifests itself differently in each child, every educator must draw from a variety of disciplines in order to appropriately modify their instructional practices: psychology, sociology, education, cognitive science, and linguistics, to name a few. Educators also need to understand that an array of biological and environmental/psychosocial factors can affect a child's acquisition and development in one or more languages.

Below is a list of potential biological and environmental/psychosocial factors that affect language learners:

BIOLOGICAL FACTORS	ENVIRONMENTAL or PSYCHOSOCIAL FACTORS
Effects of Prenatal Factors and Care Genetic Factors Health Disabilities Brain Trauma Disorders or Diseases Cognitive Functioning Issues	Socioeconomic Status (Poverty vs. Affluence) English Language Learner (ELL) status Parental Education Levels Abuse/Trauma Nutrition Rate and Frequency of Learning in the Household Cultural Factors Social Life

Recognizing Special Features of a Pupil's Language Development

California public schools serve students from a variety of cultural and linguistic backgrounds. Throughout the state, many students will be identified as English language learners (ELLs): students who are learning the language of instruction at the same time as they are learning specific state curriculum standards. A learner's ELL status and/or length of residency are two of the many special features that can help identify a student's language development as "exceptional." However, ELL and new-to-country students may also fall into other "exceptional learner" categories, such as gifted and talented, behavioral disorders, mental health conditions, physical impairments, speech or language impairments, reading disabilities, or other learning disabilities.

It is important for educators to understand the difference between "exceptional students" and "special education students" when evaluating language development:

- **Exceptional students** are students who have unusual, unique, or outstanding circumstances – such as exceptional learning types, exceptional conditions, exceptional talents, or exceptional behaviors – that affect their educational development and makes them fall outside the "normal category" of students.

- **Special education students** are a subcategory of students within the larger category of exceptionality. Special education is status given to students who have a record of a legal, documented educational disability.

Understanding the relationship(s) between these differing statuses is key to evaluating language development in the classroom.

Below is a chart of exceptional learning categories that every educator should be aware of:

CATEGORY	DEFINITION
ADHD	A common childhood disorder characterized by inattention, hyperactivity, or a combination of both. There are three types of ADHD that are common in school-age children: Inattentive ADHD: the child is easily distracted but not hyperactive/impulsive. Hyperactive ADHD: the child is not necessarily inattentive, but extremely hyperactive/impulsive. Combined ADHD: the student is both inattentive and hyperactive/impulsive.

24

CATEGORY	DEFINITION
Autism Spectrum Disorder (ASD)	A developmental disability that severely impairs a student's social skills, communication skills, or emotional regulation skills, and is characterized by repetitive behaviors, hypersensitivities, and the need for structure.
Deaf-blindness	A combination of being deaf and blind.
Deafness	Hearing loss that may significantly impact a child's educational development.
Dysgraphia	A specific learning disability that effects student writing.
Dyslexia	A specific learning disability that effects student reading.
Emotional Disturbance	Often misunderstood as trauma or a mood disorder, emotional disturbance is a term that refers to any significant chronic disruption in a student's emotions that adversely influences their educational performance. It can range from difficulties forming social relations to a general display of depression.
Intellectual Disability	A broad category that refers to below-average cognitive or intellectual functioning.
Hearing Impairment	Separate from deafness, this is a category for any hearing issues that influence academic efforts.
Multiple Disabilities	Excluding deaf-blindness, a category for when one or more disabilities affect academic performance in the classroom. For instance, a student may be orthopedically impaired and also have ADHD.
Orthopedic Impairment	A list of physical health impairments that have a direct impact on the skeletal structure of a student, such as an amputation or cerebral palsy.
Other Health Impairment (OHI)	This is a wide-ranging category for health impairments, such as diabetes, that do not fall neatly within these other categories, yet still may adversely affect student performance.
Specific Learning Disability	Dyslexia, which was previously mentioned, fits in this category. It is basically a category for specific disabilities, such as brain injuries, that impact basic learning skills like reading, writing, spelling, etc.
Speech or Language Impairment	Any impairment that negatively impacts a student's ability to speak, use their voice, or acquire/use language properly.
Traumatic Brain Injury	Brain injuries that cause complete or partial loss of brain function.
Visual Impairments (Including Blindness)	Any impactful impairment to the vision of a student.
Developmental Delay	Any child between the ages of 3 to 9 that shows signs of being behind physically, cognitively, socially, emotionally, behaviorally, or with communication skills.
Gifted and Talented	Gifted and Talented (GT) students excel exceptionally in academics or in other capacities (music, art, leadership, etc.) so they need their own high-achieving or exceptional accommodations.

CATEGORY	DEFINITION
Twice Exceptional	GT students who might have a disability, like high-functioning Autism.

Teachers should never diagnose students with exceptional circumstances or learning disabilities, but rather should monitor student behaviors and collect data to help specialists and medical professionals make diagnoses. Teachers, however, should feel empowered to properly respond and prepare for each of these categories.

Distinguishing Special Features from Interlanguage Effects

Interlanguage effects refer to the array of complications that may arise when a student is immersed within a second language setting and trying to develop new language skills. The effects are the results of the confusions, anxieties, reservations, and lack of clarity associated with learning a new language in an immersive context. Often these effects are misdiagnosed as special education designations. Part of a teacher's role in the classroom is to navigate behaviors, such as the ones listed below, and consult with diagnosticians and specialists to better understand the root of these behaviors. The last thing a teacher wants to do is mislabel or misdiagnose a student. In fact, it is not a teacher's job to diagnose behaviors, but it is their job to track behaviors for diagnostic purposes. In the chart below, some behaviors are listed with potential interlanguage or SPED explanations.

BEHAVIOR	POTENTIAL INTERLANGUAGE EFFECTS	POTENTIAL SPED EXPLANATION
The student struggles to retell stories, summarize narratives and plots, and convey sequential understanding.	The student may not fully comprehend the new vocabulary in the second language; the Lexile level of the text may be too high for the student.	There may be an exceptional circumstance or disorder preventing the student from processing or organizing information.
The student exhibits off-task behaviors and/or fails to complete word problems in math class even though they can carry out numerical calculations.	The student may not have the vocabulary or background knowledge to understand the directions of the word problems.	The student might have a relatively high level of numeracy, but may have Dyslexia or other reading complications.
The student never follows the teacher's directions, especially when they are written.	The student may not have sufficient reading comprehension skills in the second language.	The student may be exhibiting oppositional defiance.
The student avoids writing at all costs, choosing instead to doodle to their paper.	The student may have advanced reading and speaking skills, but may have beginner or intermediate writing skills.	The student may have tactile writing issues.
The student is easily distracted, displaying off-task behaviors during the heart of activities or instruction.	The student may feel overwhelming or exhausted by language immersion; the student may not comprehend, and therefore is overloaded by stimuli.	The student might have ADHD, oppositional defiance, or auditory processing delays or disorders.
The student deletes or adds words in unnecessary places when speaking or writing.	Student may not yet fully grasp vocabulary in the second language, adding and deleting words due to confusion and/or effort.	The student may have a reading disability, processing disorder, or working memory issues.

Notice how the behaviors are not assessed in absolutes – that's because behaviors are complicated and must be tracked over time and assessed professionally before a diagnosis can be given. It *may* be interlanguage effects, or it *might* be a SPED case, but only trained professionals can make those diagnoses.

Literacy

Major Descriptions of Developing Literacy

Most scholars and practitioners refer to Jeanne Chall's "Six Stages of Reading Development" (1996) framework for understanding student literacy development from birth to adulthood.

Jeanne Chall's "Six Stages of Reading Development" (1996)		
Stage	**Stage Name**	**Definition**
Stage Zero	Pre-Reading	Usually taking hold between the ages of 6 months and 6 years old, this is the stage of literacy development when young children should begin to develop phonemic awareness and identify some or all letters of the alphabet.
Stage One	Initial Reading, Writing & Decoding	Usually taking hold between the ages of 6 and 7 years old, this is the stage of literacy development where students should begin learning new letter-sound skills that allow them to manipulate phonemes and sound out new words.
Stage Two	Confirmation and Fluency	Usually taking hold between the ages of 7 and 8 years old, students will be able to read and understand short texts, learning unfamiliar words and their meanings.
Stage Three	Reading to Learn the New	Usually taking hold between the ages of 9 and 13 years old, student should begin formulating their own feelings and attitudes, which should be evident in their conversations and writings.
Stage Four	Synthesizing Information and Applying Multiple Perspectives	Usually taking hold between the ages of 14 and 17 years old, this stage should be characterized by the ability to critique, synthesize, and apply information and concepts.
Stage Five	Critical Literacy in Work and Society	Taking hold after the age of 17, reflections, readings, and writings should become more purposeful, so that students may apply their learnings to real-world settings.

Most theories of literacy development will employ some iteration of Chall's framework. However, it should be noted that most students will not progress perfectly through each of these stages and English Language Learners (ELLs) will also progress at differentiated rates. This framework should guide, not dictate, instruction. Instead, instruction should be individualized, scaffolded, and differentiated for each student's personal progression through the levels.

Continuum of English Language Acquisition

The first three years of a child's life are arguably the most intensive in terms of speech acquisition and language development. There seems to be a direct correlation between a child's vocabulary and a childhood environment rich in sights, sounds, and positive social interaction. In those beginning years, a child's **receptive vocabulary**—the words he or she can comprehend—will undoubtedly be more expansive than the child's **expressive vocabulary,** or the words he or she can use to communicate. During a child's educational career, certain language milestones need to be achieved, each building on the previous one. Children who develop a command of English language conventions, including grammar, usage, and mechanics, will be in a better position to develop more sophisticated ways to use language later.

However, continuously expanding a child's vocabulary requires much more than a command of conventions. As children grow, so does their vocabulary, especially with the introduction to reading. An environment that encourages reading and offers a variety of reading material has been shown to strengthen comprehension and expand a child's vocabulary base. An effective reading program provides increasingly more challenging texts, including informational texts, stories, poems, and historical fiction, as well as specialized texts that focus on specific disciplines. The more students are exposed to such a reading program, the greater the likelihood that they will build a foundation of knowledge in various fields of study and strengthen comprehension of the often-complex structures and elements of different texts.

Introducing students to effective reading comprehension skills is key to reading at the college level. Reading comprehension and vocabulary can be improved by encouraging students to build reading stamina and a determination to read through a text no matter the challenges it presents. Consider the following reading skills that help to improve reading comprehension and prepare students for college-level texts:

Reading Stamina	Identification of Main Idea	Paraphrasing	Annotation	Consistent Reading
Students are encouraged to read through complex texts, even if confronted with unfamiliar vocabulary.	Once the main idea has been identified, the rest of the text will begin to make more sense.	Students are encouraged to write out sections of the text in their own words. This strengthens comprehension and allows for reflection.	Students are encouraged to underline interesting ideas, circle unknown words, and use a dictionary to define the words that impede understanding.	Students who read complex and varied reading material on a regular basis are more likely to advance their reading skills and expand their expressive and receptive vocabulary.

It is clear that the more students read on a regular basis, the more prepared they will be for college-level reading, but this doesn't mean that a student has to read informational texts exclusively. Reading material that interests students also works to increase their vocabulary knowledge. When students are interested in the material, they are more likely to continue reading and will likely be motivated to learn the unfamiliar words in the text. However, it isn't just about reading. Since reading, writing, listening, and speaking are all intimately connected, when students write regularly and intentionally practice writing newly acquired words and phrases, this practice will undoubtedly reinforce their reading skills.

Phonemic Awareness

28

Phonemic awareness is the ability to isolate and understand different sound-symbol relationships embedded within a word. Phonemic awareness can be achieved through a gradual implementation of foundational practices, which should follow this general step-by-step process:

- Assist students developing a kinesthetic awareness of sounds (i.e., teaching them the mouth movements, lip motions, tongue movements, and air control associated with pronouncing words.

- Teach students how to combine two normal free morphemes to create compound words: *back* + *pack* = *backpack*

- Instruct students how to blend one-syllable words, such as car, using an auditory prompts

- Reinforcing student recognition and distinguishing of similar sounds

- Teach students how to segment one-syllable words: *tack* becomes /t-a-c/

- Teach students how to isolate initial sounds: *tack* starts with /t/

- Show students how to change initial sounds to create new words: changing /t/ to /s/ would make the word *sack*

- Demonstrate how to isolate final sounds: /c/ is the final sound of *tack*

- Show how to change the final sound to make new words: changing -ck to /p/ would create the word *tap*

- Demonstrate how to isolate medial sounds: /a/ is the medial sound of *tack*

- Show how to change the medial sound to make new words: changing /a/ to /i/ would create the word *tick*

- Teach students how to rhyme one syllable words by changing the initial sound: *tack* rhymes with *sack*, which also rhymes with *back*

Vocabulary

Context Clues

When readers encounter an unfamiliar word in text, they can use the surrounding context—the overall subject matter, specific chapter/section topic, and especially the immediate sentence context. Among others, one category of context clues is grammar. For example, the position of a word in a sentence and its relationship to the other words can help the reader establish whether the unfamiliar word is a verb, a noun, an adjective, an adverb, etc. This narrows down the possible meanings of the word to one part of speech. However, this may be insufficient. In a sentence that many birds *migrate* twice yearly, the reader can determine the word is a verb, and probably does not mean eat or drink; but it could mean travel, mate, lay eggs, hatch, molt, etc.

Some words can have a number of different meanings depending on how they are used. For example, the word *fly* has a different meaning in each of the following sentences:

"His trousers have a fly on them."

"He swatted the fly on his trousers."

"Those are some fly trousers."

"They went fly fishing."

"She hates to fly."

"If humans were meant to fly, they would have wings."

As strategies, readers can try substituting a familiar word for an unfamiliar one and see whether it makes sense in the sentence. They can also identify other words in a sentence, offering clues to an unfamiliar word's meaning.

Denotation and Connotation

Denotation refers to a word's explicit definition, like that found in the dictionary. Denotation is often set in comparison to connotation. **Connotation** is the emotional, cultural, social, or personal implication associated with a word. Denotation is more of an objective definition, whereas connotation can be more subjective, although many connotative meanings of words are similar for certain cultures. The denotative meanings of words are usually based on facts, and the connotative meanings of words are usually based on emotion. Here are some examples of words and their denotative and connotative meanings in Western culture:

Word	Denotative Meaning	Connotative Meaning
Home	A permanent place where one lives, usually as a member of a family.	A place of warmth; a place of familiarity; comforting; a place of safety and security. "Home" usually has a positive connotation.
Snake	A long reptile with no limbs and strong jaws that moves along the ground; some snakes have a poisonous bite.	An evil omen; a slithery creature (human or nonhuman) that is deceitful or unwelcome. "Snake" usually has a negative connotation.
Winter	A season of the year that is the coldest, usually from December to February in the northern hemisphere and from June to August in the southern hemisphere.	Circle of life, especially that of death and dying; cold or icy; dark and gloomy; hibernation, sleep, or rest. Winter can have a negative connotation, although many who have access to heat may enjoy the snowy season from their homes.

Word Recognition and Etymology

As students gain phonemic awareness, refine their denotation and connotation skills, and are able to comprehend new words, they will accrue a greater background knowledge that will allow for automatic **word recognition**.

This word recognition, enhanced **etymological awareness**, will allow students to *comprehend* the meanings of words in different contexts and *apply* words to new contexts. Thus, in turn, enhances the socio-cultural understanding of students.

By learning some of the etymologies (word origins) of words and their parts, readers can break new words down into components and analyze their combined meanings. For example, the root word *soph* is Greek for wise or knowledge. Knowing this informs the meanings of English words including *sophomore, sophisticated,* and *philosophy.* Those who also know that *phil* is Greek for love will realize that *philosophy* means the love of knowledge. They can then extend this knowledge of *phil* to understand *philanthropist* (one who loves people), *bibliophile* (book lover), *philharmonic* (loving harmony), *hydrophilic* (water-loving), and so on. In addition, *phob-* derives from the Greek *phobos,* meaning fear. This informs all words ending with it as meaning fear of various things: *acrophobia* (fear of heights),

30

arachnophobia (fear of spiders), *claustrophobia* (fear of enclosed spaces), *ergophobia* (fear of work), and *hydrophobia* (fear of water), among others.

Some English word origins from other languages, like ancient Greek, are found in large numbers and varieties of English words. An advantage of the shared ancestry of these words is that once readers recognize the meanings of some Greek words or word roots, they can determine or at least get an idea of what many different English words mean. As an example, the Greek word *métron* means to measure, a measure, or something used to measure; the English word meter derives from it. Knowing this informs many other English words, including *altimeter, barometer, diameter, hexameter, isometric,* and *metric.* While readers must know the meanings of the other parts of these words to decipher their meaning fully, they already have an idea that they are all related in some way to measures or measuring.

While all English words ultimately derive from a proto-language known as Indo-European, many of them historically came into the developing English vocabulary later, from sources like the ancient Greeks' language, the Latin used throughout Europe and much of the Middle East during the reign of the Roman Empire, and the Anglo-Saxon languages used by England's early tribes. In addition to classic revivals and native foundations, by the Renaissance era other influences included French, German, Italian, and Spanish. Today we can often discern English word meanings by knowing common roots and affixes, particularly from Greek and Latin.

Spelling

Homophones are words that sound the same in speech, but have different spellings and meanings. For example, *to, too,* and *two* all sound alike, but have three different spellings and meanings. Homophones with different spellings are also called **heterographs**. **Homographs** are words that are spelled identically, but have different meanings. If they also have different pronunciations, they are **heteronyms**. For instance, *tear* pronounced one way means a drop of liquid formed by the eye; pronounced another way, it means to rip. Homophones that are also homographs are **homonyms**. For example, *bark* can mean the outside of a tree or a dog's vocalization; both meanings have the same spelling. *Stalk* can mean a plant stem or to pursue and/or harass somebody; these are spelled and pronounced the same. *Rose* can mean a flower or the past tense of *rise.* Many non-linguists confuse things by using "homonym" to mean sets of words that are homophones but not homographs, and also those that are homographs but not homophones.

Indicators of Reading Fluency

Reading fluency is best defined as a student's ability to read a text with an appropriate accuracy and rate/automaticity, while also maintaining proper and meaningful phrasing and expression.

Educators assess students according to three major components of fluency:

- Accuracy
- Rate/Automaticity
- Prosody

Accuracy, quite simply, refers to a student's ability to pronounce and read words correctly. Student's with high rates of miscues and mispronunciations have lower rates of accuracy. Effective pronunciation enhances other major components of fluency, such as rate/automaticity and prosody.

Rate and automaticity are closely related components of fluency. **Rate** refers to how quickly students read a text, while **automaticity** refers to a student's ability to automatically identify a word without having to decode or process it. Accuracy and automaticity will inevitably increase the rate of student reading.

Prosody is a factor that can be evaluated when a student reads out loud. Prosody refers to the effective use of phrasing, expression, and intonation when a student reads orally. Prosodic reading is usually a good indicator of the strength of a student's reading fluency.

Decoding, Fluency, Vocabulary Knowledge, and Comprehension

Decoding is best defined as a student's ability to apply their understanding of symbol-sound relationships (i.e., how each letter or combinations of letters makes a particular sound) to properly pronounce words in text. Decoding is one of the most fundamental aspects of reading.

Vocabulary knowledge refers to the ability to decode letters rapidly and recognize words. The vaster a student's vocabulary knowledge, the more likely they are to be fluent readers.

Again, **reading fluency** is best defined as a student's ability to read a text with an appropriate accuracy and rate/automaticity, while also maintaining proper and meaningful phrasing and expression. Reading fluency is increased by decoding and vocabulary knowledge.

Reading comprehension occurs when all of these components are working together like a well-oiled machine. Comprehension goes beyond vocabulary knowledge and fluency, however, through an application of background knowledge and theoretical reasoning. Comprehension is more than pronouncing words, it is understanding their deeper meaning within an entire text.

Factors that Affect Comprehension

Reading comprehension is a cognitive process that is generally contingent upon reader-centered factors that affect learning. These reader-centered factors include:

Attention and Motivation	Background Knowledge	Vocabulary	Fluency	Active Reading	Critical Thinking
Often underestimated as a crucial factor to reading development, the attention and motivation levels of a student can either enhance or undermine the learning procession. Attention and motivation levels emerge from an array of factors, such as: biology, context, and cultural relevance.	Students come to a classroom with their own strengths and weaknesses in terms of their background knowledge, which is the ability to automatically link texts to other experiences, settings, or literary works. While a teacher cannot control the background knowledge a student brings to the classroom, they can enhance it through instructional strategies.	Mastering vocabulary enhances other reader-centered categories, such as background knowledge, fluency, and active reading. Students must be able to memorize word meanings and apply those word meanings to the texts they are reading.	Fluency enables students to read accurately and at a faster pace, which ensures that they are acquiring more knowledge and actively engaging with their materials.	Active reading, which is tied to other categories such as attention and motivation, allows students to take ownership in their reading development instead of relying on other students (or the teacher) to "do the work."	Students are only able to actively respond to a text when their critical thinking skills are enhanced and engaged. Critical thinking is a category of learning that can emerge from other sources besides texts, but then can be applied to texts.

Reading comprehension is also tied to text-based factor. While texts are inanimate objects, they have agency in the classroom – they have the ability to make or break a student's educational experience.

Below are some examples of text-based factors that affect reading comprehension:

Content	Readability	Cultural Relevance	Identity/Individual Relevance	Layout/Format
The content of the story has the potential to shape student interest – if the content is boring or irrelevant, then expect the student to disengage.	Each student has their own unique Lexile or readability range. If texts exist outside this range, they will either a) be too easy and not challenging enough to read, or b) too difficult to comprehend.	A student's culture should be reflected in the text in some capacity – if this is not the case, a student will likely not see connect to the meaning of the text.	A student's racial, ethnic, socioeconomic, and gender identity should also be reflected in the texts that they read.	Layout/format is often underestimated, but, if it looks boring or difficult, a student might perceive it as boring or difficult. For students who struggle with reading comprehension, for example, pages full of tiny text may not be the best option.

Assessment

The Processes of Learning to Read and Reading to Learn

Learning to read and reading to learn are two completely different, albeit interrelated, processes. **Learning to read** focuses mostly on decoding, and thus, all assessments should emphasize word recognition strategies: concepts of print, phonemic awareness, phonics, and sight words. Learning to read is also about building a ramp to fluency through accuracy, automaticity, and practice.

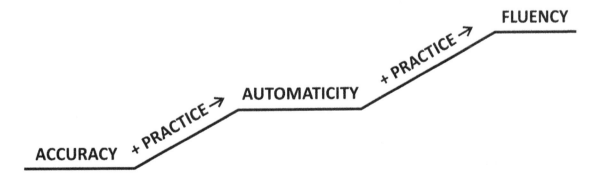

Learning to read is about sound-symbol relationships, sound conventions, and understanding sentence and syllable segments.

Reading to learn, on the other hand, is all about comprehension. It is about increasing knowledge once the conventions have already been learned. Students can graduate from terse text to full-blown expository pieces as they build academic language (background knowledge, school vocabulary, syntax, text structure) and comprehension strategies (via comprehension monitoring and (re)organizing texts).

Language development and language differences – specifically interlanguage effects – can impact this process, in both positive and negative ways. Universal language components can reinforce conventional sound-symbol techniques. However, conceptual and linguistic differences between languages can cause confusions and gaps in the knowledge of English Language Learners (ELLs). Thus, as language learners enter a new linguistic context, they can benefit from these early reading fundamentals. Language learners must move up the fluency ramp before they can ever tackle the nuances of reading comprehension.

Assessment Types

Listening, speaking, reading, writing, and vocabulary can be evaluated using a variety of assessments, methods, and tools that push both teachers and students beyond traditional standardized testing approaches. These assessments, methods, and tools include:

- **Informal Assessments:** "fly-by" assessments that may not be formally collected, but may gauge student learning and influence instructional approaches

    o Examples: Student questioning, self-assessments, journaling, reflections, surveys, votes, interviews, student conferences, social-emotional thermometers, rating, observations, personal testimonies

- Selected Response Assessments: traditional assessments that one might see on a conventional test, quiz, or standardized examination

    o Examples: True-false, word bank, yes-no, matching, multiple choice

- Constructed Response: any type of assessment in which an answer is written, drawn, mapped, charted, or illustrated (typically, but not always, by hand)

    o Examples: Visual data (charts, graphs, tables, matrices), visual maps and illustrations (flowcharts, cognitive maps, concept webs, diagrams), timelines, drawings, political cartoons, essays, short answer

- Performance Assessment: any type of nontraditional assessment that involves students performing and showing skills and knowledge through a variety of tasks

    o Examples: Prepared speeches, class debate, presentations, portfolios, prose/poetry interpretations, class discussions, exhibits

Assessment Methods

- **Diagnostic Assessments:** these assessments, which are becoming more popular, are used to diagnose such things as: behavior, academic readiness, and memory; they are used to diagnose gaps, strengths, weaknesses, or issues

- **Formative Assessments:** usually implemented more frequently to help guide instructional pacing and intervention

- **Summative Assessments:** usually implemented at the end of a chapter, unit, or semester to assess mastery of particular learning objectives

Assessment Tools

There are tons of tools, digital and traditional, that teachers can use in the classroom. Here is a list of common tools:

- Standardized Examinations
- Practice Tests
- Exams

34

- Rubrics
- Worksheets
- Quizzes
- Surveys
- Computer Technologies (which automatically compile student data)
- Lexile Scores
- Memory Tests

Non-Written and Written Communication

Conventions of Language

Sentence Structure and Formation

Four types of incomplete sentences are sentence fragments, run-on sentences, subject-verb and/or pronoun-antecedent disagreement, and non-parallel structure.

Sentence Fragments

Sentence fragments are caused by absent subjects, absent verbs, or dangling/uncompleted dependent clauses. Every sentence must have a subject and a verb to be complete. An example of a **fragment** is "Raining all night long," because there is no subject present. "It was raining all night long" is one correction. Another example of a sentence fragment is the second part in "Many scientists think in unusual ways. Einstein, for instance." The second phrase is a fragment because it has no verb. One correction is "Many scientists, like Einstein, think in unusual ways." Finally, look for "cliffhanger" words like *if, when, because,* or *although* that introduce **dependent clauses**, which cannot stand alone without an independent clause. For example, to correct the sentence fragment "If you get home early," add an independent clause: "If you get home early, we can go dancing."

Run-On Sentences

A run-on sentence combines two or more complete sentences without punctuating them correctly or separating them. For example, the following is a run-on sentence caused by a lack of punctuation:

> There is a malfunction in the computer system however there is nobody available right now who knows how to troubleshoot it.

One correction is, "There is a malfunction in the computer system; however, there is nobody available right now who knows how to troubleshoot it." Another is, "There is a malfunction in the computer system. However, there is nobody available right now who knows how to troubleshoot it."

An example of a **comma splice** of two sentences is the following:

> Jim decided not to take the bus, he walked home.

Replacing the comma with a period or a semicolon corrects this. Commas that try and separate two independent clauses without a contraction are considered comma splices.

Parallel Sentence Structures

Parallel structure in a sentence matches the forms of sentence components. Any sentence containing more than one description or phrase should keep them consistent in wording and form. Readers can easily follow writers' ideas when they are written in parallel structure, making it an important element of correct sentence construction. For example, this sentence lacks parallelism: "Our coach is a skilled manager, a clever strategist, and works hard." The first two phrases are parallel, but the third is not. The correction is: "Our coach is a skilled manager, a clever strategist, and a hard worker." Now all three phrases match in form. Here is another example:

Fred intercepted the ball, escaped tacklers, and a touchdown was scored.

This is also non-parallel. Here is the sentence corrected:

Fred intercepted the ball, escaped tacklers, and scored a touchdown.

Sentence Fluency

For fluent composition, writers must use a variety of sentence types and structures, and ensure that they smoothly flow together when they are read. To accomplish this, they must first be able to identify fluent writing when they read it. This includes being able to distinguish among simple, compound, complex, and compound-complex sentences in text; to observe variations among sentence types, lengths, and beginnings; and to notice figurative language and understand how it augments sentence length and imparts musicality. Once writers recognize superior fluency, they should revise their own writing to be more readable and fluent. They must be able to apply acquired skills to revisions before being able to apply them to new drafts.

One strategy for revising writing to increase its sentence fluency is flipping sentences. This involves rearranging the word order in a sentence without deleting, changing, or adding any words. For example, the student or other writer who has written the sentence, "We went bicycling on Saturday" can revise it to "On Saturday, we went bicycling." Another technique is using appositives. An **appositive** is a phrase or word that renames or identifies another adjacent word or phrase. Writers can revise for sentence fluency by inserting main phrases/words from one shorter sentence into another shorter sentence, combining them into one longer sentence, e.g., from "My cat Peanut is a gray and brown tabby. He loves hunting rats." to "My cat Peanut, a gray and brown tabby, loves hunting rats." Revisions can also connect shorter sentences by using conjunctions and commas and removing repeated words: "Scott likes eggs. Scott is allergic to eggs" becomes "Scott likes eggs, but he is allergic to them."

One technique for revising writing to increase sentence fluency is "padding" short, simple sentences by adding phrases that provide more details specifying why, how, when, and/or where something took place. For example, a writer might have these two simple sentences: "I went to the market. I purchased a cake." To revise these, the writer can add the following informative dependent and independent clauses and prepositional phrases, respectively: "Before my mother woke up, I sneaked out of the house and went to the supermarket. As a birthday surprise, I purchased a cake for her." When revising sentences to make them longer, writers must also punctuate them correctly to change them from simple sentences to compound, complex, or compound-complex sentences.

Skills Writers Can Employ to Increase Fluency

One way writers can increase fluency is by varying the beginnings of sentences. Writers do this by starting most of their sentences with different words and phrases rather than monotonously repeating the same ones across multiple sentences. Another way writers can increase fluency is by varying the lengths of sentences. Since run-on sentences are incorrect, writers make sentences longer by converting them from simple to compound, complex, and compound-complex sentences. The coordination and subordination involved in these also give the text more variation and interest, hence more fluency. Here are a few more ways writers can increase fluency:

- Varying the transitional language and conjunctions used
- Writing sentences with a variety of rhythms by using prepositional phrases
- Varying sentence structure

Punctuation
Rules of Capitalization
The first word of any document, and of each new sentence, is capitalized. Proper nouns, like names and adjectives derived from them, should also be capitalized. Here are some examples:

- Grand Canyon
- Pacific Palisades
- Golden Gate Bridge
- Freudian slip
- Shakespearian, Spenserian, or Petrarchan sonnet
- Irish song

Some exceptions are adjectives originally derived from proper nouns, which through time and usage are no longer capitalized, like *quixotic, herculean*, or *draconian*. Capitals draw attention to specific instances of people, places, and things. Some categories that should be capitalized include the following:

- brand names
- companies
- months
- governmental divisions or agencies
- historical eras
- major historical events
- holidays
- institutions
- famous buildings
- ships and other manmade constructions
- natural and manmade landmarks
- territories
- nicknames
- organizations
- planets
- nationalities
- tribes
- religions
- names of religious deities
- roads
- special occasions, like the Cannes Film Festival or the Olympic Games

When official titles precede names, they should be capitalized, except when there is a comma between the title and name. If a title follows or replaces a name, it should not be capitalized. For example, "the president" without a name is not capitalized, as in "The president addressed Congress." However, with a name it is capitalized, as in "President Biden addressed Congress." Some publishers and writers nevertheless capitalize President, King, Pope, etc., when they are not accompanied by names to show respect for these high offices. However, many writers in America object to this practice for violating democratic principles of equality. Occupations before full names are not capitalized, like owner Mark Cuban, director Martin Scorsese, or coach Roger McDowell.

Some universal rules for capitalization in composition titles include capitalizing the following:

- The first and last words of the title
- Forms of the verb *to be* and all other verbs

- Pronouns
- The word *not*

Universal rules for NOT capitalizing include the articles *the, a,* or *an;* the conjunctions *and, or,* or *nor;* and the preposition *to,* or *to* as part of the infinitive form of a verb. The exception to all of these is if any of them is the first or last word in the title, in which case they are capitalized. Other words are subject to differences of opinion and differences among various stylebooks or methods. These include *as, but, if,* and *or,* which some capitalize, and others do not. Some authorities say no preposition should ever be capitalized; some say prepositions five or more letters long should be capitalized. The *Associated Press Stylebook* advises capitalizing prepositions longer than three letters (like *about, across,* or *with*).

Commas

Commas separate words or phrases in a series of three or more. The **Oxford comma** is the last comma in a series. Many people omit this last comma, but doing so often causes confusion. Here is an example:

I love my siblings, the King of England and Madonna.

This example without the comma implies that the "King of England and Madonna" are the speaker's siblings. However, if the speaker was trying to say that they love their siblings, the King of England, as well as Madonna, there should be a comma after "King of England" to signify this.

Commas also separate two coordinate adjectives ("big, heavy dog") but not cumulative ones, which should be arranged in a particular order for them to make sense ("beautiful ancient ruins").

A comma ends the first of two independent clauses connected by conjunctions. Here is an example:

I ate a bowl of tomato soup, and I was hungry very shortly after.

Here are some brief rules for commas:

- Commas follow introductory words like *however, furthermore, well, why,* and *actually,* among others.

- Commas go between a city and state: Houston, Texas.

- If using a comma between a surname and Jr. or Sr. or a degree like M.D., also follow the whole name with a comma: "Martin Luther King, Jr., wrote that."

- A comma follows a dependent clause beginning a sentence: "Although she was very small, . . ."

- Nonessential modifying words/phrases/clauses are enclosed by commas: "Wendy, who is Peter's sister, closed the window."

- Commas introduce or interrupt direct quotations: "She said, 'I hate him.' 'Why,' I asked, 'do you hate him?'"

Semicolons

Semicolons are used to connect two independent clauses, but should never be used in the place of a comma. They can replace periods between two closely connected sentences, e.g., "Call back tomorrow; it can wait until then." When writing items in a series and one or more of them contains internal commas, separate them with semicolons, like the following:

People came from Springfield, Illinois; Alamo, Tennessee; Moscow, Idaho; and other locations.

Parentheses

Parentheses enclose information such as an aside or more clarifying information: "She ultimately replied (after deliberating for an hour) that she was undecided." They are also used to insert short, in-text definitions or acronyms: "His FBS (fasting blood sugar) was higher than normal." When parenthetical information ends the sentence, the period follows the parentheses: "We received new funds ($25,000)." Only put periods within parentheses if the whole sentence is inside them: "Look at this. (You'll be astonished.)" However, this can also be acceptable as a clause: "Look at this (you'll be astonished)." Although parentheses appear to be part of the sentence subject, they are not, and do not change subject-verb agreement: "Will (and his dog) was there."

Quotation Marks

Quotation marks are typically used when someone is quoting a direct word or phrase someone else writes or says. Additionally, quotation marks should be used for the titles of poems, short stories, songs, articles, chapters, and other shorter works. When quotations include punctuation, periods and commas should *always* be placed inside of the quotation marks.

When a quotation contains another quotation inside of it, the outer quotation should be enclosed in double quotation marks and the inner quotation should be enclosed in single quotation marks. For example: "Timmy was begging, 'Don't go! Don't leave!'" When using both double and single quotation marks, writers will find that many word-processing programs may automatically insert enough space between the single and double quotation marks to be visible for clearer reading. But if this is not the case, the writer should write/type them with enough space between to keep them from looking like three single quotation marks. Additionally, non-standard usages, terms used in an unusual fashion, and technical terms are often clarified by quotation marks. Here are some examples:

My "friend," Dr. Sims, has been micromanaging me again.

This way of extracting oil has been dubbed "fracking."

Apostrophes

One use of the apostrophe is followed by an *s* to indicate possession, like *Mrs. White's home* or *our neighbor's dog*. When using the *'s* after names or nouns that also end in the letter *s*, no single rule applies: some experts advise adding both the apostrophe and the *s*, like "the Jones's house," while others prefer using only the apostrophe and omitting the additional *s*, like "the Jones' house." The wisest expert advice is to pick one formula or the other and then apply it consistently. Newspapers and magazines often use *'s* after common nouns ending with *s*, but add only the apostrophe after proper nouns or names ending with *s*. One common error is to place the apostrophe before a name's final *s* instead of after it: "Ms. Hasting's book" is incorrect if the name is Ms. Hastings.

Plural nouns should not include apostrophes (e.g., "apostrophe's"). Exceptions are to clarify atypical plurals, like verbs used as nouns: "These are the do's and don'ts." Irregular plurals that do not end in *s* always take apostrophe-*s*, not *s*-apostrophe—a common error, as in "childrens' toys," which should be "children's toys." Compound nouns like mother-in-law, when they are singular and possessive, are followed by apostrophe-*s*, like "your mother-in-law's coat." When a compound noun is plural and possessive, the plural is formed before the apostrophe-*s*, like "your sisters-in-laws' coats." When two named people possess the same thing, use apostrophe-*s* after the second name only, like "Dennis and Pam's house."

<u>Usage</u>

Possessives

Possessive forms indicate possession, i.e. that something belongs to or is owned by someone or something. As such, the most common parts of speech to be used in possessive form are adjectives, nouns, and pronouns. The rule for correctly spelling/punctuating possessive nouns and proper nouns is with -*'s*, like "the woman's briefcase" or "Frank's hat." With possessive adjectives, however, apostrophes are not used: these include *my, your, his, her, its, our,* and *their,* like "my book," "your friend," "his car," "her house," "its contents," "our family," or "their property." Possessive

39

pronouns include *mine, yours, his, hers, its, ours,* and *theirs.* These also have no apostrophes. The difference is that possessive adjectives take direct objects, whereas possessive pronouns replace them. For example, instead of using two possessive adjectives in a row, as in "I forgot my book, so Blanca let me use her book," which reads monotonously, replacing the second one with a possessive pronoun reads better: "I forgot my book, so Blanca let me use hers."

Pronouns

There are three pronoun cases: subjective case, objective case, and possessive case. Pronouns as subjects are pronouns that replace the subject of the sentence, such as *I, you, he, she, it, we, they* and *who.* Pronouns as objects replace the object of the sentence, such as *me, you, him, her, it, us, them,* and *whom.* Pronouns that show possession are *mine, yours, hers, its, ours, theirs,* and *whose.* The following are examples of different pronoun cases:

- Subject pronoun: "*She* ate the cake for her birthday." "*I* saw the movie."
- Object pronoun: "You gave *me* the card last weekend." "She gave the picture to *him.*"
- Possessive pronoun: "That bracelet you found yesterday is *mine.*" "*His* name was Casey."

Adjectives

Adjectives are descriptive words that modify nouns or pronouns. They may occur before or after the nouns or pronouns they modify in sentences. For example, in "This is a big house," *big* is an adjective modifying or describing the noun *house.* In "This house is big," the adjective is at the end of the sentence rather than preceding the noun it modifies.

A rule of punctuation that applies to adjectives is to separate a series of adjectives with commas. For example, "Their home was a large, rambling, old, white, two-story house." A comma should never separate the last adjective from the noun.

Adverbs

Whereas adjectives modify and describe nouns or pronouns, adverbs modify and describe adjectives, verbs, or other adverbs. Adverbs can be thought of as answers to questions in that they describe when, where, how, how often, how much, or to what extent.

Many (but not all) adjectives can be converted to adverbs by adding *–ly.* For example, in "She is a quick learner," *quick* is an adjective modifying *learner.* In "She learns quickly," *quickly* is an adverb modifying *learns.* One exception is *fast. Fast* is an adjective in "She is a fast learner." However, *–ly* is never added to the word *fast;* it retains the same form as an adverb in "She learns fast."

Verbs

A verb is a word or phrase that expresses action, feeling, or state of being. Verbs explain what their subject is *doing.* Three different types of verbs used in a sentence are action verbs, linking verbs, and helping verbs.

Action verbs show a physical or mental action. Some examples of action verbs are *play, type, jump, write, examine, study, invent, develop,* and *taste.* The following example uses an action verb:

> Kat *imagines* that she is a mermaid in the ocean.

The verb *imagines* explains what Kat is doing: she is imagining being a mermaid.

Linking verbs connect the subject to the predicate without expressing an action. The following sentence shows an example of a linking verb:

> The mango *tastes* sweet.

40

The verb *tastes* is a linking verb. The mango doesn't *do* the tasting, but the word *taste* links the mango to its predicate, sweet. Most linking verbs can also be used as action verbs, such as *smell, taste, look, seem, grow,* and *sound.* Saying something *is* something else is also an example of a linking verb. For example, if we were to say, "Peaches is a dog," the verb *is* would be a linking verb in this sentence, since it links the subject to its predicate.

Helping verbs are verbs that help the main verb in a sentence. Examples of helping verbs are *be, am, is, was, have, has, do, did, can, could, may, might, should,* and *must,* among others. The following are examples of helping verbs:

> Jessica *is* planning a trip to Hawaii.

> Brenda *does* not like camping.

> Xavier *should* go to the dance tonight.

Notice that after each of these helping verbs is the main verb of the sentence: *planning, like,* and *go.* Helping verbs usually show an aspect of time.

Transitional Words and Phrases

In writing, some sentences naturally lead to others, whereas in other cases, a new sentence expresses a new idea. Transitional phrases connect sentences and the ideas they convey, which makes the writing coherent. Transitional language also guides the reader from one thought to the next. For example, when pointing out an objection to the previous idea, starting a sentence with "However," "But," or "On the other hand" is transitional. When adding another idea or detail, writers use "Also," "In addition," "Furthermore," "Further," "Moreover," "Not only," etc. Readers have difficulty perceiving connections between ideas without such transitional wording.

Subject-Verb Agreement

Lack of subject-verb agreement is a very common grammatical error. One of the most common instances is when people use a series of nouns as a compound subject with a singular instead of a plural verb. Here is an example:

> Identifying the best books, locating the sellers with the lowest prices, and paying for them *is* difficult.

Instead, it should say they "*are* difficult."

Additionally, when a sentence subject is compound, the verb is plural:

> He and his cousins *were* at the reunion.

However, if the conjunction connecting two or more singular nouns or pronouns is "or" or "nor," the verb must be singular to agree:

> That pen or another one like it is in the desk drawer.

If a compound subject includes both a singular noun and a plural one, and they are connected by "or" or "nor," the verb must agree with the subject closest to the verb: "Sally or her sisters go jogging daily"; but "Her sisters or Sally goes jogging daily."

Simply put, singular subjects require singular verbs and plural subjects require plural verbs. A common source of agreement errors is not identifying the sentence subject correctly. For example, people often write sentences incorrectly like, "The group of students *were* complaining about the test." The subject is not the plural "students" but the singular "group." Therefore, the correct sentence should read, "The group of students *was* complaining about the test." The converse also applies, for example, in this incorrect sentence: "The facts in that complicated court case *is* open to question." The subject of the sentence is not the singular "case" but the plural "facts." Hence the sentence would correctly be written: "The facts in that complicated court case *are* open to question." New writers should not be misled by the distance between the subject and verb, especially when another noun with a different number intervenes as in these examples. The verb must agree with the subject, not the noun closest to it.

Pronoun-Antecedent Agreement

Pronouns within a sentence must refer specifically to one noun, known as the **antecedent.** Sometimes, if there are multiple nouns within a sentence, it may be difficult to ascertain which noun belongs to the pronoun. It's important that the pronouns always clearly reference the nouns in the sentence so as not to confuse the reader. Here's an example of an unclear pronoun reference:

> After Catherine cut Libby's hair, David bought her some lunch.

The pronoun in the examples above is *her.* The pronoun could either be referring to *Catherine* or *Libby.* Here are some ways to write the above sentence with a clear pronoun reference:

> After Catherine cut Libby's hair, David bought Libby some lunch.

> David bought Libby some lunch after Catherine cut Libby's hair.

But many times the pronoun will clearly refer to its antecedent, like the following:

> After David cut Catherine's hair, he bought her some lunch.

Formal and Informal Language

Formal language is less personal than informal language. It is more "buttoned-up" and business-like, adhering to proper grammatical rules. It is used in professional or academic contexts, to convey respect or authority. For example, one would use formal language to write an informative or argumentative essay for school or to address a superior. Formal language avoids contractions, slang, colloquialisms, and first-person pronouns. Formal language uses sentences that are usually more complex and often in passive voice. Punctuation can differ as well. For example, **exclamation points (!)** are used to show strong emotion or can be used as an interjection but should be used sparingly in formal writing situations.

Informal language is often used when communicating with family members, friends, peers, and those known more personally. It is more casual, spontaneous, and forgiving in its conformity to grammatical rules and conventions. Informal language is used for personal emails and correspondence between coworkers or other familial relationships. The tone is more relaxed. In informal writing, slang, contractions, clichés, and the first- and second-person are often used.

Writing Strategies

Prewriting

Brainstorming

Before beginning the essay, read the prompt thoroughly and make sure you understand its expectations. Brainstorm as many ideas as you can think of that relate to the topic and list them or put them into a graphic organizer. Refer to this list as you organize your essay outline.

Freewriting

Like brainstorming, **freewriting** is another prewriting activity to help the writer generate ideas. This method involves setting a timer for two or three minutes and writing down all ideas that come to mind about the topic using complete sentences. Once time is up, writers should review the sentences to see what observations have been made and how these ideas might translate into a more unified direction for the topic. Even if sentences lack sense as a whole, freewriting is an excellent way to get ideas onto the page in the very beginning stages of writing. Using complete sentences can make this a bit more challenging than brainstorming, but overall it is a worthwhile exercise, as it may force the writer to come up with more complete thoughts about the topic.

Take the ideas you generated during pre-writing and organize them in the form of an outline.

Outlining

Outlines are organizational tools that arrange a piece of writing's main ideas and the evidence that supports them. After pre-writing, organize your ideas by topic, select the best ones, and put them into the outline. Be sure to include an introduction, main points, and a conclusion. Typically, it is a good idea to have three main points with at least two pieces of supporting evidence each. The following displays the format of an outline:

I. Introduction
    1. Background
    2. Thesis statement
II. Body
    1. Point A
        a. Supporting evidence
        b. Supporting evidence
    2. Point B
        a. Supporting evidence
        b. Supporting evidence
    3. Point C
        a. Supporting evidence
        b. Supporting evidence
III. Conclusion
    1. Restatement of main points
    2. Memorable ending

Drafting/Writing

Now it comes time to actually write the essay. In this stage, writers should follow the outline they developed in the brainstorming process and try to incorporate the useful sentences penned in the freewriting exercise. The main goal of this phase is to put all the thoughts together in cohesive sentences and paragraphs.

It is helpful for writers to remember that their work here does not have to be perfect. This process is often referred to as **drafting** because writers are just creating a rough draft of their work. Because of this, writers should avoid getting bogged down on the small details.

Revising

Revising involves going back over a piece of writing and improving it. Try to read your essay from the perspective of a potential reader to ensure that it makes sense. When revising, check that the main points are clearly stated, logically organized, and directly supported by the sub-points. Remove unnecessary details that do not contribute to the argument.

The main goal of the **revision phase** is to improve the essay's flow, cohesiveness, readability, and focus. For example, an essay will make a less persuasive argument if the various pieces of evidence are scattered and presented illogically or clouded with unnecessary thought. Therefore, writers should consider their essay's structure and organization, ensuring that there are smooth transitions between sentences and paragraphs. There should be a discernable introduction and conclusion as well, as these crucial components of an essay provide readers with a blueprint to follow.

Additionally, if the writer includes copious details that do little to enhance the argument, they may actually distract readers from focusing on the main ideas and detract from the strength of their work. The ultimate goal is to retain the purpose or focus of the essay and provide a reader-friendly experience. Because of this, writers often need to delete parts of their essay to improve its flow and focus. Removing sentences, entire paragraphs, or large chunks of writing can be one of the toughest parts of the writing process because it is difficult to part with work one has done. However, ultimately, these types of cuts can significantly improve one's essay.

Lastly, writers should consider their voice and word choice. The voice should be consistent throughout and maintain a balance between an authoritative and warm style, to both inform and engage readers. One way to alter voice is through word choice. Writers should consider changing weak verbs to stronger ones and selecting more precise language in areas where wording is vague. In some cases, it is useful to modify sentence beginnings or to combine or split up sentences to provide a more varied sentence structure.

Editing
Rather than focusing on content (as is the aim in the revising stage), the **editing** phase is all about the mechanics of the essay: the syntax, word choice, and grammar. This can be considered the proofreading stage. Successful editing is what sets apart a messy essay from a polished document.

Look for the following types of errors when checking over your work:

- Spelling
- Tense usage
- Punctuation and capitalization
- Unclear, confusing, or incomplete sentences
- Subject/verb and noun/pronoun agreement

One of the most effective ways of identifying grammatical errors, awkward phrases, or unclear sentences is to read the essay out loud. Listening to one's own work can help move the writer from simply the author to the reader.

During the editing phase, it's also important to ensure the essay follows the correct formatting and citation rules as dictated by the assignment.

Students will need to master the following techniques and conventions to communicate and write in standard English.

Clear and Coherent Writing
Conventional Techniques
Spelling: Students should use a near-flawless command of spelling, limiting any major homonymic or technical errors/misspellings.

Syntax: Students should maintain syntactical conventions, using appropriate sentence structures that enhance the overall tone of the piece by incorporating dramatic pauses, repetition, and an appropriate mix of sentence arrangements.

Punctuation: Students should use punctuation to enhance syntax by accurately and symbolically conveying the pace of the piece.

Structure and Sequence
Overall Structure: Students should be able to tell a story that appropriately progresses through a typical plot structure – highlighting realistic tensions, conflicts, and resolutions, while effectively conveying change over time, and introducing believable characters and settings. Additionally, the story should develop a particular point of view by teaching a lesson and/or presenting some sort of social commentary or criticism.

44

Lead/Introduction: Students should effectively paint a portrait of the setting, context, atmosphere, or situation, foreshadowing or hinting at the upcoming events, and establishing a narrative tone.

Transitions: Students should appropriately use transitional sentences, phrases, and clauses that properly convey change over time, flawlessly connecting important parts of the story.

Ending: Students should instill a sense of closure in the reader by bringing about a resolution to tensions or conflicts and revealing how characters and situations change over time. The ending should align with the targeted tone or lesson of the narrative piece.

Organization: Students, at least at the K-12 level, will adopt conventional tropes and organizational structures (i.e., a coming-of-age story or satire) to purposefully convey the overall message or meaning of the text.

Descriptive Details
Word Choice: Students should employ varied vocabulary terms that symbolically help reinforce the trope, structure, and message of the story.

Elaboration: Students should elaborate by using highly descriptive details that paint the mood and atmosphere of the story by highlighting character strengths, flaws, mannerisms, idiosyncrasies, conflicts, and tensions.

Using Technology to Produce and Publish Individual or Shared Writing Products
There are thousands of ways students can use digital technologies to publish individual or shared writing projects online. When implemented correctly, these publishing activities allow students to be active and respectful "digital global citizens," connecting with other stakeholders via the worldwide web and Internet-based apps.

While the options are plentiful, here are some recommended resources for producing and publishing online writing projects:

- **Blog Sites:** Students have plenty of online blog options, including Wordpress.com and Wix. Additionally, they can submit their writing to companies like TNPT and Time for Kids, which frequently promote student writers. Online blogging provides students with the opportunity to enhance and exhibit their writing skills.

- **Social Media:** Social media is conventionally viewed as a distraction in the classroom. However, if its power can be harnessed, and its idiosyncrasies can be explicitly taught, then it can transform from distraction to the most powerful tool in your classroom. Students must be instructed about the power and potential (and proper uses) of social media so that they can become better global citizens. They help run positive social media campaigns that garner public attention (as well as funds and donations) from the public.

- **Coding:** Coding is more than an outlet for math-minded students – it can also be a platform for publishing student writing projects. Mixing computer programming and traditional writing skills is never a bad idea. In fact, it is the epitome of interdisciplinary learning.

- **Google Drive:** Google Drive, specifically Google Docs and Google Slides, allows students to write and collaborate in real-time. This is an especially good tool for the writing process because it enables students to peer review and edit each other's work.

- **YouTube:** While not a traditional writing platform, YouTube provides students with the opportunity to showcase their writing skills by making scripts and skits.

- **E-Books:** As colleges become more competitive, students should have the opportunity to be published before ever stepping foot on campus. Today, platforms like Amazon Kindle allow anyone to publish an E-book online. This can be a great collaborative assignment or individual project.

- **The Gig Economy and Online Apps:** The growing "gig economy" presents students with an opportunity to "earn and learn" at a young age. Apps like Upwork have the potential to provide some students with access to income. Content sells at a fast rate on the worldwide web, so the gig economy could be a perfect entry point for a new career.

Writing Applications

Principles of Composition

A **paragraph** is a series of connected and related sentences addressing one topic. Writing good paragraphs benefits writers by helping them to stay on target while drafting and revising their work. It benefits readers by helping them to follow the writing more easily. Regardless of how brilliant their ideas may be, writers who do not present them in organized ways will fail to engage readers—and fail to accomplish their writing goals. A fundamental rule for paragraphing is to confine each paragraph to a single idea. When writers find themselves transitioning to a new idea, they should start a new paragraph. However, a paragraph can include several pieces of evidence supporting its single idea; and it can include several points if they are all related to the overall paragraph topic. When writers find each point becoming lengthy, they may choose instead to devote a separate paragraph to every point and elaborate upon each more fully.

An effective paragraph should have these elements:

- Unity: One major discussion point or focus should occupy the whole paragraph from beginning to end.

- Coherence: For readers to understand a paragraph, it must be coherent. Two components of coherence are logical and verbal bridges. In logical bridges, the writer may write consecutive sentences with parallel structure or carry an idea over across sentences. In verbal bridges, writers may repeat key words across sentences.

- Topic sentence: The paragraph should have a sentence that generally identifies the paragraph's thesis or main idea.

- Sufficient development: To develop a paragraph, writers can use the following techniques after stating their topic sentence:

  - Define terms
  - Cite data
  - Use illustrations, anecdotes, and examples
  - Evaluate causes and effects
  - Analyze the topic
  - Explain the topic using chronological order

A **topic sentence** identifies the main idea of the paragraph. Some are explicit, some implicit. The topic sentence can appear anywhere in the paragraph. However, many experts advise beginning writers to place each paragraph topic sentence at or near the beginning of its paragraph to ensure that their readers understand what the topic of each paragraph is. Even without having written an explicit topic sentence, the writer should still be able to summarize readily what subject matter each paragraph addresses. The writer must then fully develop the topic that is introduced or identified in the topic sentence. Depending on what the writer's purpose is, they may use different methods for developing each paragraph.

Two main steps in the process of organizing paragraphs and essays should both be completed after determining the writing's main point, while the writer is planning or outlining the work. The initial step is to give an order to the topics addressed in each paragraph. Writers must have logical reasons for putting one paragraph first, another second, etc.

The second step is to sequence the sentences in each paragraph. As with the first step, writers must have logical reasons for the order of sentences. Sometimes the work's main point obviously indicates a specific order.

To be effective, a topic sentence should be concise so that readers get its point without losing the meaning among too many words. As an example, in *Only Yesterday: An Informal History of the 1920s* (1931), author Frederick Lewis Allen's topic sentence introduces his paragraph describing the 1929 stock market crash: "The Bull Market was dead." This example illustrates the criteria of conciseness and brevity. It is also a strong sentence, expressed clearly and unambiguously. The topic sentence also introduces the paragraph, alerting the reader's attention to the main idea of the paragraph and the subject matter that follows the topic sentence.

Experts often recommend opening a paragraph with the topic sentences to enable the reader to realize the main point of the paragraph immediately. Application letters for jobs and university admissions also benefit from opening with topic sentences. However, positioning the topic sentence at the end of a paragraph is more logical when the paragraph identifies a number of specific details that accumulate evidence and then culminates with a generalization. While paragraphs with extremely obvious main ideas need no topic sentences, more often—and particularly for students learning to write—the topic sentence is the most important sentence in the paragraph. It not only communicates the main idea quickly to readers; it also helps writers produce and control information.

Composing and Analyzing Writing in Different Genres

The purpose of an **argumentative writing** is to prove or disprove a particular thesis or hypothesis, using various claims and inferences that challenge one or many previous claims or inferences. Most argumentative pieces are more formal and academic than persuasive pieces. They are not trying to persuade an audience through subjective tropes, but rather are trying to argue a particular point using objective evidence.

The purpose of **opinion writing** is to carry out the single-minding goal of voicing one's thoughts and letting one's opinion be heard. Opinion pieces differ from persuasive pieces because they are not trying to sway the readers' opinions; rather, they are simply trying to communicate their own opinion.

The purpose of **persuasive writing** is to blend person opinions with facts in order to sway or convince readers to take a particular side or stance (usually in some sort of larger societal, political, or ethical debate). Political speeches can sometimes be persuasive in nature for this reason.

The purpose of **informative or explanatory writing** is to communicate concrete intelligence to the reader. Accordingly, the tone is typically formal, and the language should be objective. Informative writing does not usually appeal to pathos, logos, or ethos. Instead, it simply aims to provide facts, evidence, observations, and objective descriptions of the subject matter in an organized, understandable fashion.

Summaries, letters, and research reports are examples of subgenres that fall within these larger genres. **Summaries** are traditionally informational/explanatory types of writing that simply remove extraneous details in order to create a shorter, less-wordy version of a particular topic, text, or other form of communication. **Letters** are interpersonal or intrapersonal forms of writing that can potentially ne argumentative, opinionated, persuasive, or informative. This category is all-encompassing because, at its core, it is a very intimate form of writing that takes on the personal goals or objectives of the author, which can range from venting to informing. **Research reports** are generally argumentative forms of writing that use thesis statements or testing hypotheses. An entirely opinionated report would likely not maintain the academic standards necessary to pass a course in college, for instance.

Writing Arguments to Support Claims

Having a command of the basics in the written structure of a language, however, is not enough to ensure a reader's comprehension. Academic writing requires a rich vocabulary and a logical order. In academic writing, the introduction should be compelling enough to draw in the audience. Within the first few sentences, the argument should be clearly stated, along with background information and subtle or overt reasons why the paper is worth reading. Once the introduction is complete, a well-organized academic paper will begin to unfold the evidence, data, and information that supports the argument. The importance of evidence cannot be overstated because the audience will immediately begin to weigh the evidence. The more objective the data, the more credible the argument. It isn't enough for the author to simply unfold the data. The data should be clearly explained and analyzed in a way that supports the argument, leaving little doubt in the reader's mind about the argument's strength. Concluding the academic paper with a concise summary, restating the evidence, and reasserting the argument without sounding redundant will add strength to the overall message and will leave the audience with a sense of closure.

Writing Narratives

Narrative writing tells a story. The most prominent examples of narrative writing are fictional novels. Here are some examples:

- Mark Twain's *The Adventures of Tom Sawyer* and *The Adventures of Huckleberry Finn*
- Victor Hugo's *Les Misérables*
- Charles Dickens' *Great Expectations, David Copperfield*, and *A Tale of Two Cities*
- Jane Austen's *Northanger Abbey, Mansfield Park, Pride and Prejudice, Sense and Sensibility*, and *Emma*
- Toni Morrison's *Beloved, The Bluest Eye*, and *Song of Solomon*
- Gabriel García Márquez's *One Hundred Years of Solitude* and *Love in the Time of Cholera*

Some nonfiction works are also written in narrative form. For example, some authors choose a narrative style to convey factual information about a topic, such as a specific animal, country, geographic region, and scientific or natural phenomenon.

Since narrative is the type of writing that tells a story, it must be told by someone who is the narrator. The narrator may be a fictional character telling the story from their own viewpoint. This narrator uses the first person (*I, me, my, mine, we, us, our*, and *ours*). The narrator may simply be the author; for example, when Louisa May Alcott writes "dear reader" in *Little Women*, she (the author) addresses us as readers. In this case, the novel is typically told in third person, referring to the characters as he, she, they, or them. Another more common technique is the omniscient narrator; i.e., the story is told by an unidentified individual who sees and knows everything about the events and characters—not only their externalized actions, but also their internalized feelings and thoughts. Second person, i.e., writing the story by addressing readers as "you" throughout, is less frequently used.

Non-Written Communication

Non-Written Genres and Traditions

Non-written genres and traditions include any oral, theatrical, or visual presentations of information or knowledge that is not completely reliant on written or typed texts (i.e., traditional essays or research papers).

Understanding these different genres and traditions of conveying knowledge is critical for engaging diverse learners and cultures. Different formats and media that can be used to enhance the implementation of these traditions in the classrooms (these formats and media are discussed below). However, beyond format and media, it is helpful for teachers to have a well-rounded understanding of the specific options made available by these non-written genres and traditions:

TYPE	DEFINITION
Storytelling	Storytelling is the process of simply sharing an oral account of something real or fictional. Oral storytelling has been around for a long time in human history, and is equally as relevant for students today. The art of storytelling is something that can enhance all aspects of students' lives – their education, their interviews, their entrepreneurial pursuits, and their political consciousness.

TYPE	DEFINITION
Oral History	Sometimes the pen never hits the paper when it comes to history. Oral history is the age-old process of recounting historical events through spoken word. Exposing students to this timeless practice can build cultural competence and historical consciousness.
Narratives	A specific form of storytelling, narratives can be defined as the ability to connect disparate events and ideas through dialogue. In the classroom, students can learn how to create narratives about their lives, narratives about their loves, and narratives about their learning. There are very few limitations to incorporating this non-written tradition in the classroom: all you need is a platform and student voice.
Persuasive Speeches	The art of persuasion can also be captured in spoken words. Persuasive speeches are specific types of speaking engagements that allow students to express their points of views in a classic, structured speech format. Although speeches usually incorporate the writing process, they can also be delivered in an impromptu, non-traditional format.
Research Presentations	Research presentations can take on different formats and utilize different media (as illustrated below). A research presentation is a non-written tradition that relies heavily on visual materials, usually some sort of digital PowerPoint slides. Exposing students to research presentations is crucial for preparing them for their next steps as students and young professionals. Although many colleges and corporations are moving away from this conventional practice, most students will have to deliver at least one research presentation in their adult life, whether at a university or corporation conference room.
TED Talks	TED Talks are more than a fad – they are an art form that students should be exposed to early and often. TED Talks are conference-style presentations captured on video that are capped at a maximum 18 minutes. They are unique because they combine all previously mentioned non-written genres and encourage students to combine digital, visual, audio, and oral formats of conveying knowledge.
Poetry Recitations	Poetry recitations are common practice within art communities and college campuses – they are defined by oral recitations of original or preexisting poems. This type of non-written tradition can help students with both memory and oratory. Some subgenres of poetry recitations include spoken word and freestyle raps. Spoken word is a rhythmic type of poetry performed in a theatrical, storytelling fashion. Freestyle rap is a blend of musical performance and symbolic, spontaneous rhyming schemes that are delivered by one or many participants, typically in a competitive manner.
Video Reviews (of Literature or Movies)	Students no longer have to write reviews with the advances of digital video technologies. Video reviews are like traditional reviews – they just take place in front of a camera. Video reviews afford students with the opportunity to analyze texts or movies in a visual and audio format.
Skits/Theatrical Productions	Skits are short-featured plays used to convey an idea, story, or message. Theatrical productions include skits, plays, spoken word, musicals, and dramas. This non-written genre often draws inspiration from written materials (i.e., scripts), but allow participants to work on other skills such as oratory, creativity, and body language.

TYPE	DEFINITION
Podcasts	Podcasts are a new take on an old art form: they are radio-style broadcasts meant for the digital age. They allow students to work on dialogue, oratory, persuasiveness, and critical thinking.

Information Presented in Diverse Media and Formats

Throughout their lives, students will have to learn to comprehend, deconstruct, and (re)construct knowledge using different types of media and formats. This allows students to become aware and contributing global citizens; it also helps them understand such concepts as objectivity, subjectivity, truth, cultural myths, and propaganda.

In order for students to fully recognize the power of each format, they must be exposed to these formats, explicitly taught about the pitfalls of these formats, and allowed to understand the motives behind each format.

Below is a list of formats that can be incorporated into the common classroom in order to prepare students to be knowledgeable global citizens:

TYPE	DEFINITION	PURPOSE/VALUE	POTENTIAL PITFALLS
Textual	Any text-based materials, printed or digital, used to convey information via the use of words Examples: Essays, Poems, Short Stories, Reflections, Newspapers, Articles, Ads, Reviews, Magazines	Allows students to build their vocabulary and convey their knowledge of language via written form	Can be potentially difficult to engage students with lower-level language development, unique learning types, or reading-based disabilities
Printed (Textual)	Any physical copy of text that utilizes traditional ink outputs, such as a printing press or computer printer Examples: Books, Textbooks, Worksheets, Printed Essays, Reflections	A more traditional way to convey one's mastery of a particular topic	May be viewed as unengaging or archaic by students who have grown up in a mostly digital world
Digital (Textual)	Sometimes referred to as an "eText," any computerized version of communication that uses digital technologies to convey words Examples: Microsoft Word, PowerPoint, Prezi, Google Docs, Digital Ads, Online Blogs, Social Media, Tweets, Pots	Helps prepare students for the digital world of communication that we live in; highly collaborative	Still relatively little research exists on the impact of digital platforms on overall learning and language acquisition

TYPE	DEFINITION	PURPOSE/VALUE	POTENTIAL PITFALLS
Visual	Any form of art or visually striking communication that incorporates words, depictions, photographs, or graphics that go beyond traditional black-ink textual representations of student knowledge Examples: Graphs, Charts, Diagrams, Photographs, Paintings, Graphic Novels, Graphic Design, Memes, Political Cartoons, Iconography, Cartoons, Sketches, Blueprints, PowerPoints, Google Slides, Sculptures, Prototypes	May help "catch the eye" of students who are more visually or artistically inclined in terms of their individualized learning types; can help reinforce language acquisition by helping students draw connections to terms that are otherwise abstract	An overreliance on visual formats has the potential to limit key college-ready skills, such as written communication and essay writing
Cinematic	Any visual presentation that emphasizes an exhibition of film or motion pictures Examples: Movies, YouTube Videos, News Interviews, Documentaries, TV Shows, Gifs, Vines, Snaps, Facebook Live, Movie Trailers, Commercials	A specific form of visual communication that relies heavily on a combination of visual, aural, textual, oral, and theatrical techniques; in a digital age with smartphones, this is an easy way to engage students	Demands the creation of explicit rules and expectations for proper video uses and ethics, especially in an age wrought with cyberbullying issues
Quantitative	Any presentation of knowledge that relies heavily on quantified, numerical data Examples: Excel Sheets, Graphs, Charts, Diagrams, Tables, Data Trackers, Data Visualization Tools, Mathematics or Science Reports, Demographic Reports, Statistics	Can help ground student ideas and theories with quantifiable data; can be used as a bridge to literacy, if incorporated properly with other formats, especially for students who tend to have more quantitative learning types	Some formats demand higher-level numeracy

TYPE	DEFINITION	PURPOSE/VALUE	POTENTIAL PITFALLS
Oral/Aural	Any type of communication that emphasizes oratory, typically devoid of exaggerated visual presentations, but also tailors a message to cater to the auditory sensitivities of an audience Examples: Speeches, TED Talks, Podcasts, Radio Broadcasts, Song, Musicals, Spoken Word, Recorded Journalistic Interviews, Entrepreneurial Pitches	In an age where Podcasts and TED Talks are becoming a preferred method of disseminating new ideas, this format offers a platform for students who want to transform their "gift of gab" into a profitable future	Can make some of your more reserved or introverted students feel uncomfortable or out of their comfort zone
Theatrical	Any type of communication related to the art of theater or drama Examples: Plays, Musicals, Skits, Movies, Roleplaying	Allows students with artistic or kinesthetic learning types to convey knowledge through an alternative, arts-based format	Many students have preconceived notions of theater and its relevance in society
Kinesthetic	Any communication or representation of information that heavily involves motion Examples: Dance, Exercises, Athletics, Yoga, Sign Language, Hand Motions, Body Language, Construction/STEM Activities, Kinesiology, Marches, Protests	Allows students to remain physically active while reinforcing otherwise abstract concepts	Can marginalize students with severe illnesses or physical disabilities

Evaluating the Motives Behind Each Type of Presentation

While the motive(s) for creating and communicating information will vary from presentation to presentation, it is helpful if students are aware of at least four major categories:

1. **Social**: focused on interpersonal relationships
2. **Commercial**: focused on economic profit or advertisement
3. **Political**: focused on perspectives on the role of government and citizenship
4. **Instructional/Academic**: focused on teaching content or skills related to traditional education

All four of these motives can manifest themselves within any of the communication formats mentioned in the chart above. For example, a digital ad can have a commercial motive or even a political motive. Some digital ads will want to sell products or services. Other digital ads will be used for political campaigning, especially during election season.

Take a look at the ways in which each motive might be potentially manifested in each format:

FORMAT TYPE	SOCIAL MOTIVES	COMMERCIAL MOTIVES	POLITICAL MOTIVES	ACADEMIC AND INSTRUCTIONAL MOTIVES
Textual	A formal invitation card about an upcoming reunion.	A print ad in the "Classifieds" that tries to sell a car in a local newspaper.	A socialist treatise that sheds light on the so-called "evils of capitalist economies."	A K-12 educational textbook on world history.
Printed (Textual)	An archive of written correspondence between two friends.	Mail that lists the most recent foreclosures and real estate opportunities in a particular neighborhood.	Adolf Hitler's *Mein Kampf* is a classic example of text-based political propaganda.	A set of printed directions about how to set up a new iPhone.
Digital (Textual)	A social media blast about an upcoming networking mixer on LinkedIn.	An email asking alumni to donate to their alma mater.	A Bernie Sanders Facebook post.	A digital article on Achieve 3000.
Visual	A visual ad about a free dating website.	A billboard trying to sell perfume.	A propaganda poster asking young women to join the army of a fascist government.	A collection of World War II photos and artefacts arranged strategically in an American history museum.
Cinematic	A gif sent out to make a group of friends laugh.	A commercial telling people to drink more Pepsi.	A campaign commercial, created by the Democratic Party that warns about the pitfalls of joining the Republican Party.	An episode of *Planet Earth*.
Quantitative	A Facebook notification that uses percentages and statistics (about views and likes) to rank which Facebook friends are their "top followers."	A PowerPoint presentation that uses BIG, BOLD sales percentages to show investors why Apple is outcompeting Microsoft.	A report that analyzes demographic breakdowns of neighborhoods in order to make suggestions in terms of campaign strategies.	A line graph that tracks trends in crime rates in 10 major metropolitan areas in Canada.
Oral/Aural	A band jamming out a song in front of a crowd on a college campus.	A radio commercial pitching the latest furniture sale.	Joe Biden's inaugural address as president.	A podcast that tells interesting stories about the history of serial killers.

FORMAT TYPE	SOCIAL MOTIVES	COMMERCIAL MOTIVES	POLITICAL MOTIVES	ACADEMIC AND INSTRUCTIONAL MOTIVES
Theatrical	A set of skits at the final day of summer camp that reflect on the funniest moments in the last six weeks.	A play at the local theater.	An election skit on SNL.	A military reenactment.
Kinesthetic	A "flash mob" that advertises for an upcoming fundraiser at a local high school.	A cheerleading routine that is being used to raise funds for a summer camp.	A silent march in solidarity against institutionalized racism.	A sign language class.

Understanding Language Development Phases

The stages of language development - which were defined a previous section - should be combined with the levels of thinking in Bloom's Taxonomy in order to create an axis of progression that helps students advance from the lowest level of language development (pre-production) to the highest level of fluency (advanced fluency).

The five stages of language development are:

1. **Pre-Production:** the silent or receptive stage where students are still learning vocab

2. **Early Production:** the "collecting" stage where students gather words and ideas to make small phrases

3. **Speech Emergence:** a "personal archive" of several thousand words helps students tap into their background knowledge to create simple sentences

4. **Intermediate Fluency:** a critical stage in which students start communicating in complex sentences and may begin processing information automatically in the new language

5. **Advanced Fluency:** students cannot only create sentences with an increased amount of complexity, but they can also apply their newfound complex sentences to unique social contexts - the student is both literate and socially/culturally aware

The six levels of thinking in Bloom's Taxonomy are:

1. **Knowledge:** students can recall or memorize terms, facts, details, or traits
2. **Comprehension:** students can summarize and paraphrase
3. **Application:** students can apply learning to different contexts than the classroom
4. **Analysis:** students can deconstruct information and unearth patterns
5. **Synthesis:** students can combine different pieces of information and/or analysis
6. **Evaluation:** students can make value propositions based on selected criteria

Bloom's Taxonomy is best synthesized with the stages of language development when teachers and students begin asking the right questions.

Analyzing Speech in Terms of Vocal Characteristics

Students and educators alike should be able to analyze student speeches, paying close attention to the following characteristics that help make a speech effective.

Vocal characteristics are oral communication factors that affect fluency. These characteristics include:

- Resonance
- Pronunciation/enunciation
- Volume
- Pitch
- Tone
- Pace/Rate

Commanding these different characteristics is critical for not only effective public speaking, but also language development in general.

Below is a rubric that defines each characteristic and offers some guiding question for analyzing each vocal characteristic in the classroom:

VOCAL CHARACTERISTIC	DEFINITION	QUESTIONS TO GUIDE ANALYSIS
Resonance	The strength, depth, and force of a person's vocal patterns	Is the speaker projecting from the lungs or chest instead of mumbling at the mouth? Is the speaker projecting so that *all* audience members can hear?
Pronunciation/Enunciation	The clarity and articulation of a speech and its words	Is the speaker avoiding the stuttering, mumbling, or slurring of words? Is the speaker accentuating each syllable of the words? Is the speaker speaking deliberately?
Volume	The loudness or quietness/softness of a speech	Is there a balance in volume? Is the speaker shifting volume for dramatic effect? Are they lowering their voice at critical points and emphasizing important content with a louder voice? Are they commanding the acoustics of their setting?
Pitch	The degree of highness or lowness of a person's tone	Is the speaker avoiding a monotone pitch? Is inflection evident? Is the pitch varied, like volume, according to content? Does the speaker seem consciously aware of their natural pitch?
Tone	The overall emotional content of a speech, which is affected by all previously mentioned factors	Is the speaker commanding the tone they want to convey? Are they adequately being perceived by the audience as excited, annoyed, lighthearted, authoritative, desperate, comical, or whatever the target tone is?
Pace/Rate	Pace or rate is the speed of a speech's delivery	Is the speaker cognizant of time limitations? Is the speaker incorporating strategic pauses to command the pace?

Fluency in speech is the ability to command ALL of these characteristics in conjunction with one another and in combination with proper vocabulary use. Advance fluency includes the ability to navigate the relationships that exist between these characteristics, with respect to a specific context and an appropriate nonverbal body language.

Integrating Nonverbal Components with Verbal Elements

Vocal characteristics cannot and should not remain in isolation from nonverbal components because the integration of these two categories is what helps students develop linguistic and cultural fluency in the classroom.

Nonverbal components are physical actions that affect verbal communications and interpersonal perceptions.

Below is a rubric that defines different nonverbal components and offers some guiding question for assessing how to well speakers integrate nonverbal components with vocal characteristic in the classroom:

NONVERBAL COMPONENT	DEFINITION	QUESTIONS TO GUIDE ANALYSIS
Body Language	Body language includes any way a person communicates with their physical characteristics: hand motions, eye contact, facial expressions, posture, and any other movements, motions, or gestures.	Does the speaker appear conscious of or in control of the way their body language affects their speaking abilities? Does the speaker avoid obvious physical distractions like slouching, fidgeting, and pacing?
Eye Contact	Eye contact refers to a strategic effort to allow the audience to see your eyes.	Does the speaker maintain eye contact with the audience, scanning the room, and making one-on-one eye contact with audience members?
Facial Expressions	Facial expressions are the movements our facial muscles, including our mouths and eyebrows, make during a speech or conversation.	Do the speaker's facial expressions match their intended tone?
Posture	Posture refers to the position of your body, particularly your back and shoulders, while standing.	Is the speaker presenting in a formal, postured manner with little slouching?
Movements/Motions/Gestures	Any physical transition with your head, hands, face, or the rest of your body.	Is the speaker controlling hand motions, gestures, and fidgets? Is the speaker avoiding distracting hand motions?

Dialects, Idiolects, and Changes in Standard Oral English Usage

Dialects are regionalized, localized, or colloquial forms of language that usually have an informal character. **Idiolects** are hyper-individualized speech patterns that are unique to a particular person, but may stem from a combination of dialect and standard language.

Standard Oral English, although difficult to define, is a generally accepted way of speaking English that certain sectors of American or British culture tend to view as "formalized," "respectable," and/or "civilized."

Decades ago, there may have been more of an emphasis on sanitizing students' tongues in order to conform with Standard Oral English. Today, with diversity at the core of American demographics, many educators are incorporating less-biased ways of viewing other styles of speaking, such as dialects or idiolects. These linguistic markers are beginning to be perceived as a positive rather than a negative. Educators are allowing students to incorporate their dialects and idiolects into their own narrative writing.

56

Nevertheless, there are still stigmas, biases, and stereotypes that pervade American society, so teachers have a moral obligation to offer students the "best of both worlds." They need to prepare them for the standardized English that still dominates the academy and business, and provide spaces and places for students to honor their own unique tongues. This balance can be taught explicitly – teachers can show students how and when to code switch, and how and when to formalize their words.

Adapting Speech to a Variety of Contexts and Tasks

Students, therefore, need to begin listing out the contexts and tasks that demand formal English and the contexts and tasks that are friendly to informal English. Have students and teachers try to list out formal vs. informal contexts like so:

FORMAL	INFORMAL
• Interviews	• Out with Friends
• Sales Pitches	• Domestic Settings
• Entrepreneurial Pitches	• Entertainment Places
• Meetings	• Public Spaces Like Parks
• Conference Calls	• The Cafeteria at School
• Presentations	• Gym Class
• Professional Conferences	• Playing Sports
• Political Campaigns	• Visiting Family
• Public Appearances	• Cookouts and Parties
• Reports	• Poetry
• Research Papers	• Music Lyrics
• Professional Emails	• Love Letters

Once students have this list down, have them try to deconstruct each setting. What makes it informal to them? What makes it formal to others? Do they see eye to eye with others? Why or why not? How can that be resurrected? *Can* it be resurrected?

The rest is **coaching**: meeting students where they are at, teaching them how to thrive in each formal context, and teaching them how to maintain their identities in all contexts.

Besides role play, students can also explore these topics in their writing, adapting their writing to a particular platform or style (i.e., professional emails vs. lyrics).

Engaging in Collaborative Discussions

Engaging in a range of collaborative discussions with diverse partners is important.

- Collaborative discussions allow students to "practice" the language they are learning.
  - Students get to practice new skills in informal, more intimate settings without the pressure of formal group norms.
- Collaborative discussions set the stage for peer-to-peer interventions.
  - Students gain access to peer-to-peer interventions, whether strategic or incidental
- Collaborative discussions enable students to deepen their analysis and understanding of a text or set of texts.
  - Students acquire a multitude of perspectives about a text, which deepens their analysis
- Collaborative discussions prepare students for 21st-century learning and work environments.
  - Students acquire collaborative skills that are necessary to thrive in 21st-century work environments

- Collaborative discussions expose students to a diverse set of ideas, identities, and cultures.
    - Students get to reinforce their own ideas, identities, and cultures, while also learning about other students' ideas, identities, and cultures

Normally, this can take place in three categories of collaborative instruction: 1) One-on-One, 2) In Groups, 3) Teacher Led.

Here are examples of different activities that can be used to meet the needs of each category:

One-on-One	In Group	Teacher Led
Examples: peer conferences, pair shares, teacher-student conferences, interviews, one-on-one debriefs	Examples: small group projects, large group debates (unmoderated), Jigsaws, Fishbowls	Examples: collaborative presentations (using digital technologies), Socratic seminars (moderated by teacher), mock trials, debates (moderated)

Research to Build and Present Knowledge

Gathering Relevant Information from Multiple Sources

Gathering relevant information from print and digital research sources is a valuable skill in writing. Strong writing uses evidence from scholarly, credible sources. These sources help bolster any arguments or claims being made in the writing. Print and digital sources are equally acceptable if they are reviewed for credibility.

Print sources include books, journals, newspapers, and any other academic material. By definition, a print source means that there is a physical copy of the source. These sources are generally found in libraries. Online catalogs can help locate where print sources are stored and whether they are accessible. Ask librarians for help accessing sources and other related resources.

Digital sources include books, journals, online articles, and any other source that can be found online or in a database. In many cases, these sources are published digitally, but often they are physical sources that have been scanned and uploaded. Digital sources may be considered easier to navigate as there is usually a search function for keywords related to the research.

Whether a source is print or digital, read it thoroughly to understand if it is appropriate for research purposes. Make notes while reading thoroughly to help determine which ideas and facts are relevant enough to use. Information is considered relevant if it can add to the research. If the source contains relevant information, it must be cited appropriately. The correct citation form depends on the citation style being used and whether the source is print or digital.

Assessing the Credibility and Accuracy of Sources

In a world inundated with content, it can be a difficult task assessing the credibility and accuracy of sources.

Credibility refers to whether the information within the sources is believable, convincing, and reputable. **Accuracy** refers to whether the information is precise or exact and can be validated by cross-referencing other resources or data.

Why is it important to explicitly teach students how to assess the credibility and accuracy of sources?

1. It teaches them critical thinking skills.
2. It enhances the credibility of their own research.
3. It prepares them for college-level research and writing.

58

4. It helps instill academic self-discipline.
5. It helps them navigate fact and fiction.

The following step-by-step guide can help students assess the credibility and accuracy of sources:

STEP 1: ORIGIN

The first step in assessing the credibility and accuracy of sources is understanding where the source comes from. In particular, you should figure out whether the source is scholarly or non-scholarly in character:

- **Scholarly sources** are vetted for credibility and accuracy by the academic community (i.e., universities, research centers, and peer-reviewed journals, books, and articles).

- **Non-scholarly sources** are not vetted for credibility or accuracy, which means they often do not maintain the same level of scrutiny as scholarly texts. Non-scholarly texts are usually considered to be more amateur in character, though this does not always affect the quality of the text.

Below is a list of guiding questions for understanding a source's origin:

- Who published the text?
- Where was the text published?
- Was it independently published or published through a particular institution?
- Is its scholarly or non-scholarly?
- Are there citations to support its claims?
- Has the content been reviewed or edited by an academic institution or publisher?
- Can you cross-reference or fact-check the information presented in the text?
- What level of objectivity and/or subjectivity exists in the text?
- Is the source written by a person or group of persons who are considered experts in the field?
- What are the credentials of the author?
- What is the context in which it was written (i.e., location, date)?

STEP 2: HISTORICITY/CURRENCY

The second step in assessing the credibility and accuracy of sources is gaining a better understanding of when the text was written and how this time period effects its arguments. Some scholars refer to this as understanding the historicity of a text – that is, understanding the historical context of the source – or understanding the currency of a text – that is, understanding how new (or old) the information is.

- **Current sources** have been published anywhere within 5-10 years. These sources tend to be "up-to-date" with trends in research.

- **Historical sources** were published outside the 5-to-10-year range, making them more inclined to be "outdated" in their arguments.

- **Historiography** refers to the entire canon of sources devoted to a particular topic or range of topics. Understanding a topic's historiography can help students gain a better understanding of how information changes – or remains the same – over time.

Below are some guiding questions for understanding a source's historicity:

- When was the text written?
- Can you tell when the information was published or revised?
- Is the text current?
- How does history influence the texts ideas?
- Are the arguments outdated?
- How does the text contribute to the overall historiography?
- Are there similar texts written about this same topic around the same time?
- What historical trends are evident in the text?

STEP 3: PURPOSE

The third step in assessing the credibility and accuracy of sources is gaining a better understanding of the author's purpose. **Purpose** refers to the reason why an author wrote a particular text; it is a combination of intent (i.e., why the text is written) and target audience (i.e., who the text is written for).

Below are some guiding questions for understanding a source's purpose:

- What is the target audience?
- Is the purpose clear?
- What is the message?
- What is the purpose?
- Are there any organizations or entities sponsoring the information?
- Are any lobby groups, special interest groups, or corporate entities associated with the message?

STEP 4: Bias/Objectivity/Subjectivity

The fourth and final step in assessing the credibility and accuracy of sources is gaining a better understanding of the level of bias in a source, and where that level of bias falls on the spectrum of objectivity and subjectivity.

- **Biased** refers to any text or form of communication that is colored by personal opinions or feelings, and therefore reads as being more embellished or subjective.

- **Unbiased** refers to any text or form of communication that is NOT colored by personal opinions or feelings, and therefore reads as being more factual, scientific, or objective.

- **Objectivity** refers to a state of being impartial, balanced, factual, and unbiased.

- **Subjectivity** refers to a state of being partial, unbalanced, non-factual, and biased. Personal tastes or prejudicial feelings are held in higher regard than factual evidence.

Below are some guiding questions for understanding a source's bias:

- Is the author in favor of a certain theory, framework, or argument?
- Are there signs of bias in the text?
- What are the signs of bias?
- What words or phrases lead you to believe the text is more objective or subjective in nature?
- Are the arguments backed by concrete, scientific evidence?

Once you have used these steps, it becomes easier to assess whether a text is credible or accurate.

Interpreting Research Findings

In order to write research papers or reports, students have to be able to synthesize their own salient points while processing salient points made by other authors; they must be able to interpret relevant evidence, through a process known as reasoning, in order to make certain claims or elucidate certain findings about the texts and ideas they encounter. Below are some helpful definitions for understanding this process:

PENULTIMATE DISPLAY OF INVESTIGATORY UNDERSTANDING	BASIC UNITS OF INFORMATION AND HUMAN KNOWLEDGE
Claims and Findings: Claims and findings are the penultimate display of the results that occurs when students filter evidence through the logical process of reasoning, and synthesize investigatory realizations with concrete details.	Details: Details are the most basic components of human knowledge and human writing; they are the foundational tidbits of information that serve as the building blocks to evidence, reasoning, and claims/findings. Details do not rest neatly within one category; rather, details span all categories mentioned in the left-hand column.
LOGICAL VETTING PROCESS Reasoning: Reasoning is the process that allows students to logically assess, contradict, underscore, or synthesize evidence; reasoning is the catalyzing process that transforms evidence into claims; it is the bridge that ties together the claim and the evidence.	
FOUNDATIONAL CLUES/KNOWLEDGE Evidence: Evidence is the qualitative or quantitative details that emerge within the salient arguments of other authors, whether written or verbalized. Evidence is the concrete set of "clues' that allow a student to agree or disagree with a certain perspective.	

In order to organize this process and make theoretically sound arguments, teachers and students must also have a solid understanding of the different types of **evidentiary operations**, the ways one can structure claims/findings after operationalizing evidence through reason. There are seven major evidential operations students and teachers can employ:

1. **Synthesis or Fusion:** synthesizing or fusing information to highlight agreements and disagreements between multiple bodies of evidence

2. **Discrediting or Contradiction:** openly adjusting, contradicting, denouncing, or discrediting the validity or credibility of a body of evidence by reducing or undermining its details

3. **Translation:** when one body of evidence is used as a lens of analysis to assess the impact or influence of a dependent theory or hypothesis

4. **Projection:** when one body of evidence, or multiple bodies of evidence, are anachronistically cast upon another temporal context, such as using history to understand the present, or using the present to predict the future

5. **Summarization:** ceaselessly paraphrasing content and eliminating extraneous details, which, in turn, creates a whole new condensed body of evidence that pays homage to the original body of evidence

6. **Gisting:** an act that is even more condensed and devoid of extraneous ideas because it pinpoints a central strand, message, or essence of a text or body of evidence

7. **Interpretation:** estimating the validity and invalidity of a text by producing a calculated statement or set of statements that evaluate truthfulness through the interrelated processes of reasoning and personal perspective

These are the seven ways that students and teachers alike can use details, evidence, reasoning, claims/findings to structure coherent reports or research papers.

Paraphrasing Data and Conclusions

Plagiarism – the act of stealing someone else's intellectual property, whether it is data, theories, or quotations – only occurs when written or communicated material is not properly paraphrased or cited.

Paraphrasing is the act of summarizing materials, using unique words instead of direct quotes; paraphrasing entails getting rid of any extraneous comments, data, or conclusions, and using one's own words to convey the core meaning of an oral statement, text, or any other form of communication.

Citation is a standardized academic procedure for honoring someone else's intellectual property by giving them credit for their work. There are many citation styles within scholarship, all of which have their own unique standards for citation.

- Proper Paraphrasing + Proper Citation = No Plagiarism
- Improper Paraphrasing + Improper Citation = Plagiarism
- Improper Paraphrasing + Proper Citation = Plagiarism
- Proper Paraphrasing + Improper Citation = Plagiarism

Plagiarism must be taken seriously in the K-12 classrooms in order to protect students and teachers from legal issues.

Integrating Technology, Multimedia, and Visual Displays into Presentations

Technology should be incorporated into all aspects of the learning environment via curriculum development. This means that technological integration should be a component of the written curriculum, the taught curriculum, and the tested curriculum of a classroom and district (along with the quality control, design, and delivery that unites each of these curricula).

Technological integration, multimedia, and visual displays should pervade all aspects of curriculum in order to increase alignment and provide more opportunities for teachers and students to clarify information, strengthen claims and evidence, and add interest.

Take a look at the graphic below to see how this is possible:

TECHNOLOGICAL INTEGRATION IN CURRICULUM		
Written	**Taught**	**Tested**
Ways to Integrate	**Ways to Integrate**	**Ways to Integrate**
➢ Align to national and state digital standards ➢ Incorporate technology into everyday learning activities ➢ Creating official rubrics for digital integration ➢ Creating official district-wide or campus-wide teacher observation assessments that make digital integration mandatory	➢ Teachers role-model proper digital technology use ➢ Technology is the heart of pedagogy as well as student activity ➢ Technology tools (i.e., videos, virtual instructors) can also carry out instruction ➢ Use online digital texts and databases ➢ Using relevant platforms like social media	➢ Using computers for diagnostic, formative, and summative assessments ➢ Allowing students to collaborate with each other and assess each other online ➢ Introducing online surveys and other interactive activities to assess student knowledge

Presenting Claims and Findings

Students should have a command of the following elements when presenting claims and findings:

SPEECH ELEMENT	EFFECTIVE IMPLEMENTATION
Resonance	Projecting from the lungs or chest instead of mumbling at the mouth Projecting so that *all* audience members can hear you
Pronunciation/Enunciation	Practice difficult-to-pronounce terms Avoid stuttering, mumbling, and slurring Accentuate each syllable Speak deliberately
Volume	Find a balance in volume; practice this balance Shift volume for dramatic effect: lower your voice at critical points and emphasize important content with a louder voice Know the acoustics of your setting
Pitch	Avoid a monotone pitch Practice inflection Vary pitch, like volume, according to content Be consciously aware of your natural pitch
Tone	Know what tone you want to convey Do you want to be perceived as excited, annoyed, lighthearted, authoritative, desperate, comical, etc.?

SPEECH ELEMENT	EFFECTIVE IMPLEMENTATION
Pace/Rate	Be conscious of time limitations Incorporate strategic pauses and practice strategic pauses
Body Language	Be conscious of your nervous "tics" and mannerisms Avoid fidgeting or repetitive motions that can be distracting
Eye Contact	Focus on people one at a time Focus on people you are comfortable with Practice vacillating the range and direction of your eye contact
Facial Expressions	Make sure your facial expressions match your targeted tone Be conscious of the way your facial expressions change when you are nervous, sad, anxious, or perturbed Study how other speakers use facial expressions to enhance their delivery
Posture	Do not "lock" your joints to the point that you faint Try not to slouch your shoulders Stand tall and take deep breaths Balance the position of your legs beneath your body
Movements/Motions/Gestures	Move a little bit, but not too much Gain command of distracting or nervous movements

Reading Comprehension and Analysis

Reading Literature

Analyzing Works from Different Literary Genres

Students should understand how to analyze works from different genres using literary elements and structural features. The table below discusses different literary genres, the features that define them, and examples of works within those genres.

Type of Literary Genre	Definition	Examples in Children's Literature	Examples of Different Representations in Diverse Cultures	Literary and Structural Elements
Folktales and Fairytales	Short stories that emerge in popular or colloquial culture that usual focus on themes such as magic, chivalry, romance, and imaginary things.	Famous collections like *Grimm's Fairy Tales* Fairytale and folktale classics like *Little Red Riding Hood, Cinderella, Jack and the Beanstalk*	Translated Latin American folktales like *Conejito: A Folktale from Panama*	Brief, succinct stories with moral lessons, usually expressed through a pithy maxim at the end of the story.

Type of Literary Genre	Definition	Examples in Children's Literature	Examples of Different Representations in Diverse Cultures	Literary and Structural Elements
Graphic Novels and Comic Books	A literary genre that tells serialized stories in visual, comic-like format.	Graphic novel adaptations of such classics as *A Wrinkle in Time*, *Fahrenheit 451*, and *The Alchemist* Marvel and DC comic books Political cartoons in history and current events	Graphic novels about immigration and the refugee experience like *Azzi In Between*	Serialized stories that employ a minimal amount of text – usually just brief dialogues, descriptions, or onomatopoeias
Novels	Book-length works of fiction.	Classic children's novels, such as the *Harry Potter* series, *Charlotte's Web*, *Charlie and the Chocolate Factory*, *James and the Giant Peach*	*The Name Jar* by Yangsook Choi, which focuses on the meaning of immigrant names in America	Classic literary arc presented over an extended period of time, following the traditional exposition, rising action, climax, falling action, and resolution/ denouement structure
Poems	A rhythmical style of verse writing that is usually known for its metaphorical scope.	Children's poems by famous authors like Shel Silverstein and Roald Dahl	Children's poems that incorporate international languages like *Salsa: Un poema para cocinar* by Jorge Argueta	Structured in stanzas, instead of paragraphs, and verses, instead of sentences
Plays/Dramas	Composed in prose or verse, this type of literary genre creates works of dramatic fiction that will be used for theatrical or cinematic production.	Child-friendly adaptions of Broadway classics like *The Lion King*, *Seussical*, and *Wicked*	Plays based on folktales from countries such as Italy, Ghana, and China, as presented in compendia such as *Multicultural Plays for Children*	Broken down into different Acts (larger sections) and scenes (minor interactions) between characters
Religious Texts	Any sacred or secular text believed to be central to the spiritual or religious beliefs of a particular group.	Children's editions of religious texts Religiously inspired short stories or tales	Children's editions of international religious texts, such as the *Quran* and the *Bhagavad Gita*	Usually broken down into a series of proverbs or stories with moral undertones; sometimes a list of rules or laws

Type of Literary Genre	Definition	Examples in Children's Literature	Examples of Different Representations in Diverse Cultures	Literary and Structural Elements
Short Stories	Short works of narrative prose fiction that are not quite book-length.	Well-known children's short stories like *Rikki-Tikki-Tavi* and *The Gift of the Magi*	Short stories that focus on racial and cultural diversity in the United States, such as *Separate is Never Equal*	Much like a novel, it follows the traditional exposition, rising action, climax, falling action, and resolution/ denouement structure, but does so in a more expedited format

Using Textual Evidence to Support Analysis

Textual evidence is any primary information provided in a work of fiction or nonfiction that can be quoted, cited, paraphrased, or referred to in order to substantiate secondary analyses, theories, interpretations, or opinions. There are two types of textual evidence: explicit evidence and implicit evidence.

Explicit evidence can be cited directly from a text, without the need for an extensive amount of interpretation or deconstruction. Explicit evidence is straightforward; the author comes right out and tells you the meaning they are trying to convey. **Implicit evidence** is subtler and more complex in character – the meaning of the text is implied and therefore demands a greater amount of audience participation, interpretation, and deconstruction. The meaning of implicit evidence is embedded within a text, but unearthed by the audience. Implicit evidence forces audiences to make inferences, using background knowledge, about the symbolism and meaning of the text. Thorough textual evidence will draw from both explicit and implicit sources, if available.

Students can use implicit evidence to make inferences, which draw from text citations and background knowledge:

IMPLICIT EVIDENCE EXAMPLE (POETRY):

"The river sweats

Oil and tar

The barges drift

With the turning tide

Red sails

Wide

To leeward, swing on the heavy spar.

The barges wash

Drifting logs

Down Greenwich reach

Subtest I: Reading, Language, and Literature

Past the Isle of Dogs."

-T.S. Eliot "The Waste Land" (1922)

Using implicit evidence in the excerpt above, students can synthesize their own arguments about "The Waste Land," mixing implicit citations with background knowledge to form inferences:

Implicit Citations	+	Background Knowledge	=	Inferences About Implicit Evidence
"The river sweats/oil and tar" *"The barges wash/Drifting logs"*	+	*I know that the Waste Land was written in 1922, after World War I, when many Modernist poets, such as T.S. Eliot, were disillusioned and frustrated with the polluted circumstances of industrialized society.*	=	*In this particular stanza, T.S. Eliot references the polluted circumstances and apocalyptic characteristics of modern society, noting the rivers filled with oil, tar, drifting logs, and other wasted natural resources. One can infer that he is lamenting the distasteful overconsumption associated with industrialized society.*

Notice how the meaning of Eliot's poem is not straightforward. He references images to make larger theoretical arguments that are implied rather than explicitly explained.

Determining Themes

The **theme** of a piece of text is the central idea the author communicates. Whereas the topic of a passage of text may be concrete in nature, by contrast the theme is always conceptual. For example, while the topic of Mark Twain's novel *The Adventures of Huckleberry Finn* might be described as something like the coming-of-age experiences of a poor, illiterate, functionally orphaned boy around and on the Mississippi River in 19th-century Missouri, one theme of the book might be that human beings are corrupted by society. Another might be that slavery and "civilized" society itself are hypocritical. Whereas the main idea in a text is the most important single point that the author wants to make, the theme is the concept or view around which the author centers the text.

Throughout time, humans have told stories with similar themes. Some themes are universal across time, space, and culture. These include themes of the individual as a hero, conflicts of the individual against nature, the individual against society, change vs. tradition, the circle of life, coming-of-age, and the complexities of love. Themes involving war and peace have featured prominently in diverse works, like Homer's *Iliad*, Tolstoy's *War and Peace* (1869), Stephen Crane's *The Red Badge of Courage* (1895), Hemingway's *A Farewell to Arms* (1929), and Margaret Mitchell's *Gone with the Wind* (1936). Another universal literary theme is that of the quest. These appear in folklore from countries and cultures worldwide, including the Gilgamesh Epic, Arthurian legend's Holy Grail quest, Virgil's *Aeneid*, Homer's *Odyssey*, and the *Argonautica*. Cervantes' *Don Quixote* is a parody of chivalric quests. J.R.R. Tolkien's *The Lord of the Rings* trilogy (1954) also features a quest.

Similar themes across cultures often occur in countries that share a border or are otherwise geographically close together. For example, a folklore story of a rabbit in the moon using a mortar and pestle is shared among China, Japan, Korea, and Thailand—making medicine in China, making rice cakes in Japan and Korea, and hulling rice in Thailand. Another instance is when cultures are more distant geographically, but their languages are related. For example, East Turkestan's Uighurs and people in Turkey share tales of folk hero Effendi Nasreddin Hodja. Another instance, which may either be called cultural diffusion or simply reflect commonalities in the human imagination, involves shared themes among geographically and linguistically different cultures: both Cameroon's and Greece's folklore tell of centaurs; Cameroon, India, Malaysia, Thailand, and Japan, of mermaids; Brazil, Peru, China, Japan,

68

Malaysia, Indonesia, and Cameroon, of underwater civilizations; and China, Japan, Thailand, Vietnam, Malaysia, Brazil, and Peru, of shape-shifters.

Two prevalent literary themes are love and friendship, which can end happily, sadly, or both. William Shakespeare's *Romeo and Juliet*, Emily Brontë's *Wuthering Heights*, Leo Tolstoy's *Anna Karenina*, and both *Pride and Prejudice* and *Sense and Sensibility* by Jane Austen are famous examples. Another theme recurring in popular literature is of revenge, an old theme in dramatic literature, e.g., Thomas Kyd's *The Spanish Tragedy* and Thomas Middleton's *The Revenger's Tragedy*. Some more well-known instances include Shakespeare's tragedies *Hamlet* and *Macbeth*, Alexandre Dumas' *The Count of Monte Cristo*, John Grisham's *A Time to Kill*, and Stieg Larsson's *The Girl Who Kicked the Hornet's Nest*.

Themes are underlying meanings in literature. For example, if a story's main idea is a character succeeding against all odds, the theme is overcoming obstacles. If a story's main idea is one character wanting what another character has, the theme is jealousy. If a story's main idea is a character doing something they were afraid to do, the theme is courage. Themes differ from topics in that a topic is a subject matter; a theme is the author's opinion about it. For example, a work could have a topic of war and a theme that war is a curse. Authors present themes through characters' feelings, thoughts, experiences, dialogue, plot actions, and events. Themes function as "glue" holding other essential story elements together. They offer readers insights into characters' experiences, the author's philosophy, and how the world works.

Dialogue and Incidents in a Work of Fiction or Drama

Dialogue is a word used to describe the conversations that occur within a work of fiction or drama. These conversations can be interpersonal (i.e., two friends chatting) or autonomous (i.e., a soliloquy).

Incidents are moments or events, which can also be interpersonal or autonomous, that contribute to the overall plot trajectory of the work of fiction or drama.

Dialogue and incidents move the action forward and/or reveals aspects of a character by:

- Informing readers about the emotions, thoughts, motivations, mannerisms, idiosyncrasies, and traits of characters

- Transforming personal feelings into verbal displays and symbols

- Creating a strong "voice" for characters who are otherwise limited by the words of the narrator; creating a sense of detachment (or union) between audience, narrator, and character

- Offering hints about the context, setting, mood, tone, and atmosphere

- Enhancing antagonistic, benevolent, and neutral connections between different characters

- Illuminating different conflicts (i.e., person vs. self, person vs. person, person vs. nature, and person vs. society) and unveiling new obstacles in the story

- Providing details about a particular evolution or transformation in character

- Making the audience feel like they are "part of the conversation"

- Intensifying suspense, humor, irony, or other dramatic effects by communicating details that are exclusive to the narrator and audience

Literary Devices in Prose and Poetry

Literary devices are techniques used by writers in literature that impact the readers' relationship to text and their understanding of the text's scope and content.

Type of Literary Device	Definition	Example
Allegory	An entire text or poem that represents a larger historical event or idea.	An oft-cited example of an allegory is George Orwell's *Animal Farm* (1945). The entire book is an allegory for the Russian Revolution, with each character representing a certain historical figure. The character Mr. Jones, for example, represents Tsar Nicholas II of Russia. The character Napoleon, on the other hand, is modeled after Joseph Stalin, the Soviet leader.
Alliteration	The repetitious use of the same sound or a similar sound in succession in a sentence or line.	The skier was sliding so softly along the slopes of snow.
Allusion	A literary reference to an important historical person, place, event, idea, or movement.	"He was a real Scrooge with his money" is a reference to Ebenezer Scrooge, the famous coldhearted miser in Charles Dickens' *A Christmas Carol* (1843).
Analogy	Comparing two completely different things in order to clarify meaning.	"Life is a journey, not a destination."
Anthropomorphism	When animals, objects, or gods reflect human traits in a poem or a novel.	Many fables, such as *Alice in Wonderland*, anthropomorphize animals, such as the Cheshire Cat.
Anachronism	A literary representation of a person, place, thing, idea, or event that is historically inaccurate.	Abraham Lincoln listening to an iPod during the Civil War.
Colloquialism	Language or a dialect of language that is informal, regional, or local in character; it is usually not considered "proper" English.	In the Anthracite Coal Region of Pennsylvania, people refer to local fire companies as "hosies."
Diction	Word choice that is characteristic of a particular poet, author, or text.	Jack Kerouac's diction relied on a lot of Beat slang and colloquialism in *On the Road* (1957).
Elegy	A poem or song written in elegiac couples that lament the loss of someone deceased.	Walt Whitman's "O Captain! My Captain!" (1865) is a classic example of an elegy. It mourns the loss of Abraham Lincoln.
Epigraph	A quotation, phrase, or poem at the beginning of a book or chapter that serves as a preface or summary of a particular theme.	A classic example of an epigraph is offered in Ernest Hemingway's *The Sun Also Rises* (1926): *"You are all a lost generation. — Gertrude Stein in conversation."*

Type of Literary Device	Definition	Example
		The epigraph is a reference to a group of disillusioned authors and youths that emerged from the heartbreaking and violent circumstances of the Great War.
Epiphany	A moment of catharsis, realization, or conscientiousness that occurs in a work of fiction, and subsequently shifts the perspective of the story.	A classic example of a literary epiphany occurs in Arthur Miller's drama, *The Crucible* (1953). Toward the end of the play, the main character, John Proctor realizes that he can finally absolve himself of his own sins, thus creating a moment of self-reconciliation.
Euphemism	Euphemisms are subtle, mild, or indirect words or phrases that are coopted by language users to create alternative messages that are rather impolite, harsh, or unpleasant. Euphemisms may be used to describe words, actions, or ideas that are normally considered taboo.	A famous example of a euphemism is the phrase "kick the bucket," which colloquially in English means "to die."
Extended Metaphor	Sometimes referred to as a "sustained metaphor" or a "conceit," it is a comparison of two unlike things that extends throughout the entirety of a paragraph, chapter, stanza, set of stanzas, poem, or novel.	A famous example is Emily Dickenson's "Hope is a Thing with Feathers" (1891). She compares hope to a bird throughout the entirety of this poem: *"'Hope' is the thing with feathers—* *That perches in the soul—* *And sings the tune without the words—* *And never stops—at all—* *And sweetest—in the Gale is heard—* *And sore must be the storm—* *That could abash the little Bird* *That kept so many warm—* *I've heard it in the chillest land* *And on the strangest Sea—* *Yet, never, in Extremity,* *It asked a crumb—of Me"*
Flashback	Much like in a movie, flashbacks occur when crucial events from the past are unraveling in present time within the plot, either sporadically or all at once. The term flashback literally means to *flash back* into time.	One classic example is *The Sound and the Fury*, written by William Faulkner in 1929. Faulkner's novel is much like a temporal jigsaw puzzle, distorting time through frequent flashbacks to previous decades and centuries.

Type of Literary Device	Definition	Example
Foreshadowing	Foreshadowing occurs in a text when an author offers hints or clues, whether embedded within descriptions or dialogues, that shed light on future events.	The death of Lennie, one of the main characters in John Steinbeck's *Of Mice and Men* (1937), is foreshadowed by George's earlier euthanasia of Candy's dog: George, in the end, kills both entities with a fatal gunshot to the back of the head.
Hyperbole	An overly exaggerated comment or statement that is typically figurative in nature.	A classic example is the statement "I am so hungry I can eat a horse!"
Idiom	An expression that has a unique, peculiar meaning that would not otherwise be deduced by separating the words involved or changing the grammatical layout of the expression.	"I want to know the truth, so please don't beat around the bush here, David."
Imagery	Any sentence, line, or phrase that is visually descriptive and/or figurative in nature.	"The sun painted the sky in a unique pallet of pinks and blues."
Irony	Using contradictory language that is meant to carry a meaning of the opposite effect, usually to create such dramatic effects as humor.	"As the man commented on how invincible he felt, he was immediately struck by lightning and perished."
Juxtaposition	Placing two words, ideas, phrases, lines, sentences, settings, characters, or texts side-by-side to create a contrasting effect.	Perhaps the most famous juxtaposition in all of literature is presented by Charles Dickens in *A Tale of Two Cities* (1859): "It was the best of times, it was the worst of times."
Malapropism	Using an incorrect word, particularly in dialog, in place of a word that has a similar sound.	"She has an extremely photogenic memory" (instead of photographic memory).
Metaphor	Comparing two things without the use of like or as.	The thunderstorm was a living nightmare.
Metonym	When one closely related word is used as a substitute for another word.	Some people refer to the Catholic Church as simply "the Vatican."
Mood	The atmospheric vibes, feelings, elements of a particular text, which is dictated by other literary devices, syntax, and word choice.	The moods in most Edgar Allen Poe poems are fairly ominous.
Onomatopoeia	A word, or set of words, that imitate a natural sound.	The bird tweeted away on the limb. The book hit the ground with a loud thump.
Oxymoron	When two contradictory terms are presented in conjunction with one another in a text.	The novel *Little Bighorn*, by John Hough, Jr., is full of oxymoronic language, much like the title.

Type of Literary Device	Definition	Example
Paradox	A juxtaposition of two seemingly contradictory concepts, ideas, propositions, or statements in a text.	John Lennon, a famous musician and member of the Beatles, once said, "It's not weird to be weird." Likewise, Socrates, the famous Greek Philosopher, once said, "I know one thing: that I know nothing." These are two famous examples of paradoxes.
Personification	Giving human-like characteristics that something that is not human	The tree wept tears of ice during the blizzard; its former radiant smile faded behind the fog.
Repetition	A word or phrase that is used multiple times for dramatic effect	Poet Allen Ginsberg uses a lot of repetition in his famous poem "Howl" (1956). In one line in the poem, he refers to people "who lit cigarettes like boxcars, boxcars, boxcars." Ginsberg was known for repeating words and ideas in a series of three.
Rhyme	When words or endings of words correspond in sound	"Cat in the Hat"
Satire	When authors use irony, comedy, or exaggeration to enhance their social commentary within their work.	Jonathan Swift's *A Modest Proposal* (1729) employs satire to make political statements about the disposition of poor people within a privileged society.
Simile	Comparing two things using like or as.	The leaves danced like a parade of acrobats.
Soliloquy	When an actor or character discusses their thoughts out loud, even though no other characters are technically listening (only the audience can hear).	William Shakespeare famously used soliloquies in *Hamlet* – in total, the main character, Hamlet, delivers seven soliloquies.
Symbolism	Using words or images (symbols) to indirectly suggest another quality or concept.	An olive branch is a traditional symbol for peace.
Synecdoche	Any figure of speech that is only presented as a part, but is representative of a whole.	One example of a synecdoche would be calling a bunch of politicians a "bunch of suits." Suits are traditionally what modern politicians wear; they are part of the job. However, here they are used as symbols to represent the whole.
Tone	The attitude of a piece of writing, as conveyed by the words, syntax, and descriptions of the author.	An author might convey a frantic tone by manipulating dialogue into run-on sentences or using descriptive adverbs, such as feverishly or pedantically, and descriptive verbs, such as panicked and stuttered.

Determining Meaning of Words and Phrases

Readers can often figure out what unfamiliar words mean without interrupting their reading to look them up in dictionaries by examining context. **Context** includes the other words or sentences in a passage. One common context clue is the root word and any affixes (prefixes/suffixes). Another common context clue is a synonym or definition included in the sentence. Sometimes both exist in the same sentence. Here's an example:

Scientists who study birds are *ornithologists*.

Many readers may not know the word *ornithologist*. However, the example contains a definition (scientists who study birds). The reader may also have the ability to analyze the suffix (*-logy*, meaning the study of) and root (*ornitho-*, meaning bird).

Another common context clue is a sentence that shows differences. Here's an example:

Birds *incubate* their eggs outside of their bodies, unlike mammals.

Some readers may be unfamiliar with the word *incubate*. However, since we know that "unlike mammals," birds incubate their eggs outside of their bodies, we can infer that *incubate* has something to do with keeping eggs warm outside the body until they are hatched.

In addition to analyzing the etymology of a word's root and affixes and extrapolating word meaning from sentences that contrast an unknown word with an antonym, readers can also determine word meanings from sentence context clues based on logic. Here's an example:

Birds are always looking out for *predators* that could attack their young.

The reader who is unfamiliar with the word *predator* could determine from the context of the sentence that predators usually prey upon baby birds and possibly other young animals. Readers might also use the context clue of etymology here, as *predator* and *prey* have the same root.

Impact of Specific Word Choices

An author's word choice can also affect the style, tone, and mood of the text. Word choices, grammatical choices, and syntactical choices can help the audience figure out the scope, purpose, and emphasis. These choices—embedded in the words and sentences of the passage (i.e., the "parts")—help paint the intentions and goals of the author (i.e., the "whole"). For instance, if an author is using strong language like *enrage*, *ignite*, *infuriate*, and *antagonize*, then they may be cueing the reader into their own rage or they may be trying to incite anger in other. Likewise, if an author is continually using rapid, simple sentences, he or she might be trying to incite excitement and nervousness. These different choices and styles affect the overall message, or purpose. Sometimes the subject matter or audience will be discussed explicitly, but often readers have to decode the passage, or "break it down," to find the target audience and intentions. Meanwhile, the impact of the article can be personal or historical, for example, depending upon the passage—it can either "speak" to you personally or "capture" an historical era.

Author's Choice of Structure

Text structure is the way in which the author organizes and presents textual information so readers can follow and comprehend it. One kind of text structure is **sequence**. This means the author arranges the text in a logical order from beginning to middle to end. There are three types of sequences:

- Chronological: ordering events in time from earliest to latest

- Spatial: describing objects, people, or spaces according to their relationships to one another in space

- Order of Importance: addressing topics, characters, or ideas according to how important they are, from either least important to most important

Chronological sequence is the most common sequential text structure. Readers can identify sequential structure by looking for words that signal it, like *first, earlier, meanwhile, next, then, later, finally;* and specific times and dates the author includes as chronological references.

Problem-Solution Text Structure

The problem-solution text structure organizes textual information by presenting readers with a problem and then developing its solution throughout the course of the text. The author may present a variety of alternatives as possible solutions, eliminating each as they are found unsuccessful, or gradually leading up to the ultimate solution. For example, in fiction, an author might write a murder mystery novel and have the character(s) solve it through investigating various clues or character alibis until the killer is identified. In nonfiction, an author writing an essay or book on a real-world problem might discuss various alternatives and explain their disadvantages or why they would not work before identifying the best solution. For scientific research, an author reporting and discussing scientific experiment results would explain why various alternatives failed or succeeded.

Comparison-Contrast Text Structure

Comparison identifies similarities between two or more things. **Contrast** identifies differences between two or more things. Authors typically employ both to illustrate relationships between things by highlighting their commonalities and deviations. For example, a writer might compare Windows and Linux as operating systems, and contrast Linux as free and open-source vs. Windows as proprietary. When writing an essay, sometimes it is useful to create an image of the two objects or events you are comparing or contrasting. Venn diagrams are useful because they show the differences as well as the similarities between two things. Once you've seen the similarities and differences on paper, it might be helpful to create an outline of the essay with both comparison and contrast. Every outline will look different because every two or more things will have a different number of comparisons and contrasts. Say you are trying to compare and contrast carrots with sweet potatoes. Here is an example of a compare/contrast outline using those topics:

- Introduction: Talk about why you are comparing and contrasting carrots and sweet potatoes. Give the thesis statement.

- Body paragraph 1: Sweet potatoes and carrots are both root vegetables (similarity)

- Body paragraph 2: Sweet potatoes and carrots are both orange (similarity)

- Body paragraph 3: Sweet potatoes and carrots have different nutritional components (difference)

- Conclusion: Restate the purpose of your comparison/contrast essay.

Of course, if there is only one similarity between your topics and two differences, you will want to rearrange your outline. Always tailor your essay to what works best with your topic.

Descriptive Text Structure

Description can be both a type of text structure and a type of text. Some texts are descriptive throughout entire books. For example, a book may describe the geography of a certain country, state, or region, or tell readers all about dolphins by describing many of their characteristics. Many other texts are not descriptive throughout but use descriptive passages within the overall text. The following are a few examples of descriptive text:

- When the author describes a character in a novel
- When the author sets the scene for an event by describing the setting
- When a biographer describes the personality and behaviors of a real-life individual

- When a historian describes the details of a particular battle within a book about a specific war
- When a travel writer describes the climate, people, foods, and/or customs of a certain place

A hallmark of description is using sensory details, painting a vivid picture so readers can imagine it almost as if they were experiencing it personally.

Cause and Effect Text Structure

When using cause and effect to extrapolate meaning from text, readers must determine the cause when the author only communicates effects. For example, if a description of a child eating an ice cream cone includes details like beads of sweat forming on the child's face and the ice cream dripping down her hand faster than she can lick it off, the reader can infer or conclude it must be hot outside. A useful technique for making such decisions is wording them in "If...then" form, e.g. "If the child is perspiring and the ice cream melting, then it may be a hot day." Cause and effect text structures explain why certain events or actions resulted in particular outcomes. For example, an author might describe America's historical large flocks of dodo birds, the fact that gunshots did not startle/frighten dodos, and that because dodos did not flee, settlers killed whole flocks in one hunting session, explaining how the dodo was hunted into extinction.

Differences in the Points of View of Characters

Point of view refers to the perspective of the narrator in a story or poem. There are four different points of view that can be incorporated into a story or poem:

The chart below defines each point of view, highlighting the different pronouns used:

FIRST PERSON	SECOND PERSON	THIRD PERSON LIMITED	THIRD PERSON OMNISCIENT
Definition: The narrator recounts the story as if they are part of the story.	**Definition:** The narrator speaks directly to the audience. Rarely used in fiction, this point of view is more likely to be found in nonfiction or instructional texts.	**Definition:** The narrator tells the story in a limited, detached manner, revealing only a few important details that they have access to, such as the protagonist's thought patterns.	**Definition:** The narrator tells the story in a detached manner, but acts as though they know *everything* about the details of the story. The word *omniscient* actually means "all-knowing" and "all-seeing." A common point of view in fiction, the third person omniscient perspective reveals the thoughts and actions of *all* characters.
Potential Pronouns: I, we, us, me, mine, our	**Potential Pronouns:** you, your	**Potential Pronouns:** he, she, they, them	**Potential Pronouns:** he, she, they, them

Depending on the point of view employed, narrators present their perspective in either a **subjective** or **objective** manner.

Objectives perspectives are observable, factual, quantifiable, unbiased, logical, reasonable, rational, and/or scientific in nature.

Subjective perspectives, on the other hand, are opinionated, debatable, questionable, biased, emotional, and, in some extreme instances, irrational or fabricated.

76

These different points of view and perspectives help generate dramatic effects – such as **suspense**, **humor**, and **dramatic irony** – for the audience. Suspense is an intense feeling – such as fear, anxiety, trepidation, or an "adrenaline rush" – that heightens the emotional sensitivities of the audience as they wait for the outcomes of certain events in a poem, play, short story, or novel. Like suspense, humor helps draw an emotional reaction from the audience; however, humor manifests itself in the form of laughter or amusement rather than fear, anxiety, or trepidation. In fact, humor can be used to distract the audience from these other emotions. Dramatic irony uses plot structure to extend irony (i.e., contradictions that occur between intended meanings and. actual meanings) throughout a text.

All three literary devices – suspense, humor, and dramatic irony – would be impossible without the strategic use of point of view. All three literary devices occur when the narrator reveals crucial pieces of information that are otherwise unknown to other characters in the text. A reader may be overwhelmed by suspense because they know a naive character is about to be murdered. They may be consumed by laughter because they are "in on a joke" only shared with the narrator, but not the characters of the story. They may even be mesmerized by the dramatic irony an author creates by juxtaposing characters and contexts that seem inherently contradictory.

While these literary devices can be incorporated into all points of view, they are especially suited for third-person narratives, which reveal details and emotions in a limited or omniscient manner.

Reading Informational Text

Structure of Informational Texts

Authors of informational texts, including popular print and digital media, structure or organize information, passages, and text features in certain ways that help readers better understand the concepts and ideas that are presented.

Reading specialists typically separate text structures into five major categories:

1. **Chronology:** This type of informational text structure follows chronological order, unveiling events in the historical order in which they happened.

   o Example: Most (but not all) history texts follow a particular chronology. They list events in the order in which they happened, using text features, such as timelines, to reinforce a particular chronology. A specific example would be a book that offers step-by-step explanations of how the United States responded to major drug-smuggling efforts during the multi-decade "War on Drugs."

2. **Comparison:** This type of informational text structure compares two or more themes, events, people, ideas, things, or movements.

   o Example: An article in the *New York Times* that compares the political stances that the Clinton and Obama Administrations took on the international "War on Drugs."

3. **Cause and Effect:** This type of informational text structure highlights how one event (the cause) influenced another event (the effect).

   o Example: A *Vox* website article that explains how President Bill Clinton's efforts to close Columbia's drug-smuggling routes in the Caribbean Sea unintentionally paved the way to Mexico's rise as the number one narco state in the world.

4. **Problem and Solution:** This type of informational text structure identifies a particular problem and offers a solution, or way to fix it.

   o Example: A High Intensity Drug Trafficking Agency (HIDTA) intelligence briefing that uses statistics to explain how a rise in fentanyl death rates in the Northeast (i.e., the problem) should be a top concern for US agencies, but also offers a ten-step action plan for bringing the "War on Drugs" to rural sectors in New England and the Mid-Atlantic.

5. **Proposition and Support:** This type of informational text structure sets forth a particular claim, thesis, or hypothesis, and uses quantitative and qualitative data to support that particular claim, thesis, or hypothesis.

   o Example: A doctoral dissertation that uses local interviews and crime statistics to claim that US drug raids in Latin America have actually led to an increase in drug-related crimes since the 1970s.

Using Textual Evidence to Support Analysis

As discussed previously, textual evidence is verified information provided in a work of fiction or nonfiction that is used to support an argument or central idea. The two types of textual evidence are explicit evidence and implicit evidence.

An example of how explicit evidence can be used to support arguments is shown below:

EXPLICIT EVIDENCE EXAMPLE (NEWSPAPER ARTICLE EXCERPT)
"...Murder rates appear to be on the rise in Milwaukee, Wisconsin. In fact, homicide rates have skyrocketed to the point where Milwaukee outpaces 96% of cities in the United States when it comes to murder. To make matters worse, Milwaukee police identified four people murdered in recent shoots in the last week..."

Using explicit evidence in the excerpt above, students can synthesize their own arguments about a particular text.

They can quote explicit evidence directly:

*According to the Milwaukee Journal Sentinel, **"homicide rates have skyrocketed to the point where Milwaukee outpaces 96% of cities in the United States when it comes to murder."***

They can paraphrase and cite explicit evidence:

*According to the Milwaukee Journal Sentinel, **homicide rates are on the rise** in Milwaukee, Wisconsin, thanks, in part to **recent shootings**.*

They can even incorporate their own ideas, while referencing explicit evidence:

Perhaps it is time for a new approach to crime in Milwaukee, Wisconsin: murder is on the rise and shootings seems commonplace.

Determining the Central Idea of an Informational Text

The **topic** of a text is the general subject matter. Text topics can usually be expressed in one word, or a few words at most. Additionally, readers should ask themselves what point the author is trying to make. This point is the **main idea** of the text, the one thing the author wants readers to know concerning the topic. Once the author has established the main idea, he or she will support the main idea by supporting details. **Supporting details** are evidence that support the main idea and include personal testimonies, examples, or statistics.

One analogy for these components and their relationships is that a text is like a well-designed house. The topic is the roof, covering all rooms. The main idea is the frame. The supporting details are the various rooms. To identify the topic of a text, readers can ask themselves what or who the author is writing about in the paragraph. To locate the main idea, readers can ask themselves what one idea the author wants readers to know about the topic. To identify supporting details, readers can put the main idea into question form and ask, "what does the author use to prove or explain their main idea?"

Let's look at an example. An author is writing an essay about the Amazon rainforest and trying to convince the audience that more funding should go into protecting the area from deforestation. The author makes the argument

78

stronger by including evidence of the benefits of the rainforest: it provides habitats to a variety of species, it provides much of the earth's oxygen which in turn cleans the atmosphere, and it is the home to medicinal plants that may be the answer to some of the world's deadliest diseases. Here is an outline of the essay looking at topic, main idea, and supporting details:

- Topic: Amazon rainforest
- Main Idea: The Amazon rainforest should receive more funding to protect it from deforestation.
- Supporting Details:
    1. It provides habitats to a variety of species
    2. It provides much of the earth's oxygen which in turn cleans the atmosphere
    3. It is home to medicinal plants that may be the answer to some of the deadliest diseases

Notice that the topic of the essay is listed in a few key words: "Amazon rainforest." The main idea tells us what about the topic is important: that the topic should be funded in order to prevent deforestation. Finally, the supporting details are what the author relies on to convince the audience to act or to believe in the truth of the main idea.

Summarizing Text

An important skill is the ability to read a complex text and then reduce its length and complexity by focusing on the key events and details. A **summary** is a shortened version of the original text, written by the reader in their own words. The summary should be shorter than the original text, and it must include the most critical points.

In order to effectively summarize a complex text, it's necessary to understand the original source and identify the major points covered. It may be helpful to outline the original text to get the big picture and avoid getting bogged down in the minor details. For example, a summary wouldn't include a statistic from the original source unless it was the major focus of the text. It is also important for readers to use their own words but still retain the original meaning of the passage. The key to a good summary is emphasizing the main idea without changing the focus of the original information.

Complex texts will likely be more difficult to summarize. Readers must evaluate all points from the original source, filter out the unnecessary details, and maintain only the essential ideas. The summary often mirrors the original text's organizational structure. For example, in a problem-solution text structure, the author typically presents readers with a problem and then develops solutions through the course of the text. An effective summary would likely retain this general structure, rephrasing the problem and then reporting the most useful or plausible solutions.

Paraphrasing is somewhat similar to summarizing. It calls for the reader to take a small part of the passage and list or describe its main points. Paraphrasing is more than rewording the original passage, though. As with summary, a paraphrase should be written in the reader's own words, while still retaining the meaning of the original source. The main difference between summarizing and paraphrasing is that a summary would be appropriate for a much larger text, while paraphrasing might focus on just a few lines of text. Effective paraphrasing will indicate an understanding of the original source, yet still help the reader expand on their interpretation. A paraphrase should neither add new information nor remove essential facts that change the meaning of the source.

Types of Informational Texts

Expository Writing

Expository writing is also known as informational writing. Its purpose is not to tell a story as in narrative writing, to paint a picture as in descriptive writing, or to persuade readers to agree with something as in argumentative writing. Rather, its point is to communicate information to the reader. As such, the point of view of the author will necessarily be more objective. Whereas other types of writing appeal to the reader's emotions, appeal to the reader's reason by using logic, or use subjective descriptions to sway the reader's opinion or thinking, expository writing seeks to simply to provide facts, evidence, observations, and objective descriptions of the subject matter. Some examples of expository writing include research reports, journal articles, articles and books about historical events or periods, academic subject textbooks, news articles and other factual journalistic reports, essays, how-to articles, and user instruction manuals.

Technical Writing

Technical writing is similar to expository writing in that it is factual, objective, and intended to provide information to the reader. Indeed, it may even be considered a subcategory of expository writing. However, technical writing differs from expository writing in that (1) it is specific to a particular field, discipline, or subject; and (2) it uses the specific technical terminology that belongs only to that area. Writing that uses technical terms is intended only for an audience familiar with those terms. A primary example of technical writing today is writing related to computer programming and use.

Persuasive Writing

Persuasive writing is intended to persuade the reader to agree with the author's position. It is also known as argumentative writing. Some writers may be responding to other writers' arguments, in which case they make reference to those authors or text and then disagree with them. However, another common technique is for the author to anticipate opposing viewpoints in general, both from other authors and from the author's own readers. The author brings up these opposing viewpoints, and then refutes them before they can even be raised, strengthening the author's argument. Writers persuade readers by appealing to the readers' reason and emotion, as well as to their own character and credibility. Aristotle called these appeals *logos*, *pathos*, and *ethos*, respectively.

Using Text Features

Textbooks that are designed well employ varied **text features** for organizing their main ideas, illustrating central concepts, spotlighting significant details, and signaling evidence that supports the ideas and points conveyed. When a textbook uses these features in recurrent patterns that are predictable, it makes it easier for readers to locate information and come up with connections. When readers comprehend how to make use of text features, they will take less time and effort deciphering how the text is organized, leaving them more time and energy for focusing on the actual content in the text. Instructional activities can include not only previewing text through observing main text features, but moreover through examining and deconstructing the text and ascertaining how the text features can aid them in locating and applying text information for learning.

Included among various text features are a table of contents, headings, subheadings, an index, a glossary, a foreword, a preface, paragraphing spaces, bullet lists, footnotes, sidebars, diagrams, graphs, charts, pictures, illustrations, captions, italics, boldface, colors, and symbols. A **glossary** is a list of key vocabulary words and/or technical terminology and definitions. This helps readers recognize or learn specialized terms used in the text before reading it. A **foreword** is typically written by someone other than the text author and appears at the beginning to introduce, inform, recommend, and/or praise the work. A **preface** is often written by the author and also appears at the beginning, to introduce or explain something about the text, like new additions. A **sidebar** is a box with text and sometimes graphics at the left or right side of a page, typically focusing on a more specific issue, example, or aspect of the subject. **Footnotes** are additional comments/notes at the bottom of the page, signaled by superscript numbers in the text.

Author's Point of View and Purpose

Authors may have many purposes for writing a specific text. They could be imparting information, entertaining their audience, expressing their own feelings, or trying to persuade their readers of a particular position. Authors' purposes are their reasons for writing something. A single author may have one overriding purpose for writing or multiple reasons. An author may explicitly state their intention in the text, or the reader may need to infer that intention. When readers can identify the author's purpose, they are better able to analyze information in the text. By knowing why the author wrote the text, readers can glean ideas for how to approach it. The following is a list of questions readers can ask in order to discern an author's purpose for writing a text:

- Does the title of the text give you any clues about its purpose?
- Was the purpose of the text to give information to readers?
- Did the author want to describe an event, issue, or individual?
- Was it written to express emotions and thoughts?
- Did the author want to convince readers to consider a particular issue?
- Do you think the author's primary purpose was to entertain?
- Why do you think the author wrote this text from a certain point of view?
- What is your response to the text as a reader?
- Did the author state their purpose for writing it?

Readers should read to interpret information rather than simply content themselves with roles as text consumers. Being able to identify an author's purpose efficiently improves reading comprehension, develops critical thinking, and makes readers more likely to consider issues in depth before accepting the writer's viewpoints. Authors of fiction frequently write to entertain readers. Another purpose for writing fiction is making a political statement; for example, Jonathan Swift wrote "A Modest Proposal" (1729) as a political satire. Another purpose for writing fiction as well as nonfiction is to persuade readers to take some action or further a particular cause. Fiction authors and poets both frequently write to evoke certain moods; for example, Edgar Allan Poe wrote novels, short stories, and poems that evoke moods of gloom, guilt, terror, and dread. Another purpose of poets is evoking certain emotions: love is popular, as in Shakespeare's sonnets and numerous others. In "The Waste Land" (1922), T.S. Eliot evokes society's alienation, disaffection, sterility, and fragmentation.

Authors seldom directly state their purposes in texts. Some readers may be confronted with nonfiction texts such as biographies, histories, magazine and newspaper articles, and instruction manuals, among others. To identify the purpose in nonfiction texts, students can ask the following questions:

- Is the author trying to teach something?
- Is the author trying to persuade the reader?
- Is the author imparting factual information only?
- Is this a reliable source?
- Does the author have some kind of hidden agenda?

To apply author purpose in nonfictional passages, readers can also analyze sentence structure, word choice, and transitions to answer the aforementioned questions and to make inferences. For example, authors wanting to convince readers to view a topic negatively often choose words with negative connotations.

Multiple Sources of Information

Books as Resources

When a student has an assignment to research and write a paper, one of the first steps after determining the topic is to select research sources. The student may begin by conducting an Internet or library search of the topic, may refer to a reading list provided by the instructor, or may use an annotated bibliography of works related to the topic. To evaluate the worth of the book for the research paper, the student first considers the book title to get an idea of its content. Then the student can scan the book's table of contents for chapter titles and topics to get further ideas of their applicability to the topic. The student may also turn to the end of the book to look for an alphabetized index. Most academic textbooks and scholarly works have these; students can look up key topic terms to see how many are included and how many pages are devoted to them.

Journal Articles

Like books, **journal articles** are primary or secondary sources the student may need to use for researching any topic. To assess whether a journal article will be a useful source for a particular paper topic, a student can first get some idea about the content of the article by reading its title and subtitle, if any exists. Many journal articles, particularly scientific ones, include abstracts. These are brief summaries of the content. The student should read the abstract to get a more specific idea of whether the experiment, literature review, or other work documented is applicable to the paper topic. Students should also check the references at the end of the article, which today often contain links to related works for exploring the topic further.

Encyclopedias and Dictionaries

Dictionaries and encyclopedias are both reference books for looking up information alphabetically. **Dictionaries** are more exclusively focused on vocabulary words. They include each word's correct spelling, pronunciation, variants, part(s) of speech, definitions of one or more meanings, and examples used in a sentence. Some dictionaries provide illustrations of certain words when these inform the meaning. Some dictionaries also offer synonyms, antonyms, and related words under a word's entry. **Encyclopedias**, like dictionaries, often provide word pronunciations and definitions. However, they have broader scopes: one can look up entire subjects in encyclopedias, not just words, and find comprehensive, detailed information about historical events, famous people, countries, disciplines of study, and many other things. Dictionaries are for finding word meanings, pronunciations, and spellings; encyclopedias are for finding breadth and depth of information on a variety of topics.

Card Catalogs

A **card catalog** is a means of organizing, classifying, and locating the large numbers of books found in libraries. Without being able to look up books in library card catalogs, it would be virtually impossible to find them on library shelves. Card catalogs may be on traditional paper cards filed in drawers, or electronic catalogs accessible online; some libraries combine both. Books are shelved by subject area; subjects are coded using formal classification systems—standardized sets of rules for identifying and labeling books by subject and author. These assign each book a **call number**: a code indicating the classification system, subject, author, and title. Call numbers also function as bookshelf "addresses" where books can be located. Most public libraries use the Dewey Decimal Classification System. Most university, college, and research libraries use the Library of Congress Classification. Nursing students will also encounter the National Institute of Health's National Library of Medicine Classification System, which major collections of health sciences publications utilize.

Databases

A **database** is a collection of digital information organized for easy access, updating, and management. Users can sort and search databases for information. One way of classifying databases is by content, i.e. full-text, numerical, bibliographical, or images. Another classification method used in computing is by organizational approach. The most common approach is a relational database, which is tabular and defines data so they can be accessed and reorganized in various ways. A distributed database can be reproduced or interspersed among different locations within a network. An object-oriented database is organized to be aligned with object classes and subclasses defining the data. Databases usually collect files like product inventories, catalogs, customer profiles, sales transactions, student bodies, and resources. An associated set of application programs is a database management system or database manager. It enables users to specify which reports to generate, control access to reading and writing data, and analyze database usage. Structured Query Language (SQL) is a standard computer language for updating, querying, and otherwise interfacing with databases.

Identifying Primary Sources in Various Media

A **primary source** is a piece of original work. This can include books, musical compositions, recordings, movies, works of visual art (paintings, drawings, photographs), jewelry, pottery, clothing, furniture, and other artifacts. Within books, primary sources may be of any genre. Whether nonfiction based on actual events or a fictional creation, the primary source relates the author's firsthand view of some specific event, phenomenon, character, place, process, ideas, field of

82

study or discipline, or other subject matter. Whereas primary sources are original treatments of their subjects, **secondary sources** are a step removed from the original subjects; they analyze and interpret primary sources. These include journal articles, newspaper or magazine articles, works of literary criticism, political commentaries, and academic textbooks.

In the field of history, primary sources frequently include documents that were created around the same time period that they were describing, and most often produced by someone who had direct experience or knowledge of the subject matter. In contrast, secondary sources present the ideas and viewpoints of other authors about the primary sources; in history, for example, these can include books and other written works about the particular historical periods or eras in which the primary sources were produced. Primary sources pertinent in history include diaries, letters, statistics, government information, and original journal articles and books. In literature, a primary source might be a literary novel, a poem or book of poems, or a play. Secondary sources addressing primary sources may be criticism, dissertations, theses, and journal articles. Tertiary sources, typically reference works referring to primary and secondary sources, include encyclopedias, bibliographies, handbooks, abstracts, and periodical indexes.

In scientific fields, when scientists conduct laboratory experiments to answer specific research questions and test hypotheses, lab reports and reports of research results constitute examples of primary sources. When researchers produce statistics to support or refute hypotheses, those statistics are primary sources. When a scientist is studying some subject longitudinally or conducting a case study, they may keep a journal or diary. For example, Charles Darwin kept diaries of extensive notes on his studies during sea voyages on the *Beagle*, visits to the Galápagos Islands, etc.; Jean Piaget kept journals of observational notes for case studies of children's learning behaviors. Many scientists, particularly in past centuries, shared and discussed discoveries, questions, and ideas with colleagues through letters, which also constitute primary sources. When a scientist seeks to replicate another's experiment, the reported results, analysis, and commentary on the original work is a secondary source, as is a student's dissertation if it analyzes or discusses others' work rather than reporting original research or ideas.

Structure and Purpose of Visual Text Features

Line Graphs

Line graphs are useful for visually representing data that vary continuously over time, like an individual student's test scores. The horizontal or x-axis shows dates/times; the vertical or y-axis shows point values. A dot is plotted on the point where each horizontal date line intersects each vertical number line, and then these dots are connected, forming a line. Line graphs show whether changes in values over time exhibit trends like ascending, descending, flat, or more variable, like going up and down at different times. For example, suppose a student's scores on the same type of reading test were 75% in October, 79% in November, 78% in December, 82% in January, 85% in February, 88% in March, and 90% in April. A line graph of these scores would look like this:

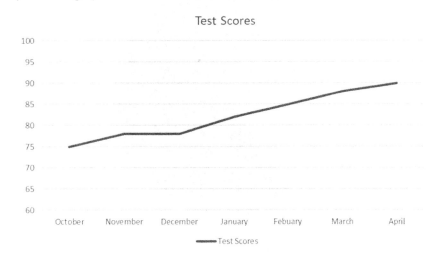

Bar Graphs

Bar graphs feature equally spaced, horizontal or vertical rectangular bars representing numerical values. They can show change over time as line graphs do, but unlike line graphs, bar graphs can also show differences and similarities among values at a single point in time. Bar graphs are also helpful for visually representing data from different categories, especially when the horizontal axis displays some value that is not numerical, like various countries with inches of annual rainfall. The following is a bar graph that compares different classes and how many books they read:

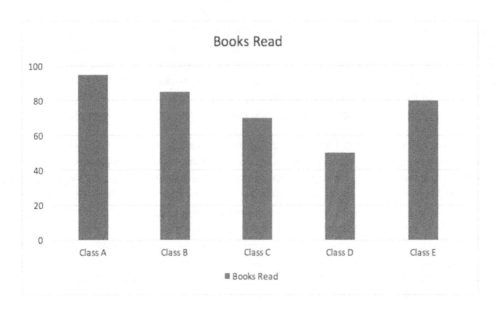

Pie Charts

Pie charts, also called circle graphs, are good for representing percentages or proportions of a whole quantity because they represent the whole as a circle or "pie," with the various proportion values shown as "slices" or wedges of the pie. This gives viewers a clear idea of how much of a total each item occupies. To calculate central angles to make each portion the correct size, multiply each percentage by 3.6 (= 360/100). For example, biologists may have information that 60% of Americans have brown eyes, 20% have hazel eyes, 15% have blue eyes, and 5% have green eyes. A pie chart of these distributions would look like this:

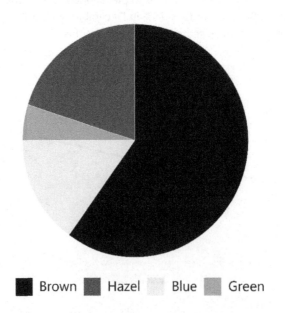

Line Plots

Rather than showing trends or changes over time like line graphs, **line plots** show the frequency with which a value occurs in a group. Line plots are used for visually representing data sets that total 50 or fewer values. They make visible features like gaps between some data points, clusters of certain numbers/number ranges, and outliers (data points with significantly smaller or larger values than others). For example, the age ranges in a class of nursing students might appear like this in a line plot:

XXXXXXXXXX	XXXXX	XX	X	XXX	XX	X
18	23	28	33	38	43	48

Pictograms

Magazines, newspapers, and other similar publications designed for consumption by the general public often use pictograms to represent data. **Pictograms** feature icons or symbols that look like whatever category of data is being counted, like little silhouettes shaped like human beings commonly used to represent people. If the data involve large numbers, like populations, one person symbol might represent one million people, or one thousand, etc. For smaller values, such as how many individuals out of ten fit a given description, one symbol might equal one person. Male and female silhouettes are used to differentiate gender, and child shapes for children. Little clock symbols are used to represent amounts of time, such as a given number of hours; calendar pages might depict months; suns and moons could show days and nights; hourglasses might represent minutes. While pictogram symbols are easily recognizable and appealing to general viewers, one disadvantage is that it is difficult to display partial symbols for in-between quantities.

Bias and Stereotyping

Biases usually occur when someone allows their personal preferences or ideologies to interfere with what should be an objective decision. In personal situations, someone is biased towards someone if they favor them in an unfair way. In academic writing, being biased in your sources means leaving out objective information that would turn the argument one way or the other. The evidence of bias in academic writing makes the text less credible, so be sure to present all viewpoints when writing, not just your own, so to avoid coming off as biased. Being objective when presenting information or dealing with people usually allows the person to gain more credibility.

Stereotypes are preconceived notions that place a particular rule or characteristics on an entire group of people. Stereotypes are usually offensive to the group they refer to or allies of that group and often have negative connotations. The reinforcement of stereotypes isn't always obvious. Sometimes stereotypes can be very subtle and are still widely used in order for people to understand categories within the world. For example, saying that women are more emotional and intuitive than men is a stereotype, although this is still an assumption used by many in order to understand the differences between one another.

Text Complexity

Understanding and assigning **text complexity** is not an exact science. A single source is not sufficient for understanding text complexity. The California Subject Examinations for Teachers (CSET) follows the recommendations of the Common Core Standards by establishing a tripartite model for evaluating text complexity. This model draws from three sources rather than one source: 1) Quantitative Tools and Measures, 2) Qualitative Dimensions, and 3) Reader and Task Variables. The goal of this model is to raise the expectations of students and teachers in terms of the complexity of the texts they select and read in the classroom.

In order to utilize this model to determine the complexity of a text, teachers have to apply their understanding and professional judgment to each of these sources, which are defined in the section below. None of these sources are sufficient when used in isolation.

Using Quantitative Tools and Measures

When determining the complexity of texts, teachers need to be familiar with quantitative measures. **Quantitative measures** are any features that can be counted in a text, such as the number of words or syllables. Quantitative measures may also be produced by certain metrics, formulas, frameworks, or rubrics that account for a combination of other quantitative and qualitative measures. For instance, quantitative measures can be used to determine the number of grade-level vocabulary terms, phrases, or sentences in a text. Additionally, the most commonly used quantitative tool is the Lexile Framework for Reading ©. The Lexile Framework for Reading © helps teachers and students determine the "readability" or "grade band equivalent" of a text. Most recent publications and online digital resources typically provide a Lexile text measure for each text. The Lexile text measure determines complexity by accounting for such factors as the word count, syntax, and the difficulty of the vocabulary in a text. Lexile text measures range quantitatively from 0L for texts for beginning readers to above 2000L for texts for advanced college-level readers. Teachers typically use these Lexile text measures to select appropriate text for their grades. Below is one example of a model teachers might use to match Lexile text measures with their appropriate grade levels:

Grade	Suggested Lexile Level
1	120L-295L
2	170L-545L
3	415L-760L
4	635L-950L
5	770L-1080L
6	855L-1165L
7	925L-1235L
8	985L-1295L
9	1040L-1350L
10	1085L-1400L
11/12	1130L-1440L

However, every student is also assigned a Lexile reader measure. There are two ways that students can be assigned a Lexile reader measure: 1) by taking a Scholastic Reading Inventory (SRI) test, which is a research-based assessment designed to calculate a students' Lexile scores, or 2) by taking another standardized examination that calculates students' reading levels. Like Lexile text measures, the higher the Lexile reading measure, the higher the student's reading level.

Knowledge of Qualitative Dimensions

Look and Layout: The look and layout of a text can dictate its complexity. In fact, look and layout are two of the first things that students respond to when they are engaging with a text. Tiny fonts and tightly packed paragraphs can cause many readers to shut down.

Levels of Meaning: Texts have different levels of meaning, ranging from straightforward facts to symbolic connotations. The more symbolic a text is, the more difficult it may be to read, especially for an English Language Learner (ELL). Symbolism carries with it a sort of intellectual depth that can only be fully grasped through advanced fluency.

Structure: Every genre and subgenre of literature possesses a unique qualitative structure that shapes its organization and meaning. For instance, poetry is usually structured in verses instead of lines and stanzas instead of paragraphs. Graphic novels are structures with more visuals and serialized dialogues that are minimalistic in nature. These structures change the ways texts are both qualitatively presented and interpreted.

Language Conventionality and Clarity: Some texts tend to be hyper-traditional, maintaining conventional language conventions. Other texts tend to be more unorthodox, experimenting with new language conventions. This type of experimentation can alter the complex dimensions of a text by introducing new styles or syntaxes. Unconventional texts are more difficult to decode, especially for English Language Learners (ELLs).

Background Knowledge: Some texts demand more background knowledge than others; they tailor their information for a niche target audience. Academic texts in many fields intentionally marginalize some readers through the use of *insider language* or *jargon*. Academics have to have a tremendous amount of background knowledge to understand the meaning of the field's jargon. Choosing texts with less jargon will be helpful for developing readers, especially English Language Learners (ELLs).

Using Text Complexity to Select Appropriate Texts

In practice, teachers should differentiate their lessons to include books or reading resources that have Lexile text levels that match each child's Lexile reading measure. The most effective classrooms will have students reading texts that are based on individual reading levels rather than grade levels. This is why quantitative measures of text complexity are so important: they scientifically and mathematically try to assess text levels and student reading levels, which makes it easier to quantifiably match these levels in curricula, lesson plans, instruction, and assessments.

Reading complex texts should not be a "sink or swim" process for students. Students will need more support as the texts become increasingly complex throughout elementary, middle, and high school. Gradual releases of responsibility are necessary for successfully preparing students for complex texts. Complex texts should not be integrated into unstructured classroom environments or lessons; rather, complex texts should be introduced in the most highly structured and highly supportive contexts. Teachers can support students in these contexts by first reading to students and reading with students (i.e., shared reading). Additionally, students must eventually approach complexity in an *active* rather than passive manner. True comprehension of complex texts can only be made possible with *active* engagement. While teachers must be structured, students must be committed. Likewise, while teachers must be strategists in the classroom, students must be risk takers in the classroom.

Below is a visual guide for gradually releasing responsibilities to students to build independence:

Student Independence

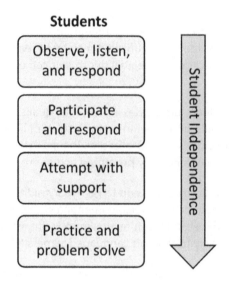

Reader Variables and Task Variables

Reader Variables

Each student in a classroom represents a unique combination of different variables: they have different language backgrounds, they come from different cultures, they have different motivations, and they possess varied ranges of background knowledge, skill levels, and experiences. Every teacher must navigate these unique combinations of individual variables while selecting and differentiating texts for each student. Additionally, teachers must be aware of collective variables, which are the variables that engage students as a social unit or set of social units in the classroom. Teachers must constantly reflect on how their students act as individuals and as a group. This type of constant reflection not only helps drive text selection and differentiation, but also reading intervention in the classroom.

Language Differences

In order to do this, teachers have to consistently understand the language backgrounds or language profiles of their students. For instance, are any students English Language Learners (ELLs)? If so, what is the level of their English comprehension? Are they fully competent in reading, writing, and speaking English? If not, what are their levels of competency for each category? Similarly, are they bilingual or trilingual? Are they living in predominantly bilingual or monolingual households? If they have a native language that is different than English, what is their comprehension level with their own language? If they are immigrants to the US, how many years have they lived in the United States? What age were they when they first moved? Are the majority of students in the class from similar linguistic backgrounds? If not, what are the demographic breakdowns of the class? These are just some of the many questions teachers need to explore when deconstructing the reader variables that influence student learning and classroom culture. Understanding these variables will help teachers to gain a better understanding of every learner's profile, and, consequently, it will help teachers select the proper texts and text complexities for each class and each student.

Cultural Backgrounds and Curricular Relevance:

Every human being has his/her own **cultural identity**. We come from different cultures, with different cultural backgrounds and variables. These backgrounds and variables affect our language abilities, motivations, background knowledge, skill levels, and experiences. Culture is often overlooked when selecting appropriate texts for students. However, it may be the most dominant of the reader variables because it is a highly influential, often-inescapable phenomenon. Students do not choose their cultures, at least not during adolescence; rather, they are merely *born into* their cultures.

Another, often overlooked, component of supporting student learning is **relevance**. Teachers must choose texts that are culturally and individually relevant to each student's identity. While many aspects of the classroom preparation are complicated, instilling relevance into reading tasks is a simplistic science: put simple, students will not care enough about reading if they are not interested in the topics they are reading. When students see no value in the texts they read, when they believe reading is dull and uninteresting, they will inevitably disengage. Selecting appropriate texts is, therefore, not only focused mastering Lexile measures, but also focused discovering relevant and engaging content for students.

Motivation

Motivation is a word used to describe an individual or collective desire to engage in a particular activity or topic. Every student and classroom has different motivation levels, which affects both behavioral and academic factors in the classroom. Many teachers passively wait to evaluate motivation levels when it comes to reading, but the most effective teachers uncover what motivates each student so that they can choose texts that match these motivations. For instance, if a student is more motivated by reading biographies about US presidents, then this platform can be used to increase Lexile reader levels and serve as a bridge to other topics.

Practice Quiz

1. Which of the following is an example of a bound morpheme that also serves as a prefix?
    a. Backpack
    b. Packing
    c. Unpack
    d. Pack

2. Which of the following scenarios would reflect a third-person omniscient perspective?
    a. An antagonistic treatise on the evident decay of industrialized society that calls out American consumer culture, employing such allegations as "You are all rotting our world from within"
    b. A letter written from a deeply personal perspective that captures significant moments in life, using "I" statements
    c. A narrative-style poem that conveys the deepest secrets and thought patterns of the characters to the readers
    d. A dramatic play that only reveals the thoughts of one character through the use of soliloquies

3. Which reader Lexile measure would likely indicate the preferred reading level of 12th grader?
    a. 170L to 545L
    b. 635L to 950L
    c. 985L to 1295L
    d. 1130L to 1440L

4. Which is the best example of argumentative writing?
    a. An article that tries to get working-class white citizens to take an anti-racist stance
    b. A letter to the editor that vents about traffic issues in Austin, Texas
    c. A monograph that uses qualitative evidence to claim that Shakespeare did not write 75% of his poems
    d. A lab report that lists data and summarizes the findings of a science experiment

5. What word can be used to describe information that "can be cited directly from a text, without the need for an extensive amount of interpretation or deconstruction"?
    a. Implicit evidence
    b. Subjective evidence
    c. Explicit evidence
    d. Stereotypical evidence

See answers on the next page.

Answer Explanations

1. C: The answer is Choice *C,* "unpack." The bound morpheme prefix is "un-" which is bound to "pack" but cannot exist on its own. Choice *A,* "backpack" is a compound word that binds two normally free morphemes, "back" and "pack." Choice *B,* "packing" adds a suffix "-ing" to "pack." Choice *D,* "pack" is a free morpheme.

2. C: The answer is Choice *C,* "A narrative-style poem that conveys the deepest secrets and thought patterns of the characters to the readers." It is third-person omniscient because it is all-seeing, highlighting the inner thoughts of characters. Choice *A* is a second person treatise because the use of "you." Choice *B* is first-person because it uses "I" statements. Choice *D* is third-person limited because it only reveals the thoughts of one character.

3. D: The answer is Choice *D,* "1130L to 1440L" because a 12th grade student would demand the highest Lexile level because these reading ranges go from lowest (Pre-K) to highest (12th grade and beyond).

4. C: The answer is Choice *C,* "A monograph that uses qualitative evidence to claim that Shakespeare did not write 75% of his poems." It is argumentative because it mixes personal interpretation and evidence. *Choice A* is persuasive because it tries to get a group to take a stance. Choice *B* is opinion because it merely vents. Choice *D* is informational because it lacks theoretical arguments.

5. C: The answer is Choice *C,* "explicit evidence" because explicit evidence is taken right from the text; it is not implied. *Choice A* is incorrect because "implicit evidence" is not direct. Choice *B* is wrong because "subjective" means emotionally driven. *Choice D* is wrong because "stereotypical" means biased and is therefore not the best choice.

Subtest I: History and Social Science

World History

Ancient Civilizations

<u>Impact of Physical Geography on Ancient Civilizations</u>

The earliest civilizations of the world were established close to the great river plains and seashores of the ancient world. Mesopotamia emerged near the Tigris and Euphrates Rivers of the Middle East. Ancient Egypt sprouted up along the Lower Nile River, while Ancient Kush called the Upper Nile River home. The Greek and Hebrew Civilizations both shared the Mediterranean Sea, albeit at different parts along the large body of water. The Greeks also dominated the seaways of the Ionian Sea, Aegean Sea, and Black Sea. Rome eventually expanded throughout the entire Mediterranean region, encompassing the old Egyptian, Greek, and Hebrew territories. It created an empire of seaways, riverways, and roadways. The Indus Civilization took hold along the Indus River Valley near modern-day India and Pakistan, while Ancient China established its first empire close to the Huang Ho (Yellow) River. These riverways and seaways helped with trade transportation, hydration, protection, and agricultural production. All early civilizations relied on water as a source of societal sustainability. Many, especially those nestled in ancient river valleys, also relied on flooding to create fertile soil for farming. When flooding threatened the livelihood of crops, these ancient civilizations began commanding the physical geography of the land by building canals and irrigation ducts. Ancient civilizations maintained a symbiotic relationship with the landforms that surrounded them. Waterways, mountains, and deserts helped form natural barriers for ancient societies across the globe. Yet, in spite of these inherent similarities, each civilization maintained its own unique relationship with the land. Physical geography, without a doubt, shaped early society. This section takes a look at each ancient civilization and its unique connection to physical geography.

Mesopotamian

The Middle East is dominated by a desert climate. However, one arc-shaped sector of land between the Persian Gulf and Mediterranean Sea offers some reprieve from this arid landscape: the Fertile Crescent. The Fertile Crescent is an agricultural masterpiece carved out in the land by the Tigris and Euphrates Rivers. The rivers, which flow from the mountains in modern-day Turkey, nourish the land with hydration. Six thousand years ago, the earliest residents of the Mesopotamian recognized the seemingly magical powers of these rivers. Whenever the Tigris and Euphrates flooded, it would enrich the land with its nutrient-rich silt. This silt created the perfect soil for the earliest harvests of the First Agricultural Revolution. The flooding of the land was so unpredictable that eventually the Mesopotamian residents – known as Sumerians – began creating primitive irrigation ditches to redirect the waters during flood season.

Egyptian

Traveling southwest from Mesopotamia, early humans were sure to encounter yet another famous river valley civilization: Ancient Egypt. Like Mesopotamia, Ancient Egypt arose along riverbanks. While Egypt was mostly surrounded by a parched desert, the Sahara, its earliest inhabitants basked in the glory and gift of the Nile River. The Nile River created a narrow ribbon of fertile land for farming. This thin ribbon of water flowed from the distant mountains and plateaus of Uganda and Ethiopia. In July, rains and melting snow would rush from the highlands to the south, causing flooding throughout the Lower Nile corridor. The rains and melting snow would instigate churning rapids, known as cataracts, sending deluges upon the lands. By October, as the great rapids receded, a new fertile black mud would emerge for Ancient Egyptian farmers. Racing against the scorching sun, Ancient Egyptians would use cattle to plow the lands and reap some harvests. Like the residents of Mesopotamia, the Ancient Egyptians learned to use the river as a lifeline; they monitored the Nile like clockwork, for it never had the same unpredictability of the Tigris and Euphrates. Predictable floods help create predictable harvests, and the rushing cataracts served as important natural barriers along the sands of the desert.

Kush

The Nubian kingdom of Kush resided just south of Egypt, along the Upper Nile River. For centuries, the Kush kingdom had served as a sort of vassal state for Ancient Egypt. When Egypt's power declined in 1000 BCE, however, Nubia established a Kushite dynasty on the Egyptian throne. Whether as a vassal state or ruling empire, whether in conflict or in peace, Kush always shared one thing with Ancient Egypt: the "Gift of the Nile." Kush's traditional boundaries began at the conflux of the Blue Nile and White Nile tributaries. But the larger Nile River was its source of sustenance. The Kush kingdom, like the Ancient Egyptian Empire to the north, used the Nile for transport and agriculture, synching its farming season with the Nile's flood patterns. The surrounding deserts and calamitous rapids served as protection from invaders.

Hebrew

The Hebrews, who eventually founded the ancient kingdoms of Judah and Israel, actually shared a region along the eastern end of the Mediterranean Sea, which later became known as Palestine, with other ancient civilizations such as the Phoenicians. The Hebrews called this land Canaan. A crossroads of many surrounding cultures, Canaan was more open to attack than other early civilizations. In fact, much of the Hebrews' history, captured in the Torah (Hebrew Bible), centers on conflicts with outside empires such as the Assyrians and Egyptians. Nevertheless, the Hebrews were a resilient culture, using the waterways of the Mediterranean Sea, Jordan River, and Dead Sea as barriers. These waterways also placed Canaan at the center of trade (as well as conflict). It was close enough to the Mediterranean Sea to access Europe, and close enough to the Red Sea to access Egypt and the Indian Ocean.

Greek

Ancient Greece created a culture that spanned the rugged mountains and the turbulent seas. Ancient Greece was comprised of a mountainous peninsula that jutted into the intricate seaways of the broader Mediterranean region. The mountain chains lent themselves to sea travel – it was often easier to traverse the Mediterranean than to navigate the jagged landscape. Some historians even claim that the Greeks did not live on land, but rather they simply lived around the sea. The Mediterranean Sea, Ionian Sea, Aegean Se, and Black Sea networks became liquid highways for Greek culture. Since Ancient Greece lacked many natural resources, due to its rocky landscape, its residents had to rely on seaways as a way to trade with the surrounding cultures of North Africa and the Middle East.

Indian

Like many other ancient civilizations, the first great Indian civilization arose near the banks of two rivers: the Indus River and the Ganges River. Less is known about the Indus River civilization than the Mesopotamian and Egyptian civilizations. Scholars have yet to fully "crack the code" of the early Indus system of writing; they have not fully deciphered its meaning. Thus, what is currently understood about the Indus River civilization stems from archeological digs and discoveries. The geography of the Indus River civilization was dominated by a great wall of mountains that separates the Indian subcontinent (modern-day India, Pakistan, Nepal, and Bangladesh) from the rest of Asia. The wall is comprised of three mountain ranges: the Hindu Kush, the Karakoram, and the Himalaya. These mountain ranges serve as a natural border for the flat and fertile plains stemming from the Indus and the Ganges Rivers. The Indus-Ganges Plain stretches 1,500 miles. The Thar Desert separates this plain from the rest of the Indian subcontinent, which is mostly comprised of high plateaus with twisting rivers. This plateaued region is called the Deccan.

Along the coast of southern India, there is yet another unique environment shaped by the geography. This coastal region creates a narrow strip of tropical lands. This interesting geographical environment is impacted each year by monsoon winds. Monsoon winds are seasonal winds that blow dry air upon the land during the winter and moist air during the summer. Much like the Egyptian and Mesopotamian civilizations, the Indus River civilization had to work with flood seasons. The flooding of the Indus River Valley, however, was unpredictable. Coupled with the unpredictability of monsoon seasons, the Indus River civilization struggled at times to produce the necessary amount of food. Nestled between the mountains and desert, the Indus River civilization also relied on trade along its waterways. Its rivers gave it access to the Mesopotamian civilization. Its coast to the south gave it access to the seafaring trades of Africa and the Middle East.

Chinese

The cradle of civilization in China was the Yellow River Valley. Like other ancient civilizations, the ancient Chinese empire arose near a river, the Yellow River. The river is therefore important historically and culturally for the Chinese nation. Given the name "Yellow River" because if its yellowish loess (silt), it served as an important natural fertilizer for the land. After flooding, the loess would be deposited in the surrounding lands, enhancing it with necessary nutrients for agriculture. A "Yellow River Civilization:" thus developed there throughout the Zhou Dynasty (1045 BCE–256 BCE). The Yellow River region continued to be an important agricultural region throughout China well into the modern era.

Roman

Rome rose from the ashes of the crumbling Greek Empire as early as 753 BCE. But the Early Roman Republic began around 600 BCE with the ascent of Etruscan as a Roman king. The legislative body of the republic, particularly its powerful senate, made it even more powerful and centralized. The Roman legion, its army of foot soldiers, eventually numbered in the hundreds of thousands. Following the Punic Wars with Carthage, Rome eventually regained control of the Mediterranean region and expanded to include territories in continental Europe, Great Britain, North Africa, and the Middle East. Eventually, under the leadership of Emperor Constantine, the Roman Empire adopted Christianity in 312 CE.

In terms of its geography, Rome rose from the rubble of the Hellenistic Period, and therefore inherited much of the same Mediterranean landscape as the Greeks. It thus relied heavily on geographic expansion and trade for its resources.

Intellectual Contributions, Artistic Forms, and Traditions
Mesopotamia

Ancient Mesopotamia eventually evolved into an expansive territory known as Persia. The Persians were known for their Zoroastrian religious system that arose around 600 BCE. Zoroastrianism taught Persian practitioners about two religious armies: one of light, and one of darkness. This Zoroastrian outlook influenced the art and architecture of the era. Later monotheistic religions eventually borrowed notions such as heaven and hell from the Zoroastrian outlook. Zoroastrians were also notoriously tolerant of other religions that emerged in the Middle East such as Judaism, Christianity, and Islam. This tolerance allowed the "Royal Road of Persia," a famous trade route that connected Mesopotamia with Anatolia, to become one of the most vibrant areas of commerce in the ancient world.

Egyptian

Even prior to Alexander the Great's conquest, the North African region of Egypt was an epicenter of scholarship, architecture, art, and commerce. The pharaohs of Egypt built immaculate temples and pyramids, some of which still exist as part of the ancient wonders of the world. Egyptian art and architecture diffused even more rapidly during the Hellenistic period, inspiring the construction of similar architectural wonders across three continents. Today, Egyptian artwork and architecture are still recognized by modern nations for their awe-inspiring characteristics. The obelisk shape of the Washington Monument in the United States, for instance, was inspired by Egyptian trends.

Kush

When Egypt fell into decline during 1000 BCE, the Kushite dynasty to the south gained more political clout in the region. Napata, the capital of Kush, consequently evolved into an ancient trade center, where Kushite artwork, pottery, and sculptures were exchanged, namely with the Egyptian Empire to the North. The Kushite dynasty was also known for its abundant supply of iron ore, shipping off iron goods to the surrounding regions. Many neighboring communities benefitted from the ironwork of the Kushite dynasty, trading luxury goods for iron bars, spearheads, and tools. The cross-cultural exchange between Kush and Egypt can be seen in the architectural and sculptural similarities between the two regions.

Hebrew

Hebrew culture continues to impact history in the form of Judaism, a monotheistic faith that defined the Hebrew kingdoms of the Near East. The Old Testament, or Hebrew Bible, still remains a foundational religious text in Judaism and Christianity (and to a lesser extent, Islam). Hebrew culture has thus affected the monotheistic religious tradition in Western civilization, perhaps more than any other religion. While much of the Hebrew art and architecture has disappeared with centuries of conflict and conquest, the religion lives on in the Jewish diaspora.

Greek

With the expansion of the Greek Empire under the leadership of Alexander the Great, an intercultural exchanged ensued between Greek, Egyptian, Persian, and Indian values and traditions. Often referred to as Hellenistic culture, this blend of Greek, Egyptian, Persian, and Indian values and traditions led to some of the most influential intellectual advancements and artistic endeavors in the ancient world. During the Hellenistic period, the African city of Alexandria became a scholarly hub. Apart from the Renaissance, this period is often viewed as the foremost era of intellectual advancement in Western civilization. The scientific advancements in astronomy, mathematics, and physics during the Hellenistic period actually laid the foundations to later scientific discoveries during the Renaissance. Astronomers like Aristarchus used Euclidian geometry to prove that the Sun was, in fact, larger than all of Greece. Archimedes of Syracuse accurately estimated the value of pi. And Eratosthenes closely calculated the Earth's true size. Greek sculptures were founded on the principles of realism (i.e., the idea that objects should be presented in their true form and features). This realistic artwork, along with the impressive Greek architecture, later inspired the movement toward realism in the Renaissance. Greek democracy also inspired later empires to adopt democratic values within their governments.

Indian

By 400 CE, after centuries of Aryan migrations, the Indus River Valley blossomed into a much larger Indian Empire. Beginning with the rise of the Gupta Empire in 400 CE, the Indian Empire began to dominant the entire subcontinent of South Asia. India became the heart of the nexus of trade that united East and West on the Silk Road. India's two biggest exports – Hinduism and Buddhism – came from the religious traditions established in the subcontinent. Buddhism in particular helped shape the philosophies and artwork of China, Southeast Asia, Korea, and eventually Japan.

Chinese

Toward the end of the Zhou Dynasty (1045 BCE–256 BCE), Chinese scholars and philosophers began adopting the values of Confucius, a scholar who was born in 551 BCE. Confucian culture and art stressed the importance of filial piety, or respect for elders. It also stressed the importance of bureaucratization, social order, education, and harmony. Confucian values deeply impacted Chinese culture well into the 20th century. Another Chinese philosophy, Daoism, arose in the 6th century, thanks to the cultural teachings of Laozi. Laozi wrote the *Dao De Ching* (*The Way of Virtue*), which urged people to seek harmony. Legalism, another contemporary philosophy founded by Han Feizi and Li Si, stood in sharp contrast to Confucianism and Daoism. It preferred harsh punishments over harmony. The Qin Dynasty that centralized China between 221 BCE and 202 BCE employed Legalism as a unifying philosophy of strict punishments. The Qin leader Shi Huangdi burned books in an effort to carry out his Legalistic doctrine. During this time, the Great Wall of China, one of the most celebrated architectural feats in human history, emerged to protect China from invading barbarians to the North. The Great Wall of China is symbolic of the art and architecture that arose during the era of philosophical strictness known as the Qin Dynasty.

Roman

Besides the impressive architectural feats that can still be seen in the ruins of Rome's amphitheaters, aqueducts, temples, and roadways, Rome's greatest contribution to history during this time was the republic, a form of government based on the power of citizens. The Roman republic, which expanded into an expansive empire, later inspired the creation of other republics, such as the United States of America. The architecture and realistic art of the

Roman republic was adopted by later republics such as the United States. The majesty of the Roman vision can still be seen in the art and architecture of capital cities across the globe, including Washington, D.C.

The Roman Empire eventually also became the biggest sponsor of Christianity in the ancient world, laying the foundation of Christian expansion during the medieval and early modern periods.

Patterns of Trade and Commerce

Even before the Silk Road connected Europe with East Asia, ancient trade routes began sprouting up throughout the entire ancient world. These land routes connected the broader Mediterranean region with other established regions of commerce, such as Central Asia, India, and East Asia. Liquid highways created a vast network of seaports and river stops along the Mediterranean Sea, Ionian Sea, Aegean Sea, Black Sea, Caspian Sea, Arabian Sea, Bay of Bengal, and Indian Ocean. It is hard to believe trade spanned from the Atlantic Ocean to the Pacific Ocean before modern-day globalization, but it did. When sailors were not capitalizing on monsoon winds to connect the Arabian Peninsula with Indonesia, they were trudging across complicated land routes that crisscrossed Central Asia and China. Certain groups, such as the Phoenicians, created resilient shipping fleets that could actual cross the Mediterranean from Palestine to the Rock of Gibraltar. Trade and commerce also influenced the diffusion of religions, art, and cultures. As spices, glass, and metals were transformed from culture to culture, these disparate groups inevitably also shared ideas and practices. Glass made from the sands of Lebanon could be transported to Carthage, which could then make its way to Ancient Rome. The period between 2000 BCE and 250 BCE set the stage for such trade routes as "The Royal Road of the Persian Empire," the "Roads of Ancient Rome," and the "Silk Road." Additionally, the sharp rises and inevitable declines of empires was accompanied by the spread of beliefs and goods. The Near East and Middle East became a crossroads of ancient civilization. There is a reason this land is considered the "Holy Land" for many ancient monotheistic religions, including Judaism, Christianity, and Islam: it felt like it was the center of the universe in ancient times, serving as the praxis of intercultural exchange, economic interchange, and perpetual conflict.

Medieval and Early Modern Times

Physical Geography and the Development of Medieval and Early Modern Civilizations
Chinese
Following the collapse of the Han Dynasty in 220 CE, the Chinese Empire fractured into tiny dynasties that split China between North and South for over 500 years. However, in 559, an emperor name Sui Wendi began unifying China to its former glory. The short-lived Sui Dynasty paved the way to a new golden era in Chinese history, which was set in motion by the rise of two subsequent powerful dynasties in the early medieval period: the Tang Dynasty and the Song Dynasty. The Tang and Song Dynasties reinstituted the old, centralized bureaucracies of the Han period. The Tang and Song Empires flourished as a result of China's newfound international notoriety as a center for trade. Great imperial armies helped guard China's Silk Road trade routes, which saw an increase in caravan trade during this period of unification. China's networks of Rivers also helped strengthen commerce. Nevertheless, China's strategic geographic position along Southeast Asia's coastline helped usher in a new era of seafaring trade. During this era, foreign traders started populating Chinese port cities, creating a new epoch of cultural exchange and diffusion. The "golden age" in China continued until the Mongol conquests overtook the region.

Japanese
Japan is an island located to the east of China. Initially, Japan's isolation as an island allowed it to form a culture entirely separate. Nevertheless, by the early medieval period, Japan began to have more contact with other empires in East Asia, including Korea and China. By the time the early medieval Heian Period took hold in the late 700s, Japan began borrowing much of its culture from China. The Heian Period, which lasted from 794 to 1185, borrowed its government, writing system, and religion (Buddhism) from China. Initially, the Heian government was strong and centralized. But, by the middle of the 11th century, a new samurai (Japanese warrior) feudal class started to rule over sectors of the mountainous island. The geography of Japan reinforced this feudal system by creating natural barriers for the newly formed samurai clans.

African

Understanding human geography in Early Modern Africa is much like understanding a historical motion picture: it is a story of migration and cultural diffusion, chiefly of the Bantu-speaking people of sub-Saharan Africa. Environmental changes, economic pressure, political and religious persecution, and technological development led to a redistribution of the Bantu-speaking people, a group interconnected by similar languages, across the continent of Africa. Between 1 CE and 1500 CE, the Bantu-speaking people, feeling the pressure of a population boom in West Africa and the looming desertification brought on by the Sahara, decided to shift to the East and South. By 1500, this group had populated most of the expansive territory in southern Africa.

Arabian

Sitting at the crossroads of three continents – Asia, Africa, and Europe – the Arabian Peninsula became the cornerstone of Middle Eastern trade by 600 CE. Surrounded by deserts, only oases and a tiny strip of fertile land in the South could sustain life. Thus, the nomadic Bedouins of the desert began to create vibrant market towns near oases. The Bedouin nomads were known for their military resilience, fighting off raids, and securing their economic opportunities along the caravan routes that tied to the Silk Roads of the east. One western city in particular became an important trade stop along these trade routes: Mecca. Medina was the home of the Ka'ba, a center of religious pilgrimage for the Arabian people. The Ka'ba became a house of worship for many gods and spirits. That is, until the Prophet Mohammed emerged in the 600s. Following a religious revelation, Mohammed became the leader and prophet of a new monotheistic religion: Islam. The desert boundaries and Bedouin military tactics of the Arabian Peninsula allowed Mohammed to spread Islam across the peninsula. Following his death in 632, an era of Muslim conquest swept across the three surrounding continents. By 1200, Islam had converted or conquered most of the regions surrounding the Arabian Peninsula, creating a giant empire for the new religion.

Mesoamerican

The Mesoamerican civilizations emerged mostly along the Yucatan Peninsula or Valley of Mexico in modern-day Mexico. Many of the Maya city-states were isolated due to the dense jungles of the region. Many of these city-states actually invaded each other, but they remained relatively separate because of the forested conditions. The Gulf of Mexico to the east also provided a natural barrier; some city-states overlooked the gulf on high cliffs. Cenotes (freshwater sinkholes) were scattered throughout the peninsula, providing water to the communities. The Maya travelled on local rivers and on the gulf. The Aztecs were located in the Valley of Mexico, a wide mountainous region of Central Mexico. The mountains offered natural defenses against invasion. Many lakes in the region, namely Lake Texcoco, which was located near the capital city of the Aztec Empire, Tenochtitlan, also offered natural boundaries and routes for transportation. Most of these lakes were extremely briny, so Aztec engineers learned to create dams along the mountains to capture fresh water. The Aztec built floating soil islands, or chinampas, to produce agriculture.

Andean Highland

The ancient Inca civilization sat atop the high ridges of the Andes Mountains, close to modern-day Cuzco-Sacred Valley region. City-states were scattered across the Andes range. These high mountains allowed the Inca to remain relatively isolated from other civilizations until the Spanish conquests. The Inca produced agriculture on tiered plateaus in the mountains that utilized complex irrigation systems. They built stone fortresses across the Sacred Valley for protection and communication. They farmed quinoa, potatoes, and fruits for the empire. They also domesticated animals such as alpacas and llamas, using the lush plateaus for grazing purposes.

European

After a brief unification of Central and Western states, under the leadership of Charlemagne, Europe once again became a region of intensified conflict. Europe was invaded from all directions between 700 CE and 1000 CE. From the North, Germanic Scandinavian tribes known as Vikings attacked Central and Western Europe. From the South and the West, an expanding Muslim Empire threatened the region from the Mediterranean, North Africa, and Al-Andalus (Spain). From the East, a nomadic group known as the Magyars threatened the region. The Vikings, Muslims, and Magyars weakened the previous geographic consolidation under Charlemagne. As a result, Europe, much like China and Japan at this time, fell under the fractured governmental structures of feudalism, a socio-political system that stratified the classes and witnessed the rise of a wealthy landed class.

The Decline of the Western Roman Empire and the Development of Feudalism
Decline of the Western Roman Empire
The gradual decline of the Western Roman Empire between 500 CE and 1500 CE occurred as a result of invading Germanic tribes. These invasions ushered in the Middle Ages, which is also known as the medieval period. Constant warfare weakened the government, culture, and economic stability of the empire. It caused disruptions in trade, which collapsed Roman businesses. Cities were abandoned as the economic epicenters of the empire. The collapse of cities forced nobles into the countryside, which laid the foundations of feudalism as a social and economic system.

The Development of Feudalism as a Social and Economic System in Europe and Japan
As previously mentioned, after a brief unification of Central and Western countries under the leadership of Charlemagne, Europe once again became a region of intensified conflict. Europe was invaded from all directions between 700 CE and 1000 CE. From the North, Germanic Scandinavian tribes known as Vikings attacked Central and Western Europe. From the South and the West, an expanding Muslim Empire threatened the region from the Mediterranean, North Africa, and Al-Andalus (Spain). From the East, a nomadic group known as the Magyars threatened the region. The Vikings, Muslims, and Magyars weakened the previous geographic consolidation under Charlemagne. As a result, Europe, much like China and Japan at this time, fell under the fractured governmental structures of feudalism, a socio-political system that stratified the classes and witnessed the rise of a wealthy landed class.

Likewise, during the medieval period, the Heian Period in Japan, which lasted from 794 to 1185, borrowed its government, writing system, and religion (Buddhism) from China. Initially, the Heian government was strong and centralized. But, by the middle of the 11th century, a new samurai (Japanese warrior) feudal class started to rule over sectors of the mountainous island. The geography of Japan reinforced this feudal system by creating natural barriers for the newly formed samurai clans.

The Art, Architecture, and Science of Pre-Columbian America
The Mayan, Aztec, and Incan Empires of pre-Columbia America became hubs of early art, architecture, and science. The classic Mayan city-states established between 250 and 900 CE had elaborate temples, palaces, and giant pyramids. The art and architecture that filled these cities served two purposes: 1) they symbolized Mayan connections with their gods, and 2) they were expressions of scientific research and discovery. One pyramid – Pyramid IV – stood at a whopping 212 feet high. This height made it the largest structure in the Western Hemisphere until the US built the Flatiron Building in New York City in 1903. Another structure, the El Caracol ("The Snail") helped the Maya study the stars. The structure looks like a modern astronomical observatory. The entire Mayan city of Chichen Itza was filled with artistic artefacts that memorialized the Mayan sacrifices to the gods. The complex art, architecture, and science of the Mayan civilization illustrated just how advanced it was as a pre-Columbian civilization. They had a written language and calendar that captured their mathematical and astronomical observations. Like the Romans, the Maya were unmatched in their command of mathematics, science, and engineering.

As the Mayan civilization faded, the Aztecs picked up where Maya had left off. They built architectural giants in their capital city of Tenochtitlan. They crafted art and artefacts to honor Quetzalcoatl, one of their major gods. They built temples and pyramids for sacrificing humans to their gods. They traded valuable materials such as obsidian, a greenish-black glossy rock. They also made artwork out of obsidian. At the heart of their city was the Pyramid of the Sun, one that honored not only the religious foundations of their empire, but the mathematical and scientific advancements of their civilization. The Aztecs created instruments for measuring time, and they, like the Maya before them, adopted a calendar.

The Incan civilization came to power in the 1300s and 1400s. Unlike the Maya and Aztecs, they built fortresses in the sky, such as the site at Machu Picchu. They recorded data on quipu, a primitive rope-like counting device. They carried out some of the most complex public works programs in the pre-Columbia period, building roads and irrigation systems to united their empire in the Andes. They used gold and silver to create masks that honored both the supernatural (their gods) and the natural (local animals like llamas). The central portion of their empire was located in modern-day Cuzco, Peru, where they build elaborate stone temples and forts.

Role of Christianity and its Expansion Beyond Europe
As Western Roman Empire crumbled in the 5th century, and fell into further disrepair during the invasions of the 7th–11th centuries, Christianity, which had become the official religion of the Roman Empire under the rule of Emperor Constantine in the 4th century, slowly progressed toward a schism between East and West. The Byzantine Empire that arose in the East thrived, making the Eastern Church in Constantinople the new epicenter of Christianity. Meanwhile, the Western Church struggled to gain power as the Vikings, Muslims, and Magyars attacked Western and Central Europe. As a result, the two churches began to diverge culturally and theologically. Eventually, an official schism occurred in 1054: Christianity became split into the Roman Catholic Church in the West and the Eastern Orthodox Church in the East.

During the Medieval period, the Eastern Orthodox Church, under the protection of the Byzantine Empire, began converting ethnic groups in Eastern Europe and Western Asia. They converted the Slavs – an ethnic group near the Black Sea – to Eastern Orthodoxy in the 9th century. Around this time, a new Russian Empire began to expand, and the Russians eventually adopted Eastern Orthodoxy as their official religion.

Between the 1000s and 1300s, the beginning of the Early Modern Period, constant attacks by the Muslims and Mongols briefly united Christians under the cause of the Crusades. Western Roman Catholic merchants and popes sent Crusaders to the Middle East to attack other religious groups. Likewise, Eastern Orthodox leaders sent Christian soldiers on Crusades against these barbarians.

Christianity began to feverishly expand beyond the boundaries of Europe during the "Age of Exploration" in the Early Modern Period. Christian explorers travelled to Africa, Asia, and the New World, carrying their doctrine of Christianity with them, and converting indigenous populations in these regions.

Role of Islam and Its Impact on Arabia, Africa, Europe, and Asia
Between the 600s and 1500s, Islam spread from its origins in the Arabian Peninsula to include a vast empire that spanned three continents: Africa, Asia, and Europe.

Islam in Arabia
Islam began in Arabia, and has influenced the region since the Prophet Mohammed first began spreading the religion there in the early 600s. The central city of Muslim life was Mecca, the place where the Prophet Mohammed first had his religious revelations. Mecca remains a pilgrimage site for members of Islam. Mohammed spread Islam throughout the Arabian Peninsula. When Mohammed died, his successors spread Islam even further throughout the Arabian region. Eventually, by 1200 Islam spread to include parts of Central Asia, Eastern Europe, North Africa, East Africa, Spain, Persia, and India.

Islam in Africa
In the 7th century, African states south of the Sahara Desert remained relatively decentralized. Historians often refer to them as "stateless societies" because they lacked centralized governments like many contemporary kingdoms at that time. North Africa, however, became a region controlled by the expansion of Islam. Following the death of the Prophet Mohammed in 632, Islam swept across modern-day Morocco, Tunisia, and Algeria, transforming the region and centralizing it under Islamic law. Muslim rulers in North Africa established theocratic Islamic states that called upon the expertise of religious scholars. Islamic law helped bring order to a region previously in flux.

The Berbers, desert dwellers who originated in North Africa, adapted Islam to their roving lifestyle. Two distinct Muslim Berber groups – the Almoravids and the Almohads – dominated the region, unifying it under Muslim rule. By the 11th century, a new dynasty emerged in North Africa: the Almoravid Dynasty. Led by a group of Berber religious scholars, the Almoravid Dynasty took over Mauritania and later the West African empire of Ghana. Under the leadership of Abd Allah Ibn Yasin, the Almoravid Dynasty also conquered parts of Spain, where they were called Moors. They founded their capital in Marrakesh, a city in Morocco. The Almohads wrested power from the Almoravid Dynasty in the mid-12th century. This group followed the teachings of another religious scholar, Ibn Tumart. By 1148, the Almohad Dynasty conquered the Moroccan capital of Marrakesh. They conquered lands in Tripoli and Tunis, spreading their empire across the Mediterranean region. The dynasty only last roughly 100 years, but unified North Africa under Muslim rule.

Islam also influenced developments in East Africa by the 14th century. Located close to the Islamic hub of the Arabian Peninsula, East African cities, such as Mogadishu, were ruled by Muslim sultans. Islamic rule in these cities contributed to the budding slave trade by exporting enslaved persons to Arabian traders from Arabia, Iraq, and Persia.

Islam in Asia

When the Gupta Empire crumbled in the 600s, it weakened the Indian subcontinent, exposing it to the potential of foreign invasion. Around this time, the Prophet Mohammed was beginning to establish the first wave of Muslim conquest across the Arabian Peninsula. Between the 600s and the 1100s, Islam begins to spread from its epicenter in Mecca to the gateway of the Indian subcontinent. The Muslim Empire was so vast at one point that it expanded from Al-Andalus (in Spain) to Southeast Asia. But it struggled to invade India. That all changed in the period from 1200 to 1500. During this time, the powerful Mongol Khanates began to convert from Islam. Likewise, two major empires helped Islam expand from Arabia to South Asia in 15th–18th centuries: the Safavids' Shi'a Empire and the Delhi Sultanate (which was later subsumed by the Mughal Empire).

Following the death of Genghis Khan in 1227, the Mongol Empire was divided into four Khanates: the Great Khan (Mongolia and China), the Golden Horde (Russia), Chagatai (Central Asia), and the Ilkhanate (Persia). Three of these — the Golden Horde, Chagatai, and the Ilkhanate — converted to Islam. They carried out campaigns in northern India, thus further spreading Islam into the subcontinent and weakening a region already in flux. This cultural diffusion and regional instability paved the way to later Muslim conquests of India.

The Safavids converted to the Shi'a branch of Islam in the 1400s; they were persecuted by the Ottoman Sunni Muslims of the Mediterranean and Arabian Peninsula. To protect themselves from being conquered by the Ottoman Turks, the Safavids built a powerful military force that spread eastward under the leadership of Ishma'il, a brilliant military general. Ishma'il eventually conquered Persia (modern-day Iran), declaring himself as the new shah and establishing Shi'a Islam as the new religion in the region. The empire eventually expanded from the Caucasus Mountains through Persia (Central Asia) and to modern-day India. The empire began to sharply decline by the 18th century. Like the Mongols, the Shi'a Muslims were able to spread the Islamic faith into India.

Islam also began to bleed into South Asia in the 1000s with the ascension of the Delhi Sultanate, which consisted of Turkish soldiers who overran the Hindu soldiers that defended the gates of the Indian subcontinent for nearly 300 years. Under the leadership of Sultan Mahmud of Ghazni, the Delhi Sultanate gained more power in India, but only formed a "loose empire." Between the 13th and 16th century, dozens of sultans ruled the territory. Eventually, the Delhi Sultanate was subsumed by the Mughal Empire due to their decentralized government. Mughal society blended Persian, Hindu, and Muslim culture, creating some of the most unique art and architecture in history, including the famous Taj Mahal. The empire eventually fell into disrepair by the 17th century, but forever infused Islam into the fabric of Indian identity.

It was only a matter of time before Islam infiltrated the gates of India. Since the centuries after Mohammed, Islam was knocking on the gates of the subcontinent. The combined forces of internal weaknesses and external conflicts - namely the expansion of the Mongol Empire, the Safavid Empire, Delhi Sultanate/Mughal Empire - broke down the Hindu barrier, forever exposing Indian culture to the power of Islam.

Islam in Europe

Islam accessed Europe from two separate entrance points: the Iberian Peninsula and Turkey. Islam first entered Europe in the early 700s when the Umayyad Dynasty established itself in Spain. The Berbers helped form a Muslim state in Spain in 732 called Al-Andalus. In Spain, the Muslims were known as the Moors. The Moors settled in a vibrant city known as Cordoba, enhancing the arts and sciences there until the years of the Spanish Inquisition.

By the 1300s, the Christian Byzantium Empire began to decline as a result of attacks from the East and the West. From the East, Byzantium was attacked by a rising empire: the Ottoman Turks. The Ottoman Turks became so powerful that they finally sacked Constantinople, the capital of Byzantium, in 1451, renaming it Istanbul. Constantinople fell thanks to the leadership of Mehmet II, a strong Turkish military leader. The Ottoman Empire eventually expanded to include the Balkans, modern-day Hungary, and parts of the Russian Empire. It later expanded to the Arabian Peninsula, Mesopotamia, and North Africa in the 16th century. The Ottoman Empire began to decline as early as the late 16th century but lasted until the end of World War I (the early 20th century). It remained a mainstay in Eastern Europe throughout six centuries.

Development of the Renaissance and Scientific Revolution in Europe

The Renaissance

Between 1300 and 1600, an explosion of creativity in Europe, which began in the urban centers of Italy, created a revolution in arts that historians refer to as the Renaissance. Three historical advantages helped Italy become the epicenter of this paradigm shift in art and architecture: its thriving merchant cities (which capitalized on the Crusades), its wealthy merchant class that arose as a result, and the region's close ties to the classical civilizations of Greece and Rome. The bubonic plague brought about economic changes that also helped spawn this "rebirth" in art and architecture. Merchants need a new source of revenue, so they looked to new economic endeavors such as art. The Renaissance – made famous by artists and sculptors such as Donatello, Michelangelo Buonarroti, Leonardo Da Vinci, and Rafael – advanced new artistic techniques such as perspective and realism. More importantly, the Renaissance, sourcing its inspirations from the ancient Greeks and Romans, shifted the focus to humanistic and secular perspectives. This helped pave the way for the subsequent Protestant reformations and scientific revolutions.

The Scientific Revolution

The Renaissance helped inspire curiosity, paving the way to a scientific revolution. The revolution witnessed the birth of modern science, which moved away from faith-based models of belief toward scientific objectivity. The scientific revolution marked the beginning of viewing the world in a dramatically different way. Translating many works from contemporary Muslim scholars and classical Greco-Roman scholars, the new scientists of the era began to see the world in a more objective way. Astronomers like Nicolaus Copernicus challenged the geocentric (earth-centered) model of the Catholic Church with his heliocentric (sun-centered) model. Other astronomers like Johannes Kepler used math to support these Copernican claims. Some of these discoveries directly challenged the Roman Catholic Church, as in the case of Galileo Galilei. Galileo Galilei used a telescope to attack Aristotelian theories. Galileo claimed that the moon and the stars were imperfect in structure, which challenged Aristotle's views of "the heavens." He was therefore brought to trial by the Catholic Church. New scientific breakthroughs helped contemporaries refine the so-called scientific method, a logical way of observing the universe. Men like Isaac Newton used the scientific method to record the laws of gravity. Other men, such as René Descartes, used it to develop a new form of analytical geometry. In all, the scientific revolution led to various discoveries in astronomy, mathematics, chemistry, and biology. The **Enlightenment** helped advance these ideals by refocusing the world's energies on the intersection between science and humanity.

Development of Early Modern Capitalism and Its Global Consequences

The develop of early modern capitalism resulted from the commercial revolution that was an outgrowth of the Age of Exploration's transatlantic **Columbian Exchange**, the global transfer of commercial goods from the New World to Africa and Europe (and vice versa). **Capitalism** is an economic system that is founded upon private ownership and investments in industry and trade. The colonization of new territories by Europeans catalyzed the growth of capitalism, offering it new lands, labor, and resources. Most European nations became extremely wealthy during this period, establishing joint-stock companies (a collective consolidation of wealth for common gain) in other countries. One of the consequences of this fast-growth model was inflation, a sharp increase in wealth accumulation and demand for goods, which also increases prices. Spain in particular suffered from inflation as a result of the dozens of galleons of gold it shipped across the Atlantic Ocean. The growth of capitalism led to a mercantile mentality in Europe that favored wealth and commerce as indicators of a nation's international prestige.

The global consequences of this new economic system included the rise of slavery as an institution, the rise of merchant classes in society, the rise of colonization as a system of economic development (and exploitation), and the growth and stratification of global populations. For the first time, the world economy felt truly international, marking the beginning of several centuries of the economic globalization that still exists today.

The Evolution of the Idea of Representative Democracy

The ascension of King John of England, following his brother Richard's death, opened up an historic opportunity for nobles to allow their voices to be heard within the systems of government in England. King John, who had lost the region of Normandy to France, was struggling to maintain the domestic theater of his great empire. The nobles, who had come of age in a feudal system, saw the kingdom's instability as an opportunity to confront the king. This confrontation paved the way for the infiltration of democratic values in a previously wholly monarchical English feudal system.

The nobles were displeased with King John's taxation system, which increased taxes to an all-time high in order to fund England's foreign wars. The nobles felt the king was trying to squeeze resources out of them, so they chartered a **Magna Carta** (Great Charter) that championed the basic political rights of all English citizens. The goal was to place more power in the hands of the nobles by limiting the king's powers. On June 15, 1215, King John reluctantly accepted the Magna Carta under the pressure of the nobles' resistance. Originally, the document only had clauses that extended rights to the nobles. However, in later years, the Magna Carta's democratic values evolved to include *all* citizens of England. These rights included such principles as: no taxation without representation, the right to a fair trial by jury, and protection of citizens by the law.

The Magna Carta was later followed by one other major democratic leap for England (and the world): the creation of Parliament. In 1295, King Edward I was struggling to maintain his last conquered lands in France. In order to raise taxes for the war, King Edward I summoned three burgesses from each English borough and two knights from every English county to form a governmental body that became known as Parliament. This bold move incidentally institutionalized a parliamentary government that would later transform into a full-fledged constitutional monarchy with a House of Commons.

While the Magna Carta served as a documented protection of democracy, the parliamentary government helped systematize democracy at large in England. The English Enlightenment of the 18th century – with its theoretical principles that focused on the expansion of inalienable rights centering on life, liberty, and the pursuit of happiness – helped further catalyze this democratic evolution. By the time of the American Revolution, they were so embedded within the English empire that it encouraged American colonists to resist the taxation efforts of King George III. The American unleashed a democratic wave of revolution upon the globe, one that spread the initial democratic reverberations of the Magna Cart and Parliament across the globe.

United States History

Early Exploration, Colonial Era, and the War for Independence

European Exploration and Settlement of North America

In what is commonly referred to as the "Age of Exploration," Europeans began exploring overseas to regions they'd never before seen. The Age of Exploration started in the early 15th century and lasted until the late 18th century, and

102

in practice, it represents the earliest stage of globalization. Technological innovation greatly facilitated European exploration, like the **caravel**—a smaller and more maneuverable ship first used by the Portuguese to explore West Africa—and the *astrolabe* and *quadrant*, which increased navigators' accuracy.

European monarchies hired explorers primarily to expand trade routes, particularly to increase access to the Indian spice markets. There were other motivating factors, however, such as the desire to spread Christianity and pursue glory.

As exploration increased, European powers adopted the policies of mercantilism and colonialism. **Mercantilism** is an economic policy that prioritizes the wealth, trade, and accumulation of resources for the sole benefit of the nation. **Colonization** was an outgrowth of mercantilism that involved establishing control over foreign people and territories. Unsurprisingly, mercantilism and colonialism were a major source of conflict between native people, colonists, and colonizers.

In 1492, Christopher Columbus arrived in the Caribbean, though he initially, and mistakenly, believed he had landed in India. Over the next two centuries, European powers established several colonies in North America to extract the land's resources and prevent their rivals from doing the same. In 1565, Spain established the first European colony in North America at St. Augustine in present-day Florida. Along with building a South and Central American empire, Spain colonized Mexico and much of the present-day American Southwest, southeast, and heartland (Louisiana Territory). Sweden colonized the mid-Atlantic region of the present-day United States in 1638, but the Netherlands conquered these colonies in 1655. France colonized Canada, Hudson's Bay, Acadia (near present-day Maine), and Newfoundland. In 1717, France assumed control over the Louisiana Territory from Spain.

In 1607, England established her first colony at Jamestown. In 1619, Jamestown colonists imported the first slaves to North America. During the rest of the 17th century, British separatist Puritans (Pilgrims) arrived on the *Mayflower* in Cape Cod, Massachusetts. Great Britain conquered New Netherlands (New York) in 1674, effectively driving the Dutch out of North America.

England's North American holdings expanded into the **Thirteen Colonies**—Connecticut, Delaware, Georgia, Maryland, Massachusetts, New Hampshire, New Jersey, New York, North Carolina, Pennsylvania, Rhode Island, South Carolina, and Virginia. Some colonies were royal colonies, while others were chartered to business corporations or proprietary local governments. The chartered colonies generally allowed for more self-government, but the Crown withdrew the charters and placed all thirteen colonies under direct royal control by the second half of the 18th century.

Cooperation and conflict among American Indians and new settlers

New settlers were able to build colonies due to the help of American Indians. They also participated in trade between the two groups. American Indian people traded with the settlers for such things as hides and knowledge of the area. They would trade different tools and weapons as well. One form of currency that was used at the time was wampum, a type of bead. The Eliot Indian Bible, a Christian Bible translated into an Indigenous language, shows another aspect of what was shared between the two groups: spiritually. This was also the first Bible printed and published in North America. Because of the Eliot Indian Bible's existence, it is believed that settlers and American Indians shared their spiritualities; however, this exchange is also a large point of conflict. Many settlers attempted to convert American Indians to Christianity, and while some did convert, many were resistant. American Indians were also resistant to the settlers' attempts to gain more land and control, though they struggled due to new diseases brought from Europe, the arrival of more settlers, and the slave trade. Most American Indian people did not want to change in the way that settlers were trying to make them, which led to growing conflict. This conflict led to a series of wars between American Indians and settler groups.

Founders of North America and Their Reasons for Colonization

Religious Reasons

There were a variety of religious reasons for colonizing the New World. However, the varying religious reasons for European settlement in the New World actually share a similar source of inspiration: many European countries and leaders wanted to spread the Christian faith to the New World. For Spain and France, the Christian faith happened to be of the Catholic variety; for England and the Netherlands, the Christian faith happened to be of the Protestant variety. These overarching religious views were further diversified by the individual and collective aspirations of each Founder and each community.

Some groups, such as the Spanish conquistadors, wanted to conquer the world in honor of the Catholic King of Spain and the Pope of the entire Catholic Church. Many Native Americans were either slaughtered or converted in the name of Catholicism.

Other groups, such as the French Jesuits of Quebec and the Great Lakes region, also wanted to converted Native Americans in masses. Yet they did so in a fashion that was more amicable (albeit still imperfect) than their Spanish Catholic predecessors. The French Jesuits tried to learn from Native Americans and work collaboratively with them to reach more converts.

The Jamestown Colony remained mostly Anglican, but its concerns were more economic than religious. Similarly, the Dutch Reform Protestants of New Netherlands focused on religious tolerance, but centered most of their energies on economics.

The Puritans of New England are, perhaps, the most iconic religious group in North America, thanks, in part, to American history's infatuation with this group as the foremost Founders of an American identity. The Puritans were escaping religious persecution in England. They tried to find refuge in the solitude of the New England. They wanted to establish a New Israel in the New World. The maintained positive relationships with the Native Americans at first, but eventually carried out wars and conflicts in the name of Christ.

Other religious groups, such as the Mennonites and Quakers of the Pennsylvania colony also sought refuge from persecution. North America, therefore, became a complex blend of those trying to escape persecution and those carrying out their own forms of persecution.

Economic Reasons

In order to understand North American colonization, students of history must first understand the Spanish colonization of the New World that preceded it. The **Age of Exploration** spawned a new era of global trade. Early Founders in the New World colonies were searching for gold, resources, and new trade routes. Spain began to establish an empire in the New World as early as 1492, with Christopher Columbus's first expedition across the Atlantic. Conquistadors, such as Hernán Cortés eventually helped Spain conquer the Aztec Empire in present-day Mexico in the early 1500s. Another conquistador, Francisco Pizarro defeated the Inca Empire in South America in 1534. As these conquistadors conquered Native American empires in the New World, they accumulated a lot of gold and artefacts. They also discovered new spices and plants. They began transporting these resources back to Spain on large Spanish galleons. Spain quickly became one of the wealthiest empires in the world. Spain acquired even more money once it established the encomienda system, which legalized the taxation of locals and forced many Native Americans into labor. Around the same time, Spain created an expansive plantation system in the Caribbean, Mexico, and South America to feed Europe's cravings for New World crops. As other countries looked to colonize North American, they eagerly sought to replicate the Spanish model of colonization. They wanted to increase the wealth of their empires.

Hoping to compete with the Spanish empire, many European countries began desperately searching for a **Northwest Passage**: they hoped to find a faster water route from the Atlantic to the Pacific via waterways along the northern Atlantic coasts of modern-day Greenland, Canada, and the United States. The English were the first to feverishly enter this race. They sent an Italian sailor, John Cabot, to search for the Northwest Passage. The English royals promised to grant a charter for any lands he discovered. Cabot embarked on two expeditions in 1497 and 1498, but few records exist documenting his journey. Many historians believe he reached the coast of Newfoundland in Canada. Cabot obviously did not find the Northwest Passage, but his journeys were certainly driven by economic hopes. Moreover, they laid the foundations for English claims to North America.

France entered the race to find the Northwest passage in 1524. They sent an Italian sailor named Giovanni da Verrazzano to North America. Verrazzano's expedition encountered land near modern-day North Carolina, and he and his crew set sail northward along the coast of the modern-day United States all the way to modern-day Maine. Hopeful that they were close to finding the Northwest Passage, France set Jacques Cartier, a French captain, on a subsequent journey to North America. Cartier famously traversed the St. Lawrence River, landing close to modern-day Montreal, Quebec.

The Dutch followed suit, sending English captain Henry Hudson, to modern-day New York in 1609. He later sailed under the English flag, claiming the Hudson Bay as yet another alleged English claim.

While none of these explorers discovered a Northwest Passage, they did set the stage for more economically inspired settlements in North America. The English, French, and Dutch colonies would later begin vying for economic power in the region. The earliest English colony was a royal charter granted to Sir Walter Raleigh, who helped found the Roanoke Colony near the coast of modern-day North Carolina. This colony, which suffered many losses, did not prove to be economically viable or safe, so its colonists eventually perished or returned to England. Jamestown, England's first successful colony, learned from the mistakes of Roanoke, finding greater success in the early 1600s. The French and Dutch colonies found similar economic successes in the New World. The French created a successful fur trade that included the Great Lakes region and stretched down the Mississippi River all the way to New Orleans. The Dutch established the Dutch West India Company and claimed lands between the Delaware and Hudson Rivers. Known as New Netherland, it had a port city, New Amsterdam, which eventually became New York City under English control.

Even Puritan New England, established at Plymouth in 1620, had an economic charter, backed by religious doctrine. Eventually this budding New England economy was strengthened by a "Great Migration" of English settlers that helped establish the Massachusetts Bay Colony. This colony not only served as a more economically driven alternative to Plymouth (which it eventually subsumed into its charter), but it also offered different economic options than Jamestown (which focused mostly on tobacco cultivation). These different economic dreams eventually led to the establishment of 13 unique colonies.

Political Reasons

Each of these European countries wanted not only to honor God and accumulate gold, but they also wanted political power. They knew that controlling the New World was one of their surest routes to controlling an increasingly globalized political landscape. The expeditions and settlements in the New World can be viewed as microcosmic displays of political power that created macrocosmic political shifts. Colonization schemes in the New World created decades of conflict between nations in the Old World. Every colonizer wanted to honor their nation, even if they were escaping it, as in the case of the Puritans. Some wanted political freedom, but this reality was not felt until the wave of revolutions in the 1700s and 1800s. The earliest years of colonization were all about honoring the Catholic and Protestant crowns of Europe.

European Colonial Rule and Its Relationship with American Indian Societies

American Indian populations were heavily affected by diseases European colonizers brought to the Americas, such as smallpox and measles. Europeans were more accustomed to experiencing these diseases and had some level of tolerance and immunity. It is estimated that as much as 90 percent of Native peoples of the Americas were killed by European diseases. Some goods introduced through trade changed the ways of American Indian societies. Europeans introduced the Native people to guns and different forms of alcohol. Native people already had some forms of alcohol in areas of the Americas prior to colonization, primarily modern-day southwest United States and Mexico. Europeans introduced liquors such as rum, which became a part of negotiations and transactions. Many Europeans wanted to change the lives of American Indians through converting them to Christianity as well, which many Native people were against. While initially there were attempts to live in peace, many factors contributed to increased tension as colonizers attempted to change Native people's ways of life. Colonizers were often violent with American Indian people and sold some of them into the slave trade.

Development and Institutionalization of African Slavery and Its Consequences

Originally, many of the European colonies in the New World, particularly the colonies of New Spain, utilized Native American slave labor to create a free supply of labor for the budding capitalist economies of colonialism. That all changed when many Native Americans began dying as a result of disease and conflict. European diseases wiped out Native American populations, creating measles, typhus, and smallpox epidemics. Millions of Native Americans died in the earliest years of colonization. Therefore, European empires had to find a new source for slavery to support its burgeoning plantation economies – it found that source in sub-Saharan Africa. By 1510, just years after Christopher Columbus's famed expedition, the Spanish government had already legalized slavery in its colonies. The Spanish and Portuguese empires of South America eventually shipped millions of slaves to the New World. The Dutch and English joined the **slave trade** as well. But the Spanish and Portuguese empires established the unprecedented pace of the slave trade. Brazil – a Portuguese colony – shipped nearly 4 million African slaves to the New World.

The slave trade had its strongest hold on the Caribbean, South America, and southern North America. The tropical climates of these places helped establish plantation economies that depended on slave labor to churn out exports to Europe. Slaves helped produce crops such as sugarcane, tobacco, and cotton in these regions, across various New World empires. In order to produce these crops, it required a lot of labor, and in order to supply the increasing demands of Europe, it required a lot of *free* labor. Along the West Coast of sub-Saharan Africa, trade posts gradually transformed into slave forts, where kidnapped slaves were sold to European sailors. European colonists would exchange goods for slaves, and they would transport them across the Atlantic Ocean. This journey became known as the Middle Passage. Many slaves would die along the way; they were forced to live in cramped and unsanitary conditions within ship hulls. Diseases spread in these coffin-like spaces, where slaves were often shackled. Many slaves died from malnutrition, dehydration, or heat exhaustion.

The slave trade had both economic and socio-cultural consequences in sub-Saharan Africa. Economically, it made the region dependent upon slave exports. While these exports benefitted some African leaders and businessmen, they mostly benefitted European empires. This made sub-Saharan Africans economically dependent upon European colonizers. In terms of socio-cultural consequences, the slave trade devastated families, stripping many sub-Saharan men, women, and children from their kin and significant others. From the start of the slave trade until the 1860s, nearly 12 million sub-Saharan Africans were displaced. Only 10 million survived the torment of the Middle Passage. The slave trade helped institutionalize racism on a global scale. Black people were believed to be an inferior race as a result of the institution. An entire African Diaspora (i.e., "a scattering of African people") took hold in the New World. Five million slaves ended up in New Spain and the Caribbean. Over 500,000 more landed in the English colonies of North America. Both sub-Saharan Africa and the African Diaspora suffered what can best be described as socio-cultural trauma: many of the original cultural systems were left "broken" by slavery, and new slave laws helped to reinforce this fragmentation.

The War for Independence

The aftermath of the French and Indian War (1756-1763) set the stage for a conflict between the American colonists and Great Britain. After defeating France and her Native American allies, England passed a series of controversial laws. First, the Proclamation of 1763 barred the colonists from settling west of the Appalachian Mountains in an effort to appease Native Americans. Second, the Quebec Act of 1774 granted protections to their recently acquired French-Canadian colonies. Third, England passed a series of taxes on the colonists to pay their war debt, including the Sugar Act (1764), Quartering Act (1765), Stamp Act (1765), Townshend Acts (1767), Tea Act (1773), and the Intolerable Acts (1774).

To the colonists, it appeared as if England was rewarding the combatants of the French and Indian War and punishing the colonists who fought for England. As a result, protests erupted, especially in New England. The most significant were those surrounding the Boston Massacre (1770) and the Boston Tea Party (1773). Colonists organized the First Continental Congress in 1774 to request the repeal of the Intolerable Acts and affirm their loyalty to the Crown. When King George III refused, the crisis escalated in April 1775 at the Battle of Lexington and Concord, the first armed conflict between British troops and colonial militias. A Second Continental Congress then met in Philadelphia, and the delegates issued Thomas Jefferson's Declaration of Independence on July 4, 1776. The Declaration of Independence declared that all people enjoyed basic rights, specifically the right to life, liberty, and the pursuit of happiness, and accused King George III of violating colonists' rights, which justified the American Revolution.

The Continental Army lost its first major offensive campaign in Quebec City in December 1775, but victories at Trenton and Saratoga boosted morale. The tides of war turned against England when the Americans and France signed the Treaty of Alliance in 1778. France sent resources and troops to support the Americans, and the Marquis de Lafayette served as a combat commander at the final decisive battle at Yorktown. On September 3, 1783, the Treaty of Paris secured American independence.

Key Ideas Embodied in the Declaration of Independence
The Declaration of Independence was drafted by the First Continental Congress on July 2, 1776 and ratified on July 4, 1776. It was a document that formally severed the American colonies' ties to the British government, declaring their rule void. The Declaration sets forth three major arguments. First, it declared that the colonists' possessed a set of unalienable, natural-born rights that could not be taken away from them by the British Crown and Parliament. The Declaration of Independence thus drew on the ideas of the Enlightenment and declared that the colonists had the right to life, liberty, and the pursuit of happiness. Second, the Declaration asserted that the kind of England, King George III, had violated the rights of the colonists by unethically taxing them without consent. Thomas Jefferson, the main author of the document, accused the king of infringing upon the rights of Americans by passing acts that interfered with the inherent liberties of the colonies. He also alleged that the quartering of soldiers had placed a burden on the American colonies and their way of life. Third, the Declaration stated that the colonists had the right to sever ties with Great Britain because King George III had violated his social contract with the colonists. It argued that King George III had failed to protect the rights of his citizens, and, therefore, the colonies had the right to rule themselves.

After the successes of the American Revolution and War for Independence, the Declaration took on a new meaning: it became a revolutionary artefact that has often been referenced within the context of other independence and civil rights movements.

The Development of the Constitution and the Early Republic

The Political System of the United States
The United States of America has three major branches in its federal government: the legislative branch, the executive branch, and the judicial branch. The legislative, executive, and judicial branches of government all must adhere to the laws and regulations set forth by the United States Constitution, which was first ratified in 1789 and last amended in 1992. The United States Constitution is a living document that has a section known as the Bill of Rights. **The Bill of Rights** ensured that the **Constitution** remained a living document by setting the precedent for making changes, known as amendments. The Bill of Rights established the first ten amendments. There have since been 27 amendments made to the United States Constitution. The Bill of Rights also helped further establish the roles of the three branches of the federal government. Additionally, it constitutionalizes the separation of powers between the branches. These branches function as follows:

Legislative Branch
The **legislative branch** creates legislation; it makes the laws. It is comprised of the two houses of Congress: **The House of Representatives** and **The Senate**. This is known as a **bicameral legislature**. As illustrated in the following

107

diagrams, Congress currently has 535 voting members. There are 435 representatives in the House of Representatives and 100 senators in the Senate. The number of senators is always restricted to two per state. The number of representatives per state is based on the population of the state. However, each state is guaranteed at least one representative. States are then split into house districts of about equal size. For example, California has a large population, and Delaware has a small population. Both states have two senators. However, because California is more populous, it has dozens of members in the House of Representatives, while Delaware only has one. The representative from Delaware is elected by and represents the entire state. However, the representatives from California are elected by and represent their district, which is a smaller area within California.

The Senate typically holds more prestige and has more media coverage. Senators serve six-year terms and representatives serve two-year terms. Senators, unlike representatives, can block legislative action through a process known as filibustering, which only requires forty-one votes.

	House of Representatives	Senate
Membership	435	100
How Representation is Determined	Population of the state	Two Senators for each state
Length of Term	2 years	6 years

Executive Branch

The **executive branch** helps the nation by carrying out the laws; it backs all legal aspects of the government with presidential power. It is composed of the president of the United States, the vice president of the United States, and the president's Cabinet. The president of the United States has vetoing power, which means he or she can block the creation of laws with their constitutional right to reject a legislative proposal made by Congress.

Judicial Branch

The **judicial branch** analyzes or interprets the law, deeming whether a law created by Congress or order enacted by the president of the United States is constitutional. The federal judicial branch is comprised of the **Supreme Court** and all lower federal courts. Nine judges preside over the Supreme Court; they are appointed by the president.

All three branches consequently keep an eye on one another through a process of **checks and balances**, ensuring that all power is separated and no branch gains too much authority over the citizens and government of the United States. The president has the power to appoint judges to the Supreme Court and veto laws made by Congress. Congress can overturn a presidential veto; it also controls the budget of the government. Additionally, Congress approves presidential court appointments and can remove judges if necessary. The Supreme Court can declare presidential acts and legislation as unconstitutional.

Articles of Confederation and the Development of the US Constitution

Enacted during the American Revolution, the **Articles of Confederation** was the original governing document of the United States. However, the Articles of Confederation was ineffective due to its weak central government. The government didn't include a president or judiciary branch, and Congress didn't have the power to tax or raise money for an army. The final straw was the Articles of Confederation's failure to handle the Shays' Rebellion (1786–1787). In May 1787, the Founding Fathers convened the **Constitutional Convention** in Philadelphia. George Washington served as the Convention's president, and James Madison wrote the draft that was the basis for the Constitution.

Slavery challenged the Constitutional Convention from the outset, foreshadowing the American Civil War. The South wanted slaves to count for representation, even though slaves couldn't vote, but not taxes, while the North advocated for the opposite. The **Three-Fifths Compromise** settled the issue by counting slaves as three-fifths of a person for taxation and representation. In addition, the delegates agreed to a compromise that allowed slave owners to capture escaped slaves in exchange for ending the international slave trade in 1808.

The delegates also debated representation in Congress. **The New Jersey Plan** proposed a single legislative body with one vote per state. In contrast, **the Virginia Plan** proposed two legislative bodies with representation decided by the states' populations. The delegates agreed to the Connecticut Compromise—two legislative bodies with one house based on population (House of Representatives) and the other granting each state two votes (Senate). Two other branches, the judiciary and executive, were also included in the final document, and a series of checks and balances divided power between all three branches. The Constitution also expressly addressed issues from the Articles of Confederation by providing for a significantly stronger central government.

The Constitution, including its interpretation by the Supreme Court of the United States, divided the powers as follows:

Exclusive federal government powers
- Coin money
- Declare war
- Establish federal courts
- Sign foreign treaties
- Expand territories and admit new states
- Regulate immigration
- Regulate interstate commerce

Exclusive state government powers
- Establish local government
- Hold and regulate elections
- Implement welfare and benefit programs
- Create and oversee public education
- Establish licensing requirements
- Regulate state corporations
- Regulate commerce within the state

Concurrent powers (shared)
- Levy taxes
- Borrow money
- Charter corporations

Nine of the thirteen states needed to ratify the Constitution before it became law, and a heated debate over the Constitution spread throughout the nation. Those in favor of the Constitution, called the Federalists, produced and distributed the *Federalist Papers*, which James Madison, Alexander Hamilton, and John Jay wrote under the pseudonym "Publius." Thomas Jefferson and Patrick Henry led the Anti-Federalists and called for the inclusion of a bill of rights. The Constitution was ratified on June 21, 1778, and three years later, the Bill of Rights was added. The Bill of Rights is the first ten amendments to the Constitution ratified together in December 1791.

Bill of Rights
- **First Amendment**: freedom of speech, freedom of press, free exercise of religion, and the right to assemble peacefully and petition the government

- **Second Amendment**: the right to bear arms

- **Third Amendment**: the right to refuse to quarter (house) soldiers

- **Fourth Amendment**: prohibits unreasonable searches and seizures and requires a warrant based on probable cause

- **Fifth Amendment**: protects due process, requires a grand jury indictment for certain felonies, protects against the government seizing property without compensation, protects against self-incrimination, and prohibits double jeopardy

- **Sixth Amendment**: the right to a fair and speedy criminal trial, the right to view criminal accusations, the right to present witnesses, and the right to counsel in criminal trials

- **Seventh Amendment**: the right to a trial by jury in civil cases

- **Eighth Amendment**: prohibits cruel and unusual punishment

- **Ninth Amendment**: establishes the existence of unnamed rights and grants them to citizens

- **Tenth Amendment**: reserves all non-specified powers to the states or people

Major Principles of Government and Political Philosophy in the Constitution

Various principles of government and political philosophy are contained within the Constitution. One of these principles is the idea of **popular sovereignty**, which means that the people are the ones who hold control of the government. Another principle contained in Article IV of the Constitution regards **republicanism**, which means that citizens can participate in electing representatives to the government. **Separation of powers** is also a part of the Constitution: each of the three branches of government split power among themselves, as each branch has its unique powers. No one branch holds more power than another. Article I of the Constitution contains information pertaining to the legislative branch (Congress), Article II contains information pertaining to the Executive branch (the president and Cabinet), and Article III contains information pertaining to the Judicial branch (the Supreme Court).

Federalism is another principle of government within the Constitution, and concerns the idea that power is to be shared between the state governments and the national government. The Founding Fathers created a decentralized federal system to protect against tyranny. The Tenth Amendment is what enshrines the principle of federalism—the separation of power between federal, state, and local government. In general, the federal government can limit or prohibit the states from enacting certain policies, and state governments exercise exclusive control over local government.

Another important principle contained within the Constitution is that everyone is bound by the Constitution, including those in positions of power. The Bill of Rights was added to the Constitution to guarantee certain personal freedoms to citizens. The concept of individual rights is an important feature of the Constitution. The Constitution was written and signed in 1787, and the Bill of Rights was added in 1791 to explicitly define individual rights.

Evolution of Political Parties
Differing Visions for the Country

The first notable division in the early years of the United States that led to the development of political parties occurred during the writing of the Constitution. This division was between Federalists and Anti-Federalists. **Federalists** preferred a strong national government over strong state governments and supported the Constitution as it was, without the Bill of Rights, which they believed to be an unnecessary addition. **Anti-Federalists** preferred strong state governments over a strong central government and wanted the Bill of Rights to be added, as they believed that the Constitution did not guarantee individual freedoms explicitly enough. The first president, George Washington, did not support the use of political parties to divide politics and advised against forming parties. His words did not stop the division. The Federalist party was founded in 1791 and was based on the Federalist viewpoint previously mentioned, favoring a strong central government. The Federalist party held power from 1798 to1801. The Republican party, renamed later to the **Democratic-Republican party**, was founded in 1792. This party believed that the Federalists' policies did not benefit most people, but rather the most affluent. They believed the federal government should not have too much power. The Republican party had control from 1801 to 1825.

Impact on Economic Development Policies

Two emerging political leaders in the Early Republic had diverging views about the nation's economic future. Their names were Alexander Hamilton and Thomas Jefferson. These differences led to larger public debates in the 1790s. Their views stemmed from their overarching political beliefs about the role of government. Hamilton was a supporter of a strong, centralized federal government. He wanted the government to help balance the perspectives of the masses and the elites. He believed that liberty could be best protected through a federal system. Jefferson believed that the people should rule the country. He presented a political model that was heavily focuses on states' rights, and the capabilities of citizens and communities to create a more democratic and benevolent society. These overarching political differences created two dramatically different economic visions of the nation.

Hamilton believed the nation should be experimenting with new economic platforms, such as manufacturing and business. He even wanted to create a competition to reward American ingenuity and the creation of new inventions/products. Hamilton's belief that America could be a manufacturing giant much like England also encouraged him to support protective tariffs. He wanted to pass higher tariffs that would protect the US from foreign competition.

Jefferson, on the other hand, was tied to the idyllic notion of an agrarian republic. He believed an agrarian economy, one that was tied to the soil and to landownership, enhanced the liberty of the nation. He believed the nation could only remain independent if its farmers lived independently on the land, and worried that manufacturing made men and women into dependent entities. Jefferson supported lower tariffs in order to protect farmers from expensive goods.

Hamilton and Jefferson's biggest point of contention, however, was the formation of a National Bank. Hamilton staunchly supported a National Bank. Jefferson fervently opposed it. Hamilton wanted to centralize the minting and banking of money. In order to protect states' rights, he even pitched a 20-year limitation on a National Bank charter. He also encouraged states to create their own banks in order to prevent the emergence of a monopoly. Jefferson – and his fellow Jeffersonian Republicans – believed this type of federal influence conflicted with the democratic ideals and liberties of the nation. Jefferson believed the creation of the bank was not legal according to the US Constitution. He thought the creation of a central bank would be unconstitutional. This meant that Jefferson's economic vision was backed by a strict interpretation of the US Constitution. Hamilton, on the other hand, argued for a looser interpretation of the US Constitution, claiming that the federal government is not fully bound by what it *does not say* and only bound by what it does say. Hamilton's vision ended up garnering more support: President George Washington and the US Congress established the First National Bank of the United States of America in hopes that it would bring economic stability to the "critical period" of the Early Republic.

Factors that Led to the Formation of Distinct Regional Identities

Historical Factors

Andrew Jackson's presidency contributed to the formation of regional differences in the United States. Regional identities often trumped national identities in this era. Three distinct regions emerged in this antebellum era of Jacksonian Democracy of the early 19th century: the North, the South, and the West. All three regions were influenced by Jackson's expansion of democratic voting rights to white voters who did not own land. These "working-class" whites transformed American democracy, and the expansion of democracy at large in the American landscape encouraged other groups (i.e., black people, Native Americans, and women) in each region to fight for their own democratic rights. Ironically, this expansion of democracy tore America into pieces, reinforcing the larger theme of sectionalism. This expansion also placed the frontier (the West) at the epicenter of a clash of values between the North and South. All eyes turned westward during Jackson's presidency, setting the state for the tensions of westward expansion.

The second (more overarching) historical factor that contributed to the creation of regions was the Industrial Revolution. One can even argue that Jacksonian Democracy was an outgrowth of the Industrial Revolution, an era in human history that witnessed the Europe and America's transition from agrarian to market/manufacturing economies.

111

The North industrialized at a much faster rate than the South. The South remained bitter at the North because of its industrial capabilities. And the West became a point of conflict for these competing industrial and agrarian values.

Cultural Factors

The agrarian lifestyle of the South helped create a genteel plantation culture that thrived on slave labor. Southern values were distinctly agrarian in nature; they tended to prefer a crop-based economy over a product-based economy. The North's culture was dominated by its industrial character. It became a hub for entrepreneurial spirits and business efforts. The elites of the North embodied cultural values that were drastically different than the elites of the South. Northern elites were more inclined to abolitionist sensitivities because they were not as dependent on slave labor as the South. Western frontiersmen valued cheap lands and agrarian independence. Culturally speaking, they were more inclined to set forth values that bolstered political platforms that centered on a combination of agrarian independence and infrastructural development.

Economic Factors

Citizens living in the North generally supported an economy that focused on manufacturing and trade. Likewise, northerners encouraged the Jackson Administration to pass protective tariffs because many American industries were threatened by the inexpensive nature of British goods. The North was the region of the country most directly affected by the Industrial Revolution. Northerners also discouraged any legislation that allowed for the sale of cheap lands in the West, fearing that the appeal would draw factory workers away from the North. Additionally, the North moved further from slavery in this era because its economy was no longer dependent on farming.

The South benefited the least from the Industrial Revolution. The South remained tied to a slave-based plantation economy. This agrarian backdrop and the rise of "King Cotton" in the South increased the need for slavery. Southerners relied heavily on British imports, so they discouraged the passage of costly tariffs. They understood that international competitors would likely raise their own tariffs in response to US increases. The South became increasingly bitter with the abolitionist efforts of the North during this period. The South also became increasingly infatuated with states' rights during this era, mostly in response to a tariff passed by Congress just prior to Andrew Jackson's inauguration. This tariff was largely supported by struggling businesses in the North. It tried to undermine the manufacturing economy of Great Britain. Southerners described it as the Tariff of Abominations because they believed it would hurt their economy. The tariff was actually signed by John Quincy Adams, not Andrew Jackson, but Jackson became a quick target for southern resentment. John C. Calhoun, a politician from South Carolina, and other southerners led a protest in the name of states' rights. These protesters threatened to have South Carolina secede from the Union. This protest, known as the **nullification crisis**, centered on Calhoun's belief that states had the right to nullify (i.e., reject) federal law if it proved to be unconstitutional. Famous debates followed, such as the Hayne-Webster debate, which pitted Robert Y. Hayne (a pro-nullification senator from South Carolina) against Daniel Webster (a pro-Union politician from Massachusetts). South Carolina even passed a Nullification Act. The crisis, which was met with stern disapproval by Andrew Jackson, finally ended in a compromised crafted by Henry Clay (a Kentucky politician). The compromise, one of many in the antebellum period, set the stage for the sectional tensions of the Civil War.

Tensions grew even worse as Andrew Jackson carried out an all-out political assault on the Second National Bank, which was establish in 1816 in the aftermath of the War of 1812. Most southerners relished in Jackson's attack on central banking, claiming that the institution was established for the benefit of business elites in the North. Some southern states even took the fight to the Supreme Court, as Maryland did in the famous *McCulloch v. Maryland* case that eventually ruled the bank as constitutional. Northerners, on the other hand, fought to keep the bank alive, passing an 1832 extension of the Bank's charter. Jackson, who had previously defended federal power, sided with the South this time. He famously claimed, "I will kill it!" in reaction to the passing of the bill. And he, indeed, kept his word. Jackson vetoed the bill and Congress failed to overrule his veto. Jackson supported state banks, moving much of the federal money to these institutions.

The West was thankful for Jackson's attack on banking. It allowed many state creditors to fund western expansion, which spawned the development the West needed at that time. The West was an odd blend of North and South – the Midwest had an emerging manufacturing economy, but the rest of the land west of the Appalachians thrived on farming, much like the South. The West's blend of North and South made it fertile soil for sectional conflicts, which, in the years leading up to the Civil War, became doused with the blood of burgeoning debates over slavery and abolition.

Geographic Factors

The history, politics, cultures, and economics of each of these regions was inspired by a larger category: geography. Geography dictated the creation of each of these categories. The North had the mountains and resources to fuel an Industrial Revolution. The South had the coastal plains necessary for a cotton economy. The West had the open sense of trans-Appalachian freedom that guided the region's sense of independence.

But the West also had a geography that became embittered in the political battles between North and South (the nation's two dominant historical regions). Both the North and South wanted a slice of the West to have as their own. They wanted the resources. They wanted to make the West either a free or enslaved region. In fact, the expansion West is really what catalyzed the Civil War: both the North and the South argued over how newly incorporated territories and states would be governed. The West, therefore, lost much of its idyllic independence in the antebellum period as it became a point of contest for civil disputes that evolved into an American Civil War.

Westward Movement

Shortly after gaining independence, the United States rapidly expanded based on **Manifest Destiny**—the belief that Americans hold special virtues, America has a duty to spread those virtues westward, and success is a certainty.

In 1803, President Thomas Jefferson purchased the Louisiana territory from France. **The Louisiana Purchase** included 828,000 square miles of land west of the Mississippi River. Unsure of what he had purchased, Jefferson organized several expeditions to explore the new territory, including the famous **Lewis and Clark Expedition**. To consolidate the eastern seaboard under American control, President James Monroe purchased New Spain (present-day Florida) in the *Adams-Onís Treaty* of 1819.

Conflict with Native Americans was constant and brutal. Great Britain allied with Native American tribes in the present-day Midwest, using them as a buffer to protect her Canadian colonies. Britain's support for Native American raids on American colonies ignited tensions and led to the War of 1812. Two years later, Great Britain and the United States signed the Treaty of Ghent, ending the war with a neutral resolution, and British support for the Native Americans evaporated. The Supreme Court's decision in *Worcester v. Georgia* (1832) later established the concept of tribal sovereignty; however, President Andrew Jackson refused to enforce the Court's decision. Consequently, Americans continued to colonize Native American land at will. President Jackson also passed the first of several Indian Removal Acts, forcing native tribes westward on the Trail of Tears.

Tensions on the American-Mexican border worsened after President John Tyler annexed Texas in 1845. That same year, James K. Polk succeeded Tyler after winning the election of 1844 on a platform of Manifest Destiny. President Polk ordered General Zachary Taylor to march his army into the disputed territory, which ignited the Mexican-American War. The United States dominated the conflict and annexed the present-day American Southwest and California through the 1848 Treaty of Guadalupe Hidalgo. Polk also settled the Oregon Country dispute with Britain, establishing the British-American boundary at the 49th parallel.

The United States purchased Alaska from Russia in 1867, and Hawaii was annexed in 1898 to complete what would become the fifty states.

The migration of settlers into these new territories was facilitated by technological innovation and legislation. Steamships allowed the settlers to navigate the nation's many winding rivers, and railroads exponentially increased the speed of travel and transportation of supplies to build settlements. Canals were also important for connecting the eastern seaboard to the Midwest. Thus, the fastest growing settlements were typically located near a major body of water or a railroad. Starting in 1862, Congress incentivized Americans to travel westward and populate the territories with a series of Homestead acts, which gave away public lands, called "homesteads," for free. In total, the United States gave away 270 million acres of public land to support the country's expansion.

Government Policies Toward American Indians and Foreign Nations

The Early Republic had one major platform for relations with American Indians in the years leading up to the Civil War: Indian Removal. As US settlers began moving in droves to the trans-Appalachian West, presidential administrations became increasingly focused on Indian Removal. No president embodied this trend better than President Andrew Jackson, who passed the **Indian Removal Act in 1830**, which led to the infamous "Trail of Tears," a long, forced migration to the West. The act authorized the removal of Native Americans from their homelands east of the Mississippi River. Congress followed suit by creating an Indian Territory in modern-day Oklahoma. Southerners like John C. Calhoun wholeheartedly supported the act. Congress even created a new government agency to enact this historical atrocity: the Bureau of Indian Affairs. Some groups resisted the forced removal by force; others took the battle to the Supreme Court. The Supreme Court decision of *Worcester v. Georgia* saw the Cherokee nation sue the state of Georgia for forcibly removing their people with its militia. The Supreme Court ruled that Georgia had no right to remove the Cherokee, and only the federal government had that right. Georgia, however, ignored the decision and maintained its violent efforts. Unfortunately, the Native Americans lost a significant amount of their battles, but not without putting up a fight. Many of the conflicts ended in one-sided treaties between Native Americans and the US government.

Policies rooted in America's expansionist efforts also affected its relationship with the international community. Skirmishes over the northern US-Canadian boundary continued in the years following the American Revolution. The United States even entered another war with Great Britain in 1812. Border disputes continued in a less-violent manner following the conclusion of the War of 1812. They continued well into the mid-19th century with Great Britain (and later Russia) in the Pacific Northwest. The US obtained an expanse of land from France through the Louisiana purchase in 1803 and settled into an agreement with Spain to control Florida from 1810-1819. As the US grew in economic power, it established tariffs in an attempt to hurt the blossoming manufacturing scene in Great Britain in the 1820s and 1830s. By the 1840s, the US had its sights set on a newly independent Texas Republic, which was annexed as a state in 1845. Additionally, following the Mexican-American War in 1848, the US gained control of modern-day New Mexico, Arizona, and California with the Mexican Cession of the Treaty of Guadalupe-Hidalgo. The last sliver of the Southwest was added by the Gadsden Purchase in 1853.

The best way to describe America's expansionist efforts during this period is "fast-growth, unilateral imperialism," which means the US sought to grow quickly into an empire in a one-sided fashion.

The Roles of Blacks, American Indians, Immigrants, Women, and Children in the New Country
Each of these groups was "otherized" in unique ways as a result of the spread of institutional prejudice and xenophobia. The country became increasingly nativist (an intense form of white, anti-immigrant nationalism) as a result of the increased immigration that stemmed from industrialization and urbanization. Slaves were discriminated against most, forced into oppression by their owners. As agriculture became mechanized in the South with the invention of Eli Whitney's cotton gin, the demand for slave labor increased. The cotton boom of the antebellum period forced African-Americans slaves into an even more brutal form of endless slavery. Free blacks were also discriminated against in both the North and South; they were forced into segregated quarters long before the Jim Crow era. Enslaved people and free blacks both suffered in poor living conditions. Yet they formed the labor backbone of the growing industrial economy in the United States. American Indians struggled to find work in an America that constantly displaced them. They often found themselves fending for their own subsistence, first in their isolated communities in the East and later on their reservations in the West. Irish immigrants and other immigrants diversified the fiber of American culture, but were also treated as the "other." Nativist sentiments attacked Irish laborers and their Catholic backgrounds. Immigrants were labeled as plagues on society, particularly in urban centers that were "bursting at the seams" because of industrial changes. Immigrants were attacked, even though they quickly surpassed black labor as the crux of American industry in the post-bellum period. Americans became so hostile with immigrants that they began passing immigrant quotas, such the Chinese Exclusion Act of 1882 that banned Chinese immigrants from entering the United States.

Civil War and Reconstruction

Origin and Evolution of the Anti-Slavery Movement
The movement to end slavery, or the abolition movement, began to really take hold in the 1830s. The abolitionist movement was not always united, but it was certainly diverse. It called upon the sentiments of religious groups like the Quakers, writers and activists such as William Lloyd Garrison who published the newspaper known as the *Liberator* and founded the American Anti-Slavery Society. Some abolitionists wanted to create a new free black colony called Liberia. Others wanted immediate emancipation within the confines of the United States. Free black Americans such as Sojourner Truth and Frederick Douglass, both former slaves, wrote about their slave experiences to bring about awareness for the need for emancipation. White women, including Angelina Grimke and Sara Grimke, two sisters from the genteel culture of the South, also began writing antislavery tracts. Many reformers saw abolition and women's suffrage as two overlapping movements. Members from all of these categories often assisted by helping fugitive slaves find refuge in the North via the **Underground Railroad**, a network of routes and hiding places for runaway

slaves. Runaway slaves would be guided by anti-slavery advocates along freedom trails that led to the North, where abolition had taken hold much more easily than the South. The most famous of these advocates was Harriet Tubman, a free black woman who escaped slavery in 1849. These runaway slaves would be hidden in the basements, barns, attics, and crawl spaces. Most travel occurred along the Underground Railroad during the night. Some slaves tried to escape the United States altogether for freer grounds across the border in Canada.

Response of Those who Defended Slavery to the Anti-Slavery Movement
While the North remained the center of the abolitionist movement, the South remained staunchly pro-slavery. White southerners argued that slavery was an important part of Southern heritage. Others argued that it was an economically vital institution. The South, proud of its states' rights advocacy, argued that northerners should not interfere with their historic way of living. Nat Turner's rebellion in 1831, which witnessed rebel slaves killing southerners, also encouraged many anti-slavery advocates to remain silent in an increasingly hostile South. The Grimke sisters – two famous female abolitionists – actually left the South at this time. The South remained dependent upon slavery, as both a culture and an economy.

Of course, like the Grimke sisters, not every person fell neatly within this North-South dichotomy. Some norther pro-slavery advocates argued that freed slaves would move to the northern states and supplant the workforce there. Some newspaper articles at that time shed light on this argument – they show that many white northerners believed that a freed black workforce would accept lower wages, undercutting the contemporary white workforce. Violent mobs took out their aggressions on abolitions, battering and murdering members of the community such as Elijah Lovejoy. Lovejoy, a reputable abolitionist, was killed by a mob in 1837 in Alton, Illinois. Other violent actions were taken out on freed blacks and abolitionists. The entire Union was being torn apart by pro-slavery and anti-slavery factions.

Causes of the Civil War
The Northern and Southern regions of the United States had major economic differences, among other disparities. The North's economy was manufacturing and industry-based, with some small-scale agriculture. The South's economy involved large-scale farming and relied heavily on enslaved people for labor. The South was concerned about what they perceived as threats to the existence of slavery, especially regarding Northern opposition to the expansion of slavery. The **Kansas-Nebraska Act**, passed in 1854, led to great debates over slavery and westward expansion. Anti-slavery factions were concerned that slavery could be extended into areas where it had previously been banned. This led to "Bleeding Kansas," during which violence occurred between pro- and antislavery groups because of debate over whether slavery should be legal in Kansas, which at the time was a potential new state.

The South was also concerned over Westward expansion's impact on slavery. California had banned the practice, but because of California's gold, Southerners still wanted California to become a state. These concerns led to the Compromise of 1850, in which other territories near California could choose for themselves whether to allow slavery. Another cause of the Civil War was popular sovereignty. This concerned the idea that the residents of a territory, rather than Congress, could choose whether slavery would be allowed or not. This was the pro-slavery faction's attempt to expand slavery into areas where it had not previously been allowed. States' rights were also an issue, as Southern states wanted the ability to override the federal government to remove laws they did not support, such as laws that could interfere with slavery.

Compromises and Acts of the Pre-Civil War Era
Congress repeatedly attempted to compromise on slavery, especially as to whether it would be expanded into new territories. The first such attempt was the **Missouri Compromise of 1820**, which included three parts. First, Missouri was admitted as a slave state. Second, Maine was admitted as a free state to maintain the balance between free and slave states. Third, slavery was prohibited north of the 36°30' parallel in new territories, but the Supreme Court overturned this in *Dred Scott v. Sandford* (1837).

The **Compromise of 1850** admitted California as a free state, allowed popular sovereignty to determine if Utah and New Mexico would be slave states, banned slavery in Washington D.C., and enforced a harsh **Fugitive Slave Law**. The

116

Kansas-Nebraska Act *of 1854* started a mini civil war, as slave owners and abolitionists rushed into the new territories. Slavery eventually caused the collapse of the Whigs, the dominant political party of the early and middle 19th century. The Northern Whigs created the anti-slavery Republican Party.

Republican Abraham Lincoln won the election of 1860. Before his inauguration, seven Southern states seceded from the United States and established the **Confederate States of America** to protect slavery.

Major Battles of the Civil War

On April 12, 1861, the first shots of the **Civil War** were fired by Confederate artillery at Fort Sumter, South Carolina. On January 1, 1863, after the particularly bloody Battle of Antietam, President Lincoln issued the **Emancipation Proclamation**, freeing the Confederacy's 3 million slaves; however, slavery continued in Union-controlled states and territories.

Later that year, the Battle of Gettysburg gave the **Union Army** a decisive victory, turning back the Confederacy's advances into the North. President Lincoln's famous **Gettysburg Address** called for the preservation of the Union and equality for all citizens. After a series of Union victories, Confederate General Robert E. Lee surrendered at Appomattox Court House and ended the Civil War in April 1865. Less than one week after Lee's surrender, John Wilkes Booth assassinated President Lincoln during a play at Ford's Theater.

Vice President Andrew Johnson assumed the presidency and battled the Radical Republicans in Congress over the Reconstruction Amendments. Federal troops were deployed across the South to enforce the new amendments, but Reconstruction concluded in 1877. Immediately after the troops withdrew, the Southern stated enacted Jim Crow laws to rollback African Americans' right to vote and enforce segregationist policies.

Comparative Strengths and Weaknesses of the Union and the Confederacy

The North's greatest strengths were its industrial economy and its larger population. With a growing population of about 22 million people, the North was strengthened by its human power, which could continue to fuel an Industrial Revolution that took on a new form as a wartime economy. In fact, it controlled 85% of the nation's industry. Its economy was more diversified mixing agriculture and manufacturing. The North's large population allowed the war economy to boom; it also gave the Union a numbers advantage in the actual war. Weapons production peaked during war time. Millions of people either joined the Union military or supported the troops with farming or factory work. The North also had stronger railroad systems, which strengthened transportation in the war. The industrial nature of the North also gave its navy an advantage over the South's navy. Most naval troops remained loyal to the Union. Lastly, the North had an established government that had been ruling its people for almost 100 years.

The North was weakened by the ongoing battle over abolition – not everyone was in ideological alignment over the issue of slavery. Some northerners believed slavery should continue. The North's war was constantly on the offensive, as it had invaded an unfamiliar territory that expanded 750,000 square miles. Although it had more soldiers on its side, it initially lacked the military brilliance to carry out this offensive. The North struggled to conquer the large territory.

The Confederacy had the advantage of defending their homeland. Most of their war was fought on a defensive front. The stubborn Confederate troops were fighting for their land, families, and properties. They were also fighting for a new national pride. Many of their soldiers and generals were skilled former US Army members who had experience in other wars.

The Confederacy was weakened by its largely agricultural economy. It was not an industrial giant like the North. It struggled to mass produce weaponry and construct railroads. It was therefore at a disadvantage in terms of its arms and transportation. Its small population of roughly 9 million struggled to maintain a constant stream of supplies for the war. Additionally, the issue of slavery weakened the South because 1/3 of its population was enslaved, making it prone to both external defeat and internal uprisings. Lastly, the South did not have the naval capabilities of the North. These evident weaknesses eventually led to the South's defeat.

Reconstruction

Reconstruction was the period following the Civil War, from the war's end in 1865 to 1877. It involved working to reintegrate the previously seceded Confederate states back into the United States, as well as incorporating people who had been enslaved into US society and its systems of labor and politics. Reconstruction may have started before the official end of the war since some enslaved people were freed and escaped to different states during the war. During this time the 13th, 14th, and 15th Amendments were passed. The 13th Amendment banned slavery "except as a punishment for a crime whereof the party shall have been duly convicted." The 14th Amendment, among other things, granted citizenship to those who were born or naturalized within the United States. The 15th Amendment prevented discrimination based on race in voting, granting all male citizens the right to vote. Due to racism and economic issues, among other factors, the Reconstruction process was eventually abandoned.

The **Compromise of 1877** is seen as the end of the Reconstruction. After this, Jim Crow laws began to rise. Initially Black Codes, which were created to control previously enslaved people following the Emancipation Proclamation, were established. They controlled all the details about what work formerly enslaved people could do, including how much money they could make. This led to many African Americans becoming indentured servants and being limited in where they could live. Even with the changes that occurred during Reconstruction, barriers still existed that prevented their ability to actively participate in society. The Fifteenth Amendment had been passed, but many Black American men could not vote due to new restrictions such as literacy tests, state laws, and threats of violence by various white supremacy groups such as the Ku Klux Klan. As Black Americans began to move into cities, Jim Crow laws continued to spread, and areas to which Black Americans moved began to be more segregated. Some areas and resources were outright prohibited for use by Black Americans.

The Rise of Industrial America

The Pattern of Urban Growth in the United States

Cities grew over the course of the 19th century due to advancements in technology during the Industrial Revolution. After the Civil War, the **American Industrial Revolution** (also known as the Second Industrial Revolution) took place, with an increase in the number and size of cities. The railroad system also expanded in the late 19th century, which allowed for materials to travel farther on land. Prior to this, manufacturing was mostly limited to areas near water. During this time, agriculture also became industrialized due to new technologies. The number of jobs increased as factories opened, which drew more people to move to cities. This included many immigrants from Europe, who largely settled in cities along the East Coast. There was a wave of immigration from Western and Northern Europe during the mid-19th century, with a large influx from Ireland due to a famine in that country. Another wave of immigration took place during the late 19th and early 20th centuries. Amid this wave, Chinese laborer immigrants were prohibited from coming to the United States for ten years with the passage of the Chinese Exclusion Act of 1882. Due to the increased movement of people into cities, public health issues arose. Poor housing and poor sanitation led to the spread of disease.

Response of Renewed Nativism

Americans who opposed immigration in the 19th century were known as nativists. They were "native-born," mostly-Protestant Americans who feared losing their jobs to immigrants, especially Irish Catholics and other European Catholics. Some nativists referred to these Catholic immigrants as papists: they believed the Catholics would have stronger allegiances with the Pope in Rome than the President in Washington. Nativists became such a powerful political contingent that they formed their own political party: the **Know-Nothing Party**. The Know-Nothing Party created a political platform that tried to place stronger restrictions on immigration. They did not want more foreigners to become US citizens. Additionally, as a predominantly Protestant group, the Know-Nothings worked to keep Catholics out of local, state, and federal offices. The group had minor successes in elections. Some even called for extreme measures such as a 21-year pathway to citizenship. Eventually their political influence waned as more immigrants assimilated to the American way of life and eventually took office.

Impact of Major Inventions

Prior to the Industrial Revolutions most residents of the United States and Europe remained famers. The major inventions of the Industrial Revolution transformed that paradigm, forcing millions of rural residents into the crowded factories of the city. The machines of the Industrial Revolution made life more efficient, but they also revolutionized the ways in which people lived, governed, and worked. The creation of inventions such as Richard Arkwright's spinning machine in 1760s led to a textile boom in the earliest years of the Industrial Revolution. Increasing the speed of textile production, Arkwright's spinning machine, and the new inventions it inspired, encouraged merchants to engineer large textile factories all over Great Britain and the United States. Men like Samuel Slater, an English immigrant to the United States, carried the secrets of Great Britain's industrial economy to American soil. Slater's machines, which he built from memory, established a new textile industry in Rhode Island. Located in Pawtucket, Rhode Island, Slater's mills inspired the invention of new cotton threads. These Rhode Island textile mills, established near rivers, created an entirely new system of work known as the Rhode Island system. Engineered from Slater's strategies, this system began hiring entire families and dividing work into simple tasks for men, women, and children. The system made industry the epicenter of the town. Company recruiters would target slums and poor farming communities, encouraging poor families to relocate in mill towns.

In Massachusetts, an entirely new system of work was established by Francis Cabot Lowell, who returned from a trip to Great Britain with the secrets of the Industrial Revolution. Like Slater, Lowell created his own machines and systems. His system, known as the Lowell system, hired thousands of unmarried women from local farms. The Lowell system thrived thanks, in part, to the creation of its boardinghouses, which housed the unmarried female employees. Both systems changed the traditional definition of family: the Rhode Island system united families in work, the Lowell system delayed the creation of families by employing women.

Another invention helped stimulate mass production: Eli Whitney's cotton gin. The cotton gin separated cotton fibers at a rapid rate to be used as textiles. The machine used interchangeable parts, which could be used on any identical cotton gin. The invention of the cotton gin not only reinforced the cotton economy of the South, but it also catalyzed the mass production of weapons and other goods in the North. It is an invention that increased the quality of life for the nation, but decreased the quality of life for slaves.

The Industrial Revolution also created a **Transportation Revolution**, which witnessed the creation of machines such as the steamboat, the steam locomotive, and railroads. Robert Fulton famously created the first steamboat in the US, which increased interstate commerce. Peter Cooper built the first steam locomotive in 1830. By the end of the 19th century, the US would subsequently be covered in railroads, including a transcontinental railroad. New fuels such as coal and oil fueled the Transportation Revolution. The expansion of railroads also made many Midwestern cities, such as Chicago, new hubs of industry. Other inventions strengthened communication between distant towns. Samuel F.B. Morse perfected a machine known as a telegraph, which could send messages over miles thousands of miles.

The impact of the Industrial Revolution and its inventions on the quality of life of American citizens varied. Slaves did not benefit from the cotton boom. Some families increased their wealth. Most workers, however, were forced into unregulated, unsafe working conditions where they earned low wages. The result was a new conflict in American history, one rooted in the capitalist battles between Big Business and laborers.

California History

The Pre-Columbian Period through the Gold Rush

The Impact of California's Physical Geography on its History

California has some of the most diverse landscapes and climates in the entire United States. While it is just one state, it has long been home to a multiplicity of cultures, landforms, and weather patterns. It is a land filled with lush redwood forests in the northwestern part of the state, bleak deserts in the western and southwestern regions, rocky coastlines

119

and sandy beaches along the eastern shores, a fruit-bearing Central Valley known to have dry spells, and the highest peaks of the continental US California experiences frequent floods, droughts, wildfires, and earthquakes, making it an awe-inspiring state with a tumultuous history of natural disasters. The sandy soil of Death Valley can heat up to a record-breaking 134 degrees, as it did at Greenland Ranch in 1913. Likewise, the verdant Central Valley tends to get scorched in the summer by temperatures that rise to well over 100 degrees. Yet residents and visitors can escape these horrid temperatures in a heartbeat, finding refuge in the steady fogs of the San Francisco Bay region or the icy peaks of the Sierra Nevada mountains. It has few natural harbors (i.e., the San Diego, San Francisco, Bodega, and Humboldt Bays), but plenty of rivers. California's geography and climate has made it both a place of refuge and a center of literary appeal. It was the home of vibrant Native American civilizations that settled across the entire state. It became the "Land of Milk and Honey" for the Dust Bowl farmers of the 1930s. It captivated the literary instincts of novelists and poets such as Bret Harte, Mark Twain, John Steinbeck, Robinson Jeffers, and John Fante. It has come to represent the American Dream at large, serving as a magnet for lost souls, hopeful immigrants, and *noir* intellectuals, moviemakers, and artists. It is a state with over 1,200 miles of shoreline and over 40 million inhabitants. It is the third-largest state in square miles, but it is first in population. Its geographic and economic magnetism have created an intense expanse of urban development, concentrated mostly along the coast. The cities of Los Angeles and San Francisco serve as its economic hubs in the global economy. But it is also the home of remote residences, such as those scattered throughout the Mohave Desert and Joshua Tree National Park.

The Geography, Economic Activities, Folklore, and Religion of California's American Indian Peoples

Many scholars believe that the first Native Americans in California crossed over a Bering Sea land bridge nearly 20,000 years ago. The original inhabitants of California had to maintain a harmonious relationship with the land they settled because they remained relatively isolated from the Native American tribes located east of the Sierra Nevada mountains and its proximal deserts. The major California Native American linguistic groups grouped together in tribes and were brought together by the trade networks they engineered throughout their isolated region. The different linguistic families tended to also group according to the geomorphic provinces of the state (represented in the second map below). This tied the Native American cultures and economic activities to the land. Scholars of Native American history claim that these tribes lived "close to the soil." While these cultures may seem simplistic or uncomplicated according to our modern-day perspectives, they were actually quite intricate. With the exception of the pottery-producing Native American groups living in the Owens Valley and the Lower Colorado River Valley, most of these linguistic groups employed sophisticated basketry techniques. Although most of the original inhabitants of California did not engage in organized agricultural efforts, they did rely on hunting-and-gathering efforts to subsist. They may not have sowed, planted, or harvested the soil, but they did forage in the surrounding environments.

Thus, they relied heavily on acorns, berries, game, and seafood for their survival. The scattered Native Californian economies relied heavily on trade with one another. Women were responsible for making baskets, dressing skins, and bedding mats. These goods would be used within each tribe or traded to neighboring tribes. Men and women used mortars and pestles to ground acorns into meal. The acorn meal was used to create an interesting form of acorn gruel. They also used baskets lined with hot stones to roast roots, salmon, vegetable greens, snakes, field mice, squirrels, wood rats, coyotes, rabbits, crows, lizards, snakes, cactus apples, wild berries, skunks, slugs, fly larvae, grubs, crickets, minnows, snails, and caterpillars. Men used elk horns and mussel-shell blades to dig out canoes. Native Americans also distilled intoxicating beverages, prepared tobacco, collected Jimson weed, and fashioned pipes. Most of their utensils and weapons were made of wood. They traded all of these goods along with watercrafts, deerskins, moccasins, sandals, and skin blankets. Some tribal groups wore and traded basketry hats, while others wore and traded hairnets.

Their folklore and religions were also tied to the land. Many of the previously mentioned foraged and crafted goods were incorporated into religious ceremonies. Special dances were carried out along rivers and other landmarks to celebrate special moments, feasts, calendar events, or occasions for mourning. In terms of folklore and religion, many of the Native American groups, especially those along California's northwest coast, called upon "spirit helpers." They believed in an animistic form of folklore and religious belief that worshipped the spiritual aspects of nature at large. According to some folkloric creation stories, these Native American groups emerged from the land – they were born from it, and forever tied to it. Prior to colonization, this social system remained intact, with few disruptions, for thousands of years. However, that all changed with the creation of the Spanish mission system.

The Impact of Spanish Exploration and Colonization

Spain's exploration and colonization of California eventually led to the demise of many Native American tribes and cultures. The Spanish *Reconquista* (re-conquest) attitude informed much of its colonization practices, establishing a mission system hyper-focused on converting all Native Americans on California soil. The mission system, however, was only loosely ruled, which allowed many Native Americans to remain settled into their homes in the West well into the late 19th century. By the 1700s, Spain tried to assert its authority over the mission system by instituting an accompanying encomienda system that forced many Native Americans into unpaid labor situations. These Native Americans provided free labor on farms and *ranchos* (ranches). They also assisted with creating artisan goods in *pueblos* (towns). Spanish colonization weakened the Native American hold on the land by introducing diseases, carrying out wars, and instituting slave-like conditions. Spain tried to fervently convert the Native Americans and make California a fully Catholic region. The Hispanic influence on the region can still be seen today. Even as Spain's influence waned with the rise of the Mexican republic in 1821, California remained a predominantly Hispanic territory. Hispanic culture still resonates there today in the form of generations of settlement and renewed immigration from Spanish-speaking countries.

Mexican Rule in California

California transferred hands from the Spanish crown to the Mexican Republic in 1821 when revolutionary leader Augustine Iturbide successfully led a revolt. Iturbide declared himself the emperor of the new Mexican government on May 19, 1822. Following this declaration, he began using the California region of North America as a dumping ground for those who went against the new revolutionary government. During this transition, the Mexican government disbanded the Spanish-Catholic missionary system in favor of a new secular system of governance. All officers from the *presidios* and all *padres* from the mission houses were obligated to pledge an oath of allegiance to the new Mexican Republic. California avoided the vortex of the revolutionary struggle of the Mexican Republic, for the most part, but absorbed much of the tumult and uncertainty of its aftermath. The era of Mexican control in California was consequently wrought with aggravated local tensions. During this era, residents witnessed periodic challenges to gubernatorial leadership. The era even created a cultural rift between northern and southern California that continues—to a certain degree—to this day. The era was also ripe with American infiltration, as settlers from the east flocked to the fruits of the Wild West. The tumult and rifts of this era thus paved the way to the eventual cessation of the California territory following the Mexican-American War.

The Causes and Consequences of the War Between Mexico and the United States

The war between the Mexican Republic and the United States of America was catalyzed by the American desire to carry forth its so-called Manifest Destiny to conquer all lands between the Atlantic Ocean and Pacific Ocean. The **Mexican-American War** was, first and foremost, a war of expansion—the United States government and its citizens focused on Texas and California as possible lands for American annexation and/or Mexican cessation. Both territories had already witnessed an impressive infiltration of Anglo-American settlers that stirred US sympathies. The Mexican-American War was also a war over resources—the United States government had their sights set on the cotton plantations of Texas and the gold, timber, crops, and minerals of California. Lastly, the Mexican-American War was a war that displaced domestic sectional tensions—the United States, on the eve of its own civil war, looked westward and southwestward in an attempt to solve the sectionalism ingrained in the American fiber. The new territories that were sought after became key players in the battle over slavery and abolition. In terms of consequences, the Mexican-American War opened up California for a brief Bear Flag Revolt that witnessed the declaration of an independent California Republic. The "Bear Flag Republic" was more romanticism than reality, however, and William Ide, the leader of the incipient skirmish, remains just a footnote in US and California history. With the signing of the Treaty of Guadalupe-Hidalgo on February 2, 1848, the Mexican-American War officially ended, and the California region officially became a part of the United States of America. The California territory remained unsettled following the war, as government power slipped from the hands of Latinos into the hands of Anglo-Americans. As a result, Hispanic culture slowly slipped into isolated shadows, only to be revealed in more vibrant colors in later decades. The ensuing gold rush brought even more white settlers to cities like Los Angeles and San Francisco, paving the way to a new era of US occupation.

The Discovery of Gold and its Effects in California

Native Americans discovered gold in California years before the Anglo-American discovery of gold there. Nevertheless, the American historical mythos traditionally points to January 24, 1848 as the paradigm-shifting date of gold discovery on the North American continent. On this date, Scotsman James Wilson Marshall gathered up and inspected gold nuggets and flakes for the first time at Johann Sutter's infamous sawmill. This "discovery" set into motion decades of movement west from the urban corridors of the northeast and Midwest to the gold mines of the Sierra Nevada mountains. The discovery was even applauded by President James K. Polk in a presidential address on December 5, 1848, creating even more of a romantic allure about the **California Gold Rush**.

By 1849, hundreds of thousands of settlers and immigrants flocked to the golden gates of San Francisco, California to try their luck in mining and/or entrepreneurship. Culturally speaking, cities like San Francisco quickly became hubs of diversity, serving as the homes of thousands of Chinese, Mexican, Black, and American Indian laborers. Socially, however, these diversities created racial tensions, leading to the persecution of "racial others" by white settlers. Wars ensued between US citizens and American Indians in the West, paving the way to the creation of more reservations. These racialized others were also exploited for railroad construction. Chinese immigrants eventually became demonized by white US politicians, leading to the passage of the xenophobic (i.e., prejudice against foreigners) exclusion acts in the late 19th century. For example, the Chinese Exclusion Act of 1882 is famous for embedding xenophobic sentiments into US law. Mexican nationals also struggled to find their place as anglicized politics and economics pushed them further to the socio-cultural margins. All residents—white and non-white—were affected by the boom-and-bust atmosphere of the gold rush. Very few residents became rich; many became broke in the staunchly capitalist tycoon environment.

The California Gold Rush stimulated a wave of migration and urban development that helped make California the epicenter of the concept of the American Dream. It helped make the Pacific Coast a nexus of economic development and (im)migrant activity. Today, California is still impacted by this cultural conception. Many people flock to cities such as San Diego, Los Angeles, and San Francisco in order to try to live out their perception of the American Dream.

Economic, Political, and Cultural Development Since the 1850's

Key Principles of The California Constitution

The California Constitution was first ratified on November 13, 1849 after convention members toiled for nearly a month to create and edit the document. One of the earliest debates of the first California constitutional convention was over the state line of demarcation—some convention members wanted the state of California to extend into the deserts surrounding the Salt Lake Basin; others wanted the state to use the crest of the Sierra Nevada mountain range as a boundary. Eventually, convention members decided to place the line of demarcation just east of the Sierra crest. Another crucial debate was over whether or not California would be admitted into the Union as a free or slave state. Following the infamous **Compromise of 1850**, convention members, influenced by the lobbying miners and gold rushers who were staunchly abolitionist, chose to make California a free state. On September 9, 1850, its statehood became official. The California Constitution of 1849, which pushed the region into statehood, was considered fundamental law in the region for nearly 30 years. After nearly 30 years as official law, the California Constitution was finally revised on September 28, 1879. The second constitutional convention included 152 convention delegates. Most delegates were either lawyers or farmers. Many delegates felt the pressure of labor demands in this era, focusing their efforts on the rise of violence and the exploitation of railroad companies. The Constitution of 1879 was also riddled with xenophobic sentiments, offering many anti-Asian clauses and condemning the act of Asiatic "coolieism" (i.e., contracted labor) as slavery. On the flip side, the Constitution of 1879 paved the way to the foundation of the University of California public university system. After 157 days of deliberation, the Constitution of 1879 was ratified as a cataloged code of laws. Since 1879, the California Constitution has been amended over 400 times. A lot of these amendments came during the Progressive Era of the early 20th century. Women did not receive suffrage, for example, until 1911, and many of the restraints on corporations did not fully come into effect until this Progressive Era. These Progressive politicians, however, still fueled Californians' xenophobia by reinforcing Asian exclusionary laws. These laws were not repealed until later decades.

Similarities and Differences Between the California Constitution and the U. S. Constitution

The California Constitution is built upon the same principles of liberty, justice, and equality as the US Constitution. However, the two constitutions differ in three major ways. First, the California Constitution limits state Supreme Court judges' terms to just 12 years; the US Constitution, on the other hand, appoints Supreme Court judges who serve for life. Second, the California Constitution does not allow the state to ratify treaties like the US Constitution allows the federal government to ratify treaties. In this sense, only the federal government has the power to resolve land disputes, violent conflicts, uprisings, and disagreements over resource allocations through treaties. The state of California cannot act as a sovereign state when it comes to such issues. For example, a treaty with local Native American groups would have to be carried out by the US government, under the auspices of the US Constitution. Third, the California Constitution requires a term limit for its congressional delegates, while the US Constitution does not. Members of the California State Assembly can only be elected only three times (for a total of six years). This provision was established in 1996. Members of the California State Senate can be elected for just two terms (for a total of eight years). This provision was established in 1998. They California Constitution and US Constitution are alike in one major way: they both restrict their executive leadership to two terms. The Governor of California and the President of the United States can only serve two terms (for a total of eight years).

Patterns of Immigration to California

Immigration has always been a key factor in the demographic growth and cultural diversity in California. This historical trend began in the mid-late 19th century with the gold rush years that brought hundreds of thousands of new immigrants to the Pacific Coast. Cultural hubs like San Francisco and Los Angeles played host to Irish, German, and Italian immigrants, leading to an impressive urban growth that reached well into the Progressive Era. Initially, thousands of Chinese and Southeast Asian immigrants flocked to the railroad industry through the Golden Gate of California, but this demographic shift eventually brought about cultural xenophobia and exclusionary politics. California witnessed even more growth during the era of the Dust Bowl and the Great Depression in the 1930s as hundreds of thousands of migrants from the Midwest and Great Plains made their way to the "Land of Milk and Honey."

These new migrants added to the diversity of California. World War II and the postwar era witnessed yet another immigrant surge, as thousands of Mexican farmers and laborers flocked to Southern California to escape Depression economics in favor for the rising prospects of the military industrial complex and agribusiness. The end of Asian exclusion and the opening of immigration channels via the Immigration Act of 1965 helped bring hundreds of thousands of Vietnamese, Korean, Japanese, Chinese, Filipino, and Pacific Islander immigrants to Los Angeles and San Francisco. This influx helped chip away at the Judeo-Christian Order, introducing East Asian religions to Californians. Latinos continue to add to the diverse fiber of the Golden State. As of 2010, Latinos make up nearly 40% of the state population. Today, many undocumented Latino immigrants flock to California for the refuge and protection of sanctuary cities such as San Francisco. This trend has catalyzed an era of divisive politics concerning undocumented immigration.

The Effects of Federal and State Law on the Legal Status of Immigrants

Both federal and state laws have both played a significant role in both excluding and integrating certain immigrant groups in US and California culture. Both the US Constitution and the California Constitution, for instance, have placed restrictions on the immigration of certain groups. Both have had a long history of anti-Asian xenophobia; both have declared Chinese exclusion as official law. Additionally, both have opened their gates to new immigrant groups, especially in the post-1960 era of American history. Today, nevertheless, a debate still wages on about "illegal immigration." To some degree, "illegal immigrants" are sometimes protected at the state and local levels in ways that they are not protected at the federal level. Likewise, state and local scare tactics, and extralegal responses, sometimes undermine federal policies regarding the human rights of undocumented immigrants. Proponents at all levels point to America's history of accepting the poor, the tired, and the hungry. Opponents at all levels claim that illegal immigration places a strain on public funds at the expense of tax-paying citizens. Laws concerning the legal status of immigrants have long been complicated and controversial in California, dating back to colonial times.

Historical and Contemporary Perspectives on Cultural Diversity

California has always been a diverse region of North America, beginning with its Native American roots. At one point in history, prior to Spanish colonization, over 300,000 Native Americans called the region home. Over 100 languages were spoken during the precolonial era. Some of these tribes still exist today, contributing to a whopping 115 remaining tribes. Nevertheless, while tribally different, this region remained ethnically similar until Spanish colonization in the 1400s and 1500s. European conquistadors, priests, ranchers, and proselytizers settled in the loosely ruled colony. By the 1700s, the Spanish made more concerted attempts to convert Native Americans to the Roman Catholic faith through the mission system. In this sense, the religious differences of the Native Americans were not tolerated. They were viewed as heathens unless they converted to the Catholic faith. The encomienda system also arose around this time, contributing to the classification of Native Americans as "the other" and their subsequent subjugation as free laborers. The Spanish influence over the land paved the way for a strong Hispanic culture that still exists to this day. Close to fifty percent of modern-day Californians are of Hispanic origin, though most are of Mexican heritage. That is because Mexico declared independence from Spain in 1821, and the region officially became part of the new Mexican Republic. *Californios* are families of Mexicans born in California between 1821 and 1848. After 1848, the region fell into hands of the United States of America, following the cessions of the Mexican-American War. Most Mexican families migrated to the region after the war. Even more have migrated in the 20th and 21st centuries. The Gold Rush of 1849 brought many immigrants to the region.

It also brought many Anglo-Americans. African-Americans also moved there in the 1840s as free people. An influx of Chinese Americans followed the initial gold rush, thanks in large part to the railroad boom. Nevertheless, relationships between Anglos and immigrants became vitriol in the late 1800s, leading to restrictions on immigration such as the Chinese Exclusion Act. This anti-immigrant sentiment is still sewn into the fabric of California culture, especially with the recent influx of Mexican, Latin American, and Asian immigrants in the 20th and 21st centuries. Following the US Immigration Act of 1965, California became one of the most diverse states in the entire US Today, California is the most populated and most diverse state. However, the citizens' sentiments about this diversity vacillates with time and transforms with culture/context. Some Californians openly embrace diversity, while others still try to fight against it.

The Development and Locations of California's Major Economic Activities

The motto for California is that there is "something for everyone." This is especially true when one thinks about the major economic activities of the state. Mining has long been a cornerstone of the California economy since the initial years of the California Gold Rush in the late 1840s. California's mining industry has annually called the Sierra Nevada mountain range and the surrounding deserts its home. Large-scale agricultural has blessed California's Central Valley, Southern California, and coastal California since the Dust Bowl migrations of the 1930s and the wartime boom of the 1940s. California's Mediterranean climate has made it an ideal location for fruit farms, vineyards, and the olive oil and tree nut industries. Recreation, as an economic industry, is scattered throughout the state, though Los Angeles, and particularly Hollywood and Disneyland, have always been beacons of American film and leisure. The motto that claim that "there is something for everyone" can also be seen in California's long history of success as a sports center. It plays host to various National Collegiate Athletic Association (NCAA) teams, major league teams, World Cup qualifying rounds, Pro Golfing Association (PGA) tours, boxing bouts, surfing events, and skateboarding events. California has even been the host of two Olympic Games. Throughout the Cold War 1980s, and even in contemporary times, California has also become well-known for its military-industrial complex and aerospace industry. Los Angeles and Silicon Valley have blossomed to become the epicenter of the global aerospace, electronics, and international trade industries. The entire Bay Area has skyrocketed its real estate prices due to this tech boom. Silicon Valley has become the home of many tech startups and industry giants (i.e., Apple and Microsoft). Places like San Francisco have now become major players in the Asian-Pacific trade economy that spans from Tokyo to the California coast.

California's Water Delivery System, and Its Relationship to California Geography

Development, migration, and civilization in California would not be made possible without the complex California water delivery system that has been built throughout the 20th and 21st centuries. After a series of bills and multi-state compacts were passed by the federal government and the western states of the US in the early 20th century, California began an impressive, multi-decade initiative with dam and canal construction. One of the crown jewels of this initiative was the creation of Hoover Dam, located in Boulder Canyon of the Colorado River system. The result was the creation of Lake Mead, a 242-mile-long artificial lake that serves as an aquatic hub for the corridor between modern Las Vegas and Los Angeles. Other dams, canals, and aqueducts followed, especially as a result of the California agricultural boom brought on by the Dust Bowl era of American history. Even today, California's farmers continue to soak up about 80% of the state's water delivery system. The system continues to sustain arid and semi-arid regions, as well as lush valleys. The delivery system has placed a strain not only on California's water resources, but also its entire geographic environment. Urban sprawl has contributed to droughts and subsequent wildfires. The system has carved the natural environment with concrete and metal, ingraining an artificial character onto the land. Today, conservationists are trying to stave off the destruction wrought by society and its insatiable thirst for water and resources in California.

Practice Quiz

1. Which event led to the first large migration of Anglo-American settlers to California?
    a. The Dust Bowl
    b. The Gold Rush
    c. The Mexican-American War
    d. The US Immigration Act of 1965

2. What is the name for Mexican families who settled in California between 1821 (the Mexican Revolution) and 1848 (US Annexation)?
    a. *Encomenderos*
    b. *Californios*
    c. *Hispanos*
    d. Conquistadors

3. Which colonial policy led to the direct subjugation of Native Americans in California via forced labor?
    a. The mission system
    b. The encomienda system
    c. The *Reconquista*
    d. The *ranchos*

4. What region of the globe can be designated as the original hub of Islamic Empire?
    a. North Africa
    b. Indian Subcontinent
    c. Western Europe (Spain)
    d. Arabian Peninsula.

5. Which inventor helped inspire the Rhode Island system of textile production?
    a. Samuel Slater
    b. Francis Cabot Lowell
    c. Robert Fulton
    d. James K. Polk

See answers on the next page.

Answer Explanations

1. B: The Gold Rush. Choice *A* is wrong because the Dust Bowl brought Anglo-American migrants to California in the 1930s, but that occurred almost 100 years after the initial migration of the Gold Rush in 1849. Choice *C,* the Mexican-American War, ceded the California territory to the United States in 1848, but Anglo-American migration was stimulated mostly by the Gold Rush of the following year. Choice *D,* the US Immigration Act of 1965 diversified California's population, adding more Asian and South American immigrants.

2. B: The Mexican families who settled California between 1821 and 1848 became known as *Californios.* *Encomenderos* is not correct because it is the name of grant recipients during the encomienda system of Spanish colonization in the region. *Hispanos* is simply as Spanish word for ALL Spanish-speaking residents. *Conquistadors* is the name given to the Spanish "conquerors" who initially colonized the region.

3. B: The encomienda forced many Native American groups into slavery. Choice *A,* the mission system, tried to convert Native Americans, but it did not directly enslave them. The *Reconquista,* choice *C,* is the name given for the Spanish "re-conquest" of the Iberian Peninsula in the 700s. Choice *D, ranchos,* is a Spanish word for ranches, which sprouted up as part of the economic system in colonial California.

4. D: The Prophet Mohammed had a revelation on the Arabian Peninsula, making him the founder and leader of the first Muslim empire, which quickly conquered the entire region. Islam did eventually expand to North Africa, the Indian Subcontinent, and Western Europe, but the original hub of the empire began on the Arabian Peninsula.

5. A: Sam Slater's mills inspired the invention of new cotton threads. Located in Pawtucket, Rhode Island, these mills created an entirely new system of work known as the Rhode Island system. Slater's system hired entire families, and made industry the epicenter of the town. Company recruiters targeted slums and poor farming communities, encouraging poor families to relocate in mill towns. Francis Cabot Lowell set up the Lowell system, which focused on hiring unmarried women. Robert Fulton invented the steam engine. James K. Polk was the US president who led Americans into the Mexican-American War.

Subtest II: Science

Physical Sciences

Structure and Properties of Matter

Physical Properties of Solids, Liquids, and Gases

The universe is composed completely of matter. **Matter** is any material or object that takes up space and has a mass. Although there is an endless variety of items found in the universe, there are only about one hundred elements, or individual substances, that make up all matter. These elements are different types of atoms and are the smallest units that anything can be broken down into while still retaining the properties of the original substance. Matter can be found in three different states: gas, liquid, or solid.

Gases

Gases have three main distinct properties. The first is that they are easy to compress. When a gas is compressed, the space between the molecules decreases, and the frequency of collisions between them increases. The second property is that they do not have a fixed volume or shape. They expand to fill large containers or compress down to fit into smaller containers. When they are in large containers, the gas molecules can float around at high speeds and collide with each other, which allows them to fill the entire container uniformly. Therefore, the volume of a gas is generally equal to the volume of its container.

The third distinct property of a gas is that it occupies more space than the liquid or solid from which it was formed. One gram of solid CO_2, also known as *dry ice,* has a volume of 0.641 milliliters. The same amount of CO_2 in a gaseous state has a volume of 556 milliliters. Steam engines use water in this capacity to do work. When water boils inside the steam engine, it becomes steam, or water vapor. As the steam increases in volume and escapes its container, it is used to make the engine run.

Liquids

A **liquid** is an intermediate state between gases and solids. It has an exact volume due to the attraction of its molecules to each other and molds to the shape of the part of the container that it is in. Although liquid molecules are closer together than gas molecules, they still move quickly within the container they are in. Liquids cannot be compressed, but their molecules slide over each other easily when poured out of a container. The attraction between liquid molecules, known as **cohesion**, also causes liquids to have surface tension. They stick together and form a thin skin of particles with an extra strong bond between them. As long as these bonds remain undisturbed, the surface becomes quite strong and can even support the weight of an insect such as a water skipper. Another property of liquids is **adhesion**, which is when different types of particles are attracted to each other. When liquids are in a container, they are drawn up above the surface level of the liquid around the edges. The liquid molecules that are in contact with the container are pulled up by their extra attraction to the particles of the container.

Solids

Unlike gases and liquids, **solids** have a definitive shape. They are similar to liquids in that they also have a definitive volume and cannot be compressed. The molecules are packed together tightly, which does not allow for movement within the substance. There are two types of solids: crystalline and amorphous. **Crystalline solids** have atoms or molecules arranged in a specific order or symmetrical pattern throughout the entire solid. This symmetry makes all of the bonds within the crystal of equal strength, and when they are broken apart, the pieces have straight edges. Minerals are all crystalline solids. **Amorphous solids**, on the other hand, do not have repeating structures or symmetry. Their components are heterogeneous, so they often melt gradually over a range of temperatures. They do not break evenly and often have curved edges. Examples of amorphous solids are glass, rubber, and most plastics.

Physical and Chemical Changes of Matter

Matter can change between a gas, liquid, and solid. When these changes occur, the change is physical and does not affect the chemical properties or makeup of the substance. Environmental changes, such as temperature or pressure changes, can cause one state of matter to convert to another state of matter. For example, in very hot temperatures, solids can melt and become a liquid, such as when ice melts into liquid water, or sublimate and become a gas, such as when dry ice becomes gaseous carbon dioxide. Liquids can evaporate and become a gas, such as when liquid water turns into water vapor. In very cold temperatures, gases can depose and become a solid, such as when water vapor becomes icy frost on a windshield, or condense and become a liquid, such as when water vapor becomes dew on grass. Liquids can freeze and become a solid, such as when liquid water freezes and becomes ice.

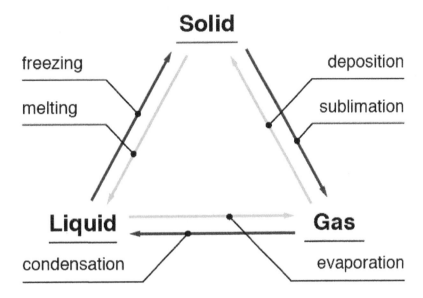

A **chemical reaction** is a process that involves a change in the molecular arrangement of a substance. Generally, one set of chemical substances, called the reactants, is rearranged into a different set of chemical substances, called the products, by the breaking and re-forming of bonds between atoms. In a chemical reaction, it is important to realize that no new atoms or molecules are introduced. The products are formed solely from the atoms and molecules that are present in the reactants. These can involve a change in state of matter as well. Making glass, burning fuel, and brewing beer are all examples of chemical reactions.

Generally, chemical reactions are thought to involve changes in positions of electrons with the breaking and re-forming of chemical bonds, without changes to the nucleus of the atoms. The three main types of chemical reactions are combination, decomposition, and combustion.

Conservations Laws

The law of conservation of mass maintains that the total mass for a chemical reaction will remain constant. In a chemical reaction, the reactant mass will be identical to the newly formed products. For example, mercury reacts with oxygen to form mercury (II) oxide. The sum of the mass of mercury and oxygen will be equal to the mass of mercury (II) oxide.

The law of conservation of energy, or the first law of thermodynamics, describes how when specific energy is converted from one type to another, the total amount of energy will stay the same. For example, a ball placed on top of a building has a specific amount of potential energy. When the ball falls off the building, its potential energy is converted to kinetic energy; the total amount of energy is conserved. The total energy of a chemical system is the sum of its potential, kinetic, and internal energy.

Atoms and Parts of an Atom

Atoms are the smallest units of all matter and make up all chemical elements. They each have three parts: protons, neutrons, and electrons. **Protons** are found in the nucleus of an atom and have a positive electric charge. They have a mass of about one atomic mass unit. The number of protons in an element is referred to as the element's **atomic number**. Each element has a unique number of protons, and therefore a unique atomic number. **Neutrons** are also found in the nucleus of atoms. These subatomic particles have a neutral charge, meaning that they do not have a positive or negative electric charge. Their mass is slightly larger than that of a proton.

Together with protons, they are referred to as the **nucleons** of an atom. The **atomic mass** number of an atom is equal to the sum of the protons and neutrons in the atom. **Electrons** have a negative charge and are the smallest of the subatomic particles. They are located outside the nucleus in **orbitals,** which are shells that surround the nucleus. If an atom has an overall neutral charge, it has an equal number of electrons and protons. If it has more protons than electrons or vice versa, it becomes an **ion.** When there are more protons than electrons, the atom is a positively charged ion, or **cation.** When there are more electrons than protons, the atom is a negatively charged ion, or **anion.**

The location of electrons within an atom is more complicated than the locations of protons and neutrons. Within the orbitals, electrons are always moving. They can spin very fast and move upward, downward, and sideways. There are many different levels of orbitals around the atomic nucleus, and each orbital has a different capacity for electrons. The electrons in the orbitals closest to the nucleus are more tightly bound to the nucleus of the atom. There are three main characteristics that describe each orbital. The first is the **principle quantum number**, which describes the size of the orbital. The second is the **angular momentum quantum number**, which describes the shape of the orbital. The third is the **magnetic quantum number,** which describes the orientation of the orbital in space.

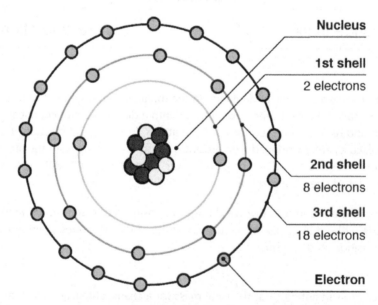

Another important characteristic of electrons is their ability to form covalent bonds with other atoms to form molecules. A **covalent bond** is a chemical bond that forms when two atoms share the same pair or pairs of electrons. There is a stable balance of attraction and repulsion between the two atoms. There are several types of covalent bonds. **Sigma bonds** are the strongest type of covalent bond and involve the head-on overlapping of electron orbitals from two different atoms. **Pi bonds** are a little weaker and involve the lateral overlapping of certain orbitals. While single bonds between atoms, such as between carbon and hydrogen, are generally sigma bonds, double bonds, such as when carbon is double bonded to an oxygen atom, are usually formed from one sigma bond and one pi bond.

130

Constituents of Molecules and Compounds

Different elements can link together to form compounds, or molecules. Hydrogen and oxygen are two examples of elements, and when they bond together, they form water molecules.

There are six major elements found in most biological molecules: carbon, hydrogen, oxygen, nitrogen, sulfur, and phosphorus. These elements link together to make up the basic macromolecules of the biological system, which are lipids, carbohydrates, nucleic acids, and proteins.

Naming Common Elements

Elements are the smallest components of matter. Every material item, both organic and inorganic substances, is made up of one or more elements. Organic substances are those that are found in living organisms; they must contain both the carbon and hydrogen elements to be considered an organic substance. Many organic substances also include the elements oxygen (O) and nitrogen (N). Organic substances are found in the air that living organisms breathe, in the macronutrients that organisms consume, and in the individual cells of an organism. Inorganic substances are those that are found in non-living materials, such as metals or salts. Common inorganic substances that are found on Earth include table salt (sodium chloride, or NaCl), precious metals, and gemstones. A number of inorganic substances are critical to human life, such as water (H_2O). Inorganic elements commonly found on Earth include oxygen (in the atmosphere), sodium (Na), chlorine (Cl), silicon (S), aluminum (Al, the most abundant metal), iron (Fe), calcium (Ca), potassium (K), and magnesium (Mg). These are found in the earth's atmosphere and crust. Some inorganic substances can contain hydrogen (such as water) or carbon (such as a diamond), but they will not contain both bonded together.

The field of chemistry utilizes basic naming conventions to name compounds. Binary compounds, or those compounds consisting of two elements only, include adding the suffix "-ide" to the second element. For example, table salt (NaCl) is comprised of sodium and chlorine, so it is named sodium chloride. Other compounds are named based on the number of atoms found per element, using the Latin prefix for the number. For example, carbon monoxide (CO) has one carbon atom and one oxygen atom. Carbon dioxide (CO_2), however, has one carbon atom and two oxygen atoms, as noted by the "di-" at the beginning of the second word. Since oxygen is the second element, it also follows the basic naming convention of ending in "-ide". Finally, if a compound is a mixture of metal and non-metal substances, the metal is named first.

Periodic Table

Today's primary model of the atom was proposed by scientist Niels Bohr. Bohr's atomic model consists of a nucleus, or core, which is made up of positively charged protons and neutrally charged neutrons. Neutrons are theorized to be in the nucleus with the protons to provide "balance" and stability to the protons at the center of the atom. More than 99 percent of the mass of an atom is found in the nucleus. Orbitals surrounding the nucleus contain negatively charged particles called electrons. Since the entire structure of an atom is too small to be seen with the unaided eye, an electron microscope is required for detection. Even with such magnification, the actual particles of the atom are not visible.

An atom has an atomic number that is determined by the number of protons within the nucleus. Some substances are made up of atoms, all with the same atomic number. Such a substance is called an **element.** Using their atomic numbers, elements are organized and grouped by similar properties in a chart called the **Periodic Table**.

The sum of the total number of protons and total number of neutrons in an atom provides the atom's mass number. Most atoms have a nucleus that is electronically neutral, and all atoms of one type have the same atomic number. There are some atoms of the same type that have a different mass number. The variation in the mass number is due to an imbalance of neutrons within the nucleus of the atoms. If atoms have this variance in neutrons, they are called **isotopes.** It is the different number of neutrons that gives such atoms a different mass number.

A concise method of arranging elements by atomic number, similar characteristics, and electron configurations in a tabular format was necessary to represent elements. This was originally organized by scientist Dmitri Mendeleev using the Periodic Table. The vertical columns on the Periodic Table are called **groups** and are sorted by similar chemical properties/characteristics, such as appearance and reactivity. This is observed in the shiny texture of metals, the softness of post-transition metals, and the high melting points of alkali earth metals. The horizontal rows on the Periodic Table are called **periods** and are arranged by electron valance configurations.

Elements are set by ascending atomic number, from left to right. The number of protons contained within the nucleus of the atom is represented by the atomic number. For example, hydrogen has one proton in its nucleus, so it has an atomic number of 1.

Since isotopes can have different masses within the same type of element, the **atomic mass** of an element is the average mass of all the naturally occurring atoms of that given element. Atomic mass is calculated by finding the relative abundance of isotopes that might be used in chemistry. A different number referred to as the mass number is found by adding the number of protons and neutrons of an atom together. For example, the mass number of one typical chlorine atom is 35: the nucleus has 17 protons (given by chlorine's atomic number of 17) and 18 neutrons. However, a large number of chlorine isotopes with a mass number of 37 exist in nature. These isotopes have 20 neutrons instead of 18 neutrons. The average of all the mass numbers turns out to be 35.5 amu, which is chlorine's atomic mass on the periodic table. In contrast, a typical carbon atom has a mass number of 12, and its atomic mass is 12.01 amu because there are not as many naturally occurring isotopes that raise the average number, as observed with chlorine.

The Periodic Table of the Elements

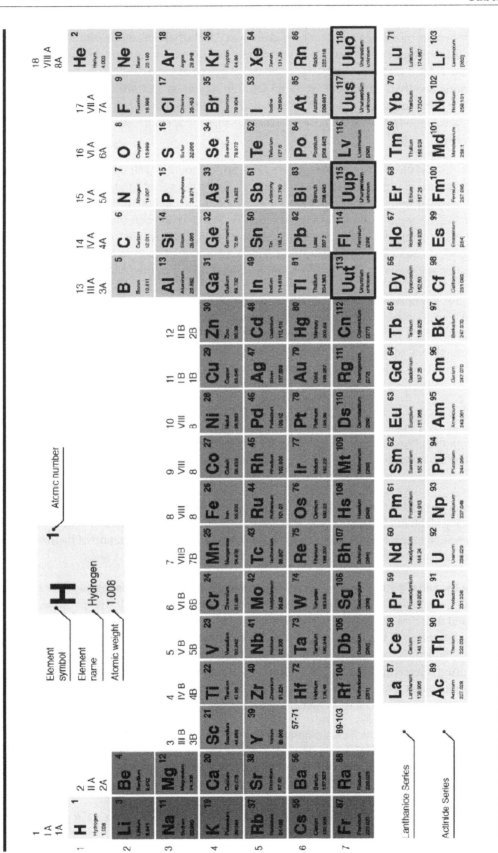

Characteristics of Solutions

A **solution** is a homogenous mixture of two or more substances. Unlike heterogenous mixtures, in solutions, the **solute**, which is a substance that can be dissolved, is uniformly distributed throughout the **solvent**, which is the substance in which the solvent dissolves. For example, when 10 grams of table salt (NaCl) is added to 100 milliliters of room temperature water and then stirred until all of the salt (the solute) has dissolved in the water (the solvent), a solution is formed. The dissolved salt, in the form of Na^+ and Cl^- ions, will be evenly distributed throughout the water. In this case, the solution is **diluted** because only a small amount of solute was dissolved in a comparatively large volume of solvent.

The saltwater solution would be said to be **concentrated** if a large amount of salt was added, stirred, and dissolved into the water, 30 grams, for example. When more solute is added to the solvent but even after stirring, some settles on the bottom without dissolving, the solution is **saturated**. For example, in 100 milliliters of room temperature water, about 35 grams of table salt can dissolve before the solution is saturated. Beyond this point—called the saturation point—any additional salt added will not readily dissolve. Sometimes, it is possible to temporarily dissolve excessive solute in the solvent, which creates a **supersaturated** solution. However, as soon as this solution is disturbed, the process of crystallization will begin and a solid will begin precipitating out of the solution.

It is often necessary, for example when working with chemicals or mixing acids and bases, to quantitatively determine the concentration of a solution, which is a more precise measure than using qualitative terms like diluted, concentrated, saturated, and supersaturated. The **molarity**, c, of a solution is a measure of its concentration; specifically, it is the number of moles of solute (represented by n in the formula) per liter of solution (V). Therefore, the following is the formula for calculating the molarity of a solution:

$$c = \frac{n}{V}$$

It is important to remember that the volume in the denominator of the equation above is in liters of solution, not solvent. Adding solute increases the volume of the entire solution, so the molarity formula accounts for this volumetric increase.

If something has a sour taste, it is considered acidic, and if something has a bitter taste, it is considered basic. Acids and bases are generally identified by the reaction they have when combined with water. An acid will increase the concentration of hydrogen ions (H^+) in water, and a base will increase the concentration of hydroxide ions (OH^-). Other methods of identification with various indicators have been designed over the years.

To better categorize the varying strength levels of acids and bases, the pH scale is employed. The pH scale is a logarithmic (base 10) grading applied to acids and bases according to their strength. The pH scale contains values from 0 through 14 and uses 7 as neutral. If a solution registers below a 7 on the pH scale, it is considered an acid. If a solution registers higher than a 7, it is considered a base. To perform a quick test on a solution, litmus paper can be used. A base will turn red litmus paper blue, and an acid will turn blue litmus paper red. To gauge the strength of an acid or base, a test using phenolphthalein can be administered. An acid will turn red phenolphthalein to colorless, and a base will turn colorless phenolphthalein to pink. As demonstrated with these types of tests, acids and bases neutralize each other. When acids and bases react with one another, they produce salts (also called **ionic substances**).

Acids and bases have varying strengths. For example, if an acid completely dissolves in water and ionizes, forming an H^+ and an anion, it is considered a strong acid. There are only a few common strong acids, including sulfuric (H_2SO_4), hydrochloric (HCl), nitric (HNO_3), hydrobromic (HBr), hydroiodic (HI), and perchloric ($HClO_4$). Other types of acids are considered weak.

An easy way to tell if something is an acid is by looking for the leading "H" in the chemical formula.

134

A base is considered strong if it completely dissociates into the cation of OH^-, including sodium hydroxide (NaOH), potassium hydroxide (KOH), lithium hydroxide (LiOH), cesium hydroxide (CsOH), rubidium hydroxide (RbOH), barium hydroxide ($Ba(OH)_2$), calcium hydroxide ($Ca(OH)_2$), and strontium hydroxide ($Sr(OH)_2$). Just as with acids, other types of bases are considered weak. An easy way to tell if something is a base is by looking for the "OH" ending on the chemical formula.

In pure water, autoionization occurs when a water molecule (H_2O) loses the nucleus of one of the two hydrogen atoms to become a hydroxide ion (OH^-). The nucleus then pairs with another water molecule to form hydronium (H_3O^+). This autoionization process shows that water is **amphoteric**, which means it can react as an acid or as a base.

Pure water is considered neutral, but the presence of any impurities can throw off this neutral balance, causing the water to be slightly acidic or basic. This can include the exposure of water to air, which can introduce carbon dioxide molecules to form carbonic acid (H_2CO_3), thus making the water slightly acidic. Any variation from the middle of the pH scale (7) indicates a non-neutral substance.

Separation of Mixtures

A **mixture** is created by combining two or more substances; however, each substance does not change its properties. Therefore, mixtures retain the ability to separate back to the individual substances that make it up. Mixtures can be separated through four primary mechanisms: chromatography, filtration, evaporation, and distillation. **Chromatography** is the process of moving a mixture through a solution in which each individual substance will respond differently. Typically, a liquid mixture will be moved across a stationary object (usually a solid) that causes each individual substance to adhere at a different rate. This difference in rate adherence separates the mixtures. Gas mixtures can also go through a chromatography process in which vaporization is used to separate the mixture by the masses of its individual parts. Filtration removes solid particles from a liquid or gas through a filter that only allows the liquid or gas through (such as in a water pitcher with a built-in filter). Evaporation focuses on removing solid particles from a liquid medium by boiling off the liquid so that only the solid particles remain (such as when reducing a sweet liquid into a thick syrup on a stovetop). Distillation is a type of purification mechanism in which a liquid is boiled and then condensed one or more times. It is commonly used in purifying liquids, such as water and hard alcohol, for drinking. Distillation can be simple or fractional. Simple distillation is a faster technique that works best for liquids that are mostly pure, and in which the individual substances have relatively small boiling point differences. For mixtures that have multiple substances that are similar in boiling point and other chemical properties, fractional distillation is used. This method distills the mixture through a fractional column. This process is commonly seen when refining crude oil into a usable energy source.

Principles of Motion and Energy

Object's Motion

On Earth, items move according to guidelines and have motion that is fairly predictable. To understand why an object moves along its path, it is important to understand what role forces have on influencing its movements. The term **force** describes an outside influence on an object. Force does not have to refer to something imparted by another object. Forces can act upon objects by touching them with a push or a pull, by friction, or without touch like a magnetic force or even gravity. Forces can affect the motion of an object.

To study an object's motion, it must be located and described. When locating an object's position, it can help to pinpoint its location relative to another known object. Comparing an object with respect to a known object is referred to as establishing a frame of reference. If the placement of one object is known, it is easier to locate another object with respect to the position of the original object.

Motion can be described by following specific guidelines called *kinematics*. Kinematics use mechanics to describe motion without regard to the forces that are causing such motions. Specific equations can be used when describing motions; these equations use time as a frame of reference. The equations are based on the change of an object's position (represented by x), over a change in time (represented by Δt). This describes an object's velocity, which is measured in meters/second (m/s) and described by the following equation:

$$v = \frac{\Delta x}{\Delta t} = \frac{x_f - x_i}{\Delta t}$$

Velocity is a vector quantity, meaning it measures the magnitude (how much) and the direction that the object is moving. Both of these components are essential to understanding and predicting the motion of objects. Velocity measures the change in position, or **displacement**, which is the shortest line between the starting point and ending point. The scientist Isaac Newton did extensive studies on the motion of objects on Earth and came up with three primary laws to describe motion:

Law 1: An object in motion tends to stay in motion unless acted upon by an outside force. An object at rest tends to stay at rest unless acted upon by an outside force (also known as the *law of inertia*).

For example, if a book is placed on a table, it will stay there until it is moved by an outside force.

Law 2: The force acting upon an object is equal to the object's mass multiplied by its acceleration (also known as $F = ma$).

For example, the amount of force acting on a bug being swatted by a flyswatter can be calculated if the mass of the flyswatter and its acceleration are known. If the mass of the flyswatter is 0.3 kg and the acceleration of its swing is 2.0 m/s^2, the force of its swing can be calculated as follows:

$$m = 0.3 \text{ kg}$$

$$a = 2.0 \text{ m/s}^2$$

$$F = m \times a$$

$$F = (0.3) \times (2.0)$$

$$F = 0.6 \text{ N}$$

Law 3: For every action, there is an equal and opposite reaction.

For example, when a person claps their hands together, the right hand feels the same force as the left hand, as the force is equal and opposite.

Another example is if a car and a truck run head-on into each other, the force experienced by the truck is equal and opposite to the force experienced by the car, regardless of their respective masses or velocities. The ability to withstand this amount of force is what varies between the vehicles and creates a difference in the amount of damage sustained.

Newton used these laws to describe motion and derive additional equations for motion that could predict the position, velocity, acceleration, or time for objects in motion in one and two dimensions. Since all of Newton's work was done on Earth, he primarily used Earth's gravity and the behavior of falling objects to design experiments and studies in free fall (an object subject to Earth's gravity while in flight). On Earth, the acceleration due to the force of gravity is measured at 9.8 meters per second^2 (m/s^2). This value is the same for anything on the Earth or within Earth's atmosphere.

Acceleration

Acceleration is the change in velocity over the change in time. It is given by the following equation:

$$a = \frac{\Delta v}{\Delta t} = \frac{v_f - v_i}{\Delta t}$$

Since velocity is the change in position (displacement) over a change in time, it is necessary for calculating an acceleration. Both of these are vector quantities, meaning they have magnitude and direction (or some amount in some direction). Acceleration is measured in units of distance over time squared (meters/second^2 or m/s^2 in metric units).

For example, what is the acceleration of a vehicle that has an initial velocity of 35 m/s and a final velocity of 10 m/s over 5.0 s?

Using the givens and the equation:

$$a = \frac{\Delta v}{\Delta t} = \frac{v_f - v_i}{\Delta t}$$

$$V_f = 10 \text{ m/s}$$

$$V_i = 35 \text{ m/s}$$

$$\Delta t = 5.0 \text{ s}$$

$$a = \frac{10 - 35}{5.0} = \frac{-25}{5.0} = -5.0 \text{ m/s}^2$$

The vehicle is decelerating at -5.0 m/s^2.

If an object is moving with a constant velocity, its velocity does not change over time. Therefore, it has no (or 0) acceleration.

How Forces Act on Objects

Newton's laws of motion describe the relationship between an object and the forces acting upon that object, and its movement responding to those forces. Although previously explained, it's helpful to again summarize **Newton's three laws of motion**:

Law of Inertia: An object at rest stays at rest and an object in motion stays in motion unless otherwise acted upon by an outside force. For example, gravity is an outside force that will affect the speed and direction of a ball; when we throw a ball, the ball will eventually decrease in speed and fall to the ground because of the outside force of gravity. However, if the ball were kicked in space where there is no gravity, the ball would go the same speed and direction forever unless it hits another object in space or falls into another gravity field.

$F = ma$: This law states that the heavier an object, the more force required to move it. This force has to do with acceleration. For example, if you use the same amount of force to push both a golf cart and an eighteen-wheeler, the golf cart will have more acceleration than the truck because the eighteen-wheeler weighs more than the golf cart.

Law of reactions: This law states that for every action, there is an opposite and equal reaction. For example, if you are jumping on a trampoline, you are experiencing Newton's third law of motion. When a book is slammed down on a table, the table pushes back up on the book with a force of equal magnitude but in the opposite direction.

As previously stated, forces act upon objects on the Earth. If an object is resting on a surface, the effect of gravity acting upon its mass produces a force referred to as *weight*. This weight touches the surface it is resting on, and the

137

surface produces a normal force perpendicular to this surface. If an outside force acts upon this object, its movement will be resisted by the surfaces rubbing on each other.

Friction is the term used to describe the force that opposes motion, or the force experienced when two surfaces interact with each other. Every surface has a specific amount with which it resists motion, called a **coefficient of friction**. The coefficient of friction is a proportion calculated from the force of friction divided by the normal force (force produced perpendicular to a surface).

$$\mu_s = \frac{F_s}{F_N}$$

There are different types of friction between surfaces. If something is at rest, it has a static (non-moving) friction. It requires an outside force to begin its movement. The coefficient of static friction for that material multiplied by the normal force would need to be greater than the force of static friction to get the object moving. Therefore, the force required to move an object must be greater than the force of static friction:

$$F_s \leq \mu_s \times F_N$$

Once the object is in motion, the force required to maintain this movement only needs to be equivalent to the value of the force of kinetic (moving) friction. To calculate the force of kinetic friction, simply multiply the coefficient of kinetic friction for that surface by the normal force:

$$F_k = \mu_k \times F_N$$

The force required to start an object in motion is larger than the force required to continue its motion once it has begun:

$$F_s \geq F_k$$

Friction not only occurs between solid surfaces; it also occurs in air and liquids. In air, it is called air resistance, or drag, and in water, it is called viscosity.

For example, what would the coefficient of static friction be if a 5.0 N force was applied to push a 20 kg crate, from rest, across a flat floor?

First, the normal force could be found to counter the force from the weight of the object, which would be the mass multiplied by gravity:

$$F_N = mass \times gravity$$

$$F_N = 20 \text{ kg} \times 9.8 \frac{\text{m}}{\text{s}^2}$$

$$F_N = 196 \text{ N}$$

Next, the coefficient of static friction could be found by dividing the frictional force by the normal force:

$$\mu_s = \frac{F_s}{F_N}$$

$$\mu_s = \frac{5.0 \text{ N}}{196 \text{ N}}$$

$$\mu_s = 0.03$$

138

Since it is a coefficient, the units cancel out, so the solution is unitless. The coefficient of static friction should also be less than 1.0.

Repulsive and Attractive Forces

Magnetic forces occur naturally in specific types of materials and can be imparted to other types of materials. If two straight iron rods are observed, they will naturally have a negative end (pole) and a positive end (pole). These charged poles follow the rules of any charged item: Opposite charges attract, and like charges repel. When set up positive to negative, they will attract each other, but if one rod is turned around, the two rods will repel each other due to the alignment of negative-to-negative poles and positive-to-positive poles. When poles are identified, magnetic fields are observed between them. If small iron filings (a material with natural magnetic properties) are sprinkled over a sheet of paper resting on top of a bar magnet, the field lines from the poles can be seen in the alignment of the iron filings, as pictured below:

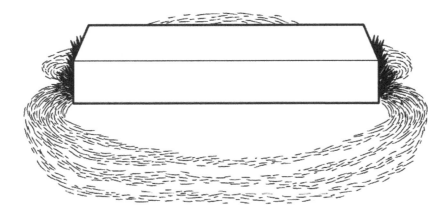

These fields naturally occur in materials with magnetic properties. There is a distinct pole at each end of such a material. If materials are not shaped with definitive ends, the fields will still be observed through the alignment of poles in the material.

For example, a circular magnet does not have ends but still has a magnetic field associated with its shape, as pictured below:

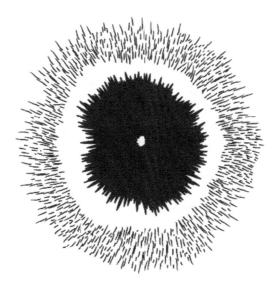

Magnetic forces can also be generated and amplified by using an electric current. For example, if an electric current is sent through a length of wire, it creates an electromagnetic field around the wire from the charge of the current. This force is from the movement of negatively charged electrons from one end of the wire to the other. This is maintained as long as the flow of electricity is sustained. The magnetic field can also be used to attract and repel other items with magnetic properties. A smaller or larger magnetic force can be generated around this wire, depending on the strength of the current in the wire. As soon as the current is stopped, the magnetic force also stops.

Magnetic energy can be harnessed, or manipulated, from natural sources or from a generated source (a wire carrying electric current). When a core with magnetic properties (such as iron) has a wire wrapped around it in circular coils, it can be used to create a strong, non-permanent electromagnet. If current is run through the wrapped wire, it generates a magnetic field by polarizing the ends of the metal core, as described above, by moving the negative charge from one end to the other. If the direction of the current is reversed, so is the direction of the magnetic field due to the poles of the core being reversed. The term **non-permanent** refers to the fact that the magnetic field is generated only when the current is present, but not when the current is stopped.

The following is a picture of a small electromagnet made from an iron nail, a wire, and a battery:

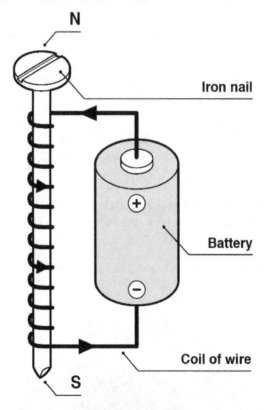

This type of **electromagnetic field** can be generated on a larger scale using more sizable components. This type of device is useful in the way it can be controlled. Rather than having to attempt to block a permanent magnetic field, the current to the system can simply be stopped, thus stopping the magnetic field. This provides the basis for many computer-related instruments and magnetic resonance imaging (MRI) technology. Magnetic forces are used in many modern applications, including the creation of super-speed transportation. Super magnets are used in rail systems and supply a cleaner form of energy than coal or gasoline.

Another example of the use of super-magnets is seen in medical equipment, specifically MRI. These machines are highly sophisticated and useful in imaging the internal workings of the human body. For super-magnets to be useful, they often must be cooled down to extremely low temperatures to dissipate the amount of heat generated from their extended usage. This can be done by flooding the magnet with a super-cooled gas such as helium or liquid nitrogen.

Much research is continuously done in this field to find new ceramic–metallic hybrid materials that have structures that can maintain their charge and temperature within specific guidelines for extended use.

Simple Machines

There are six basic machines that utilize the transfer of energy to the advantage of the user. These machines function based on an amount of energy input from the user and accomplish a task by distributing the energy for a common purpose. These machines are called **simple machines** and include the lever, pulley, wedge, inclined plane, screw, and wheel and axle.

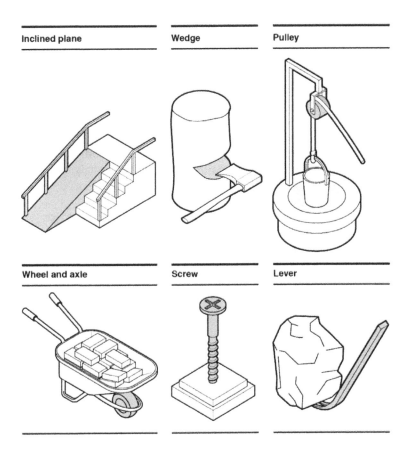

| Inclined plane | Wedge | Pulley |
| Wheel and axle | Screw | Lever |

The use of simple machines can help by requiring less force to perform a task with the same result. This is referred to as a **mechanical advantage**.

For example, if a father is trying to lift his child into the air with his arms to pick an apple from a tree, it would require less force to place the child on one end of a teeter totter and push the other end of the teeter totter down to elevate the child to the same height to pick the apple. In this example, the teeter totter is a lever.

Forms of Energy

An **electric current** is produced when electrons carry charge across a length. To make electrons move so they can carry this charge, a change in voltage must be present. On a small scale, this is demonstrated through the electrons traveling from the light switch to a person's finger in the example where the person had run their socks on a carpet. The difference between the charge in the switch and the charge in the finger causes the electrons to move. On a larger and more sustained scale, this movement would need to be more controlled. This can be achieved through batteries/cells and generators. Batteries or cells have a chemical reaction that takes place inside, causing energy to be released and charges to move freely. Generators convert mechanical energy into electric energy for use after the reaction.

For example, if a wire runs touching the end of a battery to the end of a lightbulb, and then another wire runs touching the base of the lightbulb to the opposite end of the original battery, the lightbulb will light up. This is due to a complete circuit being formed with the battery and the electrons being carried across the voltage drop (the two ends of the battery). The appearance of the light from the bulb is the visible presence of the electrons in the filament of the bulb.

Electric energy can be derived from a number of sources, including coal, wind, sun, and nuclear reactions. Electricity has numerous applications, including being transferable into light, sound, heat, or magnetic forces.

Total Energy in a System

There are two main types of energy. The first type is called **potential energy** (or gravitational potential energy), and it is stored energy, or energy due to an object's height from the ground.

The second type is called **kinetic energy**. Kinetic energy is the energy of motion. If an object is moving, it will have some amount of kinetic energy.

For example, if a roller-coaster car is sitting on the track at the top of a hill, it would have all potential energy and no kinetic energy. As the roller coaster travels down the hill, the energy converts from potential energy into kinetic energy. At the bottom of the hill, where the car is traveling the fastest, it would have all kinetic energy and no potential energy.

Another measure of energy is the total mechanical energy in a system. This is the sum (or total) of the potential energy plus the kinetic energy of the system. The total mechanical energy in a system is always conserved. The amounts of the potential energy and kinetic energy in a system can vary, but the total mechanical energy in a situation would remain the same.

The equation for the mechanical energy in a system is as follows:

$$ME = PE + KE$$

$$(Mechanical\ Energy\ =\ Potential\ Energy\ +\ Kinetic\ Energy)$$

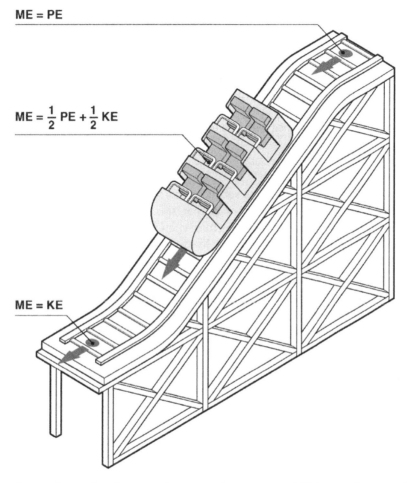

Energy can transfer or change forms, but it cannot be created or destroyed. This transfer can take place through waves (including light waves and sound waves), heat, impact, etc.

There is a fundamental law of thermodynamics (the study of heat and movement) called **conservation of energy**. This law states that energy cannot be created or destroyed, but rather energy is transferred to different forms involved in a process. For instance, a car pushed beginning at one end of a street will not continue down that street forever; it will gradually come to a stop some distance away from where it was originally pushed. This does not mean the energy has disappeared or has been exhausted; it means the energy has been transferred to different mediums surrounding the car. Some of the energy is dissipated by the frictional force from the road on the tires, the air resistance from the movement of the car, the sound from the tires on the road, and the force of gravity pulling on the car. Each value can be calculated in a number of ways, including measuring the sound waves from the tires, the temperature change in the tires, the distance moved by the car from start to finish, etc. It is important to understand that many processes factor into such a small situation, but all situations follow the conservation of energy.

Just like the earlier example, the roller coaster at the top of a hill has a measurable amount of potential energy; when it rolls down the hill, it converts most of that energy into kinetic energy. There are still additional factors such as friction and air resistance working on the coaster and dissipating some of the energy, but energy transfers in every situation.

The Difference Between Heat and Temperature

Heat and temperature are concepts that examine two separate variables; however, they do affect one another. Heat refers to how much vibrational motion (known as thermal energy) each atom or molecule in a substance has; the higher the vibrational motion, the higher the energy expenditure (or heat) there is. Temperature refers to the average of all the atomic or molecular energy expenditure that is taking place in a substance. Therefore, the more heat a substance has, the higher the measurable temperature of that substance will be. For example, a pot of water that is placed on a stovetop may be still at room temperature. When the burner underneath the water is turned on, the energy from the burner transfers to the water, causing an increase in molecular vibration in the water. The water becomes hotter as the molecules begin moving faster. It is also important to note that heat energy always transfers from a substance with more heat to a substance with less heat, and not vice versa (i.e., the room temperature water would not cool down the stovetop burner).

Heat Transfer

Heat transfers as vibrating atoms or molecules in one substance come into contact with the vibrating molecules in another substance. Heat transfers through three primary mechanisms. **Conduction** occurs when two different substances come into direct contact with one another, such as when a person holds an ice cube. The substance with more heat transfers energy to the substance with less heat. In this instance, the person's body heat from his or her hand transfers to the frozen ice cube, which consists of molecules that are vibrating extremely slowly. As the heat transfers, the ice melts. Conduction is usually the most efficient way to transfer heat from a solid. **Convection** is usually the most efficient way to transfer heat from a liquid or gas. In convection, liquid or gaseous areas with more heat energy move to areas with lower heat energy. This occurs in a cyclical manner until a relative state of equilibrium is reached. Convection is seen in the oceans, where warm water travels closer to the surface of the ocean and pushes cooler water below.

It creates a circulation motion that results in oceanic movement which contributes to the ecosystem, weather patterns, and migratory patterns of ocean life. **Radiation** is a method of transferring heat that does not require two substances to touch. Radiation results from electron activity between atoms and molecules, either through unstable activity (an electron is released, resulting in a burst of energy), or through light waves. Light waves consist of photons, or bursts of energy that continuously travel at the speed of light through space. The most commonly recognized light radiation is ultraviolet radiation from the sun; ultraviolet rays travel through space to reach Earth. High radiation levels are more dangerous to living organisms than low-level radiation, although frequent low-level radiation can cause health issues, such as cell mutation, over time.

Sources of Light

Light is a type of electromagnetic radiation that falls within a spectrum of wavelengths visible to the human eye. It is a unique source of energy in that it has some qualities of particulate matter and some qualities of an electromagnetic wave. Light production can be natural or man-made. The main source of natural light comes from stars (such as the Sun, and other stars present in the universe), which are constantly undergoing nuclear reactions and creating energy that produces light. However, this light can be reflected by other bodies that are nearby. For example, the Sun's light is cast onto the Moon, which then reflects onto Earth. Man-made sources of light are created through heating certain resources that serve as fuel, such as burning wood or oil to create fire, or burning fossil fuels to create electricity which then powers light bulbs and electronic devices. The human brain and body respond differently to the different types of light. Natural light has a different wavelength and has an effect on human circadian rhythms and mood. For example, people in the Northern hemisphere who experience decreased levels of natural light exposure during the winter months may experience trouble sleeping or mood disorders. Natural light boxes are artificial light sources that simulate natural light radiation and can serve as a form of therapy.

144

Properties of Waves

Mechanical waves are a type of wave that pass through a medium (solid, liquid, or gas). There are two basic types of mechanical waves: longitudinal and transverse.

A **longitudinal wave** has motion that is parallel to the direction the waves travel. It can best be shown by compressing one side of a tethered spring and then releasing that end. The movement travels in a bunching and then unbunching motion, across the length of the spring and back until the energy is dissipated through noise and heat.

A **transverse wave** has motion that is perpendicular to the direction the waves travel. The particles on a transverse wave do not move across the length of the wave but oscillate up and down to create the peaks and troughs observed on this type of wave.

A wave with a mix of both longitudinal and transverse motion can be seen through the motion of a wave on the ocean, with peaks and troughs, oscillating particles up and down.

Mechanical waves can carry energy, sound, and light. Mechanical waves need a medium through which transport can take place. However, an electromagnetic wave can transmit energy without a medium, or in a vacuum.

Sound travels in waves and is the movement of vibrations through a medium. It can travel through air (gas), land, water, etc. For example, the noise a human hears in the air is the vibration of the waves as they reach the ear. The human brain translates the different frequencies (pitches) and intensities of the vibrations to determine what created the noise.

A **tuning fork** has a predetermined frequency because of the size (length and thickness) of its tines. When struck, it allows vibrations between the two tines to move the air at a specific rate. This creates a specific tone (or note) for that size of tuning fork. The number of vibrations over time is also steady for that tuning fork and can be matched with a frequency (the number of occurrences over time). All sounds heard by the human ear are categorized by using frequency and measured in hertz (the number of cycles per second).

The intensity (or loudness) of sound is measured on the Bel scale. This scale is a ratio of one sound's intensity with respect to a standard value. It is a logarithmic scale, meaning it is measured by factors of ten. But the value that is $\frac{1}{10}$ of this value, the decibel, is the measurement used more commonly for the intensity of pitches heard by the human ear.

The **Doppler effect** applies to situations with both light and sound waves. The premise of the Doppler effect is that, based on the relative position or movement of a source and an observer, waves can seem shorter or longer than they are. When the Doppler effect is experienced with sound, it warps the noise being heard by the observer by making the pitch or frequency seem shorter or higher as the source is approaching and then longer or lower as the source is getting farther away. The frequency and pitch of the source never actually change, but the sound in respect to the observer's position makes it seem like the sound has changed. This effect can be observed when an emergency siren passes by an observer on the road. The siren sounds much higher in pitch as it approaches the observer and then lower after it passes and is getting farther away.

The Doppler effect also applies to situations involving light waves. An observer in space would see light approaching as being shorter wavelengths than it was, causing it to appear blue. When the light wave is getting farther away, the light would look red due to the apparent elongation of the wavelength. This is called the **red-blue shift**.

A recent addition to the study of waves is the gravitational wave. Its existence has been proven and verified, yet the details surrounding its capabilities are still under inquiry. Further understanding of gravitational waves could help scientists understand the beginnings of the universe and how the existence of the solar system is possible. This understanding could also include the future exploration of the universe.

145

Optical Properties of Waves

The dispersion of light describes the splitting of a single wave by refracting its components into separate parts. For example, if a wave of white light is sent through a dispersion prism, the light wave appears as its separate rainbow-colored components due to each colored wavelength being refracted in the prism.

Different things occur when wavelengths of light hit boundaries. Objects can absorb certain wavelengths of light and reflect others, depending on the boundaries. This becomes important when an object appears to be a certain color. The color of the object is not actually within the makeup of that object, but by what wavelengths are being transmitted by that object. For example, if a table appears to be red, that means the table is absorbing all wavelengths of visible light except those of the red wavelength. The table is reflecting, or transmitting, the wavelengths associated with red back to the human eye, and therefore, the table appears red.

Interference describes when an object affects the path of a wave, or another wave interacts with that wave. Waves interacting with each other can result in either constructive interference or destructive interference based on their positions. For constructive interference, the waves are in sync and combine to reinforce each other. In the case of deconstructive interference, the waves are out of sync and reduce the effect of each other to some degree. In scattering, the boundary can change the direction or energy of a wave, thus altering the entire wave. Polarization changes the oscillations of a wave and can alter its appearance in light waves. For example, polarized sunglasses take away the "glare" from sunlight by altering the oscillation pattern observed by the wearer.

When a wave hits a boundary and is completely reflected back or cannot escape from one medium to another, it is called **total internal reflection**. This effect can be seen in a diamond with a brilliant cut. The angle cut on the sides of the diamond causes the light hitting the diamond to be completely reflected back inside the gem and makes it appear brighter and more colorful than a diamond with different angles cut into its surface.

When reflecting light, a mirror can be used to observe a virtual (not real) image. A plane mirror is a piece of glass with a coating in the background to create a reflective surface. An image is what the human eye sees when light is reflected off the mirror in an unmagnified manner. If a curved mirror is used for reflection, the image seen will not be a true reflection, but will either be magnified or made to appear smaller than its actual size. Curved mirrors can also make an object appear closer or farther away than its actual distance from the mirror.

Lenses can be used to refract or bend light to form images. Examples of lenses are the human eye, microscopes, and telescopes. The human eye interprets the refraction of light into images that humans understand to be actual size. When objects are too small to be observed by the unaided human eye, microscopes allow the objects to be enlarged enough to be seen. Telescopes allow objects that are too far away to be seen by the unaided eye to be viewed. Prisms are pieces of glass that can have a wavelength of light enter one side and appear to be broken down into its component wavelengths on the other side, due to the slowing of certain wavelengths within the prism, more than other wavelengths.

The movement of light is described like the movement of waves. Light travels with a wave front and has an amplitude (a height measured from the neutral), a cycle or wavelength, a period, and energy. Light travels at approximately 3.00×10^8 m/s and is faster than anything created by humans.

Light is commonly referred to by its measured wavelengths, or the length for it to complete one cycle. Types of light with the longest wavelengths include radio, TV, micro, and infrared waves. The next set of wavelengths are detectable by the human eye and make up the visible spectrum. The visible spectrum has wavelengths of 10^{-7} m, and the colors seen are red, orange, yellow, green, blue, indigo, and violet. Beyond the visible spectrum are even shorter wavelengths (also called the **electromagnetic spectrum**) containing ultraviolet light, x-rays, and gamma rays. The wavelengths outside of the visible light range can be harmful to humans if they are directly exposed, especially for long periods of time.

When a wave crosses a boundary or travels from one medium to another, certain actions take place. If the wave travels through one medium into another, it experiences **refraction**, which is the bending of the wave from one medium's density to another, altering the speed of the wave.

For example, a side view of a pencil in half a glass of water appears as though it is bent at the water level. What the viewer is seeing is the refraction of light waves traveling from the air into the water. Since the wave speed is slowed in water, the change makes the pencil appear bent.

When a wave hits a medium that it cannot pass through, it is bounced back in an action called *reflection*. For example, when light waves hit a mirror, they are reflected, or bounced off, the back of the mirror. This can cause it to seem like there is more light in the room due to the doubling back of the initial wave. This is also how people can see their reflection in a mirror.

When a wave travels through a slit or around an obstacle, it is known as **diffraction**. A light wave will bend around an obstacle or through a slit and cause a diffraction pattern. When the waves bend around an obstacle, it causes the addition of waves and the spreading of light on the other side of the opening.

Conservation of Energy Resources

Renewable sources of energy are those that can be easily replenished. These are sources of energy that come from the earth or space. They include solar (coming from the Sun), wind (coming from the flow of air), hydro (coming from water), geothermal (coming from heat from the earth), and biomass (coming from organic matter from animals and plants). Solar energy methods collect ultraviolet radiation from the sun and convert this energy into electricity. Solar energy technologies have become advanced and gained popularity over the last decade, as it is a clean and abundant source. New technologies allow for solar energy to be stored and used even during night hours. Wind energy capitalizes on the constant motion of air that exists as the earth rotates. Wind is harnessed through mechanical turbines that convert it to electrical energy. It is one of the fastest growing modes of energy production across the globe. Hydropower utilizes the force of water, such as through a fast-moving body of water or through a man-made dam, to generate electricity.

Hydropower makes up a small portion of total energy production. Geothermal energy harnesses heat from five to ten feet below the earth's surface and uses that to heat buildings naturally, or converts the heat into an electrical resource. Biomass energy comes from burning wood, plant waste, and animal waste for heat or to convert heat into electricity. Biomass energy is not a clean energy source. **Non-renewable energy sources** are limited and not easily replenished. These include fossil fuels (such as coal, crude oil, and natural gas) and nuclear energy. Fossil fuels are high in carbon composition, which is released during energy production and contributes to imbalances in atmospheric carbon. Nuclear energy is derived from uranium, a finite element that is found in the earth's crust. However, small amounts of uranium can create a large amount of energy. Nuclear energy is not a clean source, as radioactive waste is highly dangerous and must be stored carefully. Natural disasters that affect nuclear power plants and their waste sites (such as the 2011 earthquake and tsunami that affected Japan's Fukushima nuclear power site) can have long-lasting and widespread health effects on living organisms in the area.

Life Sciences

Structure of Living Organisms and Their Function

Levels of Hierarchical Organization and Related Functions in Plants and Animals

All living organisms are made up of cells. **Cells** are considered the basic functional unit of organisms and the smallest unit of matter that is living. Most organisms are multicellular, which means that they are made up of more than one cell and often they are made up of a variety of different types of cells. Cells contain organelles, which are the little working parts of the cell, responsible for specific functions that keep the cell and organism alive.

Plant and animal cells have many of the same organelles but also have some unique traits that distinguish them from each other. Plants contain a cell wall, while animal cells are only surrounded by a phospholipid plasma membrane. The **cell wall** is made up of strong, fibrous polysaccharides and proteins. It protects the cell from mechanical damage and maintains the cell's shape. Inside the cell wall, plant cells also have plasma membrane. The **plasma membrane** of both plant and animal cells is made up of two layers of phospholipids, which have a hydrophilic head and hydrophobic tails. The tails converge towards each other on the inside of the bilayer, while the heads face the interior of the cell and the exterior environment. **Microvilli** are protrusions of the cell membrane that are only found in animal cells. They increase the surface area and aid in absorption, secretion, and cellular adhesion. **Chloroplasts** are also only found in plant cells. They are responsible for photosynthesis, which is how plants convert sunlight into chemical energy.

The list below describes major organelles that are found in both plant and animal cells:

- Nucleus: The nucleus contains the DNA of the cell, which has all of the cells' hereditary information passed down from parent cells. DNA and protein are wrapped together into chromatin within the nucleus. The nucleus is surrounded by a double membrane called the nuclear envelope.

- Endoplasmic Reticulum (ER): The ER is a network of tubules and membranous sacs that are responsible for the metabolic and synthetic activities of the cell, including synthesis of membranes. Rough ER has ribosomes attached to it while smooth ER does not.

- Mitochondrion: The mitochondrion is essential for maintaining regular cell function and is known as the powerhouse of the cell. It is where cellular respiration occurs and where most of the cell's ATP is generated.

- Golgi Apparatus: The Golgi Apparatus is where cell products are synthesized, modified, sorted, and secreted out of the cell.

- Ribosomes: Ribosomes make up a complex that produces proteins within the cell. They can be free in the cytosol or bound to the ER.

Human Body

There are six levels of organization that can help describe the human body. These levels, in smallest to largest size order, are chemical, cellular, tissue, organ, organ system, and organism. The **chemical level** includes atoms and molecules, which are the smallest building blocks of matter. When atoms bind together, they form molecules, which in turn make up chemicals. All body structures are made up of these small elements. **Cells** are the smallest units of living organisms. They function independently to carry out vital functions of every organism. Cells that are similar then bind together to form tissues. **Tissues** perform specific functions by having all of the cells work together. For example, muscle tissue is made up of contractile cells that help the body move. **Organs** are made up of two or more types of tissue and perform physiological functions. **Organ systems** are made up of several organs together that work to perform a major bodily function. **Organisms** include the human body as a whole and all of its structures that perform life-sustaining functions.

Structures and Related Functions of Systems in Plants and Animals

Humans are complex organisms. They have many structures and functions that work in conjunction to maintain life. The relationship of structure and function can be seen throughout living systems. For example, flagella are long whip-like structures that can move about, helping propel the cell. The small intestines contain microvilli, or small projections that significantly increase the surface area of the small intestines, which aids in absorption of nutrients. Plants have all sorts of structural adaptations that help to better serve their function. For example, root systems are far-reaching and reach underground to absorb water and minerals in the soil and anchor the plant.

Nervous System

The nervous system is often combined with the muscular system and considered the **neuromuscular system**, which is composed of all of the muscles in the human body and the nerves that control them. Every movement that the body makes is controlled by the brain. The nervous system and the muscular system work together to link thoughts and actions. Neurons from the nervous system can relay information from the brain to muscle tissue so fast that an individual does not even realize it is happening. Some body movements are voluntary, but others are involuntary, such as the heart beating and the lungs breathing.

The nervous system is made up of the **central nervous system** (**CNS**) and the **peripheral nervous system** (**PNS**). The CNS includes the brain and the spinal cord, while the PNS includes the rest of the neural tissue that is not included in the CNS. **Neurons**, or nerve cells, are the main cells responsible for transferring and processing information between the brain and other parts of the body. **Neuroglia** are cells that support the neurons by providing a framework around them and isolating them from the surrounding environment.

Reproductive System

The **reproductive system** is responsible for producing, storing, nourishing, and transporting functional reproductive cells, or **gametes**, in the human body. It includes the reproductive organs, also known as **gonads**, the **reproductive tract**, the accessory glands and organs that secrete fluids into the reproductive tract, and the **perineal structures**, which are the external genitalia. The human male and female reproductive systems are very different from each other.

Respiratory System

The **respiratory system** is responsible for gas exchange between air and the blood, mainly via the act of breathing. It is divided into two sections: the upper respiratory system and the lower respiratory system. The **upper respiratory system** comprises the nose, the nasal cavity and sinuses, and the pharynx, while the **lower respiratory system** comprises the larynx (voice box), the trachea (windpipe), the small passageways leading to the lungs, and the lungs. The upper respiratory system is responsible for filtering, warming, and humidifying the air that gets passed to the lower respiratory system, protecting the lower respiratory system's more delicate tissue surfaces.

Cardiovascular System

The **cardiovascular system** is composed of the heart and blood vessels. It has three main functions in the human body. First, it transports nutrients, oxygen, and hormones through the blood to the body tissues and cells that need them. It also helps to remove metabolic waste, such as carbon dioxide and nitrogenous waste, through the bloodstream. Second, the cardiovascular system protects the body from attack by foreign microorganisms and toxins. The white blood cells, antibodies, and complement proteins that circulate within the blood help defend the body against these pathogens. The clotting system of the blood also helps protect the body from infection when there is blood loss following an injury. Lastly, this system helps regulate body temperature, fluid pH, and water content of the cells.

Circulatory System

Circulating blood carries oxygen, nutrients, and hormones throughout the body, which are vital for sustaining life. There are two types of cardiac circulation: pulmonary circulation and systemic circulation. The heart is responsible for pumping blood in both types of circulation. The **pulmonary circulatory system** carries blood between the heart and the lungs. It works in conjunction with the respiratory system to facilitate external respiration. Deoxygenated blood flows to the lungs through the vessels of the cardiovascular system to obtain oxygen and release carbon dioxide from the respiratory system. Blood that is rich with oxygen flows from the lungs back to the heart. Pulmonary circulation occurs only in the pulmonary loop. The pulmonary trunk takes the deoxygenated blood from the right ventricle to the arterioles and capillary beds of the lungs.

Once the blood that is filling these spaces has been reoxygenated, it passes into the pulmonary veins and is transported to the left atrium of the heart. The **systemic circulatory system** carries blood from the heart to the rest of the body and works in conjunction with the respiratory system to facilitate internal respiration. The oxygenated blood

149

flows out of the heart through the vessels and reaches the body tissues, while the deoxygenated blood flows through the vessels from the body back to the heart. Unlike the pulmonary loop, the systemic loop covers the whole body. Oxygen-rich blood moves out of the left ventricle into the aorta. The aorta circulates the blood to the systemic arteries and then to the arterioles and capillary beds that are present in the body tissues, where oxygen and nutrients are released into the tissues. The deoxygenated blood then moves from the capillary beds to the venules and systemic veins. The systemic veins bring the blood back to the right atrium of the heart.

Digestive System

The **gastrointestinal system**, or digestive system, is a group of organs that work together to fuel the body by transforming food and liquids into energy. After food is ingested, it passes through the **alimentary canal**, or **GI tract**, which comprises the mouth, pharynx, esophagus, stomach, small intestine, and large intestine. Each organ has a specific function to aid in digestion. Listed below are seven steps that incorporate the transformation of food as it travels through the gastrointestinal system.

- **Ingestion**: Food and liquids enter the alimentary canal through the mouth.

- **Mechanical processing**: Food is torn up by the teeth and swirled around by the tongue to facilitate swallowing.

- **Digestion**: Chemicals and enzymes break down complex molecules, such as sugars, lipids, and proteins, into smaller molecules that can be absorbed by the digestive epithelium.

- **Secretion**: Most of the acids, buffers, and enzymes that aid in digestion are secreted by the accessory organs, but some are provided by the digestive tract.

- **Absorption**: Vitamins, electrolytes, organic molecules, and water are absorbed by the digestive epithelium and moved to the interstitial fluid of the digestive tract.

- **Compaction**: Indigestible materials and organic wastes are dehydrated and compacted before elimination from the body.

- **Excretion**: Waste products are secreted into the digestive tract.

Fundamental Principles of Chemistry of Biological Systems

The study of the chemistry of living things is called **biochemistry**. Specifically, biochemistry focuses on the molecules and compounds that make up organisms. Analyzing the multiple cycles that organisms undergo for survival is a primary part of biochemistry.

Biochemistry studies cycles such as the following:

- Photosynthesis: Plants use water and carbon dioxide to create simple sugars and oxygen. For example, in the Calvin cycle, structures in chloroplasts are involved in the fixation of carbon dioxide to produce a 6-carbon sugar. Due to its instability, it quickly hydrolyzes to two separate molecules of 3-phosphogylcerate.

- Cellular respiration: Organisms break down sugars, proteins, and starches to create energy and carbon dioxide via glycolysis, the Krebs cycle, the electron transport chain, beta oxidation, etc. For example, in the Krebs cycle, mitochondria take pyruvate molecules ($CH_3 - CO - COO^-$) and, after a series of reaction, produce energy (in the form of ATP) and carbon dioxide.

These cycles involve the production and breakdown of key components in biochemistry, described below.

Carbohydrates are known as **sugars** (COH^-). They are long chains plants create for food storage and structure. Carbohydrates can be seen in the production of shells (containing chitin) and stems (containing cellulose). Sugar is broken down in the mitochondria of a cell to power the creation of adenosine triphosphate (ATP), which is necessary for cell metabolism. Molecules of sugar are called **saccharides** and named in accordance with the number of molecules present. One molecule is called a **monosaccharide**, two molecules together is called a **disaccharide**, three molecules together is called a **trisaccharide**, and so forth. Simple sugars created through photosynthesis are called **glucose** ($C_6H_{12}O_6$). A starch is formed when several carbohydrates combine. The structural basis for most plants is a starch called **cellulose**.

Lipids are a category of molecules that do not mix well with water. This category of lipids contains fats, waxes, and cutin (plant wax that deters evaporation). Triglycerides are formed from three fatty acids, which are carbons connected in long chains, connected to a glycerol backbone. The type of bonds formed in the fatty acid structure of a triglyceride determines the properties of the fat. Saturated fats have only single bonds between carbons and are weaker than unsaturated fats, which have at least one double. Saturated fats tend to be solid at room temperature because the single bonds allow all the chains in the structure to pack in more tightly. Unsaturated fats cannot pack together as tightly because kinks are formed in the chain where there are double bonds. This looser arrangement of fatty acid chains causes most unsaturated fats to be liquid at room temperature.

Another category of lipids, called steroids, consists of a four-ring structure containing one ring of five carbons and three rings of six carbons. Steroids have very specific molecular structures, which determine their category. Cholesterol is one of the most important biological steroids, which among its many functions, is an integral constituent of cell membranes. Other steroids help form sex hormones or act as anti-inflammatories. Humans can increase their muscle and bone synthesis through anabolic steroids.

Another important area of study in biochemistry is acids. The main type, nucleic acids, are contained within the nucleus of a cell. Nucleic acids contain all the information necessary for cell replication. Specific types of nucleic acid are deoxyribonucleic acid (DNA), ribonucleic acid (RNA), messenger ribonucleic acid (mRNA), transfer ribonucleic acid (tRNA) and ribosomal ribonucleic acid (rRNA). These acids also assist in the building of proteins. DNA is a very complex and long chain composed of two nucleotide strands twisted around each other in a curved ladder configuration (double helix). DNA is the primary component of chromosomes and contains an encoded record of genetic material. This material is transferred along by RNA. DNA is more stable than RNA due to its reduction in more reactive oxygen atoms.

DNA can be broken down into building blocks (monomers), including adenine, thymine, cytosine, and guanine. Uracil is a building block contained only within RNA. All these parts are made of the following three primary components:

- Five carbon sugar; the structure of DNA is missing a hydroxyl group (OH) when compared to the structure of RNA.

- A nitrogen base; there are four, which are grouped into pyrimidines (thymine and cytosine) and purines (guanine and adenine) based on their structures.

- A phosphate ion (PO_4^{3-}), which gives DNA a negative charge.

Amino acids are long molecules made from shorter building blocks. More than five hundred amino acids have been identified, but only twenty of these appear in the genetic code. Amino acids contain a carboxyl group and are used in cells to build proteins. The carboxyl group has a carbon double-bonded to oxygen (COO^-) and a single-bonded hydroxyl (OH) group.

Amino acids (which contain the amine group, NH_2) are categorized as nonessential, conditional, or essential. The human body can synthesize nonessential amino acids such as asparagine, aspartate, and alanine. However, if the human body is stressed or unbalanced from an illness, it may not be able to produce the conditional amino acids. Conditional amino acids include glutamine, arginine, cysteine, glycine, proline, tyrosine, ornithine, and serine. The remaining amino acids must be obtained through diet and are referred to as **essential amino acids**. These include

151

isoleucine, leucine, valine, lysine, phenylalanine, methionine, threonine, and tryptophan. The human body cannot store amino acids, so a daily allowance must be taken/consumed for proper health and function. Many proteins derived from animal sources contain a full complement of the essential amino acids. Some vegetarian options, such as soy (tofu) and quinoa, can also supply the full gamut of essential amino acids, especially when paired together (for example, rice and beans).

Enzymes are catalysts that aid in the breakdown of proteins. Enzymes are necessary for most cellular metabolic processes to occur at rates fast enough to sustain life. There are specific enzymes for every individual task. Enzymes are regulated by temperature, activators, pH levels, and inhibitors.

Living and Nonliving Components in Environments

Living Things and the Characteristics of Living Organisms

Living organisms have several defining characteristics, such as growth, reproduction, sensitivity, movement, respiration, excretion, and nutrition. Growth involves the organism's ability to multiply in cell number and size. Cell division can occur through mitosis, which results in the formation of two daughter cells that have identical chromosomes count as the parent cell. The organisms can increase in size and mass. Reproduction involves the organism's ability to produce offspring. Through sexual reproduction, animals reproduce to create offspring. A male and female each contribute a sex cell (gamete cells) to reproduce. In an animal, the male donates sperm cells, which combine with ova, or female sex cells.

Organisms can also sense or detect stimuli within an external or internal environment, which allows for an appropriate response. The nose of a star-nosed mole foraging in a tunnel makes contact with an object and activates its touch receptors. Contact with an object activates a touch receptor on the nose, which allows the transmission of information to the brain via sensory nerves. Following sensory input in a simple response pathway, integration and motor output will take place. Motor output involves movement whereby an organism causes a change in position. For the mole, muscles will contract, which will allow the mole to bite down on food. The mole may move farther within the tunnel if food is not found.

Respiration involves a series of chemical reactions at the cellular level. In animals, oxygen enters and passes from the alveolus into the bloodstream. Oxygen is used in cellular respiration to create ATP energy, which is needed for motor function and other cellular processes.

In the process of excretion, metabolic waste products, excess substances, and toxic components are eliminated. During cellular respiration, carbon dioxide is released from the capillaries and diffuses out into the alveolus. Organisms must have proper nutrition throughout their lifespan. Organic or inorganic materials are constantly needed for growth/development and energy. Plants require energy from light, and animals need organic matter, water, and electrolytes to function.

Basic Needs of All Living Organisms

All living organisms on earth need nutrients (from food sources) for energy, water for cellular functioning (or for their home or respiration, such as with fish), environmental space in which to build shelters, air to breathe, and sunlight for warmth, to support metabolic functions, and to create food sources. Each species has unique ways of ensuring that their basic needs are met for survival. A critical component of survival is the environmental location in which the organism lives, and organisms will migrate to environments that have plentiful resources, and away from environments that lack them. Within an environment, organisms will establish themselves near resources such as water and food sources. They may also work cooperatively to create a shelter that helps regulate the amounts of sunlight and temperature exposure or the ability to store food for periods of time. When resources become depleted, organisms will either migrate or prepare for the period of depletion if it will be temporary. For example, bears will eat more and store nutrients during warmer periods and hibernate during cold periods when resources may be less plentiful. They will still emerge periodically to look for food, but will not die if availability is low for one season. Other animals may

152

continuously cycle migration towards warmer climates during cold periods (during which plant food dies, prey animals become scarce, and water freezes) and then return to the original location when warmer weather returns.

The Numbers and Types of Organisms an Ecosystem Can Support

An **ecosystem** can host organisms, varying in number and type, based on the resources available and the way the organisms consume the resources. The interaction between different species of organisms in an ecosystem also contributes to the supportive capabilities of an ecosystem. For example, an area with a large number of honeybee pollinators is likely to have more flowering plants and fruits that other animals can survive off of, whereas an area without a high number of pollinators is likely to become depleted faster. Additionally, all ecosystems consist of trophic levels. These categorize organisms into a hierarchical "food chain" and distinguishes what an organism may eat, as well as what organisms may consume it. Most ecosystems have five trophic levels, consisting of primary producers (i.e., plants), secondary producers (i.e., herbivores), tertiary producers (i.e., omnivores), and apex predators (which are able to consume the other subordinate levels). These must remain in relative balance in order to create enough resources for each group. For example, if one of the lower trophic groups were to die out completely, it would cause a domino effect of famine for each of the next levels. All dead organisms are eventually consumed by the decomposers of the ecosystem.

Carrying capacity of an ecosystem refers to how many organisms it can hold without becoming depleted. Factors that determine carrying capacity include the availability of resources such as accessible and usable water, food, air, sunlight, and waste removal; it also includes the rate of consumption by each organism that lives in the ecosystem. The concept of carrying capacity was altered significantly when human population rates and technologies began exploding around the time of the Industrial Revolution. Due to the influx of technological advances and innovation, especially those focused on medicine and energy consumption, humans are both living longer within ecosystems as well as consuming resources and producing waste at an unprecedented rate. It is believed that as a whole, the earth's global ecosystem has been propelled by an artificial carrying capacity that is unsustainable. While humans are creating extra resources to contribute to the high population (such as increases in food production), these can come at a high cost to human health and the environment. For example, concentrated animal farming operations increases the number of livestock that can provide food for humans, but is also associated with lower nutritional value, increased carbon production and environmental waste, and extremely poor ethical treatment of the animals.

Transfer of Energy and the Cycling of Matter

All energy transfers in an ecosystem first begin with the sun. Sunlight is utilized by plants, known as autotrophs (self-sufficient organisms) that use this energy to convert carbon dioxide in the air into nutrients for its own energy use. This process is called photosynthesis. All autotrophs are considered to be primary producers for their ecosystem, as they utilize an inorganic energy source to create an organic energy source for other consumers in the ecosystems. Consumers are those organisms that utilize the autotroph for some means. Some organisms eat the autotroph for nutritional or water value. All organisms utilize the autotrophs' waste from their carbon dioxide conversion—oxygen—in their own respiration. Other primary producers include unicellular bacteria that create wastes which are critical components of biomass. Biomass resources can be used to create energy for decomposers, which are organisms that consume biomass for energy. Examples of primary producers include all plants, including water vegetation such as algae and kelp. Examples of consumers include humans, animals, and fish. Examples of decomposers include fungi and some insects. The **food chain** consists of a hierarchical structure that shows what an organism consumes, as well as to which other organisms it may be vulnerable. When organisms in an ecosystem consume from multiple trophic levels, it creates a non-linear food web, rather than a linear food chain. **Food webs** typically encompass multiple food chains, and can show the relationships between organisms of much larger systems.

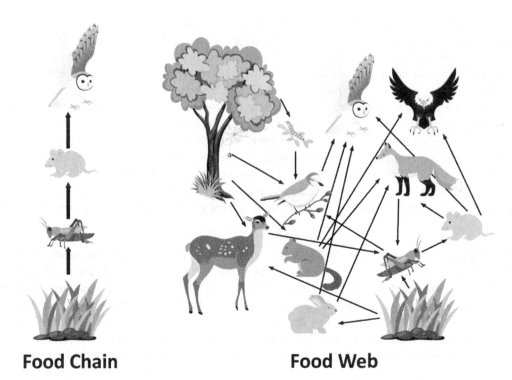

Food Chain   **Food Web**

Resources Available in an Ecosystem

An ecosystem is comprised of all the organisms and non-living entities in a specified environment. Any living item, such as plants and animals that can be prey to another animal, is considered a resource of the ecosystem. Other resources that are non-living include available water, the air, and items that could provide shelter or support thermoregulation. An ecosystem is a sum of its parts; all parts of the ecosystem are interdependent on each other. The ecosystem remains healthy and viable as long as these parts are in ecological balance. Ecological balance is supported by enough food and water resources for all organisms, a large biodiversity in flora and fauna, symbiotic relationships between living organisms, and equal rates of growth and death in living organisms that require resources from the ecosystem. Ecological balance is often disrupted when one single variable falls out of balance, which can create a domino effect within the ecosystem. For example, if a large area of forest is cut down and man-made structures are built there, the cycles of photosynthesis and availability of primary producers in the area are both disrupted. This could result in a decrease in food sources for other organisms, who may migrate away. Additionally, the introduction of new constructions and human activity brings excess waste and pollution. With less plant life and more pollution in the area, water resources can become contaminated or experience extra levels of carbon and nitrogen, which reduce the overall oxygen available in the water. This then affects the organisms in the water.

Ecosystems have varying levels of resilience and resistance, two variables that factor into overall ecosystem stability. **Resistance** refers to how well the overall ecosystem is able to maintain itself when an external disturbance (such as a tropical storm, or human activity) occurs. **Resilience** refers to how well and quickly the ecosystem can return to its natural balance after an external disturbance. The levels of resistance and resilience that an ecosystem can maintain directly correlates with the intensity, frequency, and type of external disturbance. Areas that have high biological diversity and minimal variety in disturbances are most likely to be both resistant and resilient.

How Human Activities and Natural Processes Impact the Climate

Both natural processes and human activities play a role in localized and global climate. Natural processes that affect the climate include volcanic activity, shifts in Earth's orbit around the Sun and tilt in space, and changes in solar activity. Volcanic activity releases carbon dioxide, sulfur dioxide, and other particles that can cool the immediate area by blocking sunlight. This cooling period can last months or years, depending on the intensity of volcanic activity. The Earth's tilt and rotation can take it slightly farther away or closer to the Sun, which can result in larger scale shifts in the global climate. Ice ages and warmer periods can result from these changes in the earth's relative position to the sun. Solar activity, such as the presence of sunspots and solar flares, can also cause periods of higher temperatures (when sunspots and solar flares are increased) or cooler periods (when sunspots and solar flares are decreased). Human activity is believed to contribute significantly to climate change, as rapid increases in global temperature correlate with the introduction of industrial changes, such as factory manufacturing and car usage.

These types of changes require high levels of energy, which is produced through greenhouse gas emitting activities such as the burning of fossil fuels. An increase in ocean temperatures over two degrees Celsius can cause a cascade of effects that massively disrupt ecosystems across the globe, and could cause a disruption in human food sources, clean water availability, and energy needs. Solutions primarily focus on activities that reduce the level of greenhouse gases in the atmosphere. Solutions include reducing such emissions through more efficient and clean energy sources (such as solar and wind over fossil fuels) and slowing deforestation.

Life Cycle, Reproduction, and Evolution

Life Cycles of Familiar Organisms

All living things change over time. Individual living things change over the period of a single lifespan through growth, development, and aging; entire species can change over the course of thousands of years (called species **evolution**).

Individual lifespans of organisms can last anywhere from a few hours (some species of flies) to hundreds of years (some species of ocean clams). In fact, one species of jellyfish has the ability to regenerate any injured or stressed part and could, in theory, live forever. Regardless of the lifespan, all organisms follow the basic processes of a **life cycle**, including birth, growth and development, reproduction, and death. These are typically marked by visible transitions. In humans, for example, an implanted zygote (a female egg that has been fertilized by a male sperm) transforms from a single cell into a fully formed baby over the course of nine months. After birth, different milestones mark the baby's growth and development: height, weight, head circumference, motor abilities, communication abilities, and visible understanding of the world. Puberty in adolescents indicates that reproduction is possible; pregnancy and birth provide the next generation of the species. Signs of aging may indicate that reproduction is no longer possible (i.e., menopause) or that organ systems are not functioning as well as they used to (degeneration). Eventually, all living creatures die from natural aging, disease, or trauma.

Similarly, many animals follow similar cycles, though gestation, reproductive ages, reproductive capacity, and length of lifespan varies across species. For example, a butterfly's life cycle begins when a female butterfly lays a cluster of eggs. In less than a week, these eggs hatch and a tiny caterpillar emerges. The caterpillar eats large amounts of food and grows rapidly; as it grows, it molts its outer covering (exoskeleton) approximately four to five times before growth is complete. After this period, the caterpillar creates a cocoon called a chrysalis inside which it undergoes metamorphosis. When metamorphosis is complete, the caterpillar becomes a butterfly and hatches out of the chrysalis. It takes a few hours for the butterfly to circulate blood into the wings for movement. After this period, butterflies will mate; females will lay eggs and the four-stage cycle continues again.

Mammals have slightly different cycles than butterflies. A mouse, for instance, has a lifespan of several years. Pregnant females give birth to multiple babies, and they can reproduce up to ten times annually. Mice are able to mate and reproduce two months after birth and continue the life cycle. Members of a lineage of mice may be continuously reproducing alongside older members, and a mouse population can quickly become large.

Frogs, as another unique example, have a lifespan that takes place over multiple environments. Pregnant female frogs lay numerous eggs in a body of water. If any of these eggs hatch several weeks later (they are susceptible to many different predators), tadpoles emerge. Tadpoles are aquatic; instead of legs, tadpoles have tails for swimming. They also have gills, rather than lungs, for breathing in the water. Depending on the species of frog, it can remain in a tadpole stage for weeks or months. As most species of tadpoles grow into adult frogs, they will grow legs and lungs. Female and males will live several years, and during this time, pregnant females will return to water habitats in order to lay eggs.

Factors that Affect Growth and Development of Plants

Plant growth takes place as a seedling sprouts root into soil matter and absorbs nutrients such as water, nitrogen, potassium, and phosphorus. Availability of water plays a critical role in the rate at which plants survive. Water typically comes from rainfall, but can also come from human activity (such as when homeowners manually waters plants in their yard with a garden house). Plants also take carbon dioxide from the air and need sunlight exposure to carry out photosynthesis, which provides their main source of energy for growth. Different plants also have different temperature requirements that aid in growth, in the development of reproductive structures, such as the pistil and stamen found within flowers, and in the rate of photosynthesis. For example, in very cold climates with densely packed soil or frozen water sources, it takes planted seeds relatively longer to germinate and grow upwards; in fact, these plants may struggle to grow at all, as water and nutrients move slowly in colder soil. If water within the vascular components of plants freezes, the surrounded plant cells will burst, and the plant will usually die. In warmer climates with extended periods of sunlight, plants may cycle through their lifespan much faster due to quicker cycles of photosynthesis. Additionally, some climates will only house plants that thrive in that climate. For example, cacti are primarily seen in arid deserts, while deciduous plants are unable to survive in such environments. Finally, the presence of wind and pollinators both impact plant growth and development, as these both spread pollen within plants and promote biodiversity in an area.

Sexual and Asexual Reproduction

Cellular reproduction is the process that cells follow to make new cells with the same or similar contents as themselves. This process is an essential part of an organism's life. It allows for the organism to grow larger itself, and as it ages, it allows for replacement of dying and damaged cells. The process of cellular reproduction must be accurate and precise. Otherwise, the new cells that are produced will not be able to perform the same functions as the original cell.

Mutations can occur in the offspring, which can cause anywhere from minor to severe problems. The two types of cellular reproduction that organisms can use are mitosis or meiosis. **Mitosis** produces daughter cells that are identical to the parent cell and is often referred to as asexual reproduction. **Meiosis** has two stages of cell division and produces daughter cells that have a combination of traits from their two parents. It is often referred to as sexual reproduction. Humans reproduce by meiosis. During this process, the sperm, the male germ cell, and the egg, the female germ cell, combine and form a parent cell that contains both of their sets of chromosomes. This parent cell then divides into four daughter cells, each with a unique set of traits that came from both of their parents.

In both processes, the most important part of the cell that is copied is the cell's DNA. It contains all of the genetic information for the cell, which leads to its traits and capabilities. Some parts of the cell are copied exactly during cellular reproduction, such as DNA. However, certain other cellular components are synthesized within the new cell after reproduction is complete using the new DNA. For example, the endoplasmic reticulum is broken down during the cell cycle and then newly synthesized after cell division.

Environmental and Genetic Sources of Variation

Humans carry their genetic information on structures called **chromosomes**. Chromosomes are string-like structures made up of nucleic acids and proteins. During the process of reproduction, each parent contributes a gamete that contains twenty-three chromosomes to the intermediate diploid cell. This diploid cell, which contains forty-six chromosomes, replicates itself to produce two diploid cells. These two diploid cells each then split into cells and

156

randomly divide the chromosomes so that each of the four resulting cells contains only twenty-three chromosomes, as each parent gamete does.

Each of the twenty-three chromosomes has between a few hundred and a few thousand genes on it. Each gene contains information about a specific trait that is inherited by the offspring from one of the parents. Genes are made up of sequences of DNA that encode proteins and start pathways to express the phenotype that they control. Every gene has two alleles, or variations—one inherited from each parent. In most genes, one allele has a more dominant phenotype than the other allele. This means that when both alleles are present on a gene, the dominant phenotype will always be expressed over the recessive phenotype. The recessive phenotype would only be expressed when both alleles present were recessive.

Some alleles can have codominance or incomplete dominance. **Codominance** occurs when both alleles are expressed equally when they are both present. For example, the hair color of cows can be red or white, but when one allele for each hair color is present, their hair is a mix of red and white, not pink. **Incomplete dominance** occurs when the presence of two different alleles creates a third phenotype. For example, some flowers can be red or white when the alleles are duplicated, but when one of each allele is present, the flowers are pink.

Natural and Artificial Selection

Mutations refer to a change in a cell or organism's DNA. Mutations may or may not be physically visible; they may be advantageous (an **adaptation**) or detrimental. Organisms that have detrimental mutations are less likely to survive, whereas organisms with advantageous mutations are more likely to survive and pass on their genes. This phenomenon is referred to as **natural selection**. Over time, this is how a species can evolve so that the initial mutation, which might have once been a rarity in the population, becomes common in the population. This can be beneficial to the evolved species, but it may be harmful to other species. For example, a number of bacteria have evolved to become resistant to antibiotic medications. This ensures the survival of the bacteria but can cause extreme illness or death in humans who now have less recourse for treatment. Consequently, it is possible that humans could evolve to withstand bacterial infections, as weaker groups die out and stronger ones remain in the gene pool. Adaptations typically take several generations to manifest themselves across the larger breadth of a population; however, any change that aids survival will ultimately become a dominant trait in the population. Natural selection was first theorized by biologist Charles Darwin in the early to mid-1800s.

Comparatively, Darwin also theorized the concept of artificial selection. **Artificial selection** refers to the intentional and conscious choosing of certain traits to reproduce in order to achieve a desired outcome. For centuries, farmers have utilized methods of artificial selection to manage crops and livestock yields. Rather than allowing natural cross-pollination to occur between plants, or natural mating selection to occur between livestock, farmers chose (and often still choose) to cross two organisms that would produce a desired yield. For example, the hand-selected cross-pollination of various types of flowers over many generations has resulted in many of the fruits and vegetables that people regularly consume today, such as broccoli and corn. Today's organisms have been bred to be hardier in adverse weather conditions, be larger in size, to be resistant to some pests, and have varied nutritional value than their predecessors. Many species of livestock and house pets have been selectively bred over centuries to serve as domesticated animals that could, in fact, live alongside humans. Commonly owned breeds of dogs, such as Huskies and German Shepherds, were bred from non-domesticated wolves to provide services such as transportation, herding, and protection. Selectively mating purebred animals with other purebred animals can eventually result in health issues, as genetic diversity does not exist. Genetic diversity is associated with protective traits and longer lifespans.

Fossil Record, Comparative Anatomy, and DNA Sequences

Evolution refers to the gradual genotypic and phenotypic changes that take place in a species over a period of time. It occurs as a result of natural selection or genetic variation. Darwin's theory of evolution states all living organisms on Earth have one common ancestor; as individual organisms started living in unique environments, their genes began to express or mutate in ways that provided benefits to that environment. Over time, these changes in the genetic code became permanent, and organisms began to branch off into completely new species.

Evidence of evolution exists in physical geological records and unique similarities across seemingly different species. The **fossil record** provides information relating to when organisms lived and died in Earth's history, where these organisms lived, and how they changed over a period of time. Paleontologists, who study fossils, are able to see how preserved remains that are found in deeper layers of the earth, or in older rocks, vary from those found in more superficial layers. The oldest rocks on Earth house the fossils of single-celled organisms, while the youngest rocks hold fossils of organisms that still exist today. Between these two ranges, the fossils of organisms become exceedingly more complex as the age of the rock in which it is found decreases. Evolutionary changes within a single species or group of species can be seen by comparing the anatomy of remains found in the fossil record. For example, fossil records show mammalian ear structures becoming more complex in rocks that have an age difference of approximately 20 million years. Additionally, seemingly unrelated species have undeniable anatomical similarities. For example, the bones in the paw of a tiger are similar in structure to the bones found in a bat's wing, indicating that these two species likely shared a common ancestor. Finally, DNA sequencing shows that many species of organisms share similar genetic sequences, especially when comparing the amino acids that are present. Chimpanzees, which are believed to be the closest relative to humans, do not have any variations in amino acids from humans. Most monkeys have less than a handful of amino acid variations from humans.

Natural Selection

Darwin's theory is based on descent with modification, or evolution, which describes how a population undergoes a change in genetic composition from one generation to another. **Evolution** occurs by natural selection, which is an adaptation process where organisms inherit characteristics or traits that increase their chances of survival and production in certain environments. Without those traits, the organism is less likely to survive. Since the environment often creates challenges for an organism, the organism undergoes natural selection, which can result in the creation of a distinct species.

Darwin indicated a close relationship between the formation of new species and adaptation to an environment. Darwin hypothesized that organisms living in various habitats would gradually develop diverse adaptations that allow them to fit into the environment. For example, the Galapagos Islands are home to several species of finches, which have evolved with different beaks that are adapted to their diet.

Darwin's theory is based on observations that drew two inferences. Darwin indicated that members of a population will have inherited traits that vary, and that species can create more offspring than the environment can maintain. Most offspring produced in excess will not survive and reproduce. Individuals with traits that give them a greater chance of surviving and reproducing will create more offspring than others. Since some individuals or species will reproduce and survive unequally, those with favorable traits will increase from one generation to the next.

Earth and Space Sciences

The Solar System and the Universe

Components of the Solar System

The **universe** is defined as the largest entity made by space and time, and it includes all of the smaller entities contained within it. The largest known systems within the universe are known as **galaxies**. Scientists believe there are over 100 billion galaxies within the universe. Galaxies can be made up of different gases, cosmic debris, stars, planets, moons, black holes, and other bits of matter. Billions of these entities can make up a single galaxy. They primarily appear in either spiral or elliptical shapes. Galaxies that cannot be categorized as these shapes are known as irregularly shaped galaxies. These different shapes are made based on the masses of the various entities within the galaxy. The gravitational pull of these objects upon one another creates not only the shape of the galaxy, but also influences how other systems operate within the galaxy. Galaxies can be hundreds of thousands to millions of light years across in size.

Within galaxies, the next largest system is a **solar system**. These systems contain one or more stars with a massive gravitational pull. Various planets, moons, and debris orbit the star or stars as a result. Stars form because of the gravitational collapse of explosive elements (primarily hydrogen and helium). The center of the star continues in a state of thermonuclear fusion that creates the star's internal gravitational pull. Over many thousands of years, the central thermonuclear activity will slowly cease until the star collapses, resulting in the absorption of orbiting bodies. The Earth is part of a solar system in the Milky Way galaxy.

Its solar system consists of one sun, eight planets, their moons, and other cosmic bodies, such as meteors and asteroids (including an asteroid belt that orbits the Sun in a full ring). In order of proximity to the Sun, the planets in this solar system are Mercury, Venus, Earth, Mars, Jupiter, Saturn, Uranus, and Neptune. Beyond Neptune is a dwarf planet named Pluto, and at least four other known dwarf planets. While the Earth has only a single moon, most other planets have multiple moons (although Mercury and Venus have none). Based on their mass, moons, and position from the Sun, each planet takes a different period to orbit the Sun and rotate upon its axis. The Earth takes 24 hours to rotate on its axis and 365 days to orbit the Sun.

Time Zones

Time zones are a social construct that indicate the relationship between a location on Earth and the position of the Sun. Time zones first became a global feature in the early 19th century, when train transportation became popular, and a widely accepted construct of time was needed to operate a reliable and safe train schedule. Individual countries have largely set their own time zones. Most developed and developing countries use the Coordinated Time Zone system, which is based off a longitudinal line running through Greenwich, England, as a starting point from which to create time zones. This point, which is not related to the axis or rotation of the Earth, is known as the prime meridian. It was selected due to shipping route structures and international opinion. The time changes by one hour every 15 degrees in longitude from the prime meridian; this created 24 total time zones. Not all countries, nor states within a country, follow time zones in this manner. For example, India and Sri Lanka follow a single unique time zone that encompasses the entirety of both countries. Other areas have changed time zones based on economic needs; for example, Venezuela chose to shift from the Coordinated Time Zone to allow an extra 30 minutes of daylight for work. The International Date Line is equidistant in either direction from the Prime Meridian and is an imaginary point that delineates two consecutive calendar days.

Changes in Observed Positions of the Sun, Moon, and Stars

Solar eclipses occur on Earth when the Moon's orbit appears to cross between the Earth and the Sun, while lunar eclipses occur when the Earth's orbit crosses between the Sun and the Moon. Additionally, the Moon's gravitational pull on the Earth impacts the water on the planet, causing high and low tides throughout the day. The difference in tidal height varies based on the location of the Moon in its orbit around the Earth (as well as different features of the water body and shoreline).

The positioning of the Moon between the Earth and the Sun at different positions in the Earth's orbit results in the phases of the Moon. While a common misconception is that the phases are simply caused from the shadow the Earth casts on the Moon, the different phases we see are actually due to the position of the Moon relative to the Sun. A portion of the Moon that is not visible or shadowed is turned away from the Sun. At all times, half of the Moon is illuminated while half is shadowed, yet our perception of different phases is caused by the Moon's position relative to us on Earth.

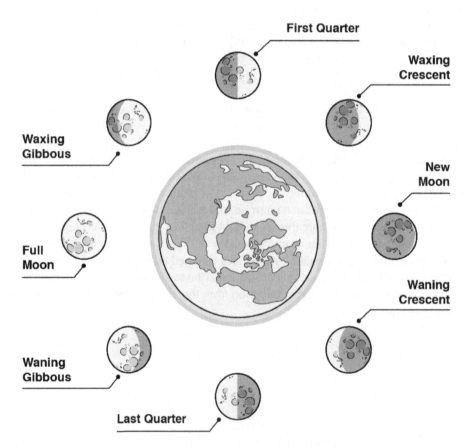

Bodies of the Universe

A **galaxy** is a system composed of dust, interstellar gas, stellar remnants, and stars, which are all gravitationally bound. Astronomical luminous objects called **stars** consist of plasma that is held by gravity. Galaxies may average 100 million stars and may have an irregular, spiral, or elliptical morphology. The **Milky Way** is described as a spiral galaxy with a diameter of 87,000 light-years and is estimated to contain, on average, 250 billion stars. The Milky Way galaxy consists of thousands of solar or planetary systems. Our solar system is found on the outer spiral arm of the Milky Way galaxy, or at a radius of 27,000 light-years to the Galactic Center.

The solar system is 4.6 billion years old, with a diameter of 287.5 billion kilometers. It contains a star called the Sun, which has a diameter of 1,329,000 kilometers. The planets in the solar system are bound to the Sun by gravity. The planets ranging from closest to farthest from the Sun are Mercury, Venus, Earth, Mars, Jupiter, Saturn, Uranus, and

160

Neptune. Pluto is a dwarf planet that is furthest from the Sun. The solar system consists of meteoroids, comets, millions of asteroids, and dozens of moons. The planets move around the sun in an elliptical orbit. The Earth is the fifth-largest planet and makes a complete orbit around the Sun in 365.25 days; the Earth's seasons are attributed to the tilt of the Earth's axis. The Earth has a radius of 12,742 kilometers.

The distance from the Earth to the Sun is one astronomical unit (AU), or about 150 million kilometers (93 million miles). The Earth's moon is approximately 239,000 miles from the Earth. From Earth, the brightness of the Sun is -26.74 mag. Non-stellar objects in the solar system, such as the Earth's moon, are -12.7 mag.

The Structure and Composition of the Earth

Formation and Observable Physical Characteristics of Minerals and Rocks

Minerals occur naturally in the Earth and are created from geological processes including heat and pressures (such as through a volcanic eruption). Minerals are inorganic, solid elements or compounds with uniform structures, distinguishable chemical characteristics, and distinct physical properties. They primarily form within the crust, the most superficial layer of the Earth. Minerals are categorized by several distinguishing factors. One main distinguishing feature of a mineral is its **relative hardness** on the Mohs Scale of Mineral Hardness, which classifies a mineral based on its ability to scratch another mineral. Talc is considered the softest mineral, while diamonds are considered the hardest. Any classified mineral can scratch another mineral that is ranked lower in hardness. Other classification factors include color, weight, luster (how well the mineral reflects light), streak (the color of the mineral in powder form), tenacity (how well the mineral resists pressure), and cleavage and fracture (how the mineral breaks upon its surface).

Most minerals are made up of the most commonly found elements in the Earth's crust: oxygen, silicon, aluminum, iron, calcium, sodium, potassium, and magnesium. Minerals containing oxygen and silicon are called silicates and make up the majority of the Earth's crust and mantle. All silicates have similar chemical composition (a tetrahedron made of silicon and oxygen atoms) but can be vastly different in color, strength, and melting points. Quartz, pyroxene, micas, and clays are commonly recognized silicates. Quartz has a tightly interwoven framework (making it feel harder and more difficult to break) with a high melting point, whereas micas and clays are more delicate in structure and have neat cleavage points. Cleavage points are areas in the mineral where atomic bonds can be cleanly broken.

Other types of minerals include oxides, in which oxygen is bonded with metal. Since oxygen can bond with a variety of other elements, oxides vary greatly in their physical characteristics. However, when oxygen bonds with iron, chromium, aluminum, and tin, the resulting compounds are quite useful in human life. For example, iron oxides are used in paint, while aluminum oxides make durable tool equipment. Sulfates and sulfides are other mineral groups that are sulfur-based and used regularly in human life. Sulfites are commonly used in preserving food, while sulfates are commonly used in cleaning products as a degreaser. Native minerals are those that are not found combined with any other mineral; they are often rare and valuable. Gold and diamonds are examples of native minerals.

Rocks are solid structures that may consist of one or more minerals, as well as other solid substances. Rocks are classified based on their composition, the texture of the particles they encompass, and how they were created. Rocks can be classified as igneous, sedimentary, or metamorphic. **Igneous rocks** are formed from magma as it cools. **Sedimentary rocks** are formed as various materials (sediments) are deposited and compacted together (such as through water pressure or weathering). **Metamorphic rocks** form after an existing rock experiences pressure or temperature that changes its physical or chemical composition.

Characteristics of Landforms

Landforms make up the solid parts of the Earth's surface. They are formed over millions of years from erosion, tectonic plate activity, and volcanic activity. The most commonly seen landforms include mountains, hills, plateaus, plains, valleys, deserts, and glaciers. **Mountains** are immense, steep, and elevated landforms typically created when two tectonic plates push together under tremendous forces and pressure, or through volcanic eruptions that deposit layers of magma and sediment upon one another. Defining whether an elevated landmass is a mountain or not is often left to the jurisdiction of the country in which it exists. Typically, most landforms under 950 feet are considered hills rather than a mountain. Mountains make up approximately 25 percent of the Earth's surface; they can exist as singular entities or as a range. **Plateaus** are elevated landmasses as well, but they are flat rather than peaked. The sides of a plateau are usually quite steep.

Plains are broad, flat areas at low elevations. They may be covered in grass or trees when inland, and may consist of sand dunes along coastlines. Similarly, **valleys** are flat areas that exist between mountains. Flat landmasses such as plains and valleys make up approximately 33 percent of the Earth's landmasses.

Glaciers consist of snow that turns into compressed mountains of ice (rather than rock) over centuries. Glacial ice is a primary source of fresh water on Earth. They comprise approximately 10 percent of Earth's landmass. Their structure changes continuously with the seasons, as they melt slightly during warmer periods and refreeze in colder periods.

75 percent of the Earth is covered by bodies of water. The largest bodies of water are five saltwater oceans (Pacific, Atlantic, Indian, Arctic, and Southern), which play a major role in climate, weather, and the carbon cycle on earth. **Oceans** are critical for maintaining balances that are critical to human life and biodiversity on Earth. Other large bodies of saltwater include **seas**, which are smaller than oceans and usually somewhat enclosed by large landmasses. For example, the Mediterranean Sea is a saltwater body which flows into the Atlantic Ocean but is largely surrounded by the African and European continents.

Large freshwater bodies include **rivers**, which move from high ground to low ground. They often originate in mountains as small flows of water that, over time, erode the area and create a larger space for more water to move down. Rivers might begin as streams or creeks, which are both smaller types of freshwater bodies that still have noticeable currents.

Lakes and **ponds** are bodies of water that are typically freshwater with less noticeable current. They form from rivers that deposit into an area where the soil is easily saturated, and the water is unable to easily flow elsewhere. Glacier melts and precipitation may also contribute to the water content of lakes and ponds.

Soil-Changing Processes and the Formation of Soil and Rock

There are three main sources that change the shape of the Earth's surface: they include weathering, erosion, and plate tectonics.

Weathering is the natural physical and chemical breakdown of rocks and the minerals within them. Some of the more common agents of weathering include changes in temperature, acids and acid rain, salts, wind, water, ice, plants, and animals. For example, water can seep into porous layers of bedrock. Because ice is less dense than water, when water freezes, it expands. Thus, the freeze-thaw cycle can cause rocks to crack and split into pieces. Once weathering has occurred, by any of its possible means, erosion can act upon the dissolved rocks and minerals and transport them away from their original site.

Erosion is caused by wind, water, and ice, and is considered a natural process that can be expedited by the effects of humans. Deforestation and overgrazing can expose soil, leading to extra erosion. In many areas, soil that is exposed can be carried away by strong winds and this changes the shape of the Earth's surface.

Glaciers contribute to erosion. They are so massive and heavy that their weight dislodges rocks. This, along with water melting and freezing in the cracks of bedrock, moves rocks that a glacier crushes back into fine rock "flour" as it slowly progresses along its path.

The Rock Cycle

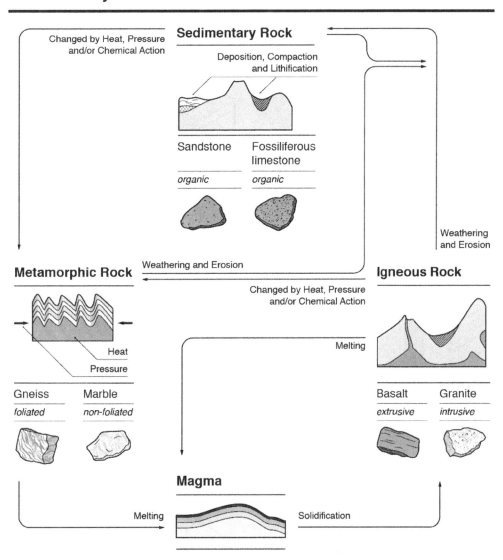

Often, **magma** (hot fluid below the earth's crust) from the Earth's mantle can find its way through cracks or boundaries between the plates in weak spots in the Earth's surface. This causes volcanoes, which can be a slow seeping action, called **shield domes**, or an explosive action at the surface, called **composite cones**. Both types of volcanoes cause corrosion of certain portions of land, but they can also add to the structure of the surface due to depositing amounts of silica upon the magma cooling, when exposed to a lower temperature atmosphere. Other types of volcanoes include the **cinder cones**, where the lava can burst up and then quickly cool and collect on the sides and lava domes, where the lava will pile up near the vent to form a steep side. There could also be a crack over the top of a lava flow, which is called a **fissure volcano**, and a volcano that keeps recreating itself within its original vent, which is called a **caldera volcano**.

Types of Volcano

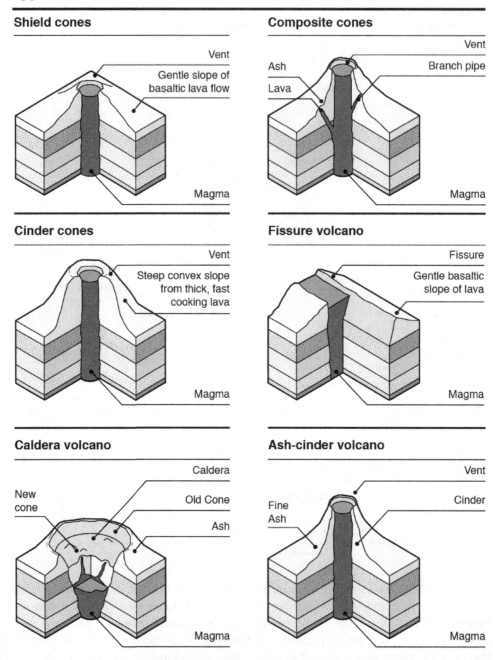

Similar to how molecules transfer heat, convection currents within the Earth's mantle cause cooling and heating of the magma, making it move in circular motions. These convection currents cause constant movement in the plates on the Earth's crust. It is **plate tectonics**—the movement of the plates past one another—that causes earthquakes. Earthquakes can be destructive by creating **craters**, which swallow up portions of the Earth and by forming **ridges**, where parts of the Earth pile up on each other. Both actions are transforming to the Earth's surface.

Layers of the Earth

The structure of the Earth has many layers. Starting with the center, or the **core,** the Earth comprises two separate sections: the inner core and the outer core. The innermost portion of the core is a solid center consisting of approximately 760 miles of iron. The outer core is slightly less than 1,400 miles in thickness and consists of a liquid nickel-iron alloy. The next section out from the core also has two layers. This section is the **mantle**, and it is split into the lower mantle and the upper mantle.

Both layers of the mantle consist of magnesium and iron, and they are extremely high in temperature. This hot temperature causes the metal contained in the lower mantle to rise and then cool slightly as it reaches the upper mantle. Once the metal begins to cool, it falls back down toward the lower mantle, restarting the whole process again. The motion of rising and falling within the layers of the mantle is the cause of plate tectonics and movement of the outermost layer of the Earth. The outermost layer of the Earth is called the **crust**. Movements between the mantle and the crust create effects such as earthquakes and volcanoes.

Mountains, Volcanoes, and Earthquakes and Their Effects

Most mountains are formed as a result of volcanic activity, tectonic activity, and erosion. Volcanic mountains are created through tectonic plate subduction or divergence where magma from the mantle is able to reach the surface. As the magma cools, it forms a relative dome or cone-like shape in which a vent still exists. Through this vent, eruptions continuously occur in which ash, volcanic gases, and rock material pile and create additional elevation. Famous volcanic mountains include Mt. Vesuvius in Italy and Krakatoa in Indonesia. The state of Hawaii in the United States is completely created from volcanic activity and still houses active volcanoes, such as Kilauea and Mauna Loa. Fold mountains are created when two continental plates collide directly into one another; the land where the two plates meet breaks, and the force of the two plates simultaneously compresses this material and pushes it upward. The most well-known range of fold mountains are the Himalayas, which are believed to have been formed when the Australian plate collided with Eurasian plate. The Himalayas continue to grow several inches each year as these plates continue to push against each other, and house Mt. Everest, the tallest mountain on Earth. Block mountains are created at fault lines, where two plates move alongside each other in opposite directions. From this force and motion, rocks along the fault line break down. Rocks upon one plate can become elevated while the other remains at the same elevation. The Sierra Nevada Mountains along the West Coast of the United States run along the well-known San Andreas fault line and are an example of block mountains.

Volcanoes and earthquakes are related, but come to be by different factors. **Volcanoes** are ruptures in the Earth's crust through which magma from the Earth's mantle emerges. Hot magma that comes through the rupture is known as lava. Volcanic mountains are formed and erupt by this continuous activity from the Earth's mantle. Ruptures through which lava flows may already be presents (such as along the edges of tectonic plates), or the force of the magma's exertion against the crust will create a rupture. **Earthquakes** can occur at this point from the force of the magma against the Earth's crust. However, earthquakes can also occur independently of volcanic activity from the drifting of tectonic plates. Fault lines are areas where two tectonic plates meet. The edges of these plates can move lengthwise against one another (a strike-slip fault line) or vertically against one another. When the plate that is lower moves further down, it is known as a normal fault. When the plate that is lower moves up, it is known as a reverse fault. When tectonic plates move against each other, stored energy is released. However, when two tectonic plates drift away from one another, this can also cause a visible crack in the Earth's surface that results in a release of energy. The more energy that is released, the stronger the earthquake. Some earthquakes may not even be felt, while others cause catastrophic destruction. Similarly, some volcanoes may experience minor eruptions that do not impact human life, while major eruptions can eliminate entire cities.

Strong earthquakes can result in tsunamis, fires, and the demolition of buildings and bridges. Another major hazard is the occurrence of avalanches and landslides. These side effects of earthquakes often cause more human and animal fatalities than the earthquake itself. Major volcanic eruptions can have significant localized and global effects. They can cause earthquakes (and the ensuing effects that result from earthquakes); heavy lava flows can be wide and will envelop and burn anything it comes across. The extreme amounts of sulfuric dust and ash that result from a volcanic

165

eruption can smother and kill living organisms instantly, or cause long-lasting respiratory problems in those who survive. Volcanic ash can also block the sun, resulting in cooling and darkness of an area that can last months or years.

Theory of Plate Tectonics

Evidence supporting the theory of plate tectonics includes the shape of the continents, the fossil record, the location of mountains, and the presence of earthquakes and volcanoes. From the earliest cartography to modern-day global positioning systems (GPS), it can be seen that the landmasses of continents appear to fit roughly together. Additionally, fossil and rock records are similar at the junctures where the continents would have originally been joined. For example, fossils of plant species that have been found along the eastern coast of South America have also been found along the western coast of Africa, indicating that these two continents were likely joined along these two coasts. As plates shifted, the continents broke away from one another. As seismic data monitoring and collection systems because more advanced, scientists were able to plot seismic activity and noticed most occurred along the same areas; volcanoes are also found in similarly grouped locations. Based on what is understood about how volcanoes form and how earthquakes occur, it is believed that their recorded data points correspond with the edges of tectonic plates.

Factors Influencing Location and Intensity of Earthquakes

Factors that influence the location and intensity of earthquakes include the Earth's rotation, the depth that the earthquake begins, the distance from the origination of the earthquake, and composition of areas nearby. The Earth's rotational speed fluctuates regularly, slowing or speeding up by milliseconds. However, this affects the intensity of seismic activity that occurs in the deeper layers of Earth, which can ultimately present as earthquakes near the crust. The **epicenter** is the point on the Earth's crust that lies directly over the point of origination of the earthquake. The **magnitude** of an earthquake measures how much energy is released at the point of origination and is measured using a seismograph. Areas that are close to the epicenter will feel stronger seismic waves, while areas farther away will experience less intensity. Finally, human activity may impact the strength of earthquakes. Some theorists say global warming may result in more frequent and stronger earthquakes, as the melting of ice caps will ultimately decrease pressure on the Earth's crust and allow more seismic activity to be felt.

Effects of Plate Tectonic Motion

It is believed that the Earth's crust, its most superficial solid layer, is comprised of large, slow-moving masses called plates. These plates float and move upon the mantle, the next layer of the Earth. The largest plate is the Pacific plate, mostly located under the Pacific Ocean. There are nine major plates and other smaller, minor pieces. Plates typically move several inches or less per year, and contribute to almost all geographical activity and features on Earth.

Plates move based on convection activity that occurs in the mantle, which causing plates that are adjacent to one another to interact in compressing, pushing, pulling, and spreading ways. Mid-ocean ridges are underwater mountain ranges that are made as two adjacent plates spread away from one another. Magma from the mantle is able to seep through these gaps; as the magma cools, new ocean floor forms. These are the youngest landmasses on Earth. Over millions of years, they may begin to emerge from the oceans as they grow. At subduction zones, plates collide rather than diverge. Depending on the type of plate, different responses can occur. If an oceanic plate, which is lighter in density, collides with a denser continental plate, the oceanic plate will move underneath (or subduct) the continental plate. This typically results in volcanic activity or earthquakes, both of which can create tsunamis along the coastline. When two continental plates collide, the edges will typically push upwards and create mountains. Seismic activity can also be affiliated with this type of collision, especially if the plates glide against each other in opposite directions.

Technological Solutions to Reduce the Impact of Earth Processes on Humans and Human Impact on Earth's Processes

Technological solutions exist and are always rapidly improving to reduce the impact of natural Earth processes on humans. Modern seismographs, which detect earthquakes, were first invented in the late 1800s and have become more complex and precise in recent decades. While these are unable to predict earthquakes, they can sense small

166

scale seismic activity which is a common precursor to larger events. Satellite and airplane tracking devices now support meteorological endeavors and help people adequately prepare for hurricanes and tornadoes. Levees and other architectural advances help prevent damage from flooding. Additionally, virtual reality tracking systems are in development to help first responders and emergency personnel help victims of natural disasters more efficiently. These systems would mimic real-time conditions within various buildings and infrastructure during times of emergency, eliminating trial-and-error rescue missions.

Human contributions to climate change are believed to be accelerating natural temperature and meteorological variation. Industrial manufacturing, pollution, the widespread use of cars and planes, livestock breeding methods, and deforestation have contributed to excess greenhouse gases in the atmosphere, which trap heat near the surface and increase temperatures. A slight change of several degrees in global temperature triggers a cascade of events that change the environment, such as stronger storms and hurricanes, drier or wetter climates in areas that are not accustomed for it, and extreme hot and cold temperatures. These can result in poor crop and food production, the death of major organisms (such as coral reef systems), and overall disruption in biodiversity. Technological changes to combat climate change include replacing fossil fuel usage with renewable energy sources (such as solar and wind power), using battery-operated vehicles, teleworking rather than commuting to work locations, and reducing concentrated animal feeding operations.

The Earth's Atmosphere

The Influence of the Sun and Oceans in Weather and Climate
The cycle of water on the Earth is called the **hydrologic cycle.** This cycle involves the water from the surface of the Earth evaporating from the oceans, lakes, and rivers, into the air. This evaporating water cools as it rises in the air. As the cooling occurs, the water condenses into clouds contained within the atmosphere, which eventually allow the water to return to the surface of the Earth in some form of precipitation. Precipitation can occur as snow, rain, hail, or sleet. Areas experiencing drought receive little or no precipitation; therefore, little to no water is available to run off into the surrounding bodies of water. The hydrologic cycle becomes imbalanced and often dormant in affected regions.

The terms *weather* and *climate* are often mistakenly interchanged, even though they describe different phenomena on Earth. **Weather** on Earth is constantly changing, while **climate** describes a long-term state. Factors that can affect the weather include latitude, elevation, wind, proximity to a large body of water, and ocean currents. Latitude influences weather based upon distance from the equator; for instance, the sections of the Earth nearest to the equator receive more direct sunlight from the positioning of the Earth on its axis, and therefore are warmer.

The higher the elevation of a location above sea level, the colder the temperature. Wind, resulting from the Earth's rotation (trade winds), can affect the temperatures of the surrounding areas. Large bodies of water can store heat, which influences the weather of surrounding areas and the effect ocean currents have on the rising and falling of warm air. This phenomenon occurs around lakes and surrounding areas; at times, for instance, areas on one side of a lake will experience heavier amounts of snowfall due to what is called "lake effect snow." This occurs when the lake is at a higher temperature than the atmosphere, and winds, picking up some of this energy, which causes a larger amount of snowfall on the other side of the lake.

Causes and Effects of Air Movements and Ocean Currents
Air movement and ocean currents both play critical factors in weather patterns and the climate over a given region. Oceans, due to their large size and ability to store, influence weather and climate through their convection patterns. Warmer ocean currents originate near the equator move toward cooler areas near both the north and south poles. Warmer water also evaporates into the atmosphere and transfers heat and moisture to the air.

Air moves due to the natural rotation of the Earth, as well as due to atmospheric temperature and pressure differences in an area. Wind moves as a result of convection or advection. Convection forces move warm air that is closer to the

167

Earth's surface to cooler areas that are higher. Advection forces move warm air horizontally to cooler areas, rather than to higher areas. Similarly, air also moves from high pressure to low pressure areas in a cyclone or anti-cyclone movement (known as the Coriolis effect). This effect is the primary precursor to hurricanes, tornadoes, and other cyclonic activities. As pressure drops, storm activity becomes stronger.

Variances in global air temperature and the occurrence of seasons result from the Earth's tilt and rotation toward or away from the Sun; the closer that a location is positioned toward the Sun, the more warming radiation it receives. During these periods, an area experiences spring and summer seasons. As an area begins to warm, both warmer ocean currents and warmer air begin the process of toward cooler pockets.

Across the globe, there exist large air masses that may be warmer or cooler relative to one another. Variations are impacted due to the placement of the air mass (for example, cooler, low pressure masses exist over mountains due to the altitude and lack of moisture, while warmer and high-pressure masses exist over the hotter parts of the ocean.) Human activity is also a contributor to the temperature of air masses. Cities that have a lot of concrete, for example, are less reflective of radiation; buildings and pollution are also able to trap and store large amounts of heat.

Importance of Technology on Predicting and Mitigating Severe Weather and Natural Hazards

Technology has significantly advanced how people are able to predict, prepare, and respond to severe weather and natural disasters. Equipment such as seismic sensors can note earthquake activity in deep parts of the ocean floor, as well as detect increasing pressure along fault lines. Meteorologists are able to collect data relating to weather, such as changes in air pressure and temperature, that indicate strengthening of storms. Satellite activity can take images of hurricanes from space and help track both its size, intensity, and directional changes. The Doppler radar is a tool that can detect the velocity and movement of precipitation, and can provide clues about incoming storms and tornadoes. Predicting natural disasters allows areas to prepare. For example, hurricane technology allows cities to evacuate, if necessary, board shelters, and stock up on supplies before a hurricane; prior to World War II and the use of airplanes to track storms, massive hurricanes often arrived as a surprise to coastal towns. Finally, technological advances have positively impacted emergency response and human survival after a natural disaster.

Data relating to a disaster (such as road closures or environmental dangers) are often available immediately; this supports responders in reaching victims safely and quickly. Medical advancements allow victims to receive treatment on-site and stabilize rather than being transported to a hospital, which can be a high-risk transition time during a natural disaster. Social media and text messaging allow people in natural disasters to stay in touch with family and responders, even when phone landlines might not work. Smartphones are also a way to disseminate information relating to natural disasters quickly. For example, many news sources and warning systems can provide continuous alerts and updates directly to individual users' smartphones. Additionally, people can program their health information into their phones, which can be extremely helpful to first responders.

The Earth's Water

Characteristics of Bodies of Water

Bodies of water come in different shapes, sizes, and compositions. Oceans are the largest bodies of water on Earth and consist of salt water. Puddles, on the other hand, are tiny bodies of water typically consisting of rain. Between these two extremes, there exist seas, rivers, streams, creeks, straits, basins, swamps, canals, dams, and many other forms of both natural and manmade bodies of water. Each body typically has its own unique ecosystem and biodiversity.

Bodies of water are primarily categorized by size. The smallest bodies of water include creeks, streams, and brooks. There are moderately flowing bodies of water that normally flow into larger bodies, such as a river. This juncture, where a smaller stream runs into a larger river, is known as an estuary. Most rivers also are adjacent to one or more deltas, a landmass of sediment deposits that accumulates from the current. Rivers typically have faster currents than creeks or streams, and they empty into a large pool of water that is enclosed by land, such as a pond or lake. These

168

types of water bodies are almost always sources of fresh water. They gain water from precipitation, melt, or natural springs found in mountainous regions.

Seas and gulfs are salty bodies of water that connect to an ocean, but are mostly surrounded by land. Narrow, inland bodies of water that are salty and connect to a sea or ocean are known as channels. A strait connects two larger bodies of water; typically, straits connect saltwater sources.

Swamps are a unique type of wetland, as they are mostly land upon which salt or freshwater collects. Swamps remain permanently wet, and host many water animals such as ducks, turtles, alligators, and fish. However, they also showcase large trees and plant life that are more commonly seen on landmasses.

Tides

Tides are waves that occur in bodies of water on Earth as a result of the Sun and Moon's gravitational pulls. They begin farther out in the body of water and move towards the coastline. As tides come in, they flood the coastline. The highest point of flooding is known as **high tide**. As tides recede, the coastline becomes more visible. The lowest point of the tidal ebb is known as **low tide**. The height difference of the water between high and low tides is known as the **tidal range**.

Different coastlines experience different tides, due to each coastline's relative location to the Sun and the Moon. Tides also change by season as the Earth tilts on its own axis. During the full and new moons each month, bodies of water experience spring tides. These tides have larger than normal tidal ranges. Rip tides are strong currents that begin at the shore and recede into the ocean at a rapid flow rate. Brown tides and red tides correspond with biological phenomenon that take place in the water. Brown tides result as excessive amounts of brownish algae grow in the water, giving the water a brown experience. Red tides also result from excessive algae growth; however, they are considerably more harmful than brown tides. While brown tides are detrimental to some forms of sea life, red tides result in toxins that can cause severe illness in humans and kill large populations of fish and other sea life. The detritus during red tides is often foul-smelling, can grow harmful bacteria, and results in beach closures that can impact local economies who depend on tourism.

Properties of Water

Water is a polar compound formed from one oxygen atom bonded to two hydrogen atoms. It has many unique properties, such as its ability to exist as a solid, liquid, and gas on Earth's surface. It is the only common substance that can exist in all three forms in this environment. Water is also self-ionizing, breaking itself up into H^+ and OH^- ions, which also makes it both an acid and a base.

The polarity of water and its attraction to other polar molecules is an important characteristic. **Cohesion** is the attraction of water molecules to each other. The slight negative charge of the oxygen atom in one molecule attracts the slightly positively charged hydrogen atoms of other water molecules. This attraction allows water to have surface tension. Insects, such as water striders, can actually walk across the surface of a pool of water. **Adhesion** is the attraction of water molecules to other molecules with which it can form hydrogen bonds. This attraction creates capillary action. **Capillary action** is the ability of water to "climb" up the side of a tube as it is attracted to the material of the tube. Its polarity also helps it break up ions in salts and bond to other polar substances, such as acids and alcohols. It is used to dissolve many substances and is often described as a **universal solvent** because of its polar attraction to other atoms and ions.

While most compounds become denser when they become solid, ice, the solid form of water, is actually less dense than the liquid form of water. The hydrogen bonds that form between the water molecules become ice crystals and more stable. The bonds remain spaced apart as the liquid freezes, creating a low density in the solid structure. Ice, therefore, floats to the top of a glass of liquid water.

Water is also a great moderator of temperature because of its high specific heat and high heat of vaporization. **Specific heat** is the amount of energy that is needed to change the temperature of one gram of a substance 1°C. When a substance has a high specific heat, it requires a lot of energy to change the temperature. Since water molecules form a lot of hydrogen bonds, it takes a lot of energy to break up the bonds. Since there are a lot of hydrogen bonds to absorb and release heat as they break and form, respectively, temperature changes are minimized. Similarly, **heat of vaporization** is the amount of energy needed to change 1 gram of liquid into gas. It takes a lot of energy to break the hydrogen bonds between liquid water molecules and turn them into water vapor.

Interactions of Earth's Hydrosphere

The Earth's hydrosphere contains all of the water on Earth; it is interdependent with the other major systems (atmosphere, biosphere, and lithosphere) of the planet. The hydrosphere is immense, as 75 percent of the Earth is water. Bodies of salt and fresh water, ice, clouds, fog, and precipitation are all a part of the hydrosphere. The water cycle explains the process of how water moves through the hydrosphere, and also provides explanation for how it interacts with the other major systems. Bodies of water on the earth's surface absorb heat in the atmosphere and evaporate (or turn into a gas in the atmosphere). Moisture in the atmosphere can also transfer heat back to the surface, during which water condenses (or returns to a solid form). This is commonly seen in the very early morning or evening hours, when dew drops form. These energy transfers can also change the relative and global climate. For example, when there is heavy moisture in the atmosphere, the air feels damp and humid; areas with limited ground or air moisture, such as deserts, are extremely arid with unique vegetation and animal life that are able to survive in these climates.

Not all evaporated water quickly condenses. Some condense over time, as warmer water vapor rises to cooler parts of the atmosphere. When it cools significantly, it may turn into tiny droplets that create a cloud. As clouds move around the globe, they can fall back to the Earth's surface as precipitation (rain, snow, hail, or ice) as air pressure and temperature drops. Precipitation returns to the soil, bodies of water, or forms of ice. As the water warms, the cycle begins again. The hydrosphere serves as an environmental habitat and source of oxygen for marine life that are included in the biosphere. It also serves as drinking water for land animals and humans; it can also be a source of energy to power electrical needs. Water is additionally a primary element of erosion and landform change in the lithosphere.

Practice Quiz

1. Which statement is true regarding atomic structure?
    a. Protons orbit around a nucleus.
    b. Neutrons have a positive charge.
    c. Electrons are in the nucleus.
    d. Protons have a positive charge.

2. Which statement regarding meiosis is correct?
    a. Meiosis produces four diploid cells.
    b. Meiosis contains two cellular divisions separated by interphase II.
    c. Meiosis produces cells with two sets of chromosomes.
    d. Crossing over occurs in the prophase of meiosis I.

3. What part of the respiratory system is responsible for regulating the temperature and humidity of the air that comes into the body?
    a. Larynx
    b. Lungs
    c. Trachea
    d. Sinuses

4. What is the difference between the isotopes of an atom?
    a. The number of protons
    b. The number of orbitals
    c. The number of neutrons
    d. The number of electrons

5. Which of the following statements is true regarding DNA?
    a. DNA is the genetic code.
    b. DNA provides energy.
    c. DNA is single-stranded.
    d. All of the above statements are true.

See answers on the next page.

Answer Explanations

1. D: Choice *D* is correct; protons have a positive charge. An atom is structured with a nucleus in the center that contains neutral neutrons and positive protons. Surrounding the nucleus are orbiting electrons that are negatively charged.

2. D: Choice *D* is the only correct answer because each chromosome set goes through a process called crossing over, which jumbles up the genes on each chromatid during meiosis I. Choice *A* is incorrect because meiosis produces haploid cells. Choice *B* is incorrect because there is no interphase II. Otherwise, gametes would be diploid instead of haploid. Choice *C* is incorrect because the resulting cells only have one set of chromosomes.

3. D: After air enters the nose or mouth, it gets passed on to the sinuses, which regulate temperature and humidity before passing the air on to the rest of the body. Volume of air can change with varying temperatures and humidity levels, so it is important for the air to be a constant temperature and humidity before being processed by the lungs. The larynx is the voice box of the body, making Choice *A* incorrect. The lungs are responsible for oxygen and carbon dioxide exchange between the air that is breathed in and the blood that is circulating the body, making Choice *B* incorrect. The trachea takes the temperature- and humidity-regulated air from the sinuses to the lungs, making Choice *C* incorrect.

4. C: The total number of protons and neutrons in an atom is the atom's mass number. The number of protons in an atom is the atomic number. If an atom has a variation in the number of neutrons, the atom's mass number changes, but the atomic number remains the same. This variation creates isotopes of the atom with the same atomic number. The number of protons, Choice *A*, is unique for each atom and does not change. The number of orbitals remains the same for atoms; therefore, Choice *B* is incorrect. The number of electrons, Choice *D*, affects the charge of the atom.

5. A: The only true statement provided is that DNA is the genetic code. Choice *B* is incorrect because DNA does not provide energy—that's the job of carbohydrates and glucose. Choice *C* is incorrect because DNA is double-stranded. Because Choices *B* and *C* are incorrect, Choice *D*, all of the above, is also incorrect.

Subtest II: Mathematics

Number Sense

Numbers, Relationships Among Numbers, and Number Systems

Base Ten Place Value

The **base-10 number system** is also called the **decimal system of naming numbers**. There is a decimal point that sets the value of numbers based on their position relative to the decimal point. The order from the decimal point to the right is the tenths place, then hundredths place, then thousandths place. From the decimal point to the left, the place value is ones, tens, hundreds, etc. The number 2,356 can be described in words as "two thousand three hundred fifty-six." In expanded form, it can be written as:

$$(2 \times 1,000) + (3 \times 100) + (5 \times 10) + (6 \times 1)$$

The expanded form shows the value each number holds in its place. The number 3,093 can be written in words as "three thousand ninety-three." In expanded form, it can be expressed as:

$$(3 \times 1,000) + (0 \times 100) + (9 \times 10) + (3 \times 1)$$

Notice that the zero is added in the expanded form as a place holder. There are no hundreds in the number, so a zero is written in the hundreds place.

Each number in the base-10 system is made of the numbers 0-9, located in different places relative to the decimal point. Based on where the numbers fall, the value of a digit changes. For example, the number 7,509 has a seven in the thousands place. This means there are seven groups of one thousand. The number 457 has a seven in the ones place. This means there are seven groups of one. Even though there is a seven in both numbers, the place of the seven tells the value of the digit. A practice question may ask the place and value of the 4 in 3,948. The four is found in the tens place, which means four represents the number 40, or four groups of ten. Another place value may be on the opposite side of the decimal point. A question may ask the place and value of the 8 in the number 203.80. In this case, the eight is in the tenths place because it is in the first place to the right of the decimal point. It holds a value of eight-tenths, or eight groups of one-tenth.

The value of a digit is found by recognizing its place relative to the rest of the number. For example, the number 569.23 contains a 6. The position of the 6 is two places to the left of the decimal, putting it in the tens place. The tens place gives it a value of 60, or six groups of ten. The number 39.674 has a 4 in it. The number 4 is located three places to the right of the decimal point, placing it in the thousandths place. The value of the 4 is four-thousandths, because of its position relative to the other numbers and to the decimal. It can be described as 0.004 by itself, or four groups of one-thousandths. The numbers 100 and 0.1 are both made up of ones and zeros. The first number, 100, has a 1 in the hundreds place, giving it a value of one hundred. The second number, 0.1, has a 1 in the tenths place, giving that 1 a value of one-tenth. The place of the number gives it the value.

Number Theory Concepts

Factorization is the process of breaking up a mathematical quantity, such as a number or polynomial, into a product of two or more factors. For example, a factorization of the number 16 is:

$$16 = 8 \times 2$$

If multiplied out, the factorization results in the original number. A **prime factorization** is a specific factorization when the number is factored completely using prime numbers only. For example, the prime factorization of 16 is:

$$16 = 2 \times 2 \times 2 \times 2$$

A factor tree can be used to find the prime factorization of any number. Within a factor tree, pairs of factors are found until no other factors can be used, as in the following factor tree of the number 84:

A factor tree

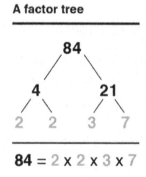

84 = 2 x 2 x 3 x 7

It first breaks 84 into 21×4, which is not a prime factorization. Then, both 21 and 4 are factored into their primes. The final numbers on each branch consist of the numbers within the prime factorization. Therefore:

$$84 = 2 \times 2 \times 3 \times 7$$

Factorization can be helpful in finding the greatest common divisors and least common denominators.

Structure of the Number System

Whole numbers are the numbers 0, 1, 2, 3, ... Examples of other whole numbers would be 413 and 8,431. Notice that numbers such as 4.13 and $\frac{1}{4}$ are not included in whole numbers. **Counting numbers**, also known as **natural numbers**, consist of all whole numbers except for the zero. In set notation, the natural numbers are the set $\{1, 2, 3, \dots\}$. The entire set of whole numbers and negative versions of those same numbers comprise the set of numbers known as **integers.** Therefore, in set notation, the integers are $\{\dots, -3, -2, -1, 0, 1, 2, 3, \dots\}$. Examples of other integers are $-4,981$ and $90,131$. A number line is a great way to visualize the integers. Integers are labeled on the following number line:

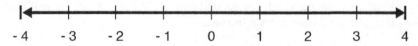

The arrows on the right- and left-hand sides of the number line show that the line continues indefinitely in both directions.

Fractions also exist on the number line as parts of a whole. For example, if an entire pie is cut into two pieces, each piece is half of the pie, or $\frac{1}{2}$. The top number in any fraction, known as the **numerator,** defines how many parts there are. The bottom number, known as the **denominator,** states how many pieces the whole is divided into. Fractions can also be negative or written in their corresponding decimal form.

174

A **decimal** is a number that uses a decimal point and numbers to the right of the decimal point representing the part of the number that is less than 1. For example, 3.5 is a decimal and is equivalent to the fraction $\frac{7}{2}$ or the mixed number $3\frac{1}{2}$. The decimal is found by dividing 2 into 7. Other examples of fractions are $\frac{2}{7}$, $\frac{-3}{14}$, and $\frac{14}{27}$.

Any number that can be expressed as a fraction is known as a **rational number.** Basically, if a and b are any integers and $b \neq 0$, then $\frac{a}{b}$ is a rational number. Any integer can be written as a fraction where the denominator is 1, so therefore the rational numbers consist of all fractions and all integers.

Ordering Real Numbers

Ordering rational numbers is a way to compare two or more different numerical values. Determining whether two amounts are equal, less than, or greater than each other is the basis for comparing both positive and negative numbers. Also, a group of numbers can be compared by ordering them from the smallest amount to the largest amount. A few symbols are necessary to use when ordering rational numbers. The equals sign, =, shows that the two quantities on either side of the symbol have the same value. For example, $\frac{12}{3} = 4$ because both values are equivalent. Another symbol that is used to compare numbers is <, which represents "less than." With this symbol, the smaller number is placed on the left and the larger number is placed on the right. Always remember that the symbol's "mouth" opens up to the larger number.

When comparing negative and positive numbers, it is important to remember that the number occurring to the left on the number line is always smaller and is placed to the left of the symbol. This idea might seem confusing because some values could appear at first glance to be larger, even though they are not. For example, $-5 < 4$ is read "negative 5 is less than 4." Here is an image of a number line for help:

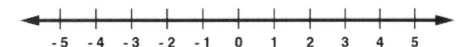

The symbol ≤ represents "less than or equal to," and it joins < with equality. Therefore, both $-5 \leq 4$ and $-5 \leq -5$ are true statements and "-5 is less than or equal to both 4 and -5." Other symbols are > and ≥, which represent "greater than" and "greater than or equal to." Both $4 \geq -1$ and $-1 \geq -1$ are correct ways to use these symbols.

Here is a chart of these four inequality symbols:

Symbol	Definition
<	less than
≤	less than or equal to
>	greater than
≥	greater than or equal to

Comparing integers is a straightforward process, especially when using the number line, but the comparison of decimals and fractions is not as obvious. When comparing two non-negative decimals, compare digit by digit, starting from the left. The larger value contains the first larger digit. For example, 0.1456 is larger than 0.1234 because the value 4 in the hundredths place in the first decimal is larger than the value 2 in the hundredths place in the second decimal. When comparing a fraction with a decimal, convert the fraction to a decimal and then compare in the same manner. Finally, there are a few options when comparing fractions. If two non-negative fractions have the same denominator, the fraction with the larger numerator is the larger value.

If they have different denominators, they can be converted to equivalent fractions with a common denominator to be compared, or they can be converted to decimals to be compared. When comparing two negative decimals or fractions, a different approach must be used. It is important to remember that the smaller number exists to the left on the number line. Therefore, when comparing two negative decimals by place value, the number with the larger first place value is smaller due to the negative sign. Whichever value is closer to 0 is larger. For instance, -0.456 is larger than -0.498 because of the values in the hundredth places. If two negative fractions have the same denominator, the fraction with the larger numerator is smaller because of the negative sign.

0 is the dividing point between the positive and negative numbers on a number line. In order to graph numbers on a number line, the number is first located on the line, and then a dot is drawn at the location of the number. For example, here is -1 graphed on a number line:

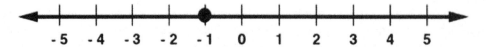

The number line can be used to add and subtract numbers. In order to add a number to a positive number, locate the first number on the number line and then move to the right the number of units corresponding to the second number. For example, $-5 + 2 = -3$. First, -5 is located on the number line. Then, moving 2 units to the right results in a value of -3.

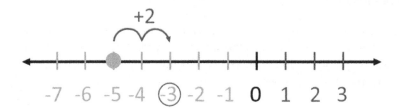

In order to add a number to a negative number, plot the first point on the number line and then move to the left the number of units corresponding to the absolute value of the second number. For example, $8 + (-2) = 6$. First, 8 is located on the number line. Then, moving $|-2| = 2$ units to the left results in a value of 6.

Because subtracting a positive number is the same as adding a negative number, this same procedure could be used to obtain $8 - 2 = 6$. Subtracting a positive number also involves moving that many units to the left on the number line.

Operations with Exponents and Scientific Notation

Rational numbers can be whole or negative numbers, fractions, or repeating decimals because these numbers can all be written as fractions. Examples of rational numbers include $\frac{1}{2}, \frac{5}{4}$, 2.75 and 8. The number 8 is rational because it can be expressed as a fraction: $\frac{8}{1} = 8$. **Rational exponents** are used to express the root of a number raised to a specific power. For example, $3^{\frac{1}{2}}$ has a base of 3 and rational exponent of $\frac{1}{2}$. The square root of 3 raised to the first power can be written as $\sqrt[2]{3^1}$.

Any number with a rational exponent can be written this way. The **numerator**, or number on top of the fraction, becomes the whole number exponent and the **denominator**, or bottom number of the fraction, becomes the root. Another example is $4^{\frac{3}{2}}$. It can be rewritten as the square root of four to the third power, or $\sqrt[2]{4^3}$. This can be simplified by performing the operations 4 to the third power, $4^3 = 4 \times 4 \times 4 = 64$, and then taking the square root of

$64, \sqrt[2]{64}$, which yields an answer of 8. Another way of stating the answer would be to power of $\frac{3}{2}$ is eight, or that 4 to the power of $\frac{3}{2}$ is the square root of 4 cubed,

$$\sqrt[2]{4}^3 = 2^3 = 2 \times 2 \times 2 = 8$$

The nth root of a is given as $\sqrt[n]{a}$, which is called a **radical.** Typical values for n are 2 and 3, which represent the square and cube roots. In this form, n represents an integer greater than or equal to 2, and a is a real number. If n is even, a must be nonnegative, and if n is odd, a can be any real number. This radical can be written in exponential form as $a^{\frac{1}{n}}$. Therefore, $\sqrt[4]{15}$ is the same as $15^{\frac{1}{4}}$ and $\sqrt[3]{-5}$ is the same as $(-5)^{\frac{1}{3}}$.

In a similar fashion, the nth root of a can be raised to a power m, which is written as $\left(\sqrt[n]{a}\right)^m$. This expression is the same as $\sqrt[n]{a^m}$. For example:

$$\sqrt[2]{4^3} = \sqrt[2]{64} = 8 = \left(\sqrt[2]{4}\right)^3 = 2^3$$

Because $\sqrt[n]{a} = a^{\frac{1}{n}}$, both sides can be raised to an exponent of m, resulting in:

$$\left(\sqrt[n]{a}\right)^m = \sqrt[n]{a^m} = a^{\frac{m}{n}}$$

This rule allows:

$$\sqrt[2]{4^3} = \left(\sqrt[2]{4}\right)^3 = 4^{\frac{3}{2}} = (2^2)^{\frac{3}{2}} = 2^{\frac{6}{2}} = 2^3 = 8$$

Negative exponents can also be incorporated into these rules. Any time an exponent is negative, the base expression must be flipped to the other side of the fraction bar and rewritten with a positive exponent. For instance, $2^{-3} = \frac{1}{2^3} = \frac{1}{8}$. Therefore, two more relationships between radical and exponential expressions are:

$$a^{-\frac{1}{n}} = \frac{1}{\sqrt[n]{a}}$$

$$a^{-\frac{m}{n}} = \frac{1}{\sqrt[n]{a^m}} = \frac{1}{\left(\sqrt[n]{a}\right)^m}$$

Thus:

$$8^{-\frac{1}{3}} = \frac{1}{\sqrt[3]{8}} = \frac{1}{2}$$

All of these relationships are very useful when simplifying complicated radical and exponential expressions. If an expression contains both forms, use one of these rules to change the expression to contain either all radicals or all exponential expressions. This process makes the entire expression much easier to work with, especially if the expressions are contained within equations.

Consider the following example: $\sqrt{x} \times \sqrt[4]{x}$. It is written in radical form; however, it can be simplified into one radical by using exponential expressions first. The expression can be written as $x^{\frac{1}{2}} \times x^{\frac{1}{4}}$. It can be combined into one base by adding the exponents as:

$$x^{\frac{1}{2}+\frac{1}{4}} = x^{\frac{3}{4}}$$

Writing this back in radical form, the result is $\sqrt[4]{x^3}$.

Scientific notation is a system used to represent numbers that are very large or very small. Sometimes, numbers are way too big or small to be written out with multiple zeros behind them or in decimal form, so scientific notation is used as a way to express these numbers in a simpler way.

Scientific notation takes the decimal notation and turns it into scientific notation, like the table below:

Decimal Notation	Scientific Notation
5	5×10^0
500	5×10^2
10,000,000	1×10^7
8,000,000,000	8×10^9
-55,000	-5.5×10^4
.00001	10^{-5}

In scientific notation, the decimal is placed after the first digit and all the remaining numbers are dropped. For example, 5 becomes "5.0×10^0." This equation is raised to the zero power because there are no zeros behind the number "5." Always put the decimal after the first number. Let's say we have the number 125,000. We would write this using scientific notation as follows: 1.25×10^5, because to move the decimal from behind "1" to behind "125,000" takes five counts, so we put the exponent "5" behind the "10." As you can see in the table above, the number ".00001" is too cumbersome to be written out each time for an equation, so we would want to say that it is "10^{-5}." If we count from the place behind the decimal point to the number "1," we see that we go backwards 5 places. Thus, the "-5" in the scientific notation form represents 5 places to the right of the decimal.

Algorithms for Addition, Subtraction, Multiplication, and Division

Addition is the combining of two numbers to find the total. The numbers being added together are the **addends**, and the resulting answer is the **sum**. Addition problems can be completed using a variety of strategies including number lines, base-10 blocks, place value, and concrete models. When adding multi-digit numbers, the numbers must be lined up by place value vertically. The problem $138 + 47$ demonstrating this type of addition involving carrying is shown below:

$$
\begin{array}{r}
1\ 3^1 8 \\
+\ \ \ 4\ 7 \\
\hline
1\ 8\ 5
\end{array}
$$

The addition of the ones column $8 + 7 = 15$, so the 5 is written beneath the ones column, and the 1 is carried over to be added to the tens column. The remaining columns are added down to provide the solution.

When adding a negative number to a positive number, the problem becomes a subtraction problem. Adding 10 and -2 becomes:

$$10 + (-2) = 10 - 2 = 8$$

When adding two negative numbers, complete the addition as usual, but the resulting total is negative,

$$-15 + (-6) = -21$$

Subtraction involves taking away or removing an amount from a number to find the difference of the two values. Addition and subtraction are related because they are inverse operations. For example, the addition problem $7 + 2 = 9$ can be changed into a subtraction problem:

$$9 - 2 = 7$$

Subtraction problems also can be solved using some of the same methods as addition including number lines and concrete models. Subtracting multi-digit numbers is slightly more complicated because they can involve **borrowing**. An example of a subtraction problem $263 - 56$ with borrowing is shown below:

$$
\begin{array}{r}
2\,^5\!6\,^1\!3 \\
-\quad 5\,6 \\
\hline
2\ 0\ 7
\end{array}
$$

In the ones column, 6 cannot be subtracted from 3; therefore, 1 is borrowed from the tens column making the ones column on the top row 13 instead of 3. The 6 in the tens column becomes 5 instead of 6. The rest of the subtraction is carried out accordingly.

When a negative number is subtracted, it creates a double negative, $13 - (-6)$. This changes the sign to a positive,
$$13 + 6 = 19$$

Multiplication is basically a short cut to repeated addition. For example, 4×5 can be thought of as adding the number 4 a total of 5 times: $4 + 4 + 4 + 4 + 4$. Both of these techniques yield the equivalent answer, 20.

Other methods to complete multiplication problems include area models, partial products, and long multiplication like the example that follows:

$$
\begin{array}{r}
2\,3 \\
\times\ 1\,4 \\
\end{array}
$$

$$
\begin{array}{r}
2\,^1\!3 \\
\times\ 1\,4 \\
\hline
9\,2
\end{array}
$$

The right column is multiplied first. In this case, $3 \times 4 = 12$ so the 2 is written below the right column, and the 1 is carried. Next, the 4 in the right column is multiplied by the 2 in the left column, and the 1 that was carried in the previous step is added:

$$(4 \times 2) + 1 = 9$$

The result is placed to the left of the 2.

$$
\begin{array}{r}
2\,^1\!3 \\
\times\ 1\,4 \\
\hline
9\,2 \\
0
\end{array}
$$

A 0 or blank space must be used for a placeholder before completing the next step of multiplication.

$$\begin{array}{r} 23 \\ \times\ 14 \\ \hline 92 \\ 230 \end{array}$$

The next line of multiplication starts with the 1 in the left column. It is multiplied starting on the right by 3 and then by 2, with the results written below the appropriate columns as shown.

$$\begin{array}{r} 23 \\ \times\ 14 \\ \hline 92 \\ 2^13 0 \\ \hline 322 \end{array}$$

The two lines of multiplication are added together to achieve the final product of 322.

When multiplying negative and nonnegative numbers, if the signs are the same, then the answer is positive. If the signs are different, then the answer is negative. These same rules apply to division as well.

Like addition and subtraction, multiplication and division are inverse operations. Division splits an amount or number into equal groups or parts. For example, $14 \div 2 = 7$ because 14 can be separated into 2 equal groups of 7. In the previous example, 14 is the **dividend**, 2 is the **divisor**, and 7 is the **quotient**, which is the term for the solution to a division problem. Division problems can be solved using arrays, area models, or equal groups of concrete objects. Division of multi-digit numbers can also be completed using long division, for example, $348 \div 6$.

$$\begin{array}{r} 58 \\ 6\,\overline{\smash{)}348} \\ 30\,\downarrow \\ \hline 48 \\ 48 \\ \hline 0 \end{array}$$

First, set up the problem. Start by dividing the first number on the left of the dividend, 3, by the divisor of 6. 3 is not divisible by 6, so the next number to the left in the dividend (the 3) comes into play. This means that 34 must be divided by 6. 6 will divide into 34 a total of 5 times, so the 5 goes above the 4.

6 multiplied by 5 equals 30, so write that below the 34. Then, subtract 30 from 34. This leaves 4. The next number to the right in the dividend must be dropped down to make 48. 48 is evenly divisible by 6, so put the quotient of that division, 8, on the top next to the 5.

The final solution is 58.

Properties of the Number System

Operations follow certain properties and rules. Addition and multiplication follow the **commutative property**. This means that the numbers can be added or multiplied in any order, and the result will be the same. For example,

180

$6 \times 3 = 18$ and $3 \times 6 = 18$. Subtraction and division are not commutative. Addition and multiplication are also associative. The **associative property** means that the grouping of numbers with parentheses does not change the answer to the problem. For example,

$$(7 + 8) + 5 = 20 \text{ and } (7 + 5) + 8 = 20$$

Another property that impacts operations is the distributive property. The **distributive property** states that when a sum or difference inside the parentheses is multiplied by a number, it is the same as multiplying both the numbers inside the parentheses by the outside number and adding or subtracting the results. For example:

$$8 \times (4 + 3) = 8 \times 7 = 56$$

and

$$8 \times 4 + 8 \times 3 = 32 + 24 = 56$$

Operations with Negative Numbers and Fractions

Once the operations are understood with whole numbers, they can be used with negative numbers. There are many rules surrounding operations with negative numbers. First, consider addition with integers. The sum of two numbers can first be shown using a number line. For example, to add $-5 + (-6)$, plot the point -5 on the number line. Adding a negative number is the same as subtracting, so move 6 units to the left. This process results in landing on -11 on the number line, which is the sum of -5 and -6. If adding a positive number, move to the right. Visualizing this process using a number line is useful for understanding; however, it is not efficient.

A quicker process is to learn the rules. When adding two numbers with the same sign, add the absolute values of both numbers, and use the common sign of both numbers as the sign of the sum. For example, to add $-5 + (-6)$, add their absolute values:

$$5 + 6 = 11$$

Then, introduce a negative number because both addends are negative. The result is -11. To add two integers with unlike signs, subtract the lesser absolute value from the greater absolute value, and apply the sign of the number with the greater absolute value to the result. For example, the sum $-7 + 4$ can be computed by finding the difference $7 - 4 = 3$ and then applying a negative because the value with the larger absolute value is negative. The result is -3. Similarly, the sum $-4 + 7$ can be found by computing the same difference but leaving it as a positive result because the addend with the larger absolute value is positive. Also, recall that any number plus 0 equals that number. This is known as the **Addition Property of 0.**

Subtracting two integers with opposite signs can be computed by changing to addition to avoid confusion. The rule is to add the first number to the opposite of the second number. The opposite of a number is the number with the same value on the other side of 0 on the number line. For example, -2 and 2 are opposites. Consider $4 - 8$. Change this to adding the opposite as follows: $4 + (-8)$. Then, follow the rules of addition of integers to obtain -4. Secondly, consider $-8 - (-2)$. Change this problem to adding the opposite as $-8 + 2$, which equals -6. Notice that subtracting a negative number functions the same as adding a positive number.

Multiplication and division of integers are actually less confusing than addition and subtraction because the rules are simpler to understand. If two factors in a multiplication problem have the same sign, the result is positive. If one factor is positive and one factor is negative, the result, known as the **product,** is negative. For example, $(-9)(-3) = 27$ and $9(-3) = -27$. Also, any number times 0 always results in 0. If a problem consists of several multipliers, the result is negative if it contains an odd number of negative factors, and the result is positive if it contains an even number of negative factors. For example:

$$(-1)(-1)(-1)(-1) = 1$$

and

$$(-1)(-1)(-1)(-1)(-1) = -1$$

These two problems are also examples of repeated multiplication, which can be written in a more compact notation using exponents. The first example can be written as $(-1)^4 = 1$, and the second example can be written as $(-1)^5 = -1$. Both are exponential expressions; -1 is the base in both instances, and 4 and 5 are the respective exponents. Note that a negative number raised to an odd power is always negative, and a negative number raised to an even power is always positive. Also, $(-1)^4$ is not the same as -1^4. In the first expression, the negative is included in the parentheses, but it is not in the second expression. The second expression is found by evaluating 1^4 first to get 1 and then by applying the negative sign to obtain -1.

Similar rules apply within division. First, consider some vocabulary. When dividing 14 by 2, it can be written in the following ways: $14 \div 2 = 7$ or $\frac{14}{2} = 7$. 14 is the **dividend,** 2 is the **divisor,** and 7 is the **quotient.** If two numbers in a division problem have the same sign, the quotient is positive. If two numbers in a division problem have different signs, the quotient is negative. For example:

$$14 \div (-2) = -7$$

and

$$-14 \div (-2) = 7$$

To check division, multiply the quotient times the divisor to obtain the dividend. Also, remember that 0 divided by any number is equal to 0. However, any number divided by 0 is undefined. It just does not make sense to divide a number by 0 parts.

Once the rules for integers are understood, move on to learning how to perform operations with fractions and decimals. Recall that a rational number can be written as a fraction and can be converted to a decimal through division. If a rational number is negative, the rules for adding, subtracting, multiplying, and dividing integers must be used. If a rational number is in fraction form, performing addition, subtraction, multiplication, and division is more complicated than when working with integers. First, consider addition. To add two fractions having the same denominator, add the numerators and then reduce the fraction. When an answer is a fraction, it should always be in lowest terms. **Lowest terms** means that every common factor, other than 1, between the numerator and denominator is divided out. For example:

$$\frac{2}{8} + \frac{4}{8} = \frac{6}{8} = \frac{6 \div 2}{8 \div 2} = \frac{3}{4}$$

Both the numerator and denominator of $\frac{6}{8}$ have a common factor of 2, so 2 is divided out of each number to put the fraction in lowest terms. If denominators are different in an addition problem, the fractions must be converted to have common denominators. The **least common denominator (LCD)** of all the given denominators must be found, and this value is equal to the **least common multiple (LCM)** of the denominators. This non-zero value is the smallest number that is a multiple of both denominators. Then, rewrite each original fraction as an equivalent fraction using the new denominator. Once in this form, apply the process of adding with like denominators.

For example, consider $\frac{1}{3} + \frac{4}{9}$.

The LCD is 9 because it is the smallest multiple of both 3 and 9. The fraction $\frac{1}{3}$ must be rewritten with 9 as its denominator. Therefore, multiply both the numerator and denominator by 3. Multiplying by $\frac{3}{3}$ is the same as multiplying by 1, which does not change the value of the fraction. Therefore, an equivalent fraction is $\frac{3}{9}$, which makes it:

$$\frac{1}{3} + \frac{4}{9} = \frac{3}{9} + \frac{4}{9} = \frac{7}{9}$$

This is in lowest terms. Subtraction is performed in a similar manner; once the denominators are equal, the numerators are then subtracted. The following is an example of addition of a positive and a negative fraction:

$$-\frac{5}{12} + \frac{5}{9} = -\frac{5 \times 3}{12 \times 3} + \frac{5 \times 4}{9 \times 4}$$

$$-\frac{15}{36} + \frac{20}{36} = \frac{5}{36}$$

Common denominators are not used in multiplication and division. To multiply two fractions, multiply the numerators together and the denominators together. Then, write the result in lowest terms. For example,

$$\frac{2}{3} \times \frac{9}{4} = \frac{18}{12} = \frac{3}{2}$$

Alternatively, the fractions could be factored first to cancel out any common factors before performing the multiplication. For example,

$$\frac{2}{3} \times \frac{9}{4} = \frac{2}{3} \times \frac{3 \times 3}{2 \times 2} = \frac{3}{2}$$

This second approach is helpful when working with larger numbers, as common factors might not be obvious. Multiplication and division of fractions are related because the division of two fractions is changed into a multiplication problem. This means that dividing a fraction by another fraction is the same as multiplying the first fraction by the reciprocal of the second fraction, so that second fraction must be inverted, or "flipped," to be in reciprocal form. For example:

$$\frac{11}{15} \div \frac{3}{5} = \frac{11}{15} \times \frac{5}{3} = \frac{55}{45} = \frac{11}{9}$$

The fraction $\frac{5}{3}$ is the reciprocal of $\frac{3}{5}$.

It is possible to multiply and divide numbers containing a mix of integers and fractions. In this case, convert the integer to a fraction by placing it over a denominator of 1. For example, a division problem involving an integer and a fraction is:

$$3 \div \frac{1}{2} = \frac{3}{1} \times \frac{2}{1} = \frac{6}{1} = 6$$

Computational Tools, Procedures, and Strategies

Order of Operations

When using operations and their properties, it is also important to remember the rule for the order of operations. When evaluating an expression, any operations inside grouping symbols must be completed first. Next, any numbers with exponents are simplified. Then, the multiplication and division portions of the expression can be evaluated. Addition and subtraction are to be completed last. A helpful mnemonic to remember these steps is *Please Excuse My Dear Aunt Sally* or **PEMDAS**. The following expression needs to be completed using the order of operations.

$$(5 - 3) \times 6 + 8$$

The numbers inside the parentheses need to be evaluated first. This gives $2 \times 6 + 8$. Next, the multiplication must be completed, $12 + 8$. Last, the addition is completed to provide a solution:

$$12 + 8 = 20$$

Rounding and Estimating

Sometimes it is helpful to find an estimated answer to a problem rather than working out an exact answer. An estimation might be much quicker to find, and it might be all that is required given the scenario. For example, if Aria goes grocery shopping and has only a $100 bill to cover all of her purchases, it might be appropriate for her to estimate the total of the items she is purchasing to determine if she has enough money to cover them. Also, an estimation can help determine if an answer makes sense. For instance, if you estimate that an answer should be in the 100s, but your result is a fraction less than 1, something is probably wrong in the calculation.

The first type of estimation involves rounding. As mentioned, **rounding** consists of expressing a number in terms of the nearest decimal place like the tenth, hundredth, or thousandth place, or in terms of the nearest whole number unit like tens, hundreds, or thousands place. When rounding to a specific place value, look at the digit to the right of the place. If it is 5 or higher, round the number to its left up to the next value, and if it is 4 or lower, keep that number at the same value. For instance, 1,654.2674 rounded to the nearest thousand is 2,000, and the same number rounded to the nearest thousandth is 1,654.267. Rounding can make it easier to estimate totals at the store. Items can be rounded to the nearest dollar. For example, a can of corn that costs $0.79 can be rounded to $1.00, and then all other items can be rounded in a similar manner and added together.

When working with larger numbers, it might make more sense to round to higher place values. For example, when estimating the total value of a dealership's car inventory, it would make sense to round the car values to the nearest thousands place. The price of a car that is on sale for $15,654 can be estimated at $16,000. All other cars on the lot could be rounded in the same manner and then added together. Depending on the situation, it might make sense to calculate an over-estimate. For example, to make sure Aria has enough money at the grocery store, rounding up for each item would ensure that she will have enough money when it comes time to pay. A $0.40 item rounded up to $1.00 would ensure that there is a dollar to cover that item. Traditional rounding rules would round $0.40 to $0, which does not make sense in this particular real-world setting. Aria might not have a dollar available at checkout to pay for that item if she uses traditional rounding. It is up to the customer to decide the best approach when estimating.

Estimating is also very helpful when working with measurements. Bryan is updating his kitchen and wants to retile the floor. Again, an over-measurement might be useful. Also, rounding to nearest half-unit might be helpful. For instance, one side of the kitchen might have an exact measurement of 14.32 feet, and the most useful measurement needed to buy tile could be estimating this quantity to be 14.5 feet. If the kitchen was rectangular and the other side measured 10.9 feet, Bryan might round the other side to 11 feet. Therefore, Bryan would find the total tile necessary according to the following area calculation: $14.5 \times 11 = 159.5$ square feet. To make sure he purchases enough tile, Bryan would probably want to purchase at least 160 square feet of tile. This is a scenario in which an estimation might be more

184

useful than an exact calculation. Having more tile than necessary is better than having an exact amount, in case any tiles are broken or otherwise unusable.

Finally, estimation is helpful when exact answers are necessary. Consider a situation in which Sabina has many operations to perform on numbers with decimals, and she is allowed a calculator to find the result. Even though an exact result can be obtained with a calculator, there is always a possibility that Sabina could make an error while inputting the data. For example, she could miss a decimal place, or misuse the parentheses, causing a problem with the actual order of operations.

A quick estimation at the beginning could help ensure that her final answer is within the correct range. Sabina has to find the exact total of 10 cars listed for sale at the dealership. Each price has two decimal places included to account for both dollars and cents. If one car is listed at $21,234.43 but Sabina incorrectly inputs into the calculator the price of $2,123.443, this error would throw off the final sum by almost $20,000. A quick estimation at the beginning, by rounding each price to the nearest thousands place and finding the sum of the prices, would give Sabina an amount to compare the exact amount to. This comparison would let Sabina see if an error was made in her exact calculation.

Using Technology for Complex Calculations

Calculators can be used to perform simple calculations, such as the operations of addition, subtraction, multiplication, and division. Also, depending on the type of calculator used, they can be utilized to evaluate more complex calculations such as expressions that involve more than one operation, trigonometric functions, exponents, and logarithms.

Scientific calculations follow order of operations (PEMDAS). For example, if $2 + 5 \times 4$ is plugged into a scientific calculator, the output would be 22. Note that multiplication is performed before addition, following PEMDAS correctly. However, if a calculator is used that is not scientific, it may not provide the correct output. It may produce the incorrect output of 28, which is the result of working operations from left to right. In this case, to be safe, parentheses can be placed around the operation that should be performed first. The correct input would be $2 + (5 \times 4)$. It is a good rule of thumb to use parentheses whenever there is any doubt.

When working with trigonometric functions, it is important to set the calculator to degrees or radians before the operation is performed. In the calculator shown above, the setting is currently in radians mode. This setting can be easily changed to degrees by pressing the DEG button. For example, if $\sin(90°)$ needed to be evaluated, the calculator would have to be in the degrees setting to have the correct output.

Algebra and Functions

Patterns and Functional Relationships

Representing Patterns Including Relations and Functions

A **relation** is any set of ordered pairs (x, y). The values listed first in the ordered pairs, known as the x-coordinates, make up the domain of the relation. The values listed second, known as the y-coordinates, make up the range. A relation in which every member of the domain corresponds to only one member of the range is known as a **function**. A function cannot have a member of the domain corresponding to two members of the range.

A **linear function** that models a linear relationship between two quantities is of the form $y = mx + b$, or in function form $f(x) = mx + b$. In a linear function, the value of y depends on the value of x, and y increases or decreases at a constant rate as x increases. Therefore, the independent variable is x, and the dependent variable is y. The graph of a linear function is a line, and the constant rate can be seen by looking at the steepness, or slope, of the line. If the line increases from left to right, the slope is positive. If the line slopes downward from left to right, the slope is negative. In the function, m represents slope. Each point on the line is an **ordered pair** (x, y), where x represents the x-coordinate of the point and y represents the y-coordinate of the point. The point where $x = 0$ is known as the y-

185

intercept, and it is the place where the line crosses the y-axis. If $x = 0$ is plugged into $f(x) = mx + b$, the result is $f(0) = b$, so therefore, the point $(0, b)$ is the y-intercept of the line. The derivative of a linear function is its slope.

Consider the following situation. A taxicab driver charges a flat fee of $2 per ride and $3 a mile. This statement can be modeled by the function $f(x) = 3x + 2$ where x represents the number of miles and $f(x) = y$ represents the total cost of the ride. The total cost increases at a constant rate of $2 per mile, and that is why this situation is a linear relationship. The slope $m = 3$ is equivalent to this rate of change. The flat fee of $2 is the y-intercept. It is the place where the graph crosses the x-axis, and it represents the cost when $x = 0$, or when no miles have been traveled in the cab. The y-intercept in this situation represents the flat fee.

Graphs, equations, and tables are three different ways to represent linear relationships. The following graph shows a linear relationship because the relationship between the two variables is constant. Each time the distance increases by 25 miles, 1 hour passes. This pattern continues for the rest of the graph. The line represents a constant rate of 25 miles per hour.

This graph can also be used to solve problems involving predictions for a future time. After 8 hours of travel, the rate can be used to predict the distance covered. Eight hours of travel at 25 miles per hour covers a distance of 200 miles. The equation at the top of the graph corresponds to this rate also. The same prediction of distance in a given time can be found using the equation. For a time of 10 hours, the distance would be 250 miles, as the equation yields:

$$d = 25 \times 10 = 250$$

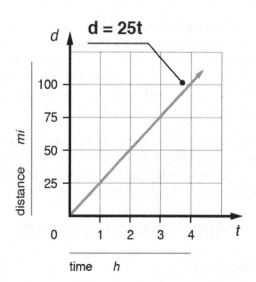

Another representation of a linear relationship can be seen in a table. In the table below, the y-values increase by 3 as the x-values increase by 1. This pattern shows that the relationship is linear. If this table shows the money earned, y-value, for the hours worked, x-value, then it can be used to predict how much money will be earned for future hours. If 6 hours are worked, then the pay would be $19. For further hours and money to be determined, it would be helpful to have an equation that models this table of values. The equation will show the relationship between x and y. The y-value can be determined by multiplying the x-value by 3, then adding 1. The following equation models this relationship:

$$y = 3x + 1$$

Now that there is an equation, any number of hours, x, can be substituted into the equation to find the amount of money earned, y.

y = 3x + 1	
x	y
0	1
1	4
2	7
4	13
5	16

Proportional Reasoning

Fractions appear in everyday situations, and in many scenarios, they appear in the real-world as ratios and in proportions. A **ratio** is formed when two different quantities are compared. For example, in a group of 50 people, if there are 33 females and 17 males, the ratio of females to males is 33 to 17. This expression can be written in the fraction form as $\frac{33}{50}$, where the denominator is the sum of females and males, or by using the ratio symbol, 33:17. The order of the number matters when forming ratios. In the same setting, the ratio of males to females is 17 to 33, which is equivalent to $\frac{17}{50}$ or 17:33. A **proportion** is an equation involving two ratios. The equation $\frac{a}{b} = \frac{c}{d}$, or $a : b = c : d$ is a proportion, for real numbers a, b, c, and d. Usually, in one ratio, one of the quantities is unknown, and cross-multiplication is used to solve for the unknown. Consider:

$$\frac{1}{4} = \frac{x}{5}$$

To solve for x, cross-multiply to obtain:

$$5 = 4x$$

Divide each side by 4 to obtain the solution:

$$x = \frac{5}{4}$$

It is also true that percentages are ratios in which the second term is 100 minus the first term. For example, 65% is 65:35 or $\frac{65}{100}$. Therefore, when working with percentages, one is also working with ratios.

Real-world problems frequently involve proportions. For example, consider the following problem: If 2 out of 50 pizzas are usually delivered late from a local Italian restaurant, how many would be late out of 235 orders? The following proportion would be solved with x as the unknown quantity of late pizzas:

$$\frac{2}{50} = \frac{x}{235}$$

Cross-multiplying results in:

$$470 = 50x$$

Divide both sides by 50 to obtain:

$$x = \frac{470}{50}$$

which in lowest terms is equal to $\frac{47}{5}$. In decimal form, this improper fraction is equal to 9.4. Because it does not make sense to answer this question with decimals (portions of pizzas do not get delivered) the answer must be rounded. Traditional rounding rules would say that 9 pizzas would be expected to be delivered late. However, to be safe, rounding up to 10 pizzas out of 235 would probably make more sense.

Comparing 2 apples to 3 oranges results in the ratio 2:3, which can be expressed as the fraction $\frac{2}{5}$. Note that order is important when discussing ratios. The number mentioned first is the antecedent, and the number mentioned second is the consequent. Note that the consequent of the ratio and the denominator of the fraction are *not* the same. When there are 2 apples to 3 oranges, there are five fruit total; two fifths of the fruit are apples, while three fifths are oranges. The ratio 2:3 represents a different relationship than the ratio 3:2. Also, it is important to make sure that when discussing ratios that have units attached to them, the two quantities use the same units. For example, to think of 8 feet to 4 yards, it would make sense to convert 4 yards to feet by multiplying by 3. Therefore, the ratio would be 8 feet to 12 feet, which can be expressed as the fraction $\frac{8}{20}$. Also, note that it is proper to refer to ratios in lowest terms. Therefore, the ratio of 8 feet to 4 yards is equivalent to the fraction $\frac{2}{5}$.

Many real-world problems involve ratios. Often, problems with ratios involve proportions, as when two ratios are set equal to find the missing amount. However, some problems involve deciphering single ratios. For example, consider an amusement park that sold 345 tickets last Saturday. If 145 tickets were sold to adults and the rest of the tickets were sold to children, what would the ratio of the number of adult tickets to children's tickets be? A common mistake would be to say the ratio is 145:345. However, 345 is the total number of tickets sold. There were $345 - 145 = 200$ tickets sold to children. Thus, the correct ratio of adult to children's tickets is 145:200. As a fraction, this expression is written as $\frac{145}{200}$, which can be reduced to $\frac{29}{40}$.

While a ratio compares two measurements using the same units, **rates** compare two measurements with different units. Examples of rates would be $200 for 8 hours of work, or 500 miles traveled per 20 gallons. Because the units are different, it is important to always include the units when discussing rates. Key words in rate problems include for, per, on, from, and in. Just as with ratios, it is important to write rates in lowest terms. A common rate in real-life situations is cost per unit, which describes how much one item/unit costs. When evaluating the cost of an item that comes in several sizes, the cost per unit rate can help buyers determine the best deal. For example, if 2 quarts of soup were sold for $3.50 and 3 quarts were sold for $4.60, to determine the best buy, the cost per quart should be found.

$$\frac{\$3.50}{2 \text{ qt}} = \$1.75 \text{ per quart}$$

and

$$\frac{\$4.60}{3 \text{ qt}} = \$1.53 \text{ per quart}$$

Therefore, the better deal would be the 3-quart option.

188

Rate of change problems involve calculating a quantity per some unit of measurement. Usually, the unit of measurement is time. For example, meters per second is a common rate of change. To calculate this measurement, find the distance traveled in meters and divide by total time traveled. The result is the average speed over the entire time interval.

Another common rate of change used in the real world is miles per hour. Consider the following problem that involves calculating an average rate of change in temperature. Last Saturday, the temperature at 1:00 a.m. was 34 degrees Fahrenheit, and at noon, the temperature had increased to 75 degrees Fahrenheit. What was the average rate of change over that time interval? The average rate of change is calculated by finding the total change in temperature and dividing by the total hours elapsed. Therefore, the rate of change was equal to:

$$\frac{75 - 34}{12 - 1} = \frac{41}{11} \text{ degrees per hour}$$

This quantity, rounded to two decimal places, is equal to 3.72 degrees per hour.

A common rate of change that appears in algebra is the slope calculation. Given a linear equation in one variable, $y = mx + b$, the **slope**, m, is equal to $\frac{rise}{run}$ or $\frac{change\ in\ y}{change\ in\ x}$. In other words, slope is equivalent to the ratio of the vertical and horizontal changes between any two points on a line. The vertical change is known as the **rise**, and the horizontal change is known as the **run**. Given any two points on a line (x_1, y_1) and (x_2, y_2), slope can be calculated with the formula:

$$m = \frac{y_2 - y_1}{x_2 - x_1} = \frac{\Delta y}{\Delta x}$$

Common real-world applications of slope include determining how steep a staircase should be, calculating how steep a road is, and determining how to build a wheelchair ramp.

Many times, problems involving rates and ratios involve proportions. A proportion states that two ratios (or rates) are equal. The property of cross products can be used to determine if a proportion is true, meaning both ratios are equivalent. If $\frac{a}{b} = \frac{c}{d}$, then to clear the fractions, multiply both sides by the least common denominator, bd. This results in $ad = bc$, which is equal to the result of multiplying along both diagonals. For example, $\frac{4}{40} = \frac{1}{10}$ grants the cross product:

$$4 \times 10 = 40 \times 1$$

This is equivalent to $40 = 40$ and shows that this proportion is true. Cross products are used when proportions are involved in real-world problems. Consider the following: If 3 pounds of fertilizer will cover 75 square feet of grass, how many pounds are needed for 375 square feet? To solve this problem, set up a proportion using two ratios. Let x equal the unknown quantity, pounds needed for 375 feet. Setting the two ratios equal to one another yields the equation:

$$\frac{3}{75} = \frac{x}{375}$$

Cross-multiplication gives:

$$3 \times 375 = 75x$$

Therefore, $1,125 = 75x$. Divide both sides by 75 to get $x = 15$. Therefore, 15 pounds of fertilizer are needed to cover 375 square feet of grass.

Another application of proportions involves similar triangles. If two triangles have corresponding angles with the same measurements and corresponding sides with proportional measurements, the triangles are said to be similar. If two angles are the same, the third pair of angles are equal as well because the sum of all angles in a triangle is equal to 180 degrees. Each pair of equivalent angles are known as **corresponding angles. Corresponding sides** face the corresponding angles, and it is true that corresponding sides are in proportion.

For example, consider the following set of similar triangles:

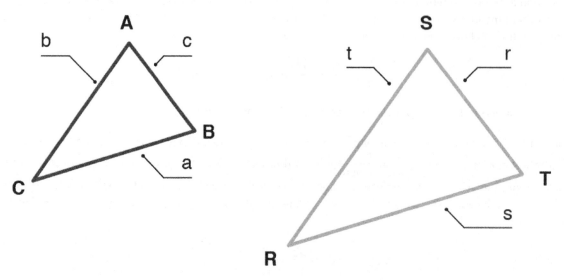

Angles A and S have the same measurement, angles C and R have the same measurement, and angles B and T have the same measurement. Therefore, the following proportion can be set up from the sides:

$$\frac{c}{r} = \frac{a}{s} = \frac{b}{t}$$

This proportion can be helpful in finding missing lengths in pairs of similar triangles. For example, if the following triangles are similar, a proportion can be used to find the missing side lengths, a and b.

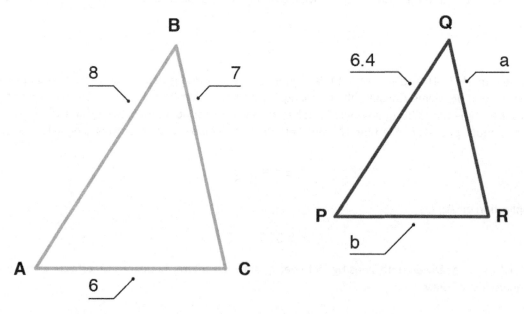

The proportions $\frac{8}{6.4} = \frac{6}{b}$ and $\frac{8}{6.4} = \frac{7}{a}$ can both be cross multiplied and solved to obtain $a = 5.6$ and $b = 4.8$.

A real-life situation that uses similar triangles involves measuring shadows to find heights of unknown objects. Consider the following problem: A building casts a shadow that is 120 feet long, and at the same time, another building that is 80 feet high casts a shadow that is 60 feet long. How tall is the first building? Each building, together with the sun rays and shadows cast on the ground, forms a triangle. They are similar because each building forms a right angle with the ground, and the sun rays form equivalent angles. Therefore, these two pairs of angles are both equal. Because all angles in a triangle add up to 180 degrees, the third angles are equal as well. Both shadows form corresponding sides of the triangle, the buildings form corresponding sides, and the sun rays form corresponding sides. Therefore, the triangles are similar, and the following proportion can be used to find the missing building length:

$$\frac{120}{x} = \frac{60}{80}$$

Cross-multiply to obtain the equation $9,600 = 60x$. Then, divide both sides by 60 to obtain $x = 160$. This means that the first building is 160 feet high.

Quantitative Relationships

Functions are most often given in terms of equations instead of ordered pairs. For instance, here is an equation of a line:

$$y = 2x + 4$$

In function notation, this can be written as:

$$f(x) = 2x + 4$$

The expression $f(x)$ is read "f of x" and it shows that the inputs, the x-values, get plugged into the function and the output is $y = f(x)$. The set of all inputs are in the domain, and the set of all outputs are in the range.

The x-values are known as the **independent variables** of the function, and the y-values are known as the **dependent variables** of the function. The y-values depend on the x-values. For instance, if $x = 2$ is plugged into the function shown above, the y-value depends on that input.

$$f(2) = 2 \times 2 + 4 = 8.$$

Therefore, $f(2) = 8$, which is the same as writing the ordered pair $(2, 8)$. To graph a function, graph it in equation form. Therefore, replace $f(x)$ with y and plot ordered pairs.

Independent variables are independent, meaning they are not changed by other variables within the context of the problem. Dependent variables are dependent, meaning they may change depending on how other variables change in the problem. For example, in the formula for the perimeter of a fence, the length and width are the independent variables, and the perimeter is the dependent variable. The formula is shown below.

$$P = 2l + 2w$$

As the width or the length changes, the perimeter may also change. The first variables to change are the length and width, which then result in a change in perimeter. The change does not come first with the perimeter and then with length and width. When comparing these two types of variables, it is helpful to ask which variable causes the change and which variable is affected by the change.

Another formula to represent this relationship is the formula for circumference shown below.

$$C = \pi \times d$$

The C represents circumference and the d represents diameter. The pi symbol is approximated by the fraction $\frac{22}{7}$, or 3.14. In this formula, the diameter of the circle is the independent variable. It is the portion of the circle that changes, which changes the circumference as a result. The circumference is the variable that is being changed by the diameter, so it is called the dependent variable. It depends on the value of the diameter.

Another place to recognize independent and dependent variables can be in experiments. A common experiment is one where the growth of a plant is tested based on the amount of sunlight it receives. Each plant in the experiment is given a different amount of sunlight, but the same amount of other nutrients like light and water. The growth of the plants is measured over a given time period and the results show how much sunlight is best for plants. In this experiment, the independent variable is the amount of sunlight that each plant receives. The dependent variable is the growth of each plant. The growth depends on the amount of sunlight, which gives reason for the distinction between independent and dependent variables.

Linear and Quadratic Equations and Inequalities

Equalities and Inequalities

When presented with a real-world problem that must be solved, the first step is always to determine what the unknown quantity is that must be solved for. Use a variable, such as x or t, to represent that unknown quantity. Sometimes there can be two or more unknown quantities. In this case, either choose an additional variable, or if a relationship exists between the unknown quantities, express the other quantities in terms of the original variable. After choosing the variables, form algebraic expressions and/or equations that represent the verbal statement in the problem.

The following table shows examples of vocabulary used to represent the different operations.

Addition	Sum, plus, total, increase, more than, combined, in all
Subtraction	Difference, less than, subtract, reduce, decrease, fewer, remain
Multiplication	Product, multiply, times, part of, twice, triple
Division	Quotient, divide, split, each, equal parts, per, average, shared

The combination of operations and variables form both mathematical expressions and equations. The difference between expressions and equations is that there is no equals sign in an expression, and that expressions are evaluated to find an unknown quantity, while equations are solved to find an unknown quantity. Also, inequalities can exist within verbal mathematical statements. Instead of a statement of equality, expressions state quantities are *less than*, *less than or equal to*, *greater than*, or *greater than or equal to*. Another type of inequality is when a quantity is said to be *not equal to* another quantity. The symbol used to represent "not equal to" is $\neq$.

The steps for solving inequalities in one variable are the same steps for solving equations in one variable. The addition and multiplication principles are used. However, to maintain a true statement when using the $<$, $\leq$, $>$, and $\geq$ symbols, if a negative number is either multiplied times both sides of an inequality or divided from both sides of an inequality, the sign must be flipped. For instance, consider the following inequality: $3 - 5x \leq 8$. First, 3 is subtracted from each side to obtain $-5x \leq 5$. Then, both sides are divided by -5, while flipping the sign, to obtain $x \geq -1$. Therefore, any real number greater than or equal to -1 satisfies the original inequality.

An **equation in one variable** is a mathematical statement where two algebraic expressions in one variable, usually x, are set equal. To solve the equation, the variable must be isolated on one side of the equals sign. The addition and

192

multiplication principles of equality are used to isolate the variable. The **addition principle of equality** states that the same number can be added to or subtracted from both sides of an equation. Because the same value is being used on both sides of the equals sign, equality is maintained. For example, the equation $2x = 5x$ is equivalent to both $2x + 3 = 5x + 3$, and $2x - 5 = 5x - 5$. This principle can be used to solve the following equation:

$$x + 5 = 4$$

The variable x must be isolated, so to move the 5 from the left side, subtract 5 from both sides of the equals sign. Therefore:

$$x + 5 - 5 = 4 - 5$$

So, the solution is $x = -1$.

This process illustrates the idea of an **additive inverse** because subtracting 5 is the same as adding -5. Basically, add the opposite of the number that must be removed to both sides of the equals sign. The multiplication principle of equality states that equality is maintained when both sides of an equation are multiplied or divided by the same number. For example, $4x = 5$ is equivalent to both $16x = 20$ and $x = \frac{5}{4}$. Multiplying both sides times 4 and dividing both sides by 4 maintains equality. Solving the equation $6x - 18 = 5$ requires the use of both principles. First, apply the addition principle to add 18 to both sides of the equals sign, which results in $6x = 23$. Then use the multiplication principle to divide both sides by 6, giving the solution $x = \frac{23}{6}$. Using the multiplication principle in the solving process is the same as involving a multiplicative inverse. A **multiplicative inverse** is a value that, when multiplied by a given number, results in 1. Dividing by 6 is the same as multiplying by $\frac{1}{6}$, which is both the reciprocal and multiplicative inverse of 6.

When solving linear equations, check the answer by plugging the solution back into the original equation. If the result is a false statement, something was done incorrectly during the solution procedure. Checking the example above gives the following:

$$6 \times \frac{23}{6} - 18 = 23 - 18 = 5$$

Therefore, the solution is correct.

Some equations in one variable involve fractions or the use of the distributive property. In either case, the goal is to obtain only one variable term and then use the addition and multiplication principles to isolate that variable. Consider the equation $\frac{2}{3}x = 6$. To solve for x, multiply each side of the equation by the reciprocal of $\frac{2}{3}$, which is $\frac{3}{2}$. This step results in $\frac{3}{2} \times \frac{2}{3}x = \frac{3}{2} \times 6$, which simplifies into the solution $x = 9$. Now consider the equation:

$$3(x + 2) - 5x = 4x + 1$$

Use the distributive property to clear the parentheses. Therefore, multiply each term inside the parentheses by 3. This step results in:

$$3x + 6 - 5x = 4x + 1$$

Next, collect like terms on the left-hand side. **Like terms** are terms with the same variable or variables raised to the same exponent(s). Only like terms can be combined through addition or subtraction. After collecting like terms, the equation is:

$$-2x + 6 = 4x + 1$$

Finally, apply the addition and multiplication principles. Add $2x$ to both sides to obtain:

$$6 = 6x + 1$$

Then, subtract 1 from both sides to obtain $5 = 6x$. Finally, divide both sides by 6 to obtain the solution:

$$\frac{5}{6} = x$$

Two other types of solutions can be obtained when solving an equation in one variable. There could be no solution, or the solution set could contain all real numbers. Consider the equation:

$$4x = 6x + 5 - 2x$$

First, the like terms can be combined on the right to obtain $4x = 4x + 5$. Next, subtract $4x$ from both sides. This step results in the false statement $0 = 5$. There is no value that can be plugged into x that will ever make this equation true. Therefore, there is no solution. The solution procedure contained correct steps, but the result of a false statement means that no value satisfies the equation. The symbolic way to denote that no solution exists is $\emptyset$. Next, consider the equation:

$$5x + 4 + 2x = 9 + 7x - 5$$

Combining the like terms on both sides results in:

$$7x + 4 = 7x + 4$$

The left-hand side is exactly the same as the right-hand side. Using the addition principle to move terms, the result is $0 = 0$, which is always true. Therefore, the original equation is true for any number, and the solution set is all real numbers. The symbolic way to denote such a solution set is $\mathbb{R}$, or in interval notation, $(-\infty, \infty)$.

Equivalent Algebraic Expressions

Two algebraic expressions are equivalent if they represent the same value, even if they look different. To obtain an equivalent form of an algebraic expression, follow the laws of algebra. For instance, addition and multiplication are both commutative and associative. Therefore, terms in an algebraic expression can be added in any order and multiplied in any order.

For instance, $4x + 2y$ is equivalent to $2y + 4x$ and $y \times 2 + x \times 4$.

Also, the distributive law allows a number to be distributed throughout parentheses, as in the following:

$$a(b + c) = ab + ac$$

The expressions on both sides of the equals sign are equivalent. Collecting like terms is also important when working with equivalent forms because the simplest version of an expression is always the easiest one to work with.

An expression is not an equation; therefore, expressions cannot undergo multiplication, division, addition, or subtraction and still have equivalent expressions. These processes can only happen in equations when the same step is performed on both sides of the equals sign.

The **distributive property** $(a(b + c) = ab + ac)$ is a way of taking a factor and multiplying it through a given expression in parentheses. Each term inside the parentheses is multiplied by the outside factor, eliminating the parentheses. The following example shows how to distribute the number 3 to all the terms inside the parentheses.

Example: Use the distributive property to write an equivalent algebraic expression:

$$3(2x + 7y + 6)$$

$$3(2x) + 3(7y) + 3(6) \qquad \text{Distributive property}$$

$$6x + 21y + 18 \qquad \text{Simplify}$$

Because $a - b$ can be written $a + (-b)$, the distributive property can be applied in the example below:

Example: Use the distributive property to write an equivalent algebraic expression.

$$7(5m - 8)$$

$$7[5m + (-8)] \qquad \text{Rewrite subtraction as addition of } -8$$

$$7(5m) + 7(-8) \qquad \text{Distributive property}$$

$$35m - 56 \qquad \text{Simplify}$$

In the following example, note that the factor of 2 is written to the right of the parentheses but is still distributed as before.

Example: Use the distributive property to write an equivalent algebraic expression:

$$(3m + 4x - 10)2$$

$$(3m)2 + (4x)2 + (-10)2 \qquad \text{Distributive property}$$

$$6m + 8x - 20 \qquad \text{Simplify}$$

Example: $\qquad -(-2m + 6x)$

In this example, the negative sign in front of the parentheses can be interpreted as $-1(-2m + 6x)$

$$-1(-2m + 6x)$$

$$-1(-2m) + (-1)(6x) \qquad \text{Distributive property}$$

$$2m - 6x \qquad \text{Simplify}$$

Real-World Problems with Algebraic Expressions and Equations

One-step problems take only one mathematical step to solve. For example, solving the equation $5x = 45$ is a one-step problem because the one step of dividing both sides of the equation by 5 is the only step necessary to obtain the solution $x = 9$. The **multiplication principle of equality** is the one step used to isolate the variable. The equation is of the form $ax = b$, where a and b are rational numbers. Similarly, the **addition principle of equality** could be the one step needed to solve a problem. In this case, the equation would be of the form $x + a = b$ or $x - a = b$, for real numbers a and b.

A **multi-step problem** involves more than one step to find the solution, or it could consist of solving more than one equation. An equation that involves both the addition principle and the multiplication principle is a two-step problem, and an example of such an equation is $2x - 4 = 5$. To solve, add 4 to both sides and then divide both sides by 2. An example of a two-step problem involving two separate equations is $y = 3x$, $2x + y = 4$. The two equations form a system that must be solved together in two variables. The system can be solved by the substitution method. Since y is already solved for in terms of x, replace y with $3x$ in the equation $2x + y = 4$, resulting in $2x + 3x = 4$. Therefore, $5x = 4$ and $x = \frac{4}{5}$. Because there are two variables, the solution consists of a value for both x and for y. Substitute $x = \frac{4}{5}$ into either original equation to find y. The easiest choice is $y = 3x$. Therefore:

$$y = 3 \times \frac{4}{5} = \frac{12}{5}$$

The solution can be written as the ordered pair $\left(\frac{4}{5}, \frac{12}{5}\right)$.

Real-world problems can be translated into both one-step and multi-step problems. In either case, the word problem must be translated from the verbal form into mathematical expressions and equations that can be solved using algebra. An example of a one-step real-world problem is the following: A cat weighs half as much as a dog living in the same house. If the dog weighs 14.5 pounds, how much does the cat weigh? To solve this problem, an equation can be used. In any word problem, the first step must be defining variables that represent the unknown quantities. For this problem, let x be equal to the unknown weight of the cat. Because two times the weight of the cat equals 14.5 pounds, the equation to be solved is: $2x = 14.5$. Use the multiplication principle to divide both sides by 2. Therefore, $x = 7.25$, and the cat weighs 7.25 pounds.

Most of the time, real-world problems require multiple steps. The following is an example of a multi-step problem: The sum of two consecutive page numbers is equal to 437. What are those page numbers? First, define the unknown quantities. If x is equal to the first page number, then $x + 1$ is equal to the next page number because they are consecutive integers. Their sum is equal to 437. Putting this information together results in the equation:

$$x + x + 1 = 437$$

To solve, first collect like terms to obtain:

$$2x + 1 = 437$$

Then, subtract 1 from both sides and then divide by 2. The solution to the equation is $x = 218$. Therefore, the two consecutive page numbers that satisfy the problem are 218 and 219. It is always important to make sure that answers to real-world problems make sense. For instance, it should be a red flag if the solution to this same problem resulted in decimals, which would indicate the need to check the work. Page numbers are whole numbers; therefore, if decimals are found to be answers, the solution process should be double-checked for mistakes.

Linear Equations and Their Properties

A linear function of the form $f(x) = mx + b$ has two important quantities: m and b. The quantity m represents the **slope** of the line, and the quantity b represents the **y-intercept** of the line. When the function represents a real-life situation or a mathematical model, these two quantities are very meaningful. The slope, m, represents the rate of change, or the amount y increases or decreases given an increase in x. If m is positive, the rate of change is positive, and if m is negative, the rate of change is negative. The y-intercept, b, represents the amount of quantity y when x is

0. In many applications, if the x-variable is never a negative quantity, the y-intercept represents the initial amount of the quantity y. The x-variable often represents time, so it makes sense that it would not be negative.

Consider the following example. These two equations represent the cost, C, of t-shirts, x, at two different printing companies:

$$C(x) = 7x$$

$$C(x) = 5x + 25$$

The first equation represents a scenario in which each t-shirt costs $7. In this equation, x varies directly with y. There is no y-intercept, which means that there is no initial cost for using that printing company. The rate of change is 7, which is the price per shirt. The second equation represents a scenario that has both an initial cost and a cost per t-shirt. The slope of 5 shows that each shirt is $5. The y-intercept of 25 shows that there is an initial cost of using that company. Therefore, it makes sense to use the first company at $7 per shirt when only purchasing a small number of t-shirts. However, any large orders would be cheaper from the second company because eventually that initial cost would become negligible.

Perpendicular Lines and Slope

Lines on a graph that intersect and form right angles (90 degrees) are called perpendicular lines. Lines will have slopes, apart from vertical lines. A slope is a number that indicates the steepness and direction of a line. The mathematical definition of a slope is given by:

$$slope = \frac{y_2 - y_1}{x_2 - x_1}$$

The coordinates (x_1, y_1) and (x_2, y_2) are two points located on one line. For two lines that are perpendicular, the slopes for each line are opposite reciprocals. For example, if the slope of line 1 is 2, then the slope of line 2 is $-\frac{1}{2}$.

Polynomials

A **polynomial** is a mathematical expression containing addition, subtraction, or multiplication of one or more constants multiplied by variables raised to positive powers. A polynomial is considered expanded when there are no variables contained within parentheses, the distributive property has been carried out for any terms that were within parentheses, and like terms have been collected.

When working with polynomials, **like terms** are terms that contain the same variables with the same powers. For example, $x^4 y^5$ and $9x^4 y^5$ are like terms. The coefficients are different, but the same variables are raised to the same powers. When adding polynomials, only terms that are considered like terms can be added. When adding two like terms, just add the coefficients and leave the variables alone. This process uses the distributive property. For example,

$$x^4 y^5 + 9x^4 y^5$$

$$(1 + 9)x^4 y^5$$

$$10x^4 y^5$$

Therefore, when adding two polynomials, simply add the like terms together. Unlike terms cannot be combined.

Subtracting polynomials involves adding the opposite of the polynomial being subtracted. Basically, the sign of each term in the polynomial being subtracted is changed, and then the like terms are combined because it is now an addition problem. For example, consider the following:

$$6x^2 - 4x + 2 - (4x^2 - 8x + 1)$$

Add the opposite of the second polynomial to obtain:

$$6x^2 - 4x + 2 + (-4x^2 + 8x - 1)$$

Then, collect like terms to obtain:

$$2x^2 + 4x + 1$$

Multiplying polynomials involves using the product rule for exponents that $b^m b^n = b^{m+n}$. Basically, when multiplying expressions with the same base, just add the exponents. Multiplying a monomial by a monomial involves multiplying the coefficients together and then multiplying the variables together using the product rule for exponents. For instance:

$$8x^2y \times 4x^4y^2 = 32x^6y^3$$

When multiplying a monomial by a polynomial that is not a monomial, use the distributive property to multiply each term of the polynomial times the monomial. For example:

$$3x(x^2 + 3x - 4) = 3x^3 + 9x^2 - 12x$$

Finally, multiplying two polynomials when neither one is a monomial involves multiplying each term of the first polynomial by each term of the second polynomial. There are some shortcuts, given certain scenarios. For instance, a binomial times a binomial can be found by using the **FOIL (Firsts, Outers, Inners, Lasts)** method shown here.

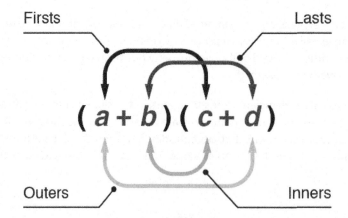

Finding the product of a sum and difference of the same two terms is simple because if it was to be foiled out, the outer and inner terms would cancel out. For instance,

$$(x + y)(x - y) = x^2 + xy - xy - y^2$$

Finally, the square of a binomial can be found using the following formula:

$$(a \pm b)^2 = a^2 \pm 2ab + b^2$$

To factor a polynomial, first determine if there is a greatest common factor. If there is, factor it out. For example, $2x^2 + 8x$ has a greatest common factor of $2x$ and can be written as $2x(x + 4)$. Once the greatest common monomial factor is factored out, if applicable, count the number of terms in the polynomial. If there are two terms, is it a difference of squares, a sum of cubes, or a difference of cubes?

If so, the following rules can be used:

$$a^2 - b^2 = (a + b)(a - b)$$

$$a^3 + b^3 = (a + b)(a^2 - ab + b^2)$$

$$a^3 - b^3 = (a - b)(a^2 + ab + b^2)$$

If there are three terms, and if the trinomial is a perfect square trinomial, it can be factored into the following:

$$a^2 + 2ab + b^2 = (a + b)^2$$

$$a^2 - 2ab + b^2 = (a - b)^2$$

If not, try factoring into a product of two binomials in the form of $(x + p)(x + q)$. For example, to factor $x^2 + 6x + 8$, determine what two numbers have a product of 8 and a sum of 6. Those numbers are 4 and 2, so the trinomial factors into $(x + 2)(x + 4)$.

Finally, if there are four terms, try factoring by grouping. First, group terms together that have a common monomial factor. Then, factor out the common monomial factor from the first two terms. Next, look to see if a common factor can be factored out of the second set of two terms that results in a common binomial factor. Finally, factor out the common binomial factor of each expression, for example:

$$xy - x + 5y - 5 = x(y - 1) + 5(y - 1)$$

$$(y - 1)(x + 5)$$

After the expression is completely factored, check the factorization by multiplying it out; if this results in the original expression, then the factoring is correct. Factorizations are helpful in solving equations that consist of a polynomial set equal to zero. If the product of two algebraic expressions equals zero, then at least one of the factors is equal to zero. Therefore, factor the polynomial within the equation, set each factor equal to zero, and solve. For example, $x^2 + 7x - 18 = 0$ can be solved by factoring into:

$$(x + 9)(x - 2) = 0$$

Set each factor equal to zero, and solve to obtain $x = -9$ and $x = 2$.

Quadratic Equations

A **quadratic equation** in standard form, $ax^2 + bx + c = 0$, can have either two solutions, one solution, or two complex solutions (no real solutions). This is determined using the determinant $b^2 - 4ac$. If the determinant is positive, there are two real solutions. If the determinant is negative, there are no real solutions. If the determinant is equal to 0, there is one real solution. For example, given the quadratic equation $4x^2 - 2x + 1 = 0$, its determinant is:

$$(-2)^2 - 4(4)(1) = 4 - 16 = -12$$

So, it has two complex solutions, meaning no real solutions.

There are quite a few ways to solve a quadratic equation. The first is by **factoring**. If the equation is in standard form and the polynomial can be factored, set each factor equal to 0, and solve using the Principle of Zero Products. For example:

$$x^2 - 4x + 3 = (x - 3)(x - 1)$$

Therefore, the solutions of $x^2 - 4x + 3 = 0$ are those that satisfy both $x - 3 = 0$ and $x - 1 = 0$, or $x = 3$ and $x = 1$. This is the simplest method to solve quadratic equations; however, not all polynomials inside the quadratic equations can be factored.

Another method is **completing the square**. The polynomial $x^2 + 10x - 9$ cannot be factored, so the next option is to complete the square in the equation $x^2 + 10x - 9 = 0$ to find its solutions. The first step is to add 9 to both sides, moving the constant over to the right side, resulting in:

$$x^2 + 10x = 9$$

Then the coefficient of x is divided by 2 and squared. This result is then added to both sides of the equation. In this example, $\left(\frac{10}{2}\right)^2 = 25$ is added to both sides of the equation to obtain:

$$x^2 + 10x + 25 = 9 + 25 = 34$$

The left-hand side can then be factored into $(x + 5)^2 = 34$. Solving for x then involves taking the square root of both sides and subtracting 5. This leads to the two solutions:

$$x = \pm\sqrt{34} - 5$$

The third method is the **quadratic formula.** Given a quadratic equation in standard form, $ax^2 + bx + c = 0$, its solutions always can be found using the formula:

$$x = \frac{-b \pm \sqrt{b^2 - 4ac}}{2a}$$

Interpreting Graphs of Equations

As mentioned, in math, a relation is a relationship between two sets of numbers. By using a rule, it takes a number from the first set and matches it to a number in the second set. A relation consists of a set of inputs, known as the **domain,** and a set of outputs, known as the **range.** A function is a relation in which each member of the domain is paired to only one other member of the range. In other words, each input has only one output.

Here is an example of a relation that is not a function:

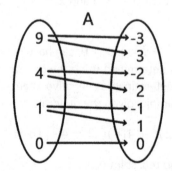

Every member of the first set, the domain, is mapped to two members of the second set, the range. Therefore, this relation is not a function.

200

In addition to a diagram representing sets, a function can be represented by a table of ordered pairs, a graph of ordered pairs (a scatterplot), or a set of ordered pairs as shown in the following:

Mapping

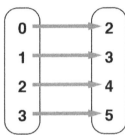

Domain — inputs

Range — outputs

Table

x	y
0	2
1	3
2	4
3	5

Graph

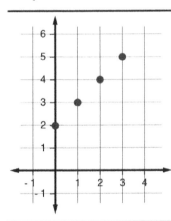

Ordered Pairs

$$\{(0,2),(1,3),(2,4),(3,5)\}$$

Note that this relation is a function because every member of the domain is mapped to exactly one member of the range.

An equation occurs when two algebraic expressions are set equal to one another. Functions can be represented in equation form. Given an equation in two variables, x and y, it can be expressed in function form if solved for y. For example, the linear equation $2x + y = 5$ can be solved for y to obtain $y = -2x + 5$, otherwise known as **slope-intercept** form. To place the equation in function form, replace y with $f(x)$, which is read "f of x." Therefore:

$$f(x) = -2x + 5$$

This notation clarifies the input–output relationship of the function. The function f is a function of x, so an x-value can be plugged into the function to obtain an output. For example:

$$f(2) = -2 \times 2 + 5 = 1$$

Therefore, an input of 2 corresponds to an output of 1.

201

Systems of Equations

An example of a system of two linear equations in two variables is the following:

$$2x + 5y = 8$$

$$5x + 48y = 9$$

A solution to a **system of two linear equations** is an ordered pair that satisfies both the equations in the system. A system can have one solution, no solution, or infinitely many solutions. The solution can be found through a graphing technique. The solution to a system of equations is equal to the point where both lines intersect. If the lines intersect at one point, there is one solution, and the system is said to be **consistent**. However, if the two lines are parallel, they will never intersect and there is no solution. In this case, the system is said to be **inconsistent**. If the two lines are the same line, there are infinitely many solutions, and the solution set is equal to the entire line. The lines are **dependent**.

Here is a summary of the three cases:

Solving Systems by Graphing

Consistent	**Inconsistent**	**Dependent**
One solution	No solution	Infinite number of solutions
Lines intersect	*Lines are parallel*	*Coincide: same line*

Consider the following system of equations:

$$\begin{cases} y + x = 3 \\ y - x = 1 \end{cases}$$

To find the solution graphically, graph both lines on the same xy-plane. Graph each line using either a table of ordered pairs, the x- and y-intercepts, or slope and the y-intercept. Then, locate the point of intersection.

The graph is shown here:

The System of Equations $\begin{cases} y + x = 3 \\ y - x = 1 \end{cases}$

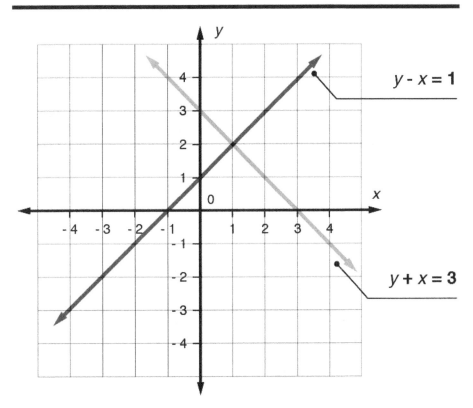

It can be seen that the point of intersection is the ordered pair $(1, 2)$. This solution can be checked by plugging it back into both original equations to make sure it results in true statements. This process results in:

$$2 + 1 = 3$$

$$2 - 1 = 1$$

Both equations are true, so the solution is correct.

The following system has no solution:

$$y = 4x + 1$$

$$y = 4x - 1$$

Both lines have the same slope and different y-intercepts, so they are parallel, meaning that they run alongside each other and never intersect.

Finally, the following solution has infinitely many solutions:

$$2x - 7y = 12$$

$$4x - 14y = 24$$

Note that the second equation is equal to the first equation times 2. Therefore, they are the same line. The solution set can be written in set notation as $\{(x, y) | 2x - 7y = 12\}$, which represents the entire line.

Measurement and Geometry

Two- and Three-Dimensional Geometric Objects

Characteristics of Two- and Three-Dimensional Figures

Shapes are defined by their angles and number of sides. A shape with one continuous side, where all points on that side are equidistant from a center point is called a **circle.** A shape made with three straight line segments is a **triangle.** A shape with four sides is called a **quadrilateral,** but more specifically a **square, rectangle, parallelogram,** or **trapezoid,** depending on the interior angles. These shapes are two-dimensional and only made of straight lines and angles.

Solids can be formed by combining these shapes and forming three-dimensional figures. While two-dimensional figures have only length and height, three-dimensional figures also have depth. Examples of solids may be prisms or spheres.

The four figures below have different names based on their sides and dimensions. Figure 1 is a **cone**, a three-dimensional solid formed by a circle at its base and the sides combining to one point at the top. Figure 2 is a **triangle**, a shape with two dimensions and three line segments. Figure 3 is a **cylinder** made up of two base circles and a rectangle to connect them in three dimensions. Figure 4 is an **oval** formed by one continuous line in two dimensions; it differs from a circle because not all points are equidistant from the center.

Shapes and Solids

1

2

3

4

The **cube** in Figure 5 below is a three-dimensional solid made up of squares. Figure 6 is a **rectangle** because it has four sides that intersect at right angles. More specifically, it is a square because the four sides are equal in length.

Figure 7 is a **pyramid** because the bottom shape is a square and the sides are all triangles. These triangles intersect at a point above the square. Figure 8 is a **circle** because it is made up of one continuous line where the points are all equidistant from one center point.

Shapes and Solids

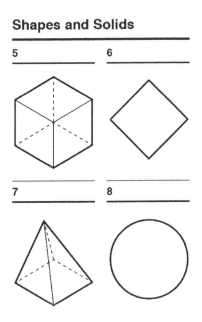

Types of Triangles

Triangles are two-dimensional objects or plane figures that contain three angles and three straight sides. When the three angles of a triangle are added together, the sum is 180 degrees. The sum of two sides of a triangle will have a length greater than the length of one side of a triangle. The difference between two sides of a triangle will be less than one side of a triangle. Triangles can be divided into three categories based on the measurement of the angle. These categories include acute, obtuse, and right-angled triangles. An acute triangle will have angles that are all less than 90 degrees. An obtuse or oblique triangle will have two angles that are less than 90 degrees and one angle greater than 90 degrees. A right-angled triangle will have one angle that is 90 degrees.

Triangles are divided into three categories based on the length of the sides. An **equilateral** triangle contains sides that are all equal in length; all angles are equal to 60 degrees. An **isosceles** triangle contains two sides that have an equivalent length; two angles are the same. A **scalene** triangle has sides that are unequal in length and angles that are unique. A single, double, and triple dash placed on the side of the triangle indicate different lengths. An equilateral triangle contains one dash on each side to illustrate that all sides are equal.

Congruence and Similarity

Two figures are **congruent** if they have the same shape and same size, meaning same angle measurements and equal side lengths. Two figures are similar if they have the same angle measurements but not side lengths. Basically, angles are congruent in similar triangles and their side lengths are constant multiples of each other. Proving two shapes are similar involves showing that all angles are the same; proving two shapes are congruent involves showing that all angles are the same and that all sides are the same. If two pairs of angles are congruent in two triangles, then those triangles are similar because their third angles have to be equal due to the fact that all three angles add up to 180 degrees.

There are five main theorems that are used to prove congruence in triangles. Each theorem involves showing that different combinations of sides and angles are the same in two triangles, which proves the triangles are congruent.

The **side-side-side (SSS) theorem** states that if all sides are equal in two triangles, the triangles are congruent. The **side-angle-side (SAS) theorem** states that if two pairs of sides and the included angles are equal in two triangles then the triangles are congruent. Similarly, the **angle-side-angle (ASA) theorem** states that if two pairs of angles and the included side lengths are equal in two triangles, the triangles are similar. The **angle-angle-side (AAS) theorem** states that two triangles are congruent if they have two pairs of congruent angles and a pair of corresponding equal side lengths that are not included. Finally, the **hypotenuse-leg (HL) theorem** states that if two right triangles have equal hypotenuses and an equal pair of shorter sides, the triangles are congruent. An important item to note is that angle-angle-angle (AAA) is not enough information to prove congruence because the three angles could be equal in two triangles, but their sides could be different lengths.

Using the Relationship Between Similarity, Right Triangles, and Trigonometric Ratios
Within two similar triangles, corresponding side lengths are proportional, and angles are equal. In other words, regarding corresponding sides in two similar triangles, the ratio of side lengths is the same. Recall that the SAS theorem for similarity states that if an angle in one triangle is congruent to an angle in a second triangle, and the lengths of the sides in both triangles are proportional, then the triangles are similar. Also, because the ratio of two sides in two similar right triangles is the same, the trigonometric ratios in similar right triangles are always going to be equal.

If two triangles are similar, and one is a right triangle, the other is a right triangle. The definition of similarity ensures that each triangle has a 90-degree angle. In a similar sense, if two triangles are right triangles containing a pair of equal acute angles, the triangles are similar because the third pair of angles must be equal as well. However, right triangles are not necessarily always similar.

The following triangles are similar:

Similar Triangles

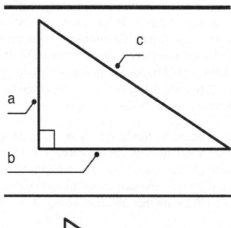

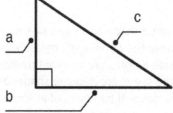

It is not always apparent at first glance, but theorems can be used to show similarity. The Pythagorean Theorem can be used to find the missing side lengths in both triangles. In the larger triangle, the missing side is the hypotenuse, c. Therefore,

$$9^2 + 12^2 = c^2$$

This equation is equivalent to $225 = c^2$, so taking the square root of both sides results in the positive root $c = 15$. In the other triangle, the Pythagorean Theorem can be used to find the missing side length b. The theorem shows that:

$$6^2 + b^2 = 10^2$$

b is then solved for to obtain $b = 8$. The ratio of the sides in the larger triangle to the sides in the smaller triangle is the same value, 1.5. Therefore, the sides are proportional. Because they are both right triangles, they have a congruent angle. The SAS theorem for similarity can be used to show that these two triangles are similar.

Different Transformations of Figures

Two-dimensional figures can undergo various types of transformations in the plane. They can be shifted horizontally and vertically, reflected, compressed, or stretched.

A **shift**, also known as a slide or a translation, moves the shape in one direction. Here is a picture of a shift:

A Translation

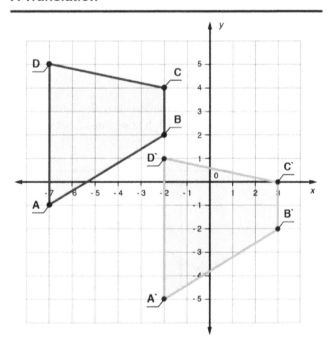

Notice that the size of the original shape has not changed at all. If the shift occurs within a **Cartesian coordinate system**, the standard x- and y-coordinate plane, it can be represented by adding to or subtracting from the x- and y-coordinates of the original shape. All vertices will move the same number of units because the shape and size of the shape do not change.

A figure can also be reflected, or flipped, over a given line known as the **line of reflection**. For instance, consider the following picture:

A Reflection Over the Y-Axis

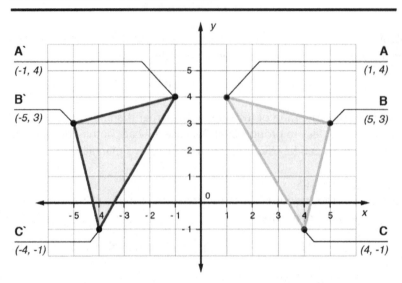

After the reflection, the original shape remains the same size and displays symmetry across the line of reflection, but the coordinates change. For instance, if a shape gets reflected over the y-axis, as above, the y-coordinate stays the same, but the x-coordinates are made negative. For example, the triangle above starts in the first and fourth quadrants, but it is reflected over y-axis to the second and third quadrants. Point A has the initial coordinates of $(1, 4)$, but in the reflection, the point A' becomes $(-1, 4)$.

Similarly, if the shape is reflected over the x-axis, the x-coordinate stays the same, but the y-coordinates are made negative. For instance, in the graphic below, the point C at $(3, 5)$ becomes C' at $(3, -5)$.

A Reflection Over the X-Axis

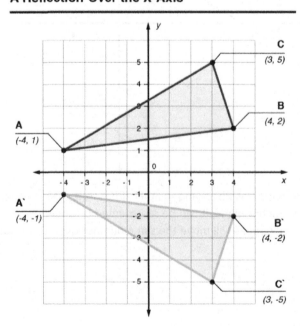

208

A compression or stretch of a figure involves changing the size of the original figure; both transformations are called **dilations**. A compression shrinks the size of the figure. We can think about this as a multiplication process by multiplying times a value between 0 and 1. A stretch of a figure results in a figure larger than the original shape. If we consider multiplication, the factor would be greater than 1. Here is a picture of a dilation that is comprised of a stretch in which the original square quadrupled in size after the length of each side increased by a factor of 2:

A Dilation with a Scale Factor of 2

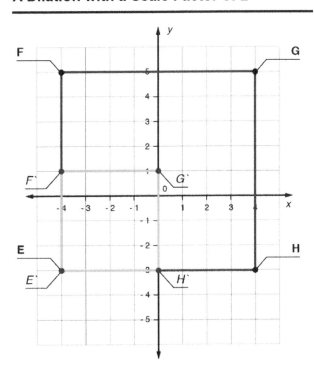

If a shape within the Cartesian coordinate system gets stretched, its coordinates get multiplied by a number greater than 1, and if a shape gets compressed, its coordinates get multiplied by a number between 0 and 1.

A figure can undergo any combination of transformations. For instance, it can be shifted, reflected, and stretched at the same time.

The Pythagorean Theorem
The **Pythagorean Theorem** expresses an important relationship between the three sides of a right triangle. It states that the square of the hypotenuse is equal to the sum of the squares of the other two sides. When using the Pythagorean Theorem, the hypotenuse is labeled as side c, the opposite is labeled as side a, and the adjacent side is side b.

The theorem can be seen in the following diagram:

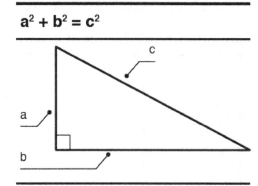

The Pythagorean Theorem

$$a^2 + b^2 = c^2$$

Both the trigonometric ratios and Pythagorean Theorem can be used in problems that involve finding either a missing side or missing angle of a right triangle. Look to see what sides and angles are given and select the correct relationship that will assist in finding the missing value. These relationships can also be used to solve application problems involving right triangles. Often, it is helpful to draw a figure to represent the problem to see what is missing.

Parallel Lines

A set of lines can be parallel, perpendicular, or neither, depending on how the two lines interact. **Parallel lines** run alongside each other but never intersect. **Perpendicular lines** intersect at a 90-degree, or a right, angle. The image below shows both an example and a non-example of each set of lines. Because the first set of lines, in the top left corner, will eventually intersect if they continue, they are not parallel. In the second set, the lines run in the same direction and will never intersect, making them parallel. The third set, in the bottom left corner, intersect at an angle that is not right, or not 90 degrees.

The fourth set is perpendicular because the lines intersect at exactly a right angle.

Lines

Not Parallel	Parallel

Not Perpendicular	Perpendicular

210

Representational Systems, Including Concrete Models, Drawings, and Coordinate Geometry

Concrete Representations of Geometric Objects

Many times, a mathematical concept or skill can be modeled using concrete materials, such as base ten blocks, pattern blocks, tiles, cubes, and chips. Concrete materials in the classroom are referred to as manipulatives. This modeling process allows for further understanding of math concepts, and once the concrete representation is used and understood, the concept can be modeled again in a semi-concrete level by using a drawing, chart, or any other representation formed with paper and pencil.

Tiles can be utilized to represent two dimensional geometric objects and can assist in the understanding of the concept of area. For instance, squares, rectangles, and other two-dimensional shapes can be built with square tiles. The area of a shape can be found by counting the number of square tiles used to form the shape. Here is a semi-concrete drawing of a rectangle, which is equivalent to the concrete representation that would be found by building it with tiles. Each individual tile is a square with side length equal to 1 cm.

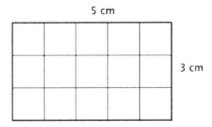

Each tile has an area of one square centimeter. The area of the rectangle is found by counting the number of squares and attaching the appropriate units. Because there are 15 squares, the rectangle has a total area of 15 square centimeters.

In a similar fashion, volume of three-dimensional shapes could be calculated using concrete representations built by cubes. The volume is equal to the number of cubes necessary to build the shape, and the units are cubic units.

Constructing Basic Geometric Figures Using a Compass and Straightedge

Straightedge and compass construction is the process by which lengths, angles, circles, and other geometric shapes are constructed with the use of a straightedge and a compass. Most often, a ruler is used as a straightedge.

The construction of most complicated figures involves the use of using these two tools to bisect both a line and an angle. To bisect a line, place the compass at one end of the line and adjust its width to be somewhat larger than half of the given line. Then, draw arcs above and below the given line. Next, move to the other side of the line and perform the same steps. Finally, place the ruler where the arcs cross and draw the line segment. Here is picture that shows the steps necessary to bisect the line AB.

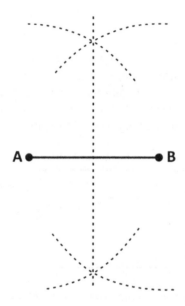

To bisect an angle, first place one of the compass points on the vertex of the angle. Then, make sure the width of the compass is a length that is not longer than the length of the ray within the angle. Use the compass to draw an arc so that the arc passes through both rays of the given angle. Then, place one side of the compass on one of the intersection points between the arc and the ray. Make sure the compass has the width to stay between the angle rays, and then, draw an arc inside the angle. Using the same width of the compass, move to the other intersection point and perform the same steps. The two new arcs should intersect. Finally, draw a line from the vertex of the angle to this intersection point. This line bisects the given angle. Here is a picture that shows the steps necessary to bisect the angle ABC, and the line BD is the bisector.

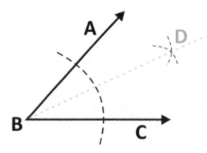

Combining and Dissecting Familiar Shapes

Basic shapes are those polygons that are made up of straight lines and angles and can be described by their number of sides and concavity. Some examples of those shapes are rectangles, triangles, hexagons, and pentagons. These shapes have identifying characteristics on their own, but they can also be decomposed into other shapes. For example, the following can be described as one hexagon, as seen in the first figure. It can also be decomposed into six equilateral triangles. The last figure shows how the hexagon can be decomposed into three rhombuses.

Decomposing a Hexagon

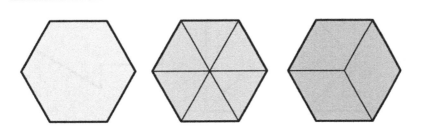

More complex shapes can be formed by combining basic shapes or lining them up side by side. Below is an example of a house. This house is one figure all together but can be decomposed into seven different shapes. The chimney is a parallelogram, and the roof is made up of two triangles. The bottom of the house is a square alongside three triangles. There are many other ways of decomposing this house. Different shapes can be used to line up together and form one larger shape. The area for the house can be calculated by finding the individual areas for each shape, then adding them all together. For this house, there would be the area of four triangles, one square, and one parallelogram. Adding these all together would result in the area of the house as a whole. Decomposing and composing shapes is commonly done with a set of tangrams. A **tangram** is a set of shapes that includes different size triangles, rectangles, and parallelograms.

A Tangram of a House

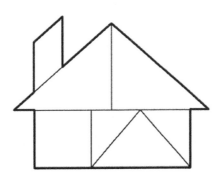

Composition of objects is the way objects are used in conjunction with each other to form bigger, more complex shapes. For example, a rectangle and a triangle can be used together to form an arrow. Arrows can be found in many everyday scenarios, but are often not seen as the composition of two different shapes. A square is a common shape, but it can also be the composition of shapes. As seen in the second figure, there are many shapes used in the making of the one square. There are five triangles that are three different sizes. There is also one square and one parallelogram used to compose this square. These shapes can be used to compose each more complex shape because

213

they line up, side by side, to fill in the shape with no gaps. This defines composition of shapes where smaller shapes are used to make larger, more complex ones.

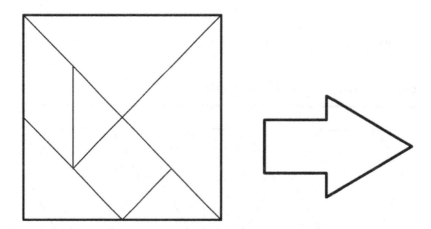

Techniques, Tools, and Formulas for Determining Measurements

Estimating and Measuring

Measuring Length

Lengths of objects can be measured using tools such as rulers, yard sticks, meter sticks, and tape measures. Typically, a ruler measures 12 inches, or one foot. For this reason, a ruler is normally used to measure lengths smaller than or just slightly more than 12 inches. Rulers may represent centimeters instead of inches. Some rulers have inches on one side and centimeters on the other. Be sure to recognize what units you are measuring in. The standard ruler measurements are divided into units of 1 inch and normally broken down to $\frac{1}{2}, \frac{1}{4}, \frac{1}{8}$, and even $\frac{1}{16}$ of an inch for more precise measurements. If measuring in centimeters, the centimeter is likely divided into tenths. To measure the size of a picture, for purposes of buying a frame, a ruler is helpful. If the picture is very large, a yardstick, which measures 3 feet and normally is divided into feet and inches, might be useful. Using metric units, the meter stick measures 1 meter and is divided into 100 centimeters. To measure the size of a window in a home, either a yardstick or meter stick would work. To measure the size of a room, though, a tape measure would be the easiest tool to use. Tape measures can measure up to 10 feet, 25 feet, or more.

Solving Problems Involving Elapsed Time, Money, Length, Volume, and Mass

To solve problems, follow these steps: identify the variables that are known, decide which equation should be used, substitute the numbers, and solve. To solve an equation for the amount of time that has elapsed since an event, use the equation $T = L - E$ where T represents the elapsed time, L represents the later time, and E represents the earlier time. For example, the Minnesota Vikings have not appeared in the Super Bowl since 1976. If the year is now 2023, how long has it been since the Vikings were in the Super Bowl? The later time, L, is 2023, $E = 1976$, and the unknown is T. Substituting these numbers, the equation is $T = 2023 - 1976$, and so $T = 47$. It has been 47 years since the Vikings have appeared in the Super Bowl. Questions involving total cost can be solved using the formula, $C = I + T$ where C represents the total cost, I represents the cost of the item purchased, and T represents the tax amount. To find the length of a rectangle given the area = 32 square inches and width = 8 inches, the formula $A = L \times W$ can be used. Substitute 32 for A, and substitute 8 for W, giving the equation $32 = L \times 8$. This equation is solved by dividing both sides by 8 to find that the length of the rectangle is 4. The formula for volume of a rectangular prism is given by the equation $V = L \times W \times H$. If the length of a rectangular juice box is 4 centimeters, the width is 2 centimeters, and the height is 8 centimeters, what is the volume of this box? Substituting in the formula we find $V =$

$4 \times 2 \times 8$, so the volume is 64 cubic centimeters. In a similar fashion as those previously shown, the mass of an object can be calculated given the formula, $Mass = Density \times Volume$.

12-Hour Clock versus Military Time

There are two different methods of telling time. The first is the 24-hour clock, or what is sometimes called **military time**. This method is shown in the format hours:minutes. The current time is the number of hours and minutes past midnight. The other main way of telling time is the use of the 12-hour clock or the AM/PM system. This takes the 24 hours in a day and divides it into the nighttime hours, which run from midnight to noon, and the daytime hours, which run from noon to midnight. The hours from midnight to noon are the AM hours, and the hours from noon to midnight are the PM hours. Rather than counting up to 24, this method counts from 1 to 12 twice in one day.

To convert between the two methods, the other important piece of information to know is that the first hour of the day in the 24-hour clock is midnight, which would read 0:00. For the AM hours starting at 1:00 AM, the two methods will yield the same time. 2:30 AM on the 12-hour clock will be the same as 2:30 in military time. However, between midnight and 1:00 AM on the 12-hour clock, 12 hours must be subtracted to convert between the two methods. For example, if it is 12:35 AM in the 12-hour clock system, then subtract 12 hours to get 00:35 hours in military time. Conversely, if it is after noon, add 12 hours to the 12-hour clock time to get the military time. For example, if it is 3:15 PM by the 12-hour clock, add 12 hours to get 15:15 in military time.

Classifying Angles Based on Their Measure

When two rays join together at their endpoints, they form an angle. Angles can be described based on their measure. An angle whose measure is ninety degrees is a right angle. Ninety degrees is a standard to which other angles are compared. If an angle is less than ninety degrees, it is an **acute angle**. If it is greater than ninety degrees, it is an **obtuse angle**. If an angle is equal to twice a right angle, or 180 degrees, it is a **straight angle**.

Examples of these types of angles are shown below:

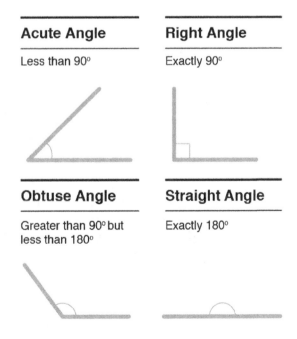

Acute Angle

Less than 90°

Right Angle

Exactly 90°

Obtuse Angle

Greater than 90° but less than 180°

Straight Angle

Exactly 180°

215

A **straight angle** is equal to 180 degrees, or a straight line. If the line continues through the **vertex,** or point where the rays meet, and does not change direction, then the angle is straight. This is shown in Figure 1 below. The second figure shows an obtuse angle. Its measure is greater than ninety degrees, but less than that of a straight angle. An estimate for its measure may be 175 degrees. Figure 3 shows an acute angle because it is just less than that of a right angle. Its measure may be estimated to be 80 degrees.

The last image, Figure 4, shows another acute angle. This measure is much smaller, at approximately 35 degrees, but it is still classified as acute because it is between zero and 90 degrees.

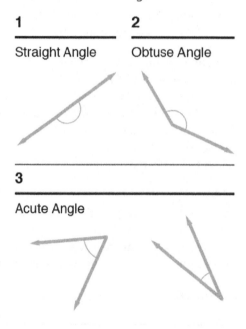

Relationships Between the Metric and the Customary Systems

Measuring length in United States customary units is typically done using inches, feet, yards, and miles. When converting among these units, remember that 12 inches = 1 foot, 3 feet = 1 yard, and 5,280 feet = 1 mile. Common customary units of weight are ounces and pounds. The conversion needed is 16 ounces = 1 pound. For customary units of volume ounces, cups, pints, quarts, and gallons are typically used. For conversions, use 8 ounces = 1 cup, 2 cups = 1 pint, 2 pints = 1 quart, and 4 quarts = 1 gallon. For measuring lengths in metric units, know that 100 centimeters = 1 meter, and 1,000 meters = 1 kilometer. For metric units of measuring weights, grams and kilograms are often used. Know that 1,000 grams = 1 kilogram when making conversions. For metric measures of volume, the most common units are milliliters and liters. Remember that 1,000 milliliters = 1 liter.

When working with dimensions, sometimes the given units don't match the formula, and conversions must be made. When performing operations with rational numbers, it might be helpful to round the numbers in the original problem to get a rough idea of what the answer should be. This system expands to three places above the base unit and three places below. These places correspond to prefixes that each signify a specific base of 10.

The following table shows the conversions:

kilo-	hecto-	deka-	base	deci-	centi-	milli-
1,000 times the base	100 times the base	10 times the base		1/10 times the base	1/100 times the base	1/1,000 times the base

To convert between units within the metric system, values with a base ten can be multiplied. The decimal can also be moved in the direction of the new unit by the same number of zeros on the number. For example, 3 meters is equivalent to 0.003 kilometers. The decimal moved three places (the same number of zeros for kilo-) to the left (the same direction from base to kilo-). Three meters is also equivalent to 3,000 millimeters. The decimal is moved three places to the right because the prefix milli- is three places to the right of the base unit.

The English Standard system, which is used in the United States, uses the base units of foot for length, pound for weight, and gallon for liquid volume. Conversions within the English Standard system are not as easy as those within the metric system because the former does not use a base ten model. The following table shows the conversions within this system.

Length	Weight	Capacity
1 foot (ft) = 12 inches (in) 1 yard (yd) = 3 feet 1 mile (mi) = 5,280 feet 1 mile = 1,760 yards	1 pound (lb) = 16 ounces (oz) 1 ton = 2,000 pounds	1 tablespoon (tbsp) = 3 teaspoons (tsp) 1 cup (c) = 16 tablespoons 1 cup = 8 fluid ounces (oz) 1 pint (pt) = 2 cups 1 quart (qt) = 2 pints 1 gallon (gal) = 4 quarts

When converting within the English Standard system, most calculations include a conversion to the base unit and then another to the desired unit. For example, take the following problem: 3 qt = ____ c. There is no straight conversion from quarts to cups, so the first conversion is from quarts to pints. There are 2 pints in 1 quart, so there are 6 pints in 3 quarts. This conversion can be solved as a proportion:

$$\frac{3 \text{ qt}}{x} = \frac{1 \text{ qt}}{2 \text{ pt}}$$

It can also be observed as a ratio 2:1, expanded to 6:3. Then the 6 pints must be converted to cups. The ratio of pints to cups is 1:2, so the expanded ratio is 6:12. For 6 pints, the measurement is 12 cups. This problem can also be set up as one set of fractions to cancel out units. It begins with the given information and cancels out matching units on top and bottom to yield the answer. Consider the following expression:

$$\frac{3 \text{ qt}}{1} \times \frac{2 \text{ pt}}{1 \text{ qt}} \times \frac{2 \text{ c}}{1 \text{ pt}}$$

It's set up so that units on the top and bottom cancel each other out:

$$\frac{3 \text{ q̶t̶}}{1} \times \frac{2 \text{ p̶t̶}}{1 \text{ q̶t̶}} \times \frac{2 \text{ c}}{1 \text{ p̶t̶}}$$

The numbers can be calculated as 3 × 2 × 2 on the top and 1 on the bottom. It still yields an answer of 12 cups.

217

This process of setting up fractions and canceling out matching units can be used to convert between standard and metric systems. A few common equivalent conversions are 2.54 cm = 1 in, 3.28 ft = 1 m, and 2.205 lb = 1 kg. Writing these as fractions allows them to be used in conversions. For the problem 5 meters = ___ ft, use the feet-to-meter conversion and start with the expression $\frac{5\ m}{1} \times \frac{3.28\ ft}{1\ m}$. The "meters" will cancel each other out, leaving "feet" as the final unit. Calculating the numbers yields 16.4 feet. This problem only required two fractions. Others may require longer expressions, but the underlying rule stays the same. When a unit in the numerator of a fraction matches a unit in the denominator, then they cancel each other out. Using this logic and the conversions given above, many units can be converted between and within the different systems.

The conversion between Fahrenheit and Celsius is found in a formula:

$$°C = (°F - 32) \times \frac{5}{9}$$

For example, to convert 78°F to Celsius, the given temperature would be entered into the formula:

$$°C = (78 - 32) \times \frac{5}{9}$$

Solving the equation, the temperature comes out to be 25.56°C. To convert in the other direction, the formula becomes:

$$°F = °C \times \frac{9}{5} + 32$$

Remember the order of operations when calculating these conversions.

Perimeter and Area

Perimeter and area are geometric quantities that describe objects' measurements. **Perimeter** is the distance around an object. The perimeter of an object can be found by adding the lengths of all sides. Perimeter may be used in problems dealing with lengths around objects such as fences or borders. It may also be used in finding missing lengths or working backwards. If the perimeter is given, but a length is missing, use subtraction to find the missing length. Given a square with side length s, the formula for perimeter is $P = 4s$. Given a rectangle with length l and width w, the formula for perimeter is $P = 2l + 2w$. The perimeter of a triangle is found by adding the three side lengths, and the perimeter of a trapezoid is found by adding the four side lengths. The units for perimeter are always the original units of length, such as meters, inches, miles, etc. When discussing a circle, the distance around the object is referred to as its circumference, not perimeter. The formula for the circumference of a circle is $C = 2\pi r$, where r represents the radius of the circle. This formula can also be written as $C = d\pi$, where d represents the diameter of the circle.

Area is the two-dimensional space covered by an object. These problems may include the area of a rectangle, a yard, or a wall to be painted. Finding the area may require a simple formula or multiple formulas used together. The units for area are square units, such as square meters, square inches, and square miles. Given a square with side length s, the formula for its area is $A = s^2$. Some other formulas for common shapes are shown below.

Shape	Formula	Graphic
Rectangle	$Area = length \times width$	width length
Triangle	$Area = \dfrac{1}{2} \times base \times height$	height base
Circle	$Area = \pi \times radius^2$	radius

The following formula, not as widely used as those shown above, but very important, is the area of a trapezoid:

Area of a Trapezoid

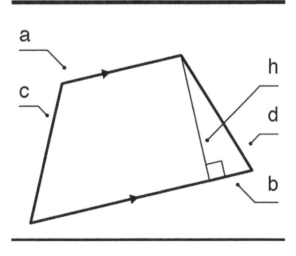

$$A = \frac{1}{2}(a + b)h$$

Geometric figures may be shown as pictures or described in words. If a rectangular playing field with dimensions 95 meters long by 50 meters wide is measured for perimeter, the distance around the field must be found. The perimeter includes two lengths and two widths to measure the entire outside of the field. This quantity can be calculated using the following equation:

$$P = 2(95) + 2(50) = 290 \text{ m}$$

The distance around the field is 290 meters.

Surface Area and Volume

Perimeter and area are two-dimensional descriptions; volume is three-dimensional. **Volume** describes the amount of space that an object occupies, but it differs from area because it has three dimensions instead of two. The units for volume are cubic units, such as cubic meters, cubic inches, and cubic millimeters. Volume can be found by using formulas for common objects such as cylinders and boxes.

The following chart shows a diagram and formula for the volume of two objects.

Shape	Formula	Diagram
Rectangular Prism (box)	$V = length \times width \times height$	height width length
Cylinder	$V = \pi \times radius^2 \times height$	radius height

Volume formulas of these two objects are derived by finding the area of the bottom two-dimensional shape, such as the circle or rectangle, and then multiplying times the height of the three-dimensional shape. Other volume formulas include the volume of a cube with side length s: $V = s^3$; the volume of a sphere with radius r: $V = \frac{4}{3}\pi r^3$; and the volume of a cone with radius r and height h:

$$V = \frac{1}{3}\pi r^2 h$$

If a soda can has a height of 5 inches and a radius on the top of 1.5 inches, the volume can be found using one of the given formulas. A soda can is a cylinder. Knowing the given dimensions, the formula can be completed as follows:

$$V = \pi(radius)^2 \times height$$

$$\pi(1.5 \text{ in})^2 \times 5 \text{ in} = 35.325 \text{ in}^3$$

220

Notice that the units for volume are inches cubed because it refers to the number of cubic inches required to fill the can.

Right rectangular prisms are those prisms in which all sides are rectangles, and all angles are right, or equal to 90 degrees. The volume for these objects can be found by multiplying the length by the width by the height. The formula is $V = lwh$. For the following prism, the volume formula is:

$$V = 6\frac{1}{2} \times 3 \times 9$$

When dealing with fractional edge lengths, it is helpful to convert the length to an improper fraction. The length $6\frac{1}{2}$ cm becomes $\frac{13}{2}$ cm. Then the formula becomes:

$$V = \frac{13}{2} \times 3 \times 9$$

$$\frac{13}{2} \times \frac{3}{1} \times \frac{9}{1} = \frac{351}{2}$$

This value for volume is better understood when turned into a mixed number, which would be $175\frac{1}{2}$ cm^3.

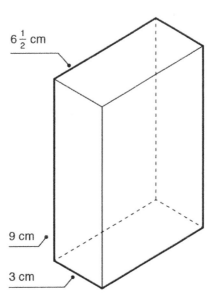

When dimensions for length are given with fractional parts, it can be helpful to turn the mixed number into an improper fraction, then multiply to find the volume, then convert back to a mixed number. When finding surface area, the conversion to improper fractions can also be helpful. The surface area can be found for the same prism above by breaking down the figure into basic shapes. These shapes are rectangles, made up of the two bases, two sides, and the front and back. The formula for surface area adds the areas for each of these shapes in the following equation:

$$SA = 6\frac{1}{2} \times 3 + 6\frac{1}{2} \times 3 + 3 \times 9 + 3 \times 9 + 6\frac{1}{2} \times 9 + 6\frac{1}{2} \times 9$$

Because there are so many terms in a surface area formula and because this formula contains a fraction, it can be simplified by combining groups that are the same. Each set of numbers is used twice, to represent areas for the opposite sides of the prism.

The formula can be simplified to:

$$SA = 2\left(6\frac{1}{2} \times 3\right) + 2(3 \times 9) + 2\left(6\frac{1}{2} \times 9\right)$$

$$2\left(\frac{13}{2} \times 3\right) + 2(27) + 2\left(\frac{13}{2} \times 9\right)$$

$$2\left(\frac{39}{2}\right) + 54 + 2\left(\frac{117}{2}\right)$$

$$39 + 54 + 117 = 210 \text{ cm}^2$$

Surface area is defined as the area of the surface of a figure. A **pyramid** has a surface made up of four triangles and one square. To calculate the surface area of a pyramid, the areas of each individual shape are calculated. Then the areas are added together. This method of decomposing the shape into two-dimensional figures to find area, then adding the areas, can be used to find surface area for any figure. Once these measurements are found, the area is described with square units. For example, the following figure shows a rectangular prism. The figure beside it shows the rectangular prism broken down into two-dimensional shapes, or rectangles. The area of each rectangle can be calculated by multiplying the length by the width. The area for the six rectangles can be represented by the following expression:

$$5 \times 6 + 5 \times 10 + 5 \times 6 + 6 \times 10 + 5 \times 10 + 6 \times 10$$

The total for all these areas added together is 280 m^2, or 280 square meters.

This measurement represents the surface area because it is the area of all six surfaces of the rectangular prism.

The Net of a Rectangular Prism

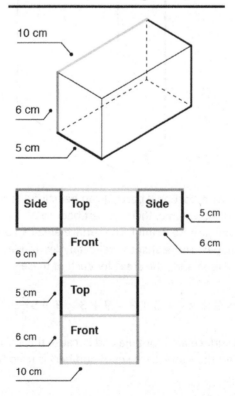

The surface area of a three-dimensional figure is the total area of each of the figure's faces. Because nets lay out each face of an object, they make it easier to visualize and measure surface area. The following figure shows a triangular prism. The bases are triangles, and the sides are rectangles. The second figure shows the net for this triangular prism. The dimensions are labeled for each of the faces of the prism. To determine the area for the two triangles, use the following formula:

$$A = \frac{1}{2}bh = \frac{1}{2} \times 8 \times 9 = 36 \text{ cm}^2$$

The rectangles' areas can be described by the equation:

$$A = lw = 8 \times 5 + 9 \times 5 + 10 \times 5 = 40 + 45 + 50 = 135 \text{ cm}^2$$

The area for the triangles can be multiplied by two, then added to the rectangle areas to yield a total surface area of 207 cm^2.

A Triangular Prism and Its Net

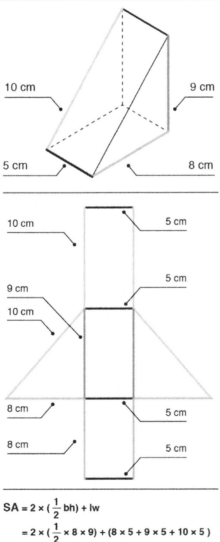

$$SA = 2 \times (\frac{1}{2}bh) + lw$$

$$= 2 \times (\frac{1}{2} \times 8 \times 9) + (8 \times 5 + 9 \times 5 + 10 \times 5)$$

$$= 207 \text{cm}^2$$

Another shape that has a surface area is a cylinder. The shapes used to make up the **cylinder** are two circles and a rectangle wrapped around between the two circles. A common example of a cylinder is a can. The two circles that make up the bases are obvious shapes. The rectangle can be more difficult to see, but the label on a can will help illustrate it. When the label is removed from a can and laid flat, the shape is a rectangle. When the areas for each shape are needed, there will be two formulas. The first is the area for the circles on the bases. This area is given by the formula

$$A = \pi r^2$$

There will be two of these areas. Then the area of the rectangle must be determined. The width of the rectangle is equal to the height of the can, h. The length of the rectangle is equal to the circumference of the base circle, $2\pi r$. The area for the rectangle can be found by using the formula:

$$A = 2\pi r \times h$$

By adding the two areas for the bases and the area of the rectangle, the surface area of the cylinder can be found, described in units squared.

Relating Proportional Reasoning to Scale Drawings and Models

Scale drawings and models can be used to analyze real-world figures. Drawings that are used to replicate real structures are usually not the same size, but they are similar. Figures are said to be similar if they have the same shape, but not the same size. Consider a real-life skyscraper and its corresponding blueprint drawing. If drawn correctly, the replication should be a scale drawing. Too many sheets of paper would be needed to draw the building using its real dimensions! The building and drawing have pairs of corresponding sides, which are sides located in the same place. By definition, if two figures are similar, the ratio of all corresponding sides are equal.

A simple example of similar shapes involves similar triangles. When two triangles are similar, the corresponding angles are the same, and the corresponding sides are proportional.

Ratios need to be used when creating scale drawings. For example, if a skyscraper was 500 feet tall, we could make a drawing that was 5 inches tall. In this case, all other dimensions used in the drawing would have to use a scale factor of $\frac{1}{100}$. For instance, if a square window was 10 ft by 10 ft, the window in the scale drawing would be $\frac{10}{100} = 0.1$ inch by 0.1 inch.

Similar situations arise in map making. Maps are representations of areas of land or sea that can be drawn on flat surfaces. They can be drawn to scale, which means that the real-life areas are reduced by a specific value, known as the scale, so that the maps are just smaller versions of the real areas. In this way, correct distances between two points on a map are maintained. The scale is always denoted in a key or legend on the graph, which shows a measurement on the map and the corresponding measurement in the real world. Here is an example of a map in which 500 miles is represented with one inch. In this case, the scale factor is 20.

1 inch

1 inch = 500 miles

Using Measures to Solve Problems

A **unit rate** is a rate with a denominator of one. It is a comparison of two values with different units where one value is equal to one. Examples of unit rates include 60 miles per hour and 200 words per minute. Problems involving unit rates may require some work to find the unit rate. For example, if Mary travels 360 miles in 5 hours, what is her speed, expressed as a unit rate? The rate can be expressed as the following fraction:

$$\frac{360 \text{ miles}}{5 \text{ hours}}$$

The denominator can be changed to one by dividing by five. The numerator will also need to be divided by five to follow the rules of equality. This division turns the fraction into:

$$\frac{72 \text{ miles}}{1 \text{ hour}}$$

This can now be labeled as a unit rate because one unit has a value of one. Another type of question involves the use of unit rates to solve problems. For example, if Trey needs to read 300 pages and his average speed is 75 pages per hour, will he be able to finish the reading in 5 hours? The unit rate is 75 pages per hour, so the total of 300 pages can be divided by 75 to find the time. After the division, the time it takes to read is four hours. The answer to the question is yes, Trey will finish the reading within 5 hours.

Statistics, Data Analysis, and Probability

Collection, Organization, and Representation of Data

Representing Data through Graphs, Tables, and Charts

Graphs, tables, and charts all organize, categorize, and compare data, and they come in different shapes and sizes. Each type has its own way of showing information, whether through a column, shape, or picture. To answer a question relating to a table, chart, or graph, some steps should be followed. First, the problem should be read thoroughly to determine what is being asked to determine what quantity is unknown. Then, the title of the table, chart, or graph should be read. The title should clarify what data is actually being summarized in the table. Next, look at the key and labels for both the horizontal and vertical axes, if they are given. These items will provide information about how the data is organized. Finally, look to see if there is any more labeling inside the table. Taking the time to get a good idea of what the table is summarizing will be helpful as it is used to interpret information.

Tables are a good way of showing a lot of information in a small space. The information in a table is organized in columns and rows. For example, a table may be used to show the number of votes each candidate received in an election. By interpreting the table, one may observe which candidate won the election and which candidates came in second and third. In using a bar chart to display monthly rainfall amounts in different countries, rainfall can be compared between counties at different times of the year. Graphs are also a useful way to show change in variables over time, as in a line graph, or percentages of a whole, as in a pie graph.

The table below relates the number of items to the total cost. The table shows that one item costs $5. By looking at the table further, five items cost $25, ten items cost $50, and fifty items cost $250. This cost can be extended for any number of items. Since one item costs $5, then two items would cost $10. Though this information is not in the table, the given price can be used to calculate unknown information.

Number of Items	1	5	10	50
Cost ($)	5	25	50	250

A **bar graph** is a graph that summarizes data using bars of different heights. It is useful when comparing two or more items or when seeing how a quantity changes over time. It has both a horizontal and vertical axis. To interpret bar graphs, recognize what each bar represents and connect that to the two variables. The bar graph below shows the scores for six people during three different games. The different colors of the bars distinguish between the three games, and the height of the bar indicates their score for that game. William scored 25 on game 3, and Abigail scored 38 on game 3. By comparing the bars, it is obvious that Williams scored lower than Abigail.

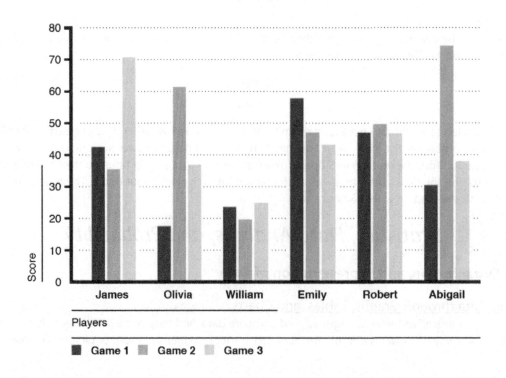

A **line graph** is a way to compare two variables that are plotted on opposite axes of a graph. The line indicates a continuous change as it rises or falls. The line's rate of change is known as its slope. The horizontal axis often represents a variable of time. Audiences can quickly see if an amount has grown or decreased over time. The bottom of the graph, or the x-axis, shows the units for time, such as days, hours, months, etc. If there are multiple lines, a comparison can be made between what the two lines represent. For example, as shown previously, the following line graph shows the change in temperature over five days. The top line represents the high, and the bottom line represents the low for each day. Looking at the top line alone, the high decreases for a day, then increases on Wednesday. Then it decreases on Thursday and increases again on Friday. The low temperatures have a similar trend, shown in the bottom line. The range in temperatures each day can also be calculated by finding the difference between the top line and bottom line on a particular day.

On Wednesday, the range was 14 degrees, from 62° F to 76° F.

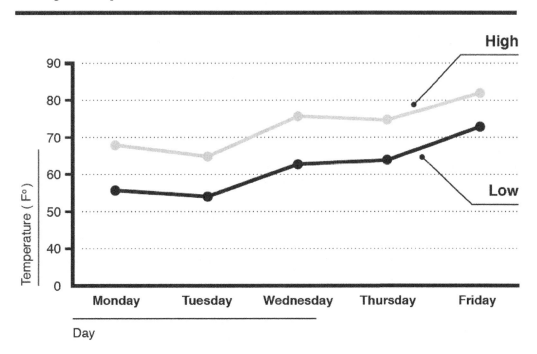

Daily Temperatures

Pie charts are used to show percentages of a whole, as each category is given a piece of the pie, and together all the pieces make up a whole. They are a circular representation of data which are used to highlight numerical proportion. It is true that the arc length of each pie slice is proportional to the amount it individually represents. When a pie chart is shown, an audience can quickly make comparisons by comparing the sizes of the pieces of the pie. They can be useful for comparison between different categories. The following pie chart is a simple example of three different categories shown in comparison to each other.

Light gray represents cats, dark gray represents dogs, and the medium shade of gray represents other pets. These three equal pieces each represent just more than 33 percent, or $\frac{1}{3}$ of the whole. Values 1 and 2 may be combined to represent $\frac{2}{3}$ of the whole. In an example where the total pie represents 75,000 animals, then cats would be equal to $\frac{1}{3}$ of the total, or 25,000. Dogs would equal 25,000 and other pets would also equal 25,000.

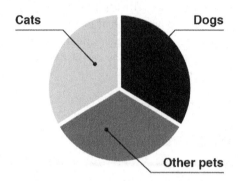

Since circles have 360 degrees, they are used to create pie charts. Because each piece of the pie is a percentage of a whole, that percentage is multiplied times 360 to get the number of degrees each piece represents. In the example above, each piece is $\frac{1}{3}$ of the whole, so each piece is equivalent to 120 degrees. Together, all three pieces add up to 360 degrees.

Stacked bar graphs, also used fairly frequently, are used when comparing multiple variables at one time. They combine some elements of both pie charts and bar graphs, using the organization of bar graphs and the proportionality aspect of pie charts. The following is an example of a stacked bar graph that represents the number of students in a band playing drums, flute, trombone, and clarinet. Each bar graph is broken up further into girls and boys.

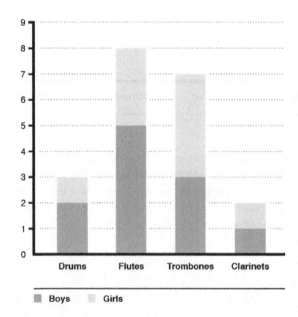

To determine how many boys play trombone, refer to the darker portion of the trombone bar, resulting in 3 students.

A **scatterplot** is another way to represent paired data. It uses Cartesian coordinates, like a line graph, meaning it has both a horizontal and vertical axis. Each data point is represented as a dot on the graph. The dots are never connected with a line. For example, the following is a scatterplot showing the connection between people's ages and heights.

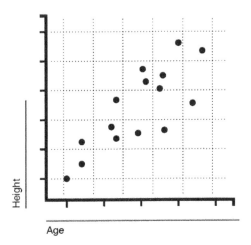

A scatterplot, also known as a **scattergram**, can be used to predict another value and to see if an association, known as a **correlation,** exists between a set of data. If the data resembles a straight line, the data is **associated.** The following is an example of a scatterplot in which the data does not seem to have an association:

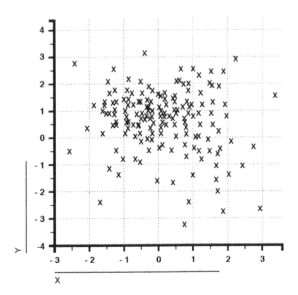

Sets of numbers and other similarly organized data can also be represented graphically. Venn diagrams are a common way to do so. A **Venn diagram** represents each set of data as a circle. The circles overlap, showing that each set of data is overlapping. A Venn diagram is also known as a **logic diagram** because it visualizes all possible logical combinations between two sets. Common elements of two sets are represented by the area of overlap. The following is an example of a Venn diagram of two sets A and B:

Parts of the Venn Diagram

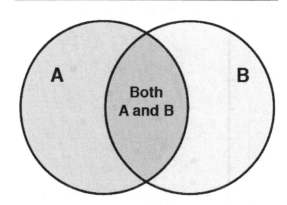

Another name for the area of overlap is the **intersection.** The intersection of A and B, $A \cap B$, contains all elements that are in both sets A and B. The **union** of A and B, $A \cup B$, contains all elements in sets A and B. Finally, the **complement** of $A \cup B$ is equal to all elements that are not in either set A or set B. These elements are placed outside of the circles.

The following is an example of a Venn diagram in which 30 students were surveyed asking which type of siblings they had: brothers, sisters, or both. Ten students only had a brother, seven students only had a sister, and five had both a brother and a sister. Therefore, five is the intersection, represented by the section where the circles overlap. Two students did not have a brother or a sister. Two is therefore the complement and is placed outside of the circles.

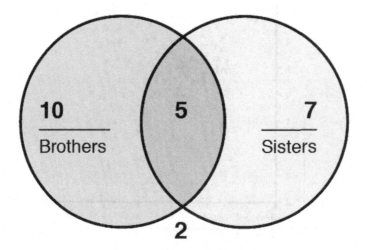

Mean, Median, Mode, and Range

One way information can be interpreted from tables, charts, and graphs is through statistics. The three most common calculations for a set of data are the mean, median, and mode. These three are called **measures of central tendency**, which are helpful in comparing two or more different sets of data.

The **mean** refers to the average and is found by adding up all values and dividing the total by the number of values. In other words, the mean is equal to the sum of all values divided by the number of data entries. For example, if you bowled a total of 532 points in 4 bowling games, your mean score was:

$$\frac{532}{4} = 133 \text{ points per game}$$

Students can apply the concept of mean to calculate what score they need on a final exam to earn a desired grade in a class.

The **median** is found by lining up values from least to greatest and choosing the middle value. If there is an even number of values, then calculate the mean of the two middle amounts to find the median. For example, the median of the set of dollar amounts $5, $6, $9, $12, and $13 is $9. The median of the set of dollar amounts $1, $5, $6, $8, $9, $10 is $7, which is the mean of $6 and $8.

The **mode** is the value that occurs the most. The mode of the data set {1, 3, 1, 5, 5, 8, 10} actually refers to two numbers: 1 and 5. In this case, the data set is bimodal because it has two modes. A data set can have no mode if no amount is repeated. Another useful statistic is range.

The **range** for a set of data refers to the difference between the highest and lowest value.

In some cases, numbers in a list of data might have weights attached to them. In that case, a **weighted mean** can be calculated. A common application of a weighted mean is GPA. In a semester, each class is assigned a number of credit hours, its weight, and at the end of the semester each student receives a grade. To compute GPA, an A is a 4, a B is a 3, a C is a 2, a D is a 1, and an F is a 0. Consider a student that takes a 4-hour English class, a 3-hour math class, and a 4-hour history class and receives all B's. The weighted mean, GPA, is found by multiplying each grade times its weight, number of credit hours, and dividing by the total number of credit hours.

Therefore, the student's GPA is:

$$\frac{3 \times 4 + 3 \times 3 + 3 \times 4}{11} = \frac{33}{1} = 3.0$$

The following bar chart shows how many students attend a cycle class on each day of the week. To find the mean attendance for the week, add each day's attendance together:

$$10 + 7 + 6 + 9 + 8 + 14 + 4 = 58$$

Then divide the total by the number of days:

$$58 \div 7 = 8.3$$

The mean attendance for the week was 8.3 people. The median attendance can be found by putting the attendance numbers in order from least to greatest: 4, 6, 7, 8, 9, 10, 14, and choosing the middle number: 8 people. This set of data has no mode because no numbers repeat. The range is 10, which is found by finding the difference between the lowest number, 4, and the highest number, 14.

Design of Surveys and Samples

Statistics is the branch of mathematics that deals with the collection, organization, and analysis of data. A statistical question is one that can be answered by collecting and analyzing data. When collecting data, expect variability. For example, "How many pets does Yanni own?" is not a statistical question because it can be answered in one way. "How many pets do the people in a certain neighborhood own?" is a statistical question because, to determine this answer, one would need to collect data from each person in the neighborhood, and it is reasonable to expect the answers to vary.

Identify these as statistical or not statistical:

- How old are you?
- What is the average age of the people in your class?

- How tall are the students in Mrs. Jones' sixth grade class?
- Do you like Brussels sprouts?

The first and last questions are not statistical, but the two middle questions are.

Data collection can be done through surveys, experiments, observations, and interviews. A **census** is a type of survey that is done with a whole population. Because it can be difficult to collect data for an entire population, sometimes, a sample survey is used. In this case, one would survey only a fraction of the population and make inferences about the data and generalizations about the larger population from which the sample was drawn. Sample surveys are not as accurate as a census, but this is an easier and less expensive method of collecting data. An **experiment** is used when a researcher wants to explain how one variable causes changes in another variable. For example, if a researcher wanted to know if a particular drug affects weight loss, he or she would choose a treatment group that would take the drug, and another group, the control group, that would not take the drug.

Special care must be taken when choosing these groups to ensure that bias is not a factor. **Bias** occurs when an outside factor influences the outcome of the research. In observational studies, the researcher does not try to influence either variable, but simply observes the behavior of the subjects. Interviews are sometimes used to collect data as well. The researcher will ask questions that focus on her area of interest in order to gain insight from the participants. When gathering data through observation or interviews, it is important that the researcher be well trained so that he or she does not influence the results and so that the study is reliable. A study is reliable if it can be repeated under the same conditions and the same results are received each time.

Inferences, Predictions, and Arguments Based on Data

Interpreting Graphs, Tables, and Charts

A **histogram** is a bar graph used to group data into "bins" that cover a range on the horizontal, or x-axis. Histograms consist of rectangles whose heights are equal to the frequency of a specific category. The horizontal axis represents the specific categories. Because they cover a range of data, these bins have no gaps between bars, unlike the bar graph above. In a histogram showing the heights of adult golden retrievers, the bottom axis would be groups of heights, and the y-axis would be the number of dogs in each range. Evaluating this histogram would show the height of most golden retrievers as falling within a certain range. It also provides information to find the average height and range for how tall golden retrievers may grow.

The following is a histogram that represents exam grades in a given class. The horizontal axis represents ranges of the number of points scored, and the vertical axis represents the number of students. For example, approximately 33 students scored in the 60 to 70 range.

Results of the exam

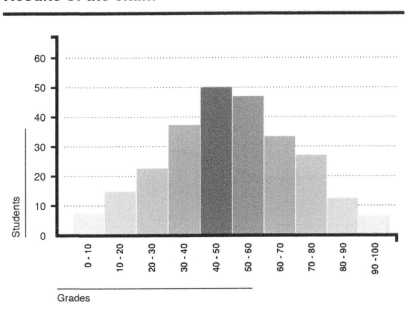

Certain measures of central tendency can be easily visualized with a histogram. If the points scored were shown with individual rectangles, the tallest rectangle would represent the mode. A bimodal set of data would have two peaks of equal height. Histograms can be classified as having data **skewed to the left, skewed to the right,** or **normally distributed**, which is also known as **bell-shaped**. These three classifications can be seen in the following chart:

Measures of central tendency images

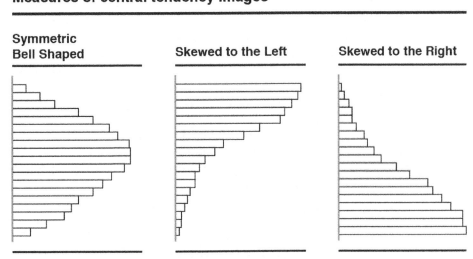

When the data is normal, the mean, median, and mode are very similar because they all represent the most typical value in the data set. In this case, the mean is typically considered the best measure of central tendency because it includes all data points. However, if the data is skewed, the mean becomes less meaningful because it is dragged in the direction of the skew. Therefore, the median becomes the best measure because it is not affected by any outliers.

The measures of central tendency and the range may also be found by evaluating information on a line graph.

The line graph shows the daily high and low temperatures:

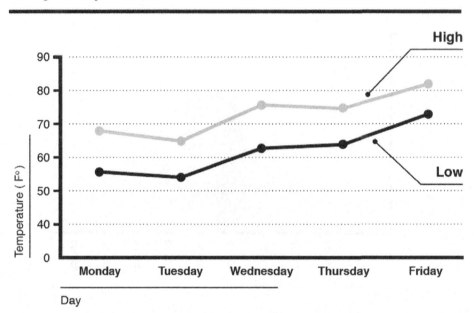

The average high temperature can be found by gathering data from each day on the triangle line. The days' highs are 69, 65, 75, 74, and 81. To find the average, add them together to get 364, then divide by 5 (because there are 5 temperatures). The average high for the five days is 72.8. If 72.8 degrees is found on the graph, it will fall in the middle of all the values. The average low temperature can be found in the same way.

Given a set of data, the **correlation coefficient**, r, measures the association between all the data points. If two values are correlated, there is an association between them. However, correlation does not necessarily mean causation, or that one value causes the other. There is a common mistake made that assumes correlation implies causation. Average daily temperature and number of sunbathers are both correlated and have causation. If the temperature increases, that change in weather causes more people to want to catch some rays. However, wearing plus-size clothing and having heart disease are two variables that are correlated but do not have causation. The larger someone is, the more likely he or she is to have heart disease. However, being overweight does not cause someone to have the disease.

The value of the correlation coefficient is between −1 and 1, where −1 represents a perfect negative linear relationship, 0 represents no relationship between the two data sets, and 1 represents a perfect positive linear relationship. A negative linear relationship means that as x-values increase, y-values decrease. A positive linear relationship means that as x values increase, y values increase.

The formula for computing the correlation coefficient is:

$$r = \frac{n\sum xy - (\sum x)(\sum y)}{\sqrt{n(\sum x^2) - (\sum x)^2}\sqrt{n(\sum y^2) - (y)^2}}$$

n is the number of data points. The closer r is to 1 or −1, the stronger the correlation. A correlation can be seen when plotting data. If the graph resembles a straight line, there is a correlation.

Relationships in Bivariate Data

Independent and dependent are two types of variables that describe how they relate to each other. The **independent variable** is the variable controlled by the experimenter. It stands alone and is not changed by other parts of the experiment. This variable is normally represented by x and is found on the horizontal, or x-axis, of a graph. The **dependent variable** changes in response to the independent variable. It reacts to, or depends on, the independent variable. This variable is normally represented by y and is found on the vertical, or y-axis of the graph.

The relationship between two variables, x and y, can be seen on a scatterplot.

The following scatterplot shows the relationship between weight and height. The graph shows the weight as x and the height as y. The first dot on the left represents a person who is 45 kg and approximately 150 cm tall. The other dots correspond in the same way. As the dots move to the right and weight increases, height also increases. A line could be drawn through the middle of the dots to move from bottom left to top right. This line would indicate a **positive correlation** between the variables. If the variables had a **negative correlation**, then the dots would move from the top left to the bottom right.

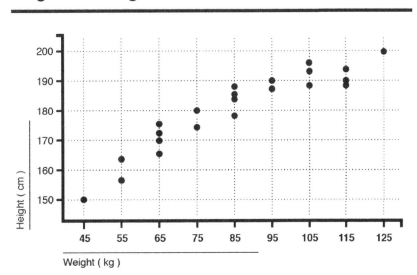

Height and Weight

A scatterplot is useful in determining the relationship between two variables, but it is not required. Consider an example where a student scores a different grade on his math test for each week of the month. The independent variable would be the weeks of the month. The dependent variable would be the grades because they change depending on the week. If the grades trended up as the weeks passed, then the relationship between grades and time would be positive. If the grades decreased as the time passed, then the relationship would be negative. (As the number of weeks went up, the grades went down.)

The relationship between two variables can further be described as strong or weak. The relationship between age and height shows a strong positive correlation because children grow taller as they get older. In adulthood, the relationship between age and height becomes weak, and the dots will spread out. People stop growing in adulthood, and their final heights vary depending on factors like genetics and health. The closer the dots on the graph, the stronger the relationship. As they spread apart, the relationship becomes weaker. If they are too spread out to determine a correlation up or down, then the variables are said to have no correlation.

Variables are values that change, so determining the relationship between them requires an evaluation of who or what changes them. If the variable changes because of a result in the experiment, then it's dependent. If the variable changes before the experiment, or is changed by the person controlling the experiment, then it's the independent variable. As they interact, one is manipulated by the other. The manipulator is the independent, and the manipulated is the dependent. Once the independent and dependent variables are determined, they can be evaluated to have a positive, negative, or no correlation.

Data rarely fits into a straight line. Usually, we must be satisfied with approximations and predictions. Typically, when considering linear data with some sort of trend or association, the scatter plot for the data set appears to "fit" a straight line, and this line is known as the **line of best fit**. For instance, consider the following set of data which shows test scores for 10 students in a classroom on a final exam based on the number of hours each student studied: {$(8, 89), (7, 78), (7, 77), (6, 76), (5, 76), (5, 65), (4, 88), (4, 72), (4, 64), (3, 61)$}. Within each ordered pair, the first coordinate is the number of hours studied and the second coordinate is the test score. Graphing these in a scatterplot yields the following:

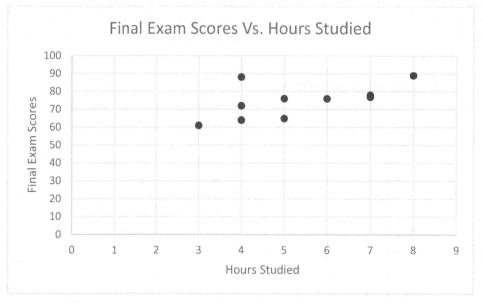

Note that the data does not follow a straight line exactly; however, a straight line can be drawn through the points as shown in the following plot:

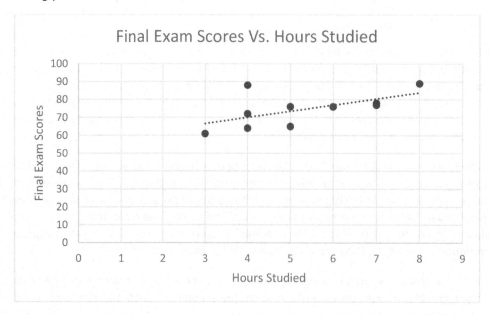

The inserted line is called the **line of best fit**, and it runs through the middle of the points. It can be found using technology, such as Excel® or a graphing calculator. In our example, Excel® was used for the scatter plot, and that function allowed us to add a **linear trend line**, which is another name for line of best fit. **Linear regression line** is another term that means line of best fit. Once you obtain the line, you can predict other points identifying other ordered pairs that the line runs through. For instance, the plot can be used to predict that a student who studied for 5.5 hours should receive close to a 75 on the final exam.

Draw Conclusions about a Population from a Random Sample

In statistics, a **population** contains all subjects being studied. For example, a population could be every student at a university or all males in the United States. A **sample** consists of a group of subjects from an entire population. A sample would be 100 students at a university or 100,000 males in the United States. **Inferential statistics** is the process of using a sample to generalize information concerning populations. **Hypothesis testing** is the actual process used when evaluating claims made about a population based on a sample.

A **statistic** is a measure obtained from a sample, and a **parameter** is a measure obtained from a population. For example, the mean SAT score of the 100 students at a university would be a statistic, and the mean SAT score of all university students would be a parameter.

The beginning stages of hypothesis testing starts with formulating a **hypothesis**, a statement made concerning a population parameter. The hypothesis may be true, or it may not be true. The experiment will help answer that question. In each setting, there are two different types of hypotheses: the **null hypothesis**, written as H_0, and the **alternative hypothesis**, written as H_1. The null hypothesis represents verbally when there is not a difference between two parameters, and the alternative hypothesis represents verbally when there is a difference between two parameters.

Consider the following experiment: A researcher wants to see if a new brand of allergy medication has any effect on drowsiness of the patients who take the medication. He wants to know if the average hours spent sleeping per day increases. The mean for the population under study is 8 hours, so $\mu = 8$. In other words, the population parameter is μ, the mean. The null hypothesis is $\mu = 8$ and the alternative hypothesis is $\mu > 8$. When using a smaller sample of a population, the **null hypothesis** represents the situation when the mean remains unaffected, and the **alternative hypothesis** represents the situation when the mean increases. The chosen statistical test will apply the data from the sample to actually decide whether the null hypothesis should or should not be rejected.

When measuring or calculating a specific quantity in mathematics, the obtained value is not always equal to the exact quantity. In this case, an error occurs, which is the difference between the exact value and the obtained value. In any scenario, there are a few potential sources of error. If the quantity is a measurement, the measuring tool might not be accurate enough to obtain an exact amount. For instance, if you wanted to weigh yourself to the nearest ounce, but your scale at home weighs only in pounds, there would be a difference between your exact weight and the amount seen on your scale. A more accurate scale would have to be used to obtain a weight in ounces. Rounding can also be a source of error. If you did have a very accurate scale at home that measured weight to the nearest ounce, but always rounded to the nearest pound, there would be rounding error involved.

Bias can also occur in calculations. Bias is when a tool consistently undervalues or overvalues a quantity, causing the measured quantity to lean in a certain direction. When bias occurs, there is a difference in the calculation versus what was expected. For instance, if you wanted to calculate the average temperature in your classroom for each month of the year, but a heat source consistently warmed the room every Monday due to the heat being turned off over the weekend, the results would be biased. The actual average would be higher that what was expected.

Basic Notions of Chance and Probability

Understanding Probability

Probability describes how likely it is that an event will occur. Probabilities are always a number from zero to 1. If an event has a high likelihood of occurrence, it will have a probability close to 1. If there is only a small chance that an event will occur, the likelihood is close to zero. A fair six-sided die has one of the numbers 1, 2, 3, 4, 5, and 6 on each side. When this die is rolled there is a one in six chance that it will land on 2. This is because there are six possibilities and only one side has a 2 on it. The probability then is $\frac{1}{6}$ or 0.167. The probability of rolling an even number from this die is three in six, which is $\frac{1}{2}$ or 0.5. This is because there are three sides on the die with even numbers (2, 4, 6), and there are six possible sides. The probability of rolling a number less than 10 is 1; since every side of the die has a number less than 6, it would be impossible to roll a number 10 or higher. On the other hand, the probability of rolling a number larger than 20 is zero. There are no numbers greater than 20 on the die, so it is certain that this will not occur, thus the probability is zero.

If a teacher says that the probability of anyone passing her final exam is 0.2, is it highly likely that anyone will pass? No, the probability of anyone passing her exam is low because 0.2 is closer to zero than to 1. If another teacher is proud that the probability of students passing his class is 0.95, how likely is it that a student will pass? It is highly likely that a student will pass because the probability, 0.95, is very close to 1.

Calculating Probabilities of Events

A probability experiment is a repeated action that has a specific set of possible results. The result of such an experiment is known as an **outcome**, and the set of all potential outcomes is known as the **sample space.** An **event** consists of one or more of those outcomes. For example, consider the probability experiment of tossing a coin and rolling a six-sided die. The coin has two possible outcomes—a heads or a tails—and the die has six possible outcomes—rolling each number 1–6. Therefore, the sample space has twelve possible outcomes: a heads or a tails paired with each roll of the die.

A **simple event** is an event that consists of a single outcome. For instance, selecting a queen of hearts from a standard fifty-two-card deck is a simple event; however, selecting a queen is not a simple event because there are four possibilities.

Classical, or **theoretical, probability** is when each outcome in a sample space has the same chance to occur. The probability for an event is equal to the number of outcomes in that event divided by the total number of outcomes in the sample space. For example, consider rolling a six-sided die. The probability of rolling a 2 is $\frac{1}{6}$, and the probability of rolling an even number is $\frac{3}{6}$, or $\frac{1}{2}$, because there are three even numbers on the die. This type of probability is based on what should happen in theory but not what actually happens in real life.

Empirical probability is based on actual experiments or observations. For example, if a die is rolled eight times, and a 1 is rolled two times, the empirical probability of rolling a 1 is $\frac{2}{8} = \frac{1}{4}$, which is higher than the theoretical probability. The Law of Large Numbers states that as an experiment is completed repeatedly, the empirical probability of an event should get closer to the theoretical probability of an event.

Probabilities range from 0 to 1. The closer the probability of an event occurring is to 0, the less likely it will occur. The closer it is to 1, the more likely it is to occur.

The **addition rule** is necessary to find the probability of event A or event B occurring, or both occurring at the same time. If events A and B are **mutually exclusive** or **disjoint,** they cannot occur at the same time:

$$P(A \text{ or } B) = P(A) + P(B)$$

238

If events A and B are not mutually exclusive, $P(A \text{ or } B) = P(A) + P(B) - P(A \text{ and } B)$ where $P(A \text{ and } B)$ represents the probability of event A and B both occurring at the same time. An example of two events that are mutually exclusive are rolling a 6 on a die and rolling an odd number on a die. The probability of rolling a 6 or rolling an odd number is:

$$\frac{1}{6} + \frac{3}{6} = \frac{4}{6} = \frac{2}{3}$$

Rolling a 6 and rolling an even number are not mutually exclusive because there is some overlap. The probability of rolling a 6 or rolling an even number is:

$$\frac{1}{6} + \frac{3}{6} - \frac{1}{6} = \frac{3}{6} = \frac{1}{2}$$

The **multiplication rule** is necessary when finding the probability that event A occurs in a first trial and event B occurs in a second trial, which is written as $P(A \text{ and } B)$. This rule differs if the events are independent or dependent. Two events A and B are **independent** if the occurrence of one event does not affect the probability that the other will occur. If A and B are not independent, they are **dependent,** and the outcome of the first event somehow affects the outcome of the second. If events A and B are independent, $P(A \text{ and } B) = P(A)P(B)$, and if events A and B are dependent, $P(A \text{ and } B) = P(A)P(B|A)$, where $P(B|A)$ represents the probability event B occurs given that event A has already occurred.

$P(B|A)$ represents **conditional probability**, or the probability of event B occurring given that event A has already occurred. $P(B|A)$ can be found by dividing the probability of events A and B both occurring by the probability of event A occurring using the formula $P(B|A) = \frac{P(A \text{ and } B)}{P(A)}$ and represents the total number of outcomes remaining for B to occur after A occurs. This formula is derived from the multiplication rule with dependent events by dividing both sides by $P(A)$. Note that $P(B|A)$ and $P(A|B)$ are not the same. The first quantity shows that event B has occurred after event A, and the second quantity shows that event A has occurred after event B. Incorrectly interchanging these ideas is known as **confusing the inverse**.

Consider the case of drawing two cards from a deck of fifty-two cards. The probability of pulling two queens would vary based on whether the initial card was placed back in the deck for the second pull. If the card is placed back in, the probability of pulling two queens is:

$$\frac{4}{52} \times \frac{4}{52} = 0.00592$$

If the card is not placed back in, the probability of pulling two queens is:

$$\frac{4}{52} \times \frac{3}{51} = 0.00452$$

When the card is not placed back in, both the numerator and denominator of the second probability decrease by 1. This is due to the fact that, theoretically, there is one less queen in the deck, and there is one less total card in the deck as well.

Expressing Probabilities

Probability is a numerical description of the likelihood of an event. When the probability is expressed as a ratio, two quantities of the same type are compared and may take the form of a/b, a:b, or a to b. If there are six cats and four dogs, the ratio of cats to dogs is 6:4, or 3:2 in reduced form. A probability may be expressed as a proportion, which is an equation that states two ratios are the same. The properties of a proportion are given by:

$$\frac{a}{b} = \frac{c}{d}; \ a, b, c, and \ d \ are \ nonzero$$

Suppose that Neighbor A has $a = 6$ cats and $b = 4$ dogs and that Neighbor B has $c = 12$ cats. If each neighbor has the same proportion of cats to dogs, then $d = 8$ dogs: $6/4 = 12/8$. A ratio is not a fraction, since ratios compare two or more numbers. Fractions are mathematical expressions that show part of a whole.

Probability may also be decimal since it is a fraction. The top of the fraction represents the desirable outcomes, while the denominator represents all possible outcomes. Consider the probability of choosing a dog from Neighbor A, who has four dogs and six cats. The desirable outcome is four, and the possible outcome is ten. The probability is less than one when expressed as a decimal.

$$Probability = \frac{4}{10} = 0.4$$

Probabilities may be expressed as a percent, which is a fraction of a hundred. A percent is expressed as a percent, a%, or a*100%, where a is a fraction. If Neighbor A has ten pets, six of which are cats, then the percentage of cats is:

$$\% \ cats = \frac{number \ of \ cats}{number \ of \ pets} \times 100 = \frac{6}{10} \times 100\% = 60\%$$

The probability that a cat will be chosen from the mix of pets is 60 percent.

Using Various Representations to Show Compound Events

A **two-way frequency table** displays categorical data with two variables, and it highlights relationships that exist between those two variables. Such tables are used frequently to summarize survey results and are also known as **contingency tables**. Each cell shows a count pertaining to that individual variable pairing, known as a **joint frequency**, and the totals of each row and column also are in the table.

Consider the following two-way frequency table:

Distribution of the Residents of a Particular Village

	70 or older	69 or younger	Totals
Women	20	40	60
Men	5	35	40
Total	25	75	100

Table 1 shows the breakdown of ages and sexes of 100 people in a particular village. The end of each row or column displays the number of people represented by the corresponding data, and the total number of people is shown in the bottom right corner. For instance, there were 25 people age 70 or older and 60 women in the data. The 20 in the first cell shows that out of 100 total villagers, 20 were women aged 70 or older. The 5 in the cell below shows that out of 100 total villagers, 5 were men aged 70 or older.

A two-way table can also show relative frequencies by indicating the percentages of people instead of the count. If each frequency is calculated over the entire total of 100, the first cell would be 20% or 0.2. However, the relative frequencies can also be calculated over row or column totals. If row totals were used, the first cell would be:

$$\frac{20}{60} = 0.333 = 33.3\%$$

If column totals were used, the first cell would be:

$$\frac{20}{25} = 0.8 = 80\%$$

Such tables can be used to calculate conditional probabilities, which are probabilities that an event occurs, given another event. Consider a randomly selected villager. The probability of selecting a male 70 years old or older is $\frac{5}{100} = 0.05$ because there are 5 males over the age of 70 and 100 total villagers.

Probability Models

A **uniform probability distribution** exists when there is constant probability. Each random variable has equal probability, and its graph looks like a rectangle because the height, representing the probability, is constant.

A **normal probability distribution** has a graph that is symmetric and bell-shaped; an example using body weight is shown here:

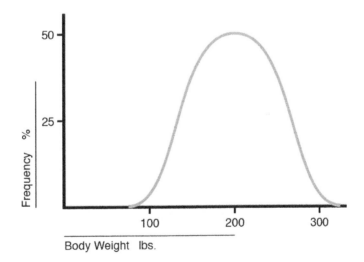

Body Weight lbs.

Population percentages can be estimated using normal distributions. For example, the probability that a data point will be less than the mean is 50 percent. The Empirical Rule states that 68 percent of the data falls within 1 standard deviation of the mean, 95 percent falls within 2 standard deviations of the mean, and 99.7 percent falls within 3 standard deviations of the mean. A **standard normal distribution** is a normal distribution with a mean equal to 0 and standard deviation equal to 1. The area under the entire curve of a standard normal distribution is equal to 1.

Tree Diagrams

In probability, a **tree diagram** can be used to determine the outcome of an event and can represent independent or dependent events. An independent event is one that doesn't change the probability of another event. Flipping a coin or drawing a marble that is subsequently replaced is an independent event. In a dependent event, the outcome of an event affects the outcome of another event.

Practice Quiz

1. What is the solution to the equation $10 - 5x + 2 = 7x + 12 - 12x$?
    a. $x = 12$
    b. No solution
    c. $x = 0$
    d. All real numbers

2. Paul took a written driving test, and he answered 12 questions correctly. If he answered 75% of the total questions correctly, how many questions were on the test?
    a. 25
    b. 16
    c. 20
    d. 18

3. Which of the following represents the correct sum of $\frac{14}{15}$ and $\frac{2}{5}$, in lowest possible terms?
    a. $\frac{20}{15}$

    b. $\frac{4}{3}$

    c. $\frac{16}{20}$

    d. $\frac{4}{5}$

4. The number of members of the House of Representatives varies directly with the total population in a state. If the state of New York has 19,800,000 residents and has 27 total representatives, how many should Ohio have with a population of 11,800,000?
    a. 10
    b. 16
    c. 11
    d. 5

5. The mass of the Moon is about 7.348×10^{22} kilograms, and the mass of Earth is 5.972×10^{24} kilograms. How many times greater is Earth's mass than the Moon's mass?
    a. 8.127×10^{1}
    b. 8.127
    b. 812.7
    d. 8.127×10^{-1}

See answers on the next page.

Answer Explanations

1. D: First, like terms are collected to obtain:

$$12 - 5x = -5x + 12$$

Then, if the addition principle is used to move the terms with the variable, $5x$ is added to both sides and the mathematical statement $12 = 12$ is obtained. This is always true; therefore, all real numbers satisfy the original equation.

2. B: The unknown quantity is the number of total questions on the test. Let x be equal to this unknown quantity. Therefore, $0.75x = 12$. Divide both sides by 0.75 to obtain $x = 16$.

3. B: Common denominators must be used to add fractions. The least common denominator is 15, and $\frac{2}{5} = \frac{6}{15}$. Therefore, $\frac{14}{15} + \frac{6}{15} = \frac{20}{15}$. In lowest terms, the answer is $\frac{4}{3}$. A common factor of 5 was divided out of both the numerator and denominator.

4. B: The number of representatives varies directly with the population, so the equation necessary is $N = k \times P$, where N is number of representatives, k is the variation constant, and P is total population in millions. Plugging in the information for New York allows k to be solved for. This process gives $27 = k \times 19.8$, so $k = 1.36$. Therefore, the formula for number of representatives given total population in millions is:

$$N = 1.36 \times P$$

Plugging in $P = 11.8$ for Ohio results in $N = 16.05$, which rounds to 16 total representatives.

5. A: Division can be used to solve this problem. The division necessary is:

$$\frac{5.972 \times 10^{24}}{7.348 \times 10^{22}}$$

To compute this division, divide the numbers written in decimal form first and then use algebraic laws of exponents to divide the exponential expression.

This results in about 0.8127×10^2, which, written in scientific notation, is 8.127×10^1.

Subtest III: Physical Education

Movement Skills and Movement Knowledge

Basic Movement Skills

Elementary age students are expected to learn, and eventually master, various movement skills as part of a well-rounded physical education curriculum. These skills are the building blocks each student will use when learning the more specific movements and skills necessary to participate in athletic activities, sports, and social events (such as dances) throughout childhood, adolescence, and adulthood. Early education in these simple concepts and abilities supports the student's sense of confidence and self-esteem when learning more advanced skills. The final goal of the program is to prepare the student to confidently live a physically active life during adulthood.

Failure to master these skills may lead to embarrassment, or even feelings of inadequacy, while the student struggles to build upon insecure foundations to learn socially useful physical activities.

Movement Concepts

The idea of **movement concepts** categorizes the different ways students engage in movement exploration into three general categories: body awareness, effort, and relationships. Remember that these movement concepts are *not* the physical skills that children learn. Rather, they are different *ways* children may make use of a learned skill.

Body awareness broadly describes the student's ability to be aware and in control of the ways and places in which their body moves. This movement concept is demonstrated through elements such as *direction* (up and down, left and right), *pathways* (running in a straight line as opposed to running in a zigzag pattern), and *space awareness* (personal space, general play space). Teachers can help students master these body awareness elements through movement activities that require the student to move in accord with one or more elements. For example, a game of tag where students must leap over a crouching "out" player to get back in the game uses the concept of direction in going *over* the student.

The concept of **effort** describes how much energy is used when the student implements a physical skill. Effort contains elements such as *force* (whether that's light skipping or a full-strength leap), and *speed* (moving quickly, moving suddenly, or moving slowly). Students demonstrate this concept through activities such as Red Light, Green Light, where the participant must begin motion and suddenly stop.

Finally, the concept of **relationships** describes how the body, objects, and other participants in an activity interact with one another. This concept is particularly important for its social aspects. *Leading, following,* and *mirroring* movements with other people are all significant aspects of activities children may be expected to learn in the future (such as dances, marches, and games).

Each movement concept category is used in context to define the ways students should engage in their basic physical skills. For example, skipping toward the teacher and then sprinting away from them makes use of both *direction* and *force,* among other elements of body awareness and effort.

Locomotor, Non-Locomotor, and Manipulative Skills

Students in elementary physical education are expected to learn a cohort of basic **locomotor** and **non-locomotor** skills. These physical skills are the *actions* students learn and practice as part of an elementary physical education curriculum. The movement concepts then describe the manner in which these actions are carried out (for example, slowly, in such-and-such direction, and so on).

Locomotor skills describe how students move around, such as by walking, running, skipping, or hopping. Non-locomotor skills describe motions practiced in a static position, such as balancing, twisting, turning, jumping, or transferring weight from one part of the body to another. As the student grows more competent and confident in their physical skills, these skills are combined for use in more advanced ways. For example, the triple jump event in track and field combines running, jumping, hopping, and balance into a single physical skill.

Manipulative skills describe students' ability to move and use objects effectively. An individual's ability to use objects dexterously improves over time, but the basic ability to coordinate perceptions and bodily movements should be taught and reinforced from an early age. This category includes skills such as throwing, catching, and kicking. Learning basic manipulative skills at an early age helps students learn to play popular games such as baseball, basketball, or soccer in later years.

Biomechanics

One important thing to remember when teaching movement skills to children is that after they achieve initial success, they should repeat the activity until it becomes a habit. If the student can complete the activity successfully, but is not using all steps of the skill to be mastered, they may develop bad habits that lead to challenges when learning more advanced skills. For example, a child who learns to hop forward on one foot, but does not swing their opposite leg for increased momentum, may struggle when learning to perform a *layup* in basketball. This skill's effectiveness is closely connected with how much forward momentum the individual can generate before throwing the basketball.

These childhood bad habits often arise through the student's incorrect use of **biomechanics.** This concept describes how the students can maximize the body's movements when performing a physical skill through use of gravity, momentum, and so on. Some examples include:

- Following through the arm motion while throwing a ball overhand.
- Swinging the arms while running.
- Swinging the opposite leg while hopping.

Correcting stiff, awkward, or incorrect movements during childhood helps support the student's later ability to learn new, more complex physical skills that make use of similar biomechanical functions to maximize performance. For example, the full-body twisting motion of hitting a baseball makes use of the same biomechanical concepts as stepping forward when kicking a ball.

Exercise Physiology: Health and Physical Fitness

One important function of a physical education curriculum for students of all ages is teaching the core elements of keeping themselves physically active throughout their entire lives. By learning about these principles and internalizing them, students reduce their risk of developing any of the chronic illnesses that are brought about by sedentary lifestyles.

Components of Physical Fitness

The **American College of Sports Medicine** (ACSM) identifies five key components to consider when evaluating an individual's physical fitness:

- **Body composition:** The ratio of lean mass to fat mass in an individual's body
- **Cardiorespiratory endurance:** The ability to engage in ongoing aerobic exercise
- **Flexibility:** The ability to stretch, twist, and move without distress
- **Muscular endurance:** The ability to use one's muscles consistently for long periods of time
- **Muscular strength:** The ability to output short, significant bursts of power with one's muscles

Each of the five components is important to consider within a holistic approach to evaluating an individual student's health. A student with good flexibility may struggle with muscular endurance, or a student with good muscular

246

strength may struggle with maintaining a healthy body composition. When evaluating a student's overall physical fitness and choosing appropriate exercises to improve their health, it is important for teachers and coaches to consider the individual's weaknesses *and* strengths. A person-centered exercise curriculum is more likely to benefit the student because encouraging their strengths increases their motivation to complete the program.

One key concept when considering different forms of exercise is **aerobic** versus **anaerobic** exercise. Aerobic exercise takes place when the exercise requires increased oxygen intake to continue energy production in the muscles. This form of exercise focuses on improving cardiorespiratory endurance as the lungs and heart continue bringing oxygen into the body. Common forms of aerobic exercise include jogging, biking, and playing soccer. On the other hand, anaerobic exercise takes place when a majority of the muscle power for the exercise is generated without oxygen playing a significant role. Anaerobic exercise focuses on improving the individual's muscular strength. Typical anaerobic exercises include weightlifting or wrestling.

Most forms of exercise have an impact on multiple physical fitness components. For example, jogging improves cardiorespiratory endurance, but it also exercises the individual's muscular endurance. No single component works alone to achieve physical fitness and maintain a healthy lifestyle.

The FITT Principle
Teachers can remember how to select the best exercises and activities for specific components of physical fitness with the acronym **FITT:**

- **Frequency:** How often an individual performs an exercise
- **Intensity:** The amount of exertion required for the exercise
- **Time:** The duration of the exercise
- **Type:** An exercise that targets the correct muscle group, or correct component of fitness

Altering one or more of these aspects of a physical fitness regimen leads to continuous improvement of the student's physical fitness. The teacher must match the correct element of FITT to the student's fitness goal to see positive results. For example, a student who seeks to increase the number of consecutive pushups they can do should be assigned weightlifting exercises with *intensity* that increases as the student's muscular strength increases, because this contributes best to their goal. On the other hand, changing up the aspect of FITT an exercise regimen focuses on can help the student continue to improve once benefits from a prior regime become stagnant. For another example, assigning the same student different *types* of weightlifting exercises that focus on multiple muscle groups in the arms and abdomen may help them achieve their pushup goal through the development of less-used muscles.

Benefits of Lifelong Physical Activity
Educating students about physical fitness increases the likelihood that they will choose to live a physically active lifestyle in adulthood. Physical activity reduces an individual's risk of experiencing various illnesses.

During childhood, ongoing participation in a physical education program supports the student's physical development. Through play, sports, and exercise, the student becomes increasingly aware of the ways their body can move and is able to strengthen their muscular and skeletal growth. Thirty to sixty minutes of activity daily also reduces the risk of childhood obesity. Frequent exercise also improves certain chronic illnesses, such as asthma, in some youth.

Physically active adults reduce their risk of obesity, which in turn reduces their risk of developing type 2 diabetes, heart disease, high blood pressure, and related chronic ailments. Consistent activity also improves flexibility and reduces the risk of inflammatory diseases, such as arthritis or gout, in old age.

At all ages, physical activity carries a risk of injury. Typically, exercise injuries are minor, involving muscular strain or cramping, but at times they can be serious. Students should be taught not only to exercise frequently, but also how to exercise *safely*. Safety in both class and individual exercise can be improved through gentler warm-up exercises and cool-downs, such as stretching or walking, after a workout. Appropriate form, rest, and awareness of one's body during physical activity are all important parts of a well-rounded physical education curriculum.

Movement Forms: Content Areas

Physical skills, and the movement concepts which may modify them, are best taught to children using a variety of traditional and nontraditional activities. **Traditional** activities are the ones each generation teaches through oral methods to the next (for example, *tag*). Some children may be introduced to one game or another by a teacher, but in general, children are first exposed to games, dances and music, marches, and other physical activities common in their culture through parents, non-parental adults, and peers.

Nontraditional activities are those a teacher devises for the sake of practicing a particular physical skill or skills (for example, an obstacle course). They also might include activities that are traditional to another culture, which the student should spend time learning. Early exposure to multicultural activities prepares the student for participation in a plural society as an adult.

The Function of Sportsmanship

One important function of early physical education is teaching children how to interact together during both competitive and non-competitive activities. Learning **sportsmanship**—appropriate social etiquette about how to behave with fairness and respect during competitive activities—at an early age reinforces the likelihood the student will engage in sportsmanlike conduct as they grow older. This impacts their social behavior both in physical activities and in social events generally.

The sense of fairness and respect required to instill this subjective feeling into young students requires proactive support by the teacher. Ensuring consistent application of activity and class rules, positively reinforcing treating other participants well, and negatively reinforcing students who wish to shun or tease another participant all contribute to developing the child's internal sense that games should be played in a certain way. Note that developing a sense of sportsmanship does *not* necessitate competitive activities. Games and activities that encourage students to move and participate are equally capable of teaching sportsmanship.

Childhood Games

Teachers are expected to be familiar with traditional childhood games their students play, and to devise their own activities so students can practice using a variety of physical skills.

Many popular games make good use of locomotor, non-locomotor, and manipulative skills. Some frequent favorites include tag (and variations, such as freeze tag or kick the can), hide and seek, and hopscotch. These games are popular among elementary students due to their simple rules, which make the game easy to learn and play with their peers.

As students grow older and their physical and cognitive abilities improve, they become able to participate in increasingly complicated activities. These activities are characterized by an increased focus on teamwork and competition. Education in basic rule-following and social etiquette regarding sportsmanship at an early age increases the students' ability to participate in these team activities successfully. Traditional examples of team games played by older children, adolescents, and adults include basketball, baseball, and football. The teacher's knowledge of these and similar team games is important because oral teaching of the rules from child to child does not always present the formal rules—as adjudicated by associations for a given sport, such as the National Football League (NFL)—that are required for participation as an adult with strangers.

Nontraditional activities devised by the teacher, or by a physical education curriculum, also help students master their physical skills. These activities increase in complexity as a student grows older. For example, a first-grade student's obstacle course might include three different challenges, while a course for ninth grade students might include ten or more. Some nontraditional physical activities students should become familiar with include gymnastic activities (such as tumbling, vaulting, and rolling), manipulative activities such as juggling or corn hole, and games such as ultimate frisbee or pickleball.

Remember, the distinction between traditional and nontraditional activities is cultural, and may change over time. As a sport, game, or activity becomes increasingly popular, children will naturally mimic their elders and engage in the activity on their own. Nontraditional activities are not necessarily difficult or obscure.

Selecting Activities

As a general principle, teachers of physical education should focus on **participation** over competition. The goal of a physical education curriculum is not to train athletes, but to prepare all students for living a physically active adult life. It is especially important during elementary physical education to select activities which keep all students moving and engaged for the duration of the class session. Setting this early precedent encourages students to continue active participation during physical education as they grow older. Games such as dodgeball, where some students may be "out" for the majority of an activity, are a less effective choice because not all students have similar opportunities for exercise and practicing skill mastery.

When selecting activities, physical education teachers should also keep opportunities in mind to integrate other academic subjects into the exercise. This is especially effective for student learning during elementary school because providing fun, physical ways to engage with educational material improves both a student's motivation to learn and their retention of material. For example, setting out a variety of numbered stations and playing a game where students must run to the station whose number is the answer to a math problem would integrate math and physical activity for a combined benefit to the students.

Physical education teachers should also make use of nontraditional games—such as those found in textbooks but not played independently by children—and traditional games drawn from other cultures. This provides children an opportunity to use their physical and social skills in new ways. It also provides a hands-on way for young children to learn about cultural differences from the American mainstream in a method of play they can experience directly. For example, students might play *vaputta* to learn about the Native American Pima people or dance the flamenco to learn about Spain.

Self-Image and Personal Development

Physical Growth and Development

From birth through childhood and adolescence, children are constantly growing. One aspect of physical education is to help students adjust to their changing bodies. Developing coordination between a student's perceptions and their body increases confidence in their ability to perform physical activities appropriately. Mastering age-appropriate physical skills in early childhood correlates with the student's willingness to participate in physical activities during adolescence and adulthood. To this end, it is important for teachers of physical education to understand how their students grow and change.

Elementary Students

By the time children enter elementary school, they have grown more than double their size and weight at birth. Elementary children are fully capable of crawling, walking, and running. They further develop their motor skills over the following years, refining a sense of balance and coordination. These skills develop from the trunk outward. By the end of elementary school, students are able to use their fingers for fine motor skills (such as writing with a pencil) without difficulty.

During childhood, students grow about 2 inches per year. While slower than the dramatic growth of infancy and the preschool years, this rate of growth is steady enough to require students to continually adjust how they move and coordinate their bodies through gross motor skills. They should be able to perform a variety of physical skills—such as skipping, kicking, or galloping—without difficulty coordinating the movement of legs and arms.

Puberty

The most significant period of physical change experienced by a majority of students is **puberty**. This is a process that typically begins between the ages of twelve and fifteen where changes in hormone production—**estrogen** for girls, **testosterone** for boys—trigger growth spurts and the development of primary and secondary sex characteristics.

Puberty's growth spurt is commonly characterized by a student's increased feelings of clumsiness or awkwardness with their own body. They may express frustration with their inability to perform physical skills they had previously mastered as their body outgrows their ability to keep pace with the changes. During puberty, students may grow up to 4 inches in a year. This increase in height is accompanied by an increase in muscle mass. Students may take pride in newfound strength or other physical abilities but may also experience a period of crisis and lower self-esteem due to the associated coordination difficulties.

It is important during puberty and adolescence that students have both an appropriate amount of exercise and an appropriate amount of rest. These factors, combined with appropriate nutrition, provide the student with the greatest opportunity to maximize their development into a physically healthy and capable adult.

Risk Factors

A number of risk factors can inhibit potential growth. The factors most frequently experienced by American students include:

- **Maltreatment:** Harmful choices by adults in the student's life—such as neglect or physical abuse—can hinder physical growth. Malnutrition is a common symptom of abuse that directly inhibits growth.

- **Mental health challenges:** Students who struggle with the symptoms of mental health difficulties are at increased risk for delays or reduced physical growth outcomes due to their inability to care for themselves. For example, a student with depression whose appetite has diminished might lose too much weight.

- **Stress:** The drive to achieve in academics, in athletics, and in the eyes of one's peers is a significant stressor on many adolescents. While learning to perform effectively under stress is an important emotional skill, chronic stress inhibits physical and mental development.

- **Substance abuse:** The frequent use of common intoxicating substances (such as alcohol, nicotine, and prescription drugs) has a negative influence beyond addiction or the social and legal troubles to which substance abuse frequently leads. Heavy use of drugs hinders development of the brain and limits a youth's potential height. Substance abuse can have lifelong effects on development, such as growing slightly shorter than the individual's potential height, or even significant mental impairments.

Bodies in crisis or stress—such as a student experiencing malnutrition due to neglect—expend fewer resources on growth to save resources for survival. It is important for teachers to identify and address risk factors to provide the student with the best chance to grow and develop.

Role of Physical Education

The function of frequent physical education throughout a student's school years is to support their ability to use their changing body, and to offer them sufficient exercise and activity to remain healthy throughout childhood. If a physical education curriculum is effective, the students will remain confident in their physical abilities and become adults who habitually participate in social activities typical of their community. This might include joining a pick-up game of soccer or a night out dancing with friends. Physical education provides exercise needed for proper development of the body, and practice in coordinating the body so the student feels skilled and confident in their ability to move a variety of ways as an adult.

Self-Image

A strong physical education curriculum encourages development of a positive **self-image** for the student. The psychological benefits students gain from **participation** in a combined program of physical activity and physical education prepare them for lifelong engagement in exercise activities.

Each student has their own individual perception of their self. This concept combines aspects of personality, physical appearance, and confidence in one's own abilities. Self-image is best thought of as an internal "mirror" held up to examine themselves, although external factors (such as peer opinions) also have an impact. Teachers bolster a student's self-image by encouraging **goal-setting**, which in turn increases a sense of **achievement**.

Physical education encourages students to set individual, measurable goals, and then provides the tools—such as the FITT principle—for the student to accomplish their objective. During goal-setting, the teacher should consider the student's physical, mental, and social abilities, and take care that objectives are person-centered. Focusing on creating goals the student *wants* to achieve supports their motivation and overall development. For example, a 200-pound deadlift goal is not appropriate for a twelve-year-old male, whereas running 3 miles in under 30 minutes is an appropriate goal for a fourteen-year-old female who wants to join the cross country team next year.

Goal-setting is a teaching process that improves the student's self-image through the feeling of achievement after they accomplish their goals. Including the student's choices in the goal-setting process improves motivation and teaches them how to break down larger ambitions into smaller objectives. This extends the skills learned during physical education into other aspects of the student's academic (and non-academic) life.

Teachers can also support a positive self-image in students during physical education through individualized support. Praise, encouragement, and coaching techniques all encourage the student's growth. Throughout, the teacher should ensure their student interactions focus on the individual's goals.

Fostering positive self-image in children and teenagers encourages students toward lifelong engagement in physical activity. This reduces the likelihood that the student will develop diseases related to inactivity, including heart disease, type 2 diabetes, and obesity, during their lifetime. Lifelong physical activity also improves psychological health, which reduces the likelihood of anxiety and depression in children, teenagers, and adults.

Social Development

Social Aspects of Physical Education

Beyond providing opportunities for exercise and mastery of new physical skills, a school's physical education curriculum also plays an important part in the students' social skill development. This is reflected in a variety of ways, including relatively simple concepts about social etiquette such as **sharing** or **sportsmanship**, as well as complex tasks such as **group problem-solving**. Games and other physical activities provide teaching moments around the use of social skills. Students can put these skills to further use by students outside of the classroom. For example, they might be able to resolve conflicts during recess or while playing with friends after school.

As with physical skills, an appropriate approach to social skills as part of the physical education curriculum is informed by accurate expectations of student behavior based on age, culture, and individual ability or disability. Social skills are less capable of universalization than physical skills because communication styles vary from one culture (and one home within a culture) to another. Further, some students experience a form of disability and struggle to learn appropriate methods of peer communication through regular instruction. Teachers should be aware of various cognitive, emotional, learning, and communication disabilities their students may have. These difficulties may make learning and following rules more challenging for such individuals, requiring additional patience, attention, and direction from educators. On the other hand, the process by which a child grows larger and develops physical skills such as running or skipping, are cross-cultural experiences—and are often growth experiences shared by individuals struggling with disabilities.

The best approach for teaching social skills is to begin with **observation.** Observation of how students interact with one another allows the teacher to develop a student-centered curriculum. Additional resources, such as discussions during parent-teacher conferences, provide the teacher opportunities to understand how a student has learned to communicate outside of formal education. Rather than imposing external learning objectives on a student (or a class), the teacher should seek to learn through close observation what skills an individual would benefit from practicing.

Cooperative or Competitive Activities

In general, teachers ought to choose activities which practice **cooperation** during the first years of elementary school, and slowly increase the extent to which student **compete** with one another as the students grow older and improve both their physical and their social skills. Practicing cooperative social skills at a young age increases prosocial attitudes and behavior among students, and reduces misconduct. This provides the student with a useful foundation for controlling their emotions. Simple cooperative activities and team-building activities (for example, two students walking a certain distance while pressing a balloon between their shoulders) encourage students to communicate with a partner, or members of a larger team, to achieve a mutual objective. These exercises should require the students to practice their physical skills alongside their social skills. In contrast, activities designed to practice social skills in the general elementary classroom do not necessarily have this physical component.

Some other types of activities which encourage cooperation among elementary students include line games and relay games. The general objective of such activities is to keep all students engaged—both physically and socially—in the lesson, and to avoid win or loss states in the activity. Instead, the class should focus on *completing* the activity. This avoids some of the negative emotions of more competitive activities and allows the students to share a sense of accomplishment after completion. This shared sense of success is an emotional cornerstone for **teamwork.**

Competition emerges naturally among students of all ages, and does not need to be discouraged outright. For example, children will naturally race to see who can reach a sign first, or compete to see who can jump highest. However, with elementary students, it is best for the teacher to provide activities that may not have a clear "winner" or "loser," and focus on continuous participation instead. A game like tag, for example, allows students to compete with one another—practicing emotional skills such as being respectful after tagging someone, or handling frustration upon being tagged—without lauding a victor, or leading a student to feel negatively about themselves due to a loss. During tag, all students can continue participating in the activity while *also* competing to tag one another.

This principle can be further applied to team games, relay games, and so on. For example, a possible activity has the class divided into two groups for a basketball line game, in which the two students at the head of each line compete to make a basket first. Whoever fails goes to the other group's line. This activity continues until all students are in the same group, or until it has continued for a certain duration. By transferring students from one group to another, this activity provides a competitive element, while avoiding a student being called "out," and no longer allowed to participate.

Progression of Complexity

Simpler activities like the one above help students practice physical and social skills which they will put to use in more complex activities. A standard objective is playing team sports during high school. Typical examples in a physical education class include basketball, baseball, or flag football. Participation in competitive small group or one-on-one activities (like tennis or badminton) also provides an important opportunity to learn a sport which is simpler to participate in spontaneously in young adulthood. Learning to play a team sport by its formal rules is a complex process, requiring several stages of education. This typically begins with practicing specific elements included within the sport—such as swinging at a baseball on a tee, or racing another student while dribbling a basketball—and then combining these portions together over time.

These activities, midway between playing a sport by "adult" rules and learning the physical skills piecemeal, provide the teacher with diverse opportunities to practice social skills. At this stage, students are equipped to practice increasingly competitive activities. Competition provides a testing ground for students to experience social conflicts and practice resolving problems, either together or with adult assistance. Some example conflicts which arise in physical education include encouraging respectful or sportsmanlike behavior, adjudicating rules fairly, and coping with the student's internal experience of success or failure. Learning to be gracious to other participants, to admire a competitor's success, and to be kind in victory are all important social abilities which the student will use in all aspects of their life—personal, social, vocational, and so on—as an adult.

Social Development Objectives

Developing competence through an effective physical education curriculum provides students with a source of **self-confidence** and **self-expression**. The student's knowledge that they can move their body freely and effectively empowers them to pursue ongoing engagement in physical activities. For many, athletic competence in one or more physical pursuits becomes a source of pride. Alternatively, activities such as dancing, acrobatics, or even sleight-of-hand tricks or juggling provide a physical way for the student to build self-esteem and express their unique personality.

Throughout a student's education, the exercise of social skills within physical education has notable positive outcomes for their adult life. Emotional control, social problem-solving, and cooperation are all internal abilities that are important for a student to master so they can engage effectively in society as an adult. Students who struggle to learn these lessons in their youth find themselves at heightened risk for antisocial behavior during adolescence and young adulthood.

Cultural and Historical Aspects of Movement Forms

Physical education as an intentional regime of movement and exercise—as opposed to engaging in physical activity through daily chores and games—began in ancient Greece. This tradition inspired the first physical education curricula in the United States during the 1800s, which has continued in one shape or another to present day. Like in ancient Greece, one significant factor in the historical development of physical education was concern with preparing young men for military activity. This concern was emphasized by draftees' high failure rates on physical fitness tests during World War II. The modern physical education movement began in response to this crisis. Today, politicians and educators continue to debate about the importance of physical education in the context of maintaining a population of young adults fit for military service.

However, as physical education curricula continued to be developed across the country, the program's emphasis has changed. Rather than focusing on preparedness for wartime, most physical education programs are concerned with supporting healthy child development. This has grown increasingly important in the last decades as childhood rates of obesity increased. The dominant philosophy of physical education presently is to help prepare students to live a physically active life. Due to the increase in sedentary work and leisure activities, it is important for students to develop a habit of physical exercise. On a national level, educators and politicians alike hope this intervention will reduce rates of obesity and related diseases.

The most effective focus of physical education for long-term outcomes is teaching activities—typically sports—which students will continue to enjoy participating in as adults. Finding personal pleasure in physical activity increases the likelihood that a student will continue participating in that activity during adulthood. For example, a student who enjoyed learning tennis during physical education classes may continue playing tennis with friends each Saturday morning. This provides social activity, pleasure, and exercise in a single activity.

To this end, it is important for teachers to provide education to their students in a variety of activities, and to select activities which are culturally relevant to their students. Different cultures within modern America hold different types of physical activities to be important, popular, or pleasurable. For example, the activities that members of a community of socioeconomically well-off Black people enjoy might be different from what a community of poorer white people enjoy. Rather than presuming a given culture or community will prefer a certain activity based on ethnic or socioeconomic categories, teachers should adopt a student-centered approach. By observing community norms and directly asking students and parents, teachers can empower themselves to make culturally sensitive physical education choices.

Practice Quiz

1. Leticia is planning a game for her physical education students to play. It involves having the student run from one marker to another carrying a ball and then turning and throwing the ball to another player, who will then run to another marker. What type of skill(s) does this game involve?
    a. Locomotor and non-locomotor
    b. Locomotor and manipulative
    c. Non-locomotor and manipulative
    d. Locomotor only

2. When designing a physical fitness program, it is important to include both aerobic and anaerobic exercises. Which of the following is an example of a good, balanced routine?
    a. Running on a treadmill followed by lifting weights
    b. A triathlon of running, swimming, and biking
    c. Jogging to the park and playing soccer with the kids
    d. Warming up with some weightlifting before wrestling with the team

3. Elizabeth has noticed that one of her students does not seem to be doing very well in physical education class. He used to be a happy, active child, but as he has gotten older, he seems more withdrawn. The lunchroom monitor says that he has not been eating lunch, even though it is available to him, and he is losing weight. Elizabeth knows that she must monitor her students for signs of potential risk factors that could inhibit their growth and development. What might this student be experiencing?
    a. Malnutrition
    b. Substance abuse
    c. Puberty
    d. Mental health challenges or stress

4. Which of the following activities can help promote sportsmanship and group problem-solving skills?
    a. Rope climbs
    b. Playing tag
    c. Racing while swimming laps
    d. Relay races

5. Which of the following activities would be best for helping young elementary students develop body awareness in a physical education class?
    a. Playing tag
    b. Long-jump contests
    c. Running an obstacle course
    d. Dodgeball

See answers on the next page.

Answer Explanations

1. B: The running portion of this game uses locomotor skills, and the passing of the ball uses manipulative skills. Non-locomotor skills, Choices *A* and *C*, involve movement while in a static position, such as balancing and twisting. Choice *D* is incorrect because the throwing of the ball is a manipulative skill, not a locomotor skill.

2. A: Running on a treadmill is an aerobic activity, while lifting weights is anaerobic. Choices *B* and *C* include only forms of aerobic activity and not any anaerobic exercises. Choice *D* includes only anaerobic exercises with no aerobic activity.

3. D: Loss of appetite and becoming withdrawn can be signs that a student is experiencing mental health problems and/or is under unmanageable stress. Because the student does have food available to him, malnutrition, Choice *A*, is not likely the problem. Common signs of substance abuse, Choice *B*, have also not been reported, making this unlikely as well. While puberty, Choice *C*, does come with certain challenges for many children, a loss of appetite and becoming more withdrawn are not typical symptoms.

4. D: Relay races allow children to work in teams, deciding which teammates should run in which leg of the race, which helps develop group problem-solving skills. Competing with other teams develops sportsmanship. Choice *A* is a more solitary activity, and while Choices *B* and *C* can promote sportsmanship, there are no problem-solving skills involved in these activities.

5. C: Body awareness refers to students' ability to be aware of and in control of the ways their bodies move. Games that ask children to move in certain directions or specific pathways help create this awareness and control. Obstacle courses can be created that encourage students to move over, under, and around obstacles, as well as running in specific patterns or directions. The games in Choices *A*, *B*, and *D* do not require students to create this type of specific body awareness and movement.

Subtest III: Human Development

Cognitive Development from Birth Through Adolescence

Cognitive Development

Cognition is the human capacity to learn, reason, and comprehend information acquired through perception. The process of **cognitive development** is the maturation of this capacity from simple experience of sense-data toward increasingly abstract thought processes in adolescence and adulthood. Throughout this process, children learn to understand their perceptions and construct an internal representation of the external world through concepts such as **space**, **time**, and **memory**.

Teachers should understand this process to help them understand student behavior. Students learn within diverse cultural and socioeconomic contexts. Studies have shown that the process of cognitive development is similar for children with varying personal histories. Cognitive development is often described in stages. While thinking about stages of development may assist comprehension, it may also impede teaching students whose development is slower, or more advanced, than other children of the student's age. Be mindful that cognitive development is a complex process unique to each individual child.

Teachers should remember the **multiple intelligences** of individuals while considering their students' cognitive development and preparing coursework. This concept proposes a triarchic framework whereby all individuals—not just children and adolescents, but adults as well—are evaluated using **analytic**, **creative**, and **practical intelligences**. Traditional testing often measures a student's **memory**, not their intelligence. Viewing students through this lens encourages teachers to identify strengths in disadvantaged children and to use the teacher's limited emotional, financial, and temporal resources in the most effective way.

Infancy and Early Childhood

Cognitive development in infants is characterized by children learning to understand their perceptions and the distinction between themselves and an external world. This process continues alongside the development of social and physical skills, such as crawling or speaking. Infants explore their environment through observation and repetitive action. A well-known example is **object permanence**. As this concept develops, the infant begins to understand that parents, toys, and other items continue to exist, even outside of their own vision. Another common behavior is dropping objects repeatedly; through this behavior, the child comes to understand gravity.

Early childhood is characterized by **egocentrism** and flawed attempts at causal reasoning. Egocentrism is the child's assumption that other people experience the same perceptions, feelings, and thoughts as themselves; note that this is *not* identical with the concept of selfishness. This tendency diminishes during the elementary years as the child achieves the ability to perform more complex mental operations.

This learning process also impacts the child's perceptual understanding of the difference between themselves and another individual. Beginning with a form of magical thinking sometimes called **transductive reasoning**, the child attempts to use inductive and deductive processes to manipulate their ideas about objects and persons and create hypotheses to understand their world. However, children often fail to create meaningful connections between symbolic observations. For example, a boy frightened by his older sister while holding the family cat might come to associate cats with fear, or consider them scary. While erroneous, the child's cognition represents a mental process which eventually results in the adult's process of observation, hypothesis, experimentation, and conclusion.

Another element of early cognitive development is the child's preparation to learn language and begin communicating with their parents. The ability to hear is a prenatal development and establishes the infant's preference for their mother's voice. In turn, this encourages the child's interaction with their mother. A cycle of vocalizations

257

followed by behavioral responses on the part of both parent and child reinforces continuation of both adult baby-talk and the child's nonverbal responses to adult speech, laying the foundation for the back-and-forth of linguistic communication.

This cycle develops into speech during the child's preschool years. Language development begins with nonsense language (which nonetheless may hold some private meaning for the child and parent), transitions into a combination of single words with gestures, and finally into short sentences. Young children are often better at understanding adults with **receptive speech** than making their own wants known with **expressive speech**.

Middle Childhood

Children's cognition continues to explore concepts of space, time, and reasoning during their elementary school years (roughly between the ages of six and twelve). They develop mental symbols—first while learning language—and begin to manipulate these symbols with increasing complexity through **concrete operations**. Children who use this type of thinking are capable of various counting, organizing, and reasoning tasks. They continue to develop these capacities through practicing **classification** and **reversibility**.

The ability to classify an object as belonging to one or several larger sets due to its properties is typical of an elementary school student's cognitive development. An example of this ability is identifying that an apple belongs to both "red objects" and "fruits." Operative learning activities—learning concepts through practical manipulation of objects—support the student's comprehension of increasingly abstract categories. The transition from classifying physical objects into increasingly abstract categories prepares the student for formal operations in adolescence.

Reversibility is the cognitive function through which a person imagines reversing a mental or physical operation. An elementary school child's comprehension of this principle is illustrated through their understanding of **conservation** of volume.

Conservation of Volume

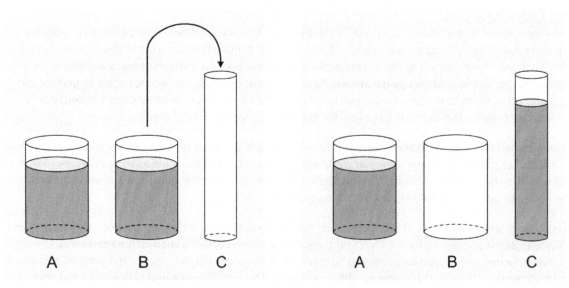

After watching this process, children who do not yet understand reversibility believe that the taller jar has greater volume. Older children intuitively understand that each container's volume is the same because the water can be poured back and forth (although they may struggle to describe this verbally).

When shown the procedure above, a child who struggles to understand conservation will say that the taller glass holds more liquid despite seeing liquid poured from one glass to the other. However, most elementary school students can mentally reverse this process.

Children's cognitive development is strongly supported by play. This includes both play activities that are structured to support the student's development—such as the use of building blocks to explore basic concepts of geometry—and unstructured opportunities for play, such as recess. Recess and occasional breaks from academic work have been shown to improve attention and retention for elementary students.

During these years, the child's speech increases in syntactic complexity. While vocabulary is important, students in elementary school focus more on understanding the grammar and **pragmatics**—nonverbal expressive elements, such as facial expression, proximity to other speakers, and gesturing—of their native language.

Adolescence

As students near adulthood, they begin to think using **formal operations**. Teenage students demonstrate cognitive flexibility and the ability to use increasingly abstract ideas to form hypotheses when problem-solving. At this point in cognitive development, the student begins to explore concepts such as tyranny, freedom, or justice. This change in the structure of thought while entering adolescence contributes to teenage idealism and egocentrism.

It is important to note that egocentrism in adolescence expresses itself differently from the egocentrism of early childhood. Rather than assuming other persons share the adolescent's perspective, thoughts, and feelings, adolescents often assume that they themselves are the subject of peer and adult scrutiny. Hyper-self-consciousness contributes to an internal narrative of personal uniqueness. In turn, this can lead to an adolescent student's feelings of isolation (accompanied by statements such as, "No one has ever felt anger the way I do").

During adolescence, students become increasingly capable of absorbing information through traditional methods of **figurative learning**, such as reading, listening to lectures, and other stereotypical "academic" activities. Adolescent cognition functions similarly to that of adults. However, teenagers still lack the quantity of knowledge available to adults, and often struggle with **executive functions** coordinating their cognition, knowledge, emotions, social skills, and self-control.

An adolescent's use of language also improves. Grammar and vocabulary use resembles the speech of adults, although often with the inclusion of slang and other coded language that emphasizes the student's independence from adult social groups.

Development of Moral Judgment

Moral sentiments, knowledge, and judgment each tend to develop throughout childhood in three broad stages:

- **Preconventional morality:** The individual is largely self-interested. They are concerned with appropriate behavior due to fear of punishment or seeking rewards. This stage is commonly associated with early childhood.

- **Conventional morality:** The individual cares about the well-being of those in their immediate social vicinity. This may be restricted to family and a few friends, or it may grow to encompass a whole community. Associated with middle childhood and early adolescence, conventional morality means individuals often focus on concepts like respect or sympathy, which reflect empathetic and sympathetic modes of care.

- **Postconventional morality:** The individual's moral judgments seek to be universally valid. At this stage— associated with late adolescence and adulthood—the individual considers broad values such as justice or tolerance which have impacts beyond the individual's immediate acquaintances or the laws of their society.

These stages remain controversial and have been the subject of ongoing criticism. Studies indicate that all three modes of moral judgment are used by individuals in a variety of gender, ethnic, and socioeconomic groups. One source of this controversy is that those concepts held in esteem by individuals using the "postconventional" stage depend on each person's background. However, there is a strong tendency for adults in diverse societies to use moral judgments which are intended for universal application. One example is the statement, "All human life is precious."

Well-adjusted individuals develop moral judgment through these stages via mechanisms of positive and negative reinforcement. Common sources of reinforcement are parents, teachers, and peers. However, unlike physical or cognitive stages of development, moral development is less directly associated with the individual's chronological age. Further, adults occasionally vary the stage of moral development they use while considering different instances of moral concern.

Social and Physical Development from Birth Through Adolescence

Social Development

Social development is the process through which a child comes to understand and internalize normative behavior for their culture through interactions with parents, peers, and non-parental adults. This development takes place alongside changes in the child's cognition. As an individual progresses through infancy, childhood, and adolescence, changes in their thought processes make an increasingly complex and nuanced understanding of social environments possible. In general, the child moves through this process from a position of dependence and attachment to independence and autonomy.

Infancy and Early Childhood

Early childhood is exemplified by the development of the child's **theory of mind**. This is the gradual understanding shared by nearly all individuals that other persons they interact with are true **agents** with their own thoughts, beliefs, and desires. It is important that the child internalizes this concept because it is essential to meaningful communication and interaction with other people. The inability to imaginatively conceive of another person's mental world is called **mind blindness**. The lack of this capacity, to some extent, is symptomatic of individuals on the autism spectrum. However, a child's theory of mind continues to change and grow throughout the social development process.

Infants and preschool children learn their initial social cues and behaviors primarily from watching their parents' behavior. Observation also shapes the child's development of basic social concepts such as gender, identity, and body language. Preschool children then practice these behaviors during play with same-aged peers. Experiencing play helps the child move away from an egocentric viewpoint of others. This manifests externally through improved sharing, sympathy, and teamwork skills during play.

Middle Childhood

Social activity during elementary school and before adolescence are characterized by **friendships** and the development of **social status** as children engage in mutual socialization and play. This play is not merely fun; it is the learning process through which children begin acquiring the social skills they'll need during adolescence and adulthood. A child's first friendships emphasize mutual interests (such as shared sports interests or imaginative games), and develop into strong peer attachments to a few close friends.

Unfortunately, both positive and negative elements of adult society can be found in the microcosm of childhood socialization. In particular, elementary school-aged children begin to exercise ideas about preferred playmates, and ostracize children considered "annoying," "gross," or other pejoratives. When this behavior leads to a pattern of abuse, it is considered **bullying.**

During middle childhood, students remain attached to their parents. The importance of non-parental mentors—especially teachers or coaches—grows alongside their emotional connection to family. Children assert their autonomy through challenging behaviors, but do not generally seek independence from parental authority.

Adolescence

In adolescence, youth begin to value their relationships with peers over their relationships with adults. This is a natural part of asserting their independence and individuality separate from the family unit. In most families, this creates mild, but persistent, friction between the parents and the adolescent as each party navigates the teenager's increased need for personal choice and autonomy in their day-to-day life.

Teenagers' high valuation on same-aged relationships, and the need to belong within a society of like-minded individuals, leads to the experience of **peer pressure**. Stereotypically, peer pressure is an overt encouragement to engage in antisocial (or at least anti-parental) behavior. Classic examples include sexual activity and substance use. However, research indicates that teenagers experience peer pressure more often as the force of "expectations" about their behavior, rather than through attempts to verbally persuade. In addition, peer pressure is as likely to have a positive or neutral influence as it is to have a negative influence. Teenagers report experiencing peer pressure to dress certain ways, speak certain ways, and otherwise fit into a **clique** of peers with similar interests. The negative influence of peer pressure beyond that scope is overstated.

During late adolescence, the influence of peer pressure diminishes as the youth becomes better able to assert their own personality within the context of both family and peer relationships. This typically leads to the parent-child relationship becoming less fractious in young adulthood, transforming from childhood attachment into the mutual respect and affection of adult families.

Romance is an important fixation throughout the adolescent years. These interests typically first arise during puberty. The teenager begins to spend time in mixed-gender groups of friends, and then develops individual connections as they and their peers explore dating and romantic relationships. The nature of these new relationships changes during adolescence, generally moving from prioritizing mutual interests and fun toward trust and emotional intimacy.

As teenagers become involved in romantic behavior, the likelihood they will engage in sexual behavior increases. This has associated risks, such as **pregnancy** and **sexually transmitted infections (STIs)** which can hinder the adolescent's potential academic and vocational outcomes in early adulthood. Open conversations between parents, mentors, and teenagers about sexual activity and safe sex practices (for example, condom use) reduces the risk of these negative results if the teen does decide to engage in sexual activity with romantic partners.

Physical Development

The process of **physical development** entails the ongoing growth and development of a child's nervous, muscular, and skeletal systems from birth through adolescence. This is most strongly typified by rapid development during infancy and early childhood, and again during puberty and adolescence. While muscular and skeletal growth typically ends between the ages of fifteen and seventeen, depending on gender, ethnicity, nutrition, and other factors, the final development of the brain's regions that process reasoning, judgment, and language is not finished until an individual's early twenties.

Before birth, and during infancy and early childhood, the sense organs and nervous system lay the foundation for the individual's future ability to coordinate their perceptions and motor skills. The body grows a layer of **myelin** along the nervous system. Myelin is a fatty coating that insulates the nerves like rubber around an electric cord. This coating grows from the head down toward the feet, beginning with the thickest nerves. Once the smallest nerves have been covered in myelin—typically around the start of adolescence—the youth is capable of fine-tuning their eye-hand coordination and other motor skills.

Skeletal growth takes place as bones move from a soft, cartilaginous state to the firm bone of adulthood. The edges of each bone—sometimes called the **epiphyses**—remain soft until growth is complete, sometime during adolescence. Muscular growth occurs alongside skeletal growth. Together, these factors describe why adequate nutrition and physical activity are important for healthy physical development during childhood.

Puberty and Adolescence

Entering puberty marks the beginning of adolescence. This change is brought about through the generation of various hormones in the brain, most notably **estrogen** and **testosterone**. These hormones trigger the adolescent growth spurt. During puberty, the child will grow taller and heavier, closer to their adult height and weight. They develop **primary** and **secondary sex characteristics**, transitioning from a child to a young adult who is physically capable of reproduction. These characteristics include:

- **Primary characteristics:** Changes in the sex organs directly related to reproductive functions. These begin a girl's menstrual cycle, and enable a boy to produce viable sperm.

- **Secondary characteristics:** Muscular development and fat accumulation emphasizes stereotypical distinctions between adult males and females. Boys and girls alike begin to grow underarm hair and pubic hair, while boys additionally begin growing facial hair.

The physical changes of puberty typically end between the ages of fifteen and seventeen. However, the emotional and social development connected with these hormonal changes continues throughout adolescence and into early adulthood.

Developmental Difficulties

Many childhood or psychological disorders are caused by delayed or inhibited physical development. While some disorders appear to have a genetic cause, other disabilities are caused by prenatal or birthing trauma, or have causes that are unknown. Some important examples include:

- **Autism spectrum disorder (ASD):** The cause of ASD is the subject of ongoing debate. Many researchers believe this condition is caused by genetic factors that shape the individual's brain during early childhood, leading to the disorder's characteristic difficulties communicating with and understanding other people.

- **Cerebral palsy:** Most cases of cerebral palsy are the result of trauma to the brain during either gestation or the birthing process. Difficulty breathing after birth and being born prematurely both increase the risk of cerebral palsy. This disability, like ASD, presents with a spectrum of mild to severe impairments. Individuals with cerebral palsy often have delayed or inadequate development of muscles and tendons, difficulties with executive function, or intellectual disabilities.

- **Down syndrome:** This disorder occurs when an individual's DNA has an extra **chromosome**. It is characterized by mild intellectual disability and delays in physical development. While Down syndrome impacts individuals throughout their whole life, many people with this condition are capable of living meaningful and impactful lives with appropriate support and education.

- **Drug use during pregnancy:** Use of alcohol, tobacco, cannabis, and other intoxicating or restricted substances while pregnant increases the risk of various disorders in the child, including being born addicted to the substance. One such disorder is **fetal alcohol syndrome**.

Influences on Development from Birth Through Adolescence

Influences on Development

The healthy growth and development of children can be supported—or hindered—by a variety of **biological, sociocultural,** and **socioeconomic** influences. Proactive systems of support during a child's development consistently encourage greater independence, academic performance, and vocational success throughout their life. Teachers should remember that negative developmental influences need not result in negative outcomes for the individual's adulthood life. In general, the earlier support is implemented for a disadvantaged individual, the more effective the system's results will be.

Biological Influences

A child's biological makeup has a significant impact upon their development. Influences on development which are innately part of the child are typically genetic, but some environmental factors (such as **fetal alcohol syndrome**) can fall into this category.

There is an important distinction between **mental disabilities** and **learning disabilities**. Mental disabilities generally reflect a difference in one or several aspects of the individual's intelligence. Children with learning disabilities often are just as intelligent as their peers, but struggle with comprehending new information in one or more academic fields. Many mental disabilities and learning disabilities can be considered biological. For example, Down syndrome and dyslexia are both conditions with neurological foundations. Neither disability prevents adulthood success.

The hormones released during puberty also play an important role in influencing a child's development. In addition to triggering the various physical changes associated with puberty, they also have significant impacts on the individual's social and emotional development. **Precocious puberty**—when hormones trigger puberty during middle childhood instead of adolescence—increases feelings of isolation and dissatisfaction as the child seeks interaction with more "mature" youths. The timing of puberty, and the physical changes associated with it, contribute to a young adolescent's risk factors for sexual activity and drug use, as well as mental health disorders lacking typical teenage co-morbidities.

Research is divided on the extent to which a child's intelligence—in particular their academic, analytic intelligence—is founded in the individual's genetics and neurology. Nature and nurture both seem to play an important role in determining the developing individual's ability to learn, grow, and acclimate to their social environment as a well-adjusted and successful adult.

Sociocultural Influences

From birth through middle childhood, the family is the most significant influence on a child's behavior. Children watch and imitate their parents' speech, emotions, and choices. While parents have the most important impact, both positive and negative interactions with siblings and extended family contribute to the child's development as well.

The role of family and extended community shapes a child's sense of belonging and identity. Ethnicity and cultural heritage wield influence on each family's approach to raising children. Some cultures emphasize the child's individual accomplishments (such as learning to read), while others emphasize the child's role as a community member (such as helping in the home). Positive or negative reactions to the child's behaviors during early childhood play an important role in their development. By reinforcing the child's behavior in positive or negative ways, parents help the child develop an early understanding of gender identity and relationships, family relationships, and moral behavior. Parents and other adults model how they expect the child to interact with individuals based on the child's gender. Stereotypes about gendered behavior, feelings, and needs are imitated and then internalized. These stereotypes are then reinforced or subverted by broader cultural values as the child enters social life through the education system.

Children who do not receive appropriate behavior reinforcement during early childhood are at increased risk of social skill disorders during adolescence and adulthood. For example, parents might consider toddler misbehavior "cute" or give in frequently to tantrums or other oppositional behavior.

As a young person enters adolescence, they seek additional independence as they assert their individual personality. Teenagers often value the opinions and judgment of their peers over that of their parents, teachers, and other adults in their life. They are also more likely to look up to adults in "glamorous" careers—such as musicians and athletes—and to see them as role models. This is compounded by the adolescent's pursuit of novelty, expressed by using new slang, listening to new music, or other engagements in cultural (and often countercultural) trends.

Socioeconomic Influences

The economic situation of a child's family has the potential for lasting consequences on all aspects of their developmental process. Children from financially stable families generally experience improved academic and social success. Likewise, children raised in situations of economic adversity demonstrate increased difficulties due to their parents' financial situation.

Some economic advantages commonly available to children of stable or wealthy families include improved parental involvement in the child's life, consistent nutrition, non-parental childcare, and ease of access to extracurricular activities, or additional academic supports. In some cases, children of well-off families attend school districts with superior financial and administrative resources. These advantages reduce the stressors children experience, which in turn reduces the likelihood of behavioral or academic difficulty in adolescence and adulthood.

In contrast, families which struggle with poverty experience many stressors. The most obvious challenge experienced by children of impoverished families is **malnutrition**. Malnutrition in the United States typically takes one of two forms: inability to afford sufficient food, or inability to afford sufficiently nutritious food. The latter contributes to the rising rates of **childhood obesity.** Food stress in both forms inhibits physical and cognitive development because the body is unable to spend the required energy—or lacks appropriate nutrients—to continue usual developmental processes.

The mental health struggles of impoverished parents are another notable stressor. Parents experiencing stress, depression, or anxiety brought about by financial difficulties often struggle to provide warm and nurturing relationships with their children. Some additional stressors children living in poverty experience include lack of stimulation in the home, inability to participate in social activities (such as extracurricular sports), and even parental neglect.

These socioeconomic stressors contribute to a number of negative developmental outcomes. In particular, children experiencing these difficulties often struggle with academic achievement and are at an increased risk of displaying antisocial behavior (such as conduct disorder, or oppositional defiant disorder). Early intervention and social support—such as the Department of Education's **Head Start** program—improves rates of academic and vocational success in adulthood.

Social supports should keep in mind the family's cultural, ethnic, and religious relationships. Youth facing socioeconomic difficulties disproportionately come from Black, Hispanic, or other minority backgrounds. A support that is sensitive and effective support for one family may not be appropriate for another.

Maltreatment, and Influence on Developmental Outcomes

The umbrella term **maltreatment** is used to cover a variety of different forms of abuse children and vulnerable adults experience. Research indicates that the typical perpetrator of abuse is the child's immediate caregivers, most often a parent. Specific rates of abuse vary depending on the type of abuse and the age of the youth. Apart from caregivers, other adults—such as teachers, coaches, and extended family—are the most frequent perpetrators of abuse.

Understanding different types of abuse is important because all teachers are **mandatory reporters** and are required to report suspected maltreatment to Child Protective Services. The most significant categories of maltreatment are:

- **Physical abuse:** When a caretaker strikes, wounds, burns, or otherwise causes intentional physical injury to the child's body.

- **Emotional abuse:** When the child is subjected to demeaning language, such as insults, shame, or rejection, that damages the child's sense of self-worth.

- **Sexual abuse:** Any time a child is forced to engage in sexual activity, or exposed to sexual activity happening in their environment.

- **Neglect:** The willful choice by a caretaker to not meet the child's physical, emotional, or developmental needs.

Children subjected to abuse are at increased risk for mental health difficulties including (but not limited to) depression, post-traumatic stress disorder, and reactive attachment disorder. Fortunately, studies indicate that children's **resilience**—the capacity to endure adversity, and move forward in a healthy way—often enables an abused individual to still develop into a well-adjusted adult if they receive support. Teachers must pay attention to children's injuries, how they interact with adults, and changes in their demeanor to be vigilant against potential incidents of abuse.

Practice Quiz

1. Anthony is planning an activity for his third-grade class. He has collected several items of varying size, shape, and color that he will have the children group according to different directions, such as grouping all of the green items. What type of development is this activity fostering?
    a. Concrete operations
    b. Reversibility
    c. Classification
    d. Conservation

2. A child who respects and cares about the well-being of those close to them, such as their friends and family, is demonstrating what stage of moral development?
    a. Preconventional
    b. Conventional
    c. Postconventional
    d. Social contract

3. A child who seems to lack the capacity to conceive of another person's individual thoughts and beliefs may be experiencing what?
    a. Theory of mind
    b. Egocentrism
    c. Mind blindness
    d. Cognitive function

4. A child whose hormones have triggered sexual maturation during middle childhood rather than during adolescence is experiencing what type of developmental disorder?
    a. Precocious puberty
    b. Diabetes
    c. Growth hormone deficiency
    d. ADHD

5. A young child who imitates her parents' speech patterns, a child who pretends to be vacuuming the house with his mother, and a pre-teen who puts up posters of well-known athletes and musicians are all experiencing what type of developmental influence?
    a. Biological
    b. Socioeconomic
    c. Peer pressure
    d. Sociocultural

See answers on the next page.

Answer Explanations

1. C: When children learn to group like objects based on different characteristics or features, they are practicing classification. Concrete operations, Choice *A*, involve the manipulation of mental information, as in counting and reasoning. Reversibility, Choice *B*, is the ability to imagine the reverse of an image or physical act. Conservation, Choice *D*, is the understanding that volume does not change based on the size of the container.

2. B: A child who has entered the conventional morality stage begins to care about the well-being of those around them, including friends, family, schoolmates, and even the community they live in. Choice *A* refers to the first stage of moral development, in which the child is largely self-interested. Postconventional morality, Choice *C*, is the final stage, in which children begin to apply values to the broader world on a more universal basis. Choice *D*, social contract, is a substage of postconventional morality in which expected standards of behavior are viewed as variable social agreements.

3. C: Mind blindness is when a child lacks the ability to imaginatively conceive of another person's mental states. These children may be on the autism spectrum, but they may also simply be developing this understanding a bit slower. Theory of mind, Choice *A*, refers to the development of the child's understanding that other people are individuals with their own thoughts and feelings. Choices *B* and *D* are not relevant answers.

4. A: Precocious puberty occurs when hormones trigger puberty earlier than is typical, during middle childhood rather than later during adolescence. Choices *B*, *C*, and *D* are all conditions caused by hormonal imbalances in young children, but they do not cause early puberty.

5. D: Sociocultural influences are those created by the people and society around the child, including the child's immediate family, as well as friends and the world at large. Biological influences, Choice *A*, are those factors that affect the child's biological makeup. These are usually genetic factors. Socioeconomic influences, Choice *B*, include things like the family's ability to provide a safe place to live and adequate food for the child. Peer pressure, Choice *C*, is a term that refers to the often-negative influence of other children of similar age, such as a teen's friends pressuring her to drink or do drugs.

Subtest III: Visual and Performing Arts

Dance

Movement

Improvising movement from various stimuli can be a challenge when one has only known how to create dancing motion from music, but the fundamental rules behind dancing to music can also apply to creating movement from many other different sources. At its core, creating movement from stimuli involves acting on impulse and trusting yourself to let go and move in reaction to what you are experiencing. Below are examples of how one might draw motion and improvised dancing from various stimuli.

Moving from Words

Words are an easier concept to start thinking about dancing from, as they still involve auditory stimuli, and many songs that people already create improvisational dance to have words within them in the form of lyrics. The key to moving to words in an impactful way often relies on finding the "rhythm" of the words, or the cadence that the speech invokes. Because of this, easy, non-musical collections of words for your students to use as dance inspiration can include lists of actions, soliloquies or monologues in a play, or spoken word poems.

The key is to start in a localized way. Students should attempt to react to the rhythm of the words in your prompted speech and represent that rhythm in a specific body part, such as the legs. The act of transferring that rhythm to their arms and then the rest of their body gets them more in tune with the rhythm of the words and helps them embody it as they continue to improvise.

Ask your students to consider the imagery that arises in their mind as they hear the words. They should listen to the verbs that are emphasized in the speech and allow these images and actions to guide their movements. They should search for the tones of the speech. Are the words and delivery sharp or smooth? Meek or bombastic? Erudite or pedestrian? Ask your students to represent the actions and imagery of the speech with the energy of its tones, and let the rest come naturally. Improvisational movement is, after all, a reactionary exercise.

Moving from Images

A raw image can be a tricky source for dance inspiration, and it requires the dancer to have a basic understanding of visual art comprehension. The image can be a painting, a photograph, even a sculpture, but the key is to identify the techniques used by the artist to guide the viewer's movement. Does the image follow some sort of spatial pattern, such as a spiral or motion to a focal point? If so, moving in such a pattern is a great start.

With nothing but a single image to inspire an entire dance, repeating motions and patterns is key to unlocking the rest of the dance. Your students should continue observing the image as they go through these motions and pay attention to how their body might begin to alter the patten on its own. Have them lean into these instinctual adjustments; adaptations are natural in the improvisational process. If there is a central focal point of the image, such as a structure, a person, an item, or a creature, have your students try to embody it, both in shape and in mood. Images with sad shapes and color schemes should be met with more melancholy and flowing movements, lower to the ground. Vibrant images with warm color schemes should be more dynamic, with grander and sharper motions. Ideally, your students will understand what emotions the art invokes in them personally and move in a way that expresses that impact using whatever patterns or focal points they have identified in the image.

Above all else, students should play with positioning and variance. An image does not change, so the patterns, shapes, and emotions they will find in it should be expressed in as many ways as possible to maintain variation in the dance. Have them try switching the body parts used to convey different emotions, attempting to communicate the image's essence while on the floor or sitting down, or seeing how the dance feels while moving at various speeds and paces.

268

Moving from Tasks

Creativity tends to flourish in a box, which is why task-based movement often involves a fixed prompt upon which an improvisational dance can be built. These prompts often involve simple motions and a tonal or technique-based command, such as "move from one wall to the next, starting high in your motions and ending low to the ground," or "You can only turn at right angles, and you must lead all movements with your right hand."

These prompts often force your students' brains to think about what motions are possible at all with these restrictions, which will force them to think outside the box. As they become more comfortable with the prompt, further instinctive creativity should follow.

Moving from Everyday Senses

Any and all of the five primary senses can inspire motion at any given time. The foundational premise is simple: react with motions that embody the sensation one experiences. However, the technique to developing a dance routine via these sensations lies in experimenting with different levels and types of a given sensation.

If you eat something sweet and pay close attention to how it makes you feel, allowing that feeling to inspire a certain type of movement, you should also try eating something sour or spicy or bitter and going through the same process. If the sensation of being cold inspires motion in you, experiment with the sensation of being uncomfortably hot for a while. Understanding how various stimuli make your students feel and ensuring that they know how their bodies want to creatively react to such stimuli is excellent practice for eventually being able to develop meaningful improvisational dances from nearly anything.

Moving in a Story

Reacting to stimuli is a core aspect of making improvisational dances, but it is important to remember that every dance is a small story or journey of sorts. In the same way that a writer uses the structure of rising tension, a climax, and a resolution to retain a reader's attention, so too must a dance have some semblance of a beginning, a middle, and an end. Your students should not begin their improvisational dances with the absolute embodiment of the most powerful emotions they intend to convey, though that may commonly happen in a first attempt. Oftentimes, starting slower, softer, or in a more contained manner gives one room to escalate later on in the dance. Middle portions of a dance should communicate more of the central themes of a dance. If the dance is vibrant and boisterous, large leaps and great ranges of motion are ideal for the middle of your students' routine.

There is often the most variance of tone towards the ending of dances; some feel it appropriate to wind down their themes, motions, and techniques to a state similar to the dance's introduction, while others would rather end the dance at its absolute tonal apex, embodying the peak of their inspiriting sensations just as the dance ends. Neither choice is incorrect, but both should be made with intention. Do your students want to shock the audience with a rush of emotion, or ease them down from the experience? Does the stimulus they wish to convey leave them with a feeling of peace, intensity, or something else? Your students' tailoring of the "story" of their dance to the emotions they receive and the emotions they wish to convey is a critical aspect of creating motion that will effectively impact and communicate with others.

Technical Skills

Rhythm

Arguably the most important foundation of dancing, **rhythm** is used to describe the often-steady beat of whatever sounds you are dancing to. Most music has a rhythm composed of down beats and up beats, but many different rhythmic structures can be made with these two elements.

Some dances have set rhythmic structures that are fairly consistent across an entire genre, such as the two up beats followed by a down beat, which comprises most waltz music. Other dances use songs with intentionally complex or inconsistent rhythmic structures. In the best cases, these departures from conventional rhythm are done with artistic

purpose, but overall, dancing in accordance with your music's rhythm is critical to developing a greater dance routine; the rhythm is the skeleton of your dance upon which you build something that fits well within the respective music.

Tempo

Tempo is often confused for rhythm, but while rhythm refers to the composition of a sound's beat, tempo describes the speed or rate at which this beat is performed. **Tempo** is often measured in beats per minute (bpm) and can be made as slow or fast as is realistically possible for the song's musicians or dancers.

Musicians tend to categorize tempo into 3 primary types. A fast tempo (above 120 bpm) is referred to as presto, a medium-rate tempo (between 76 and 120 bpm) is called moderato, and a slower tempo (between 60 and 76 bpm) is called adagio. It is possible to go faster than presto or slower than adagio, but these tempos are extreme to the point of falling outside primary consideration. Keeping a solid sense of both rhythm and tempo is foundational to dancing in time with any type of music.

Posture, Poise, Frame

These three concepts are closely related, and you often need to consider the other two when accounting for any one of them. **Posture** refers to the structural alignment of your body. Good posture aligns your head, your shoulders, your hips, and your ribs in such a way that they compose a straight throughline.

Poise is used to refer to your body's directional weight, or its weight in relation to your feet. Leaning forward would give you forward-positioned poise. Attempting to balance on one leg with forward-positioned poise would likely result in you falling forward. The same applies for backward-positioned and left- or right-positioned poise. Proper poise is such that your body weight is equally distributed and primed for ideal balance and movement.

Frame refers to the way you hold your arms and torso when dancing. Frame can shift frequently throughout a dance or stay in one position for an entire routine. Adjusting the positioning of your chest, shoulder blades, and arms are all parts of shifting one's frame, and in couples' dances, frame changes are often used to nonverbally lead and communicate with your dance partner.

Balance

Balance refers to the symmetry of your body in a dance. The better your balance is, the less likely you are to shift, tilt, or fall in a dance routine. Though a certain type of balance can be displayed when standing or posing perfectly still, true balance in dancing involves constantly adjusting your body's alignment throughout a routine in such a way that the poses and momentum of the dance do not result in stumbles or other positional mistakes.

Flexibility

Flexibility measures the tension and the range of motion in your body's muscles. More flexible dancers can create a wider range of motion that allows for a wider variety of movements and positions when dancing. **Flexibility** also refers to your body's ability to withstand these movements and positions safely, which is why regular stretching is critical. Common dance moves such as high kicks require regular flexibility training to perform without tearing muscles or sustaining other injuries. For safety reasons, it is critical that dancers do not attempt moves which require a higher level of flexibility than they currently have. Flexibility is built during stretching, not in the moment of a dance.

Coordination

A well-coordinated dancer can smoothly use different body parts in unison while dancing. **Coordination** is the control and efficiency with which you utilize multiple parts of your body without needing to look at all of them in the moment. Working towards better coordination is an effective way to improve other technical skills in dancing such as spatial awareness, balance, and posture. Better-coordinated dancers develop better instincts for moving gracefully and intentionally.

Kinesthetic Awareness

Also called your "sixth sense," your **kinesthetic awareness** is your ability to "feel" your own body. It is your ability to understand the positioning and motion of your muscles and joints without relying on your primary five senses. Building up your kinesthetic awareness involves a lot of exercises that reinforce a strong muscle memory, which can be instinctually accessed with enough practice during a dance routine. A kinesthetically aware dancer can accurately and intuitively predict how much force is needed behind various motions such as jumps and spins in order to get a body part to a desired location without overextending or underextending.

Spatial Relationships

Dancers can have spatial relationships with many aspects of a routine such as props, set pieces, and other dancers, but all dancers have at least one spatial relationship: the relationship between the dancer and the physical space in which they dance. Understanding where you are in relation to the space in which you dance is an important factor to consider, especially when improvising a dance.

Are your students in the center of their space, so as to give the most even view of your dancing? If not, why not? What are the boundaries of the space in which they are allowed to dance? How much motion is required to approach the corner of their space, or grab the prop behind them, or reach the dance partner on the other side of the space? Keeping one's spatial relationships in mind while dancing leads to an increase in one's ability to gracefully react to the sometimes-moving locations of the things with which one holds these relationships.

Analysis

As is true of any art form, analyzing a dance with any measure of legitimacy requires a degree of subjectivity along with an idea of the work's context.

Intent and Meaning

There is merit to the idea of all art being subjective and fully different in the eye of each person who beholds it, but for serious, meaningful, and helpful analysis of a dance, one should also have the creator's intent in mind when observing.

Sometimes, more professional dance institutions will directly provide this context, or a dancer might outright declare the subject matter that inspired the work. However, in lieu of this information, one can arrive at some sort of thoughtful conclusion by asking themselves the right questions while observing a dance. Some helpful questions for your students to ask when analyzing a dance are as follows:

- How is the dance structured? Is there a clear beginning, middle, and end? When do the dance's crescendos happen? Why?

- What technical dance characteristics are the dancers displaying? Is this dance most characteristic of a jazz dance? A tap dance? A ballet?

- In what ways does the dance differ from its primary characterization? Why do you think the choreography used these departures from form?

- Are you enjoying the dance? Why or why not? What aspects of the dance can you point to that specifically affect your personal enjoyment of it? Often, a better understanding of why you enjoy what you enjoy can lead to more meaningful analyses of art in general.

- Is there a narrative in the dance routine? If so, were you able to understand all of it?

Identifying the purpose of a dance is far easier once your students have a more thorough idea of what kind of dance they're watching, the artistic decisions being made, and how they are personally reacting to it.

Context

As is often the case with art, the piece of art in front of your students is more than just what they are looking at; art always carries its context and influences with it. These influences can be emotional and personal, but they can also be historical, regional, and cultural. Helpful questions for your students to ask before and during a viewing of a dance are as follows:

- Is the purpose of this dance an artistic one, or is it recreational or ceremonial?

- Was this dance choreographed by a named person, or was it passed down via a cultural tradition?

- If the dance was choreographed by a named person, who are they? How close are they with the culture the dance is interacting with? How much of the dance is the history of the choreographer versus the history of a people?

- Do you already know this type of dance to be associated with a particular culture? What are that culture's values? What parts of the dance reinforce or otherwise interact with those values, and what is the statement being made about them?

Above all else, it is important for your students to bear in mind the difference between analysis and criticism of dance. When analyzing art, "good" and "bad" are not especially useful terms. Analysis is about discerning the point of the dance and the process by which it is performed; it is not about determining the quality or artistic merit of the piece. When personally responding to an analysis, ask your students to keep in mind the difference between "How do I feel about this?" and "Is this good?"

Music

Elements of Music

Pitch

In the most technical sense, **pitch** refers to the frequency of a sound, or where it lies in the known range of sound wave frequencies. It is measured in hertz (Hz), with higher-pitch sounds measuring at higher Hz levels. However, in much western music, certain frequencies have been attributed to measured, lettered pitches (e.g., the pitch of 440 Hz is what we know as a middle C note). Notes range from A to G, and then restart in a different octave, meaning the same series of notes in a higher or lower tone. On the staff of sheet music, these notes are represented by a central five lines and the four spaces between them, which indicate the notes E, F, G, A, B, C, D, E and F in ascending order.

Some people possess a skill known as **absolute pitch** or perfect pitch, in which they are able to replicate sounds at specific pitches from memory alone. However, most people with perfect pitch are born with the talent, so it is not recommended that teachers try to cultivate this ability in students. Instead, the use of pitch-reference resources such as pitch pipes should be encouraged in a musical curriculum. If a person has a starting pitch to a song fresh in their mind, it is then far easier to stay "on key" when performing a song.

Tonality

The "tone" of a song refers to the focal pitch of the song, otherwise known as its **key**. The tonality of a song describes the note at which the song is most at rest, the note from which the rest of a traditional song is built. When reading sheet music, you can identify the key of a song as the note one degree above the final sharp in a key signature. When the key signature features flats, the key can be identified as the note of the penultimate flat. When no flats are present, the key is C major, and when one flat is present, the key is F major. Presenting various key signatures such as the ones below and asking for their respective keys is a quick and efficient way to teach students how to identify the key of a song just by reading it.

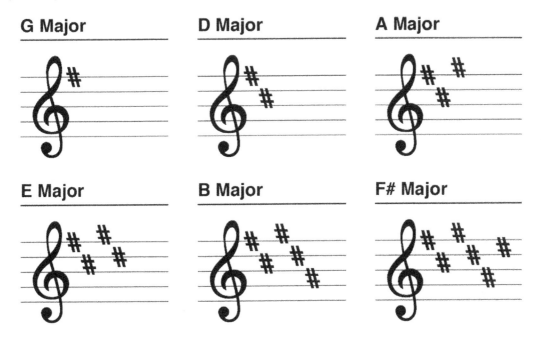

Melody

Melody is the central point of attention when listening to the way notes develop in music. It is the series of tones that stands out as a single musical throughline. Though songs will often have multiple series of tones on top of one another, you are most likely to remember the melody as the part that would be hummed along to in order to indicate the song.

The most important part of a strong and effective melody is keeping it complementary to the song's key, or its tonality. A well-made melody will sound wrong if played in a song in a different key than the one for which the melody was written. Learning basic scales can be an effective way to improvise melodic ideas. Scales teach us what successions of notes sound good next to each other in a given key, and moving up and down various kinds of scales in a specific key can often create melodies pleasing to the ear.

Harmony

Harmony is often the support behind the melody. **Harmonies** are series of tones that are designed to accompany a melody and complement it with tonal depth. Popular harmonies are often three or five notes above the melody's note, but when you get a sense for what notes sound good with other notes, many other opportunities for harmony can open up. It is easy to identify what harmonies work and which ones do not via trial and error, as bad harmonies will be discordant with the melody and create unpleasant sounds. In music with many instruments or singers working in tandem, a single melody can be backed by potentially dozens of harmonic progressions, creating a sound of immense depth.

Rhythm

In music, rhythm refers to the pattern of sound against silence. This pattern is temporal, and songs are usually structured around a singular rhythm that instructs other musicians when to play and at what rate. Rhythm is most often kept with a percussion instrument of some sort, but any kind of sound with a purposeful beat can indicate rhythm in a composition. Rhythm can speed up or slow down in tempo mid-song, but generally speaking, a song will only follow one rhythm at a time.

When improvising rhythmic patterns, it is critical to understand the baseline rhythm upon which you are improvising. Many different rhythmic patterns can be made from a single "measure" of song and can be broken down into theoretically infinite sections. If a single measure is broken into two notes, they are called "half notes." Breaking it into four notes renders quarter notes, breaking into eights makes eighth notes, and so on. The smaller the notes become in the measure, the more quickly they start and end. Additionally, these notes do not need to make sound, as the absence of sound on rhythmic beats also contributes to a song's rhythmic structure. These silent pauses in rhythm are called rests. As long as the final result of a measure adds fully up to "1," the rhythmic structure is valid (e.g., one half note and two quarter notes, or one eighth note, followed by a quarter note and a half note, ended with another eighth note).

Often, students will be able to "feel" rhythm to a certain extent; what sounds good in a rhythmic structure will be obvious. As long as they know the tempo of a piece, improvising rhythm can be quite easy. For students that do not have a good internal sense of rhythm, having them break a measure into various kinds of note compositions can provide a more academic, theory-based way to make rhythmic structure.

Meter

We now understand that rhythm is a pattern of sound. With this knowledge, we can make sense of meter, which is simply the way in which rhythm is measured. A song's **meter** sets the pace for the rhythmic rules it will follow, and this indicator is usually represented by two numbers at the beginning of a line of music, one on top of the other. These two numbers are called a **time signature**. The top number in a time signature indicates how many beats comprise a measure in this song, and the bottom number indicates what kind of note is given a single beat. For example, a 4/4 time signature means that a measure is given four beats before it is completed, and quarter notes are what indicate those beats. If that signature changes to ¾, that means we still count beats in quarter notes, but the measure now only holds three quarter notes.

Musical Ideas and Connections

Using Your Life Experience

There is no such thing as an original idea, especially when it comes to art. Everything that humans create is derived from something else, be it another artistic piece, a person you knew, something you were once told, even a piece of trash on the street. With the knowledge in mind that all art is derivative, it is helpful to teach your students to consider their influences when making art. Some questions to have them ask are as follows:

- Are my inspirations musical at all? Are they instead verbal or visual? If they are not musical, how can I use my knowledge of music to encapsulate the essence of something nonmusical in music?

- What mood do I want to convey with my music? What other art do I enjoy that conveys similar moods? What about that work brings that mood out? How can I make those factors my own and build from there?

- Will my music have lyrics? What inspires the lyrics? Does the song have a message that the lyrics will convey, or are the lyrics an aid to the mood of the song, just like every other instrument?

- What is unique about my own perspective and abilities in contrast with my influences? How can I apply my own strengths and interests to make my work distinct from its influences?

It is less important that students have prepared answers to each of these questions and more important that they are simply asking themselves these questions throughout the creative process. Someone experienced in answering these questions will become acutely aware of their own artistic taste, which in turn will aid their progress in continually growing their artistic voice.

Perhaps the most concrete and reliable activity that can hone and strengthen one's musical ear is **active listening**. Music is often an accompaniment to our daily lives, whether we are driving, studying, or going grocery shopping. When you engage in active listening, you consciously remove other stimuli from your environment and direct all of your attention to a piece of music. This exercise is effective in developing a better understanding of your own tastes and will allow you to focus more on why your reactions are what they are. Did you like the chorus? Why? What parts of the chorus made it enjoyable? Was it the melody? The rhythm? The way in which the two interacted? Identify what makes this more enjoyable than a similar piece of work that you might react to differently. If your students are asking and answering these questions when discussing music, it is a good indicator that they have a good understanding of their taste, which, once again, will strengthen their artistic voice. Teachers are encouraged to allow for these moments in class, in which everyone listens to a song in silence, and the teacher does not attempt to interrupt mid-song with instruction.

Your students should also be encouraged to listen to different types of music and attempt to create interesting rhythms, melodies, and harmonies with whatever new inspirations they come across, no matter how small. If a poem that a student enjoys is without musical accompaniment, perhaps they might write a melody and some harmonies for the background that match the poem's mood. Perhaps someone could experiment with adding different layers of percussion to tweak the rhythmic structures of songs. All of these activities, regardless of how "original" they are, serve to further hone the artistic ear.

Music and Culture

To understand musical creation, one must at least acknowledge multiple aspects of culture and its influence. As the primary shaper of artistic direction for all of human history, the culture of a given type of music is inseparable from the music itself, and deepening one's understanding of a culture that is attached to a given type of music will always aid in one's ability to better create similar music.

Doing some research can often improve and deepen a listener's understanding of a piece of music. This can be research on the artist as an individual, such as learning about personal anecdotes they have given involving their life experiences, which give further weight and meaning to their music. However, this can also be research on the art's origins beyond the individual that directly made it. Questions to ask in these instances are as follows:

- What cultures does the artist come from? These cultures can be regional, ethnic, religious, economic, or any other source that might act as a lens on how one views the world. How do those cultures intersect? What parts of the music can you find that clearly originate from these cultural influences?

- Is this music cultural by active or passive influence? Active influence means that the music is giving acknowledgement of various possible backgrounds or traditions within the work itself. Is this acknowledgement as direct as a lyrical reference, or something more subtle, such as a distinct instrument that comes from a particular group of people?

- Does the music juxtapose its cultural influences with newer content with less cultural significance? What is the result of that clash? What culture does this other aspect of the song come from? What does it mean to be at such an intersection?

Particularly creative or observant students might have this idea before they are told, but all music students should know that they each have a unique blend of cultural influences, and that no two people will have the same answers to the questions above. Seeing how other musicians express their cultural influences will also aid a student's sense of originality, because everyone's personal cultural influences are made up of different combinations and are bound to be unique to the individual musician.

In specific instances, cultural pieces will be more stringent than simply being an influence on someone's original work. In instances where songs and dances and instruments are used in clearly defined pieces, passed down through generations, the intention becomes different. Appropriate questions for students to ask in these instances are as follows:

- What is the original purpose of this music, if not to entertain? Is it to tell a story, teach a lesson, or perhaps to honor or commune with a higher power?

- Are there lyrics or a dance involved with the song, and what role do they play in aiding the music's original purpose?
- With what instruments is this song being performed? Do people still commonly use this instrument? If not, what makes this instrument so culturally significant? How does its use contribute to the song as a whole?

Often, the constraints of specifically passed-down music can inspire further creativity in musicians. If your students know how a certain group of people has communicated a story throughout history, especially a group of people with which the student is not already familiar, it can lead to different ways of thinking about creation. Experiencing music from different cultures makes musicians practiced in viewing art from different angles and with different lenses. This better equips them to make more meaningful music.

Selecting Music

As a Listener

Students who spend enough time doing active listening exercises will eventually develop a very specific understanding of their own musical tastes. As in dance, it is critical to understand the difference between "Do I like this?" and "Is this good?" when taking in music. Students should be encouraged to understand what they enjoy about the music that they like. A student who understands their artistic tastes well should be able to answer the following questions:

- What are some of the trademark musical aspects of your favorite musicians? What do they do with their music that draws you to it?

- How much of your interest in a given song is critical, and how much of it is subjective? Personal attachments to the subject matter of a song are valid reasons to enjoy it, but they do not aid in critically understanding music. Music need not always be critically understood, but a good active music listener understands the difference between their ear for technique and their personal sentiments.

- What don't you like about your favorite musicians? Art is subjective, but nothing is perfect. Are there any aspects that you don't like in music that is otherwise enjoyable to you? Do you know how you would do it differently?

- In what context do you listen to this music? Is this a song you listen to more often when you exercise or when you study? Do you like listening to this song around your friends or do you prefer listening to it alone? Would you enjoy listening to it around your parents? What role does this song play in various aspects of your life in this way?

As a Creator

Understanding how you select music as a listener helps you understand how to create it. We have thoroughly discussed how to create based on one's influences, but when a student can break down the reasons behind the influences, they arrive at their own taste, and can create based on their raw interests.

Students that can create music based on their raw interests, divorced from the proper nouns attached to influences, will do so with a better understanding of their fundamental taste. These students should know how to evoke moods with sounds and lyrics on a creative level. If the technical theory aspect of properly writing music is not yet developed in a student, this is the time to encourage a student to experiment more with composition. Often, collaboration can also be helpful, and students who are more versed in technical music theory can work with students who are more instinctively creative, eventually creating something with musical signatures that reflect both of them.

Sometimes, one might draw musical inspiration from more of a concrete life event than a general desire to capture a particular sound. Struggles, triumphs, tragedies, and even regular interactions with someone you know can spur inspiration, and if you've trained your sense of artistic expression enough, these experiences can be translated into music in more ways than just lyrical. Students who wish to make music based on their own life experiences should consider their mental and emotional states during said experiences. An experience that left one's heart racing might be made with a consistent and quick tempo, and the general mood of the event can shape the musical mood of the

276

song as anything from tense to jubilant to meandering to overtly aggressive. It is often easy to simply represent stories and experiences through lyrics, but a song backed with expressions of an experience through every musical aspect makes for a stronger message and a fuller intent behind one's music.

Theatre

Creating a Story

Characters

Theatre, more than any other story medium, relies on interesting characters to determine quality. On the stage, characters are often the most realistic thing an audience member will see, and any set design or prop quality is engineered to strengthen the story of the characters. When writing characters, your students should consider the following:

- Establish your character's voice. This is more than just deciding whether the main character will be speaking in first or third person; character voice comprises the uniqueness of the character's dialogue patterns. A reader of the script should be able to differentiate two characters with well-established voices without seeing their names or knowing anything else about the character. Do they use a type of slang? Do they speak in run-on sentences? Do they use placeholder words like "like" or "um"? Most importantly, what do these tendencies say about the character as a person?

  o   It is worth noting that a character's artistic voice is more than simply how they talk. A character's voice also comes across in ways that they differ from other characters beyond just the messages they are communicating in their lines. Nonverbal gestures, or "secondary acting," also largely contribute to character voice. What is revealed about a character if they always have their arms crossed? What does it mean if a character is always fidgeting with their hands? How does a character who reacts with large expressions differ in essence from a character with intentionally more muted reactions?

- Give a character some motivations. An interesting character is usually in motion in some capacity. Audience members do not care about a character who already has everything they want. A good character is driven by a powerful motivation, usually revealed early in the story so it can move the character through the plot.

- Give your characters flaws. Do they have a crippling fear? Does their temper go through the roof when faced with a particular subject? Do they have a soft spot for a particular person or thing, and would they be willing to compromise their morals in order to protect them? Perfect characters are for power fantasies and stories without depth. Make sure the people you are writing are human, in that they are flawed in some way—ideally a way that makes for interesting conflict within the scope of your plot.

Plot

Plot is defined as the interrelated sequence of events that the audience is made to focus on in a play. It is what drives any story forward and makes things happen within the narrative. With a few exceptions, a plot should follow a series of story beats that build and release tension, as explained in the graphic below:

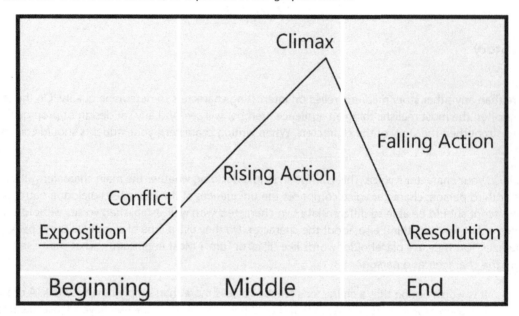

Students should be thoroughly familiar with this diagram before they begin writing plots on their own.

With few exceptions, stories generally have a beginning, a middle, and an end, usually in that order. In the beginning of a play, the writer should communicate most of the important information that is needed in order to follow along with the events of the play. In the middle of a play, complications tend to arise, and conflict starts to build. One of the key facets of theatrical writing is this dramatic tension, which will be brought to a climax somewhere between the late middle and early end of the play. In the climax, all of the established tension and conflict are expressed in their apex and are usually resolved in one way or another. Note that resolving a point of tension does not mean things will work out well for the protagonist of the play; not all stories have a happy ending. Tension simply must resolve in one way or another, which brings the audience to the end of the play, where no further tension is added, and some level of resolution is reached.

To practice this skill of plot writing, students should write down the bare bones of any and all stories that come to their mind with minimal detail, whether in bullet points or in a literal plot diagram. This "skeleton plot" will help you as a teacher understand if they grasp the basic fundamentals of building a plot.

The Technical Crew

No play with any standard of quality can be performed with actors alone. A massive portion of good theatre rests on the shoulders of the various members of the technical crew. Below are explanations of the major players on an average tech crew, followed by their responsibilities.

Set

Set designers are in charge of sculpting the space in which the play takes place; the dressing of the stage and any other physical objects or constructs that help communicate the setting of the play fall under the purview of the set designer. Set designers often require the help of stagehands, who are in charge of moving around aspects of the set between scenes. Without a good set designer and stagehands, the physical-space component of the story the play tells will have considerably less impact.

Lights

A lighting specialist's job is to plan out and manage the lighting effects throughout the show. Lighting and set design often work hand in hand, as lighting is used to communicate the environment in which the characters exist (e.g., warm, yellow lights communicate daytime or firelight; cold blues communicate nighttime). However, lighting can also be used to emphasize mood and expression. Deep red lights are effective at conveying a scene's intensity or violence. Gentle pinks and purples can emphasize romance and passion. To effectively create lighting scripts, students should have a basic understanding of color theory and which colors emphasize what moods.

In addition to being aware of the play's tone and energy, lighting technicians should also be aware of the scale of the theater in which they plan to put on a show. Your students should consider both the height and the depth of the space before going forward with a lighting script. Set lights should cover the entire stage unless an intentional choice is made not to do so. This means that on a deeper stage where more actors can be considerably farther back (or "upstage"), lights must be angled from higher up to shine farther back. Theater height mustn't always be filled, but it must always be considered, because if your students have a tall space in which to work, but only keep the first 10–12 feet of the stage's height lit, that creates a considerable and noticeable void above the actors that should only be done as an intentional artistic decision.

Sound

Sound design has two primary purposes. First, on a technical level, it aids actors in being heard in larger spaces. Microphone mixing and sound control from the actors themselves are paramount to making sure everyone in an audience gets a complete experience of a show. Second, and more artistically, sound design can aid greatly in creating an immersive environment. The passive sounds of walking horses and general chatter can go quite far in establishing an old town square.

Props

A prop is any object that is not a part of a costume or the set in a play. Well-made props help add immersion to the narrative and spectacle of the show, but they also often make things easier for actors; for example, handling an actual ball in a game of catch is easier than trying to mime the presence of a ball that is not there. Skilled prop artists have a good sense of artistic design, detail, and—sometimes— construction.

Costume/Makeup

Like props, most costume work is not necessary in theatre, but it can significantly help establish immersion and authenticity. Especially elaborate makeup can also be considered part of a costume, but actors should typically have at least a base of foundation and eyeliner to make their features and expression pop distinctly on stage. All students who are actors, regardless of gender, should understand the basics of applying foundation and a basic layer of eyeliner, as dedicated makeup artists are rare in lower-budget theatrical spaces unless the play calls for elaborate, costumed makeup.

Improvisation and Design

Improvisational performances come in a wide variety of formats, of which theatre is only one. Developing a strong sense of improv and an understanding of the different ways it manifests can help your students think on their feet when they end up on stage.

Poetry/Spoken Word

As in all improvisation, one of the key skills to improvisational poetry is to accept what is on the page and move forward with it. Nitpicking over the quality of every line is antithetical to the nature of improvisation. The hardest part will be writing the first line, and afterword your students should primarily be concerned about just saying "yes" to whatever their previous line was and letting their next line be guided by what came before it.

Music

Depending on your students' talents and the way they process information, music could be the easiest or the hardest medium in which to improvise. Musical improvisation requires some degree of developed musical instinct—enough to at least know what sounds good in the moment. Practicing with various types of scales and various instruments can be a good way to get started with musical improvisation.

Storytelling/Theatre

Telling an improvised story, especially on stage in front of an audience, requires a good sense of story structure (see the plot diagram above) and an understanding of live audience feedback.

Oftentimes, especially when improvising, the purpose of telling a story is to capture the attention of your audience and keep them interested, so when improvising stories, students should pay attention not only to maintaining a beginning, middle, and end of their story with a proper climax, but also to how the audience is reacting. Students should focus on what aspects of the story hook the audience members because every crowd is going to react in a slightly different way. Does this group react better to comedy? Do they appreciate the tension of drama? Do descriptions of violence make them uncomfortable? Understanding how to read a crowd in this way will be paramount to your students' ability to retain a crowd's attention on the spot.

When performing with another person, the most important rule for students to remember in improvisation is the "yes, and" rule. Shutting down the improvised input of scene partners is considered poor form in improv. Your students should understand that it is essential to accept the story beat that they are given and then learn to push the story forward in some way with their response to their scene partner's input.

Comedy

Improvised comedy can be especially tough, because performing comedy requires a sense of knowing what is funny in the first place, which is often subjective and can change from crowd to crowd. Your students should first and foremost understand who they're performing for and make decisions informed by that. Beyond that, the best pieces of advice for improvising comedy are as follows:

- Always listen to your scene partners. Improv is not about proving that you are the funniest person in the room; if your students are only conceiving their own jokes and looking for places to insert them, that quickly becomes bad improv. Understand the choices your partners are making in the moment and reinforce them with your own reactions; see the "yes, and" discussion above.

- Follow your instincts. Improv is best when you maintain a sense of momentum and pausing to think about your next line is antithetical to that momentum. Not every line will be solid gold, but it is more important that you keep a scene going. Within boundaries of human decency, trusting your first instinct in improv is often the best decision, and the more you engage in improv, the better that first instinct will become.

Non-Representational Design

Non-representational materials are assorted objects that are used to create specific props or costumes. Whereas representational props and costumes would include actual outfits, blunted metal swords, purchased masks, etc., non-representational costumes and props require a little more homemade effort and are often more symbolic than realistic. However, they are effective when one is preparing for shows with small budgets or short run times and that require something that might not ever be used. Your students should understand how to use non-representational materials to make both costumes and props.

Non-Representational Costumes

If the realistic costume that a given character would wear in a scene is not an option, or if your students wish for something more sensationalized or absurdist, non-representational costumes are a good idea.

280

Spare fabrics, streamers, ribbons, etc. can be attached to otherwise regular-looking clothing to evoke specific moods. Particularly vibrant characters can be decorated in strips of bright, multicolored cloth. Characters meant to be large and intimidating can have their shoulders and headgear extended with felt or other types of sturdy cloth. Wealthy or royal characters can be outfitted with large or numerous craft rhinestones. The important part is that your costume crew understands the symbolism of the costume pieces they are putting together and how these pieces reinforce the narrative idea of the character.

Applied with the right artistic touch, paints and dyes can also be great non-representational materials when used on regular articles of clothing to demarcate character traits such as disposition and faction. A classic example might be a minimalist telling of *Romeo and Juliet* in which all of the Montagues wear basic clothing that is dyed blue, and all of the Capulets wear clothing dyed red.

Non-Representational Props

Non-representational props allow your more hands-on students to display their creativity and craftsmanship. Common craft materials such as cardboard, paper mâché, and recycled materials can allow for a wide variety of props that may not otherwise be available to your group. Weapons can be crafted from wood and tinfoil, crowns can be made from cardboard and glossy paint, and puppets can be made from anything from felt to cardboard to plastic bottles, depending on how elaborate and creative your needs are.

Most often, non-representational props will not come off as realistic on stage, especially when compared to specialized representational props. However, given the technical and financial restraints on theatre, especially student theatre, realism is not always the goal. Your students should primarily be concerned about the mood that their props should evoke, and any narrative symbolism they need to portray. A sword made of cardboard and tinfoil might look strange in the hand of a character in a fully time-period-accurate doublet and breastplate, but if the majority of the play is non-representational, such props contribute to the overall mood of the play and still lend themselves to a sound performance.

Contextual Analysis

To understand what good theatre looks like, your students must be able to analyze the theatre that they watch. As in all art, there are many perspectives from which people can and should attempt to view art. Below are some primary examples.

Cultural/Social Perspective

When your students analyze art from a cultural or social perspective, they are looking for direct or indirect commentary of or influence from a particular cultural angle. What about this play is unique to its particular culture? How might the playwright, actors, or director have been influenced by their own culture in a way that impacts what appears on the stage? Does this play have something to say about the culture it comes from, or is it just passively shaped by the culture of the play's creators? If the play has something to say about the culture, what stance does it take? Does the play hold admiration and respect for its culture, or is it more critical? What specific technical and non-technical aspects of the play contribute to that statement?

Since all art is derivative of the artists' cultures in some way, students should always be able to answer this question to some degree. If your students share any of the cultures being observed, they should be encouraged to explain how their personal understanding of the play's culture impacted their opinion of the play and how they were able to critically analyze it.

Global Perspective

Analyzing from a global perspective asks your students to consider where in the world this work comes from or takes place. If the play does not take place in a culture or society familiar to your students, this might require some research. How are the topics presented in the play viewed in the relevant culture? How are the values weighed? Do these values differ from what your students regularly experience? What insight could this play provide about the cultural and social space it comes from? What is expressed or discussed in this play that is particularly unique to its respective culture that could not faithfully be done in the same way in a different part of the world?

Understand that different students might have different cultural backgrounds, and what might be a "global play" for one student could be a personally significant cultural piece for another. Because of this, you should attempt to share plays from multiple global cultures with your students to ensure that everyone gets an opportunity to analyze a play from a culture outside of their own.

Historical Perspective

Analyzing from a historical perspective requires that your students ask "when," rather than "where." How was society viewed differently during the time in which the play takes place? How were cultural values different? Do the creators of this play appear to have a particular stance on any pressing issues of the time? How do they immerse a modern audience in a narrative space that is distinctly non-modern?

Your students should ask similar questions as they would when analyzing from a cultural/social perspective—partly because different time periods often have as many cultural differences as different global locations do, but also because there are many historical plays that are also from different cultures. Often a play will be from both a different time and place than what your students are familiar with.

Visual Art

Tools, Materials, and Techniques

Techniques
- **Drawing** refers to visual art mostly practiced with dry materials such as graphite pencils, charcoal, or chalk, most often done on a paper surface. With the exceptions of those made with pastels and markers, drawings are less likely to have as much color as paintings. Drawings can also serve as the foundations or guidelines for paintings.

- **Painting** is most often done with wet materials such as oils and acrylics and is usually done on a canvas surface rather than paper. The exception is watercolor, which is most often done on paper. Whereas drawings are typically flat, paintings can have more texture, with thick blobs of glistening oil paint or long, thin, rippled brushstrokes.

- **Sculpting** refers to visual art crafted from three-dimensional materials. Sculptures can be crafted out of anything from clay to glass to paper mâché to trash from the recycling bin. Whereas sculptures can lack the complexity of shading and tone control that drawings and paintings can provide, sculptures are not bound by the dimensions of a sheet of paper or a canvas, and can be built to any shape, size, and scale desired, materials allowing.

Materials
- **Charcoal** is used for drawings with powerful grayscales and is known for its easy, residual strokes. Charcoal is a hard material and is incredibly brittle, so proper charcoal care is necessary to teach your students if they are to handle it.

  Students should always be mindful of the pressure they are applying to charcoal, as breaking charcoal sticks is incredibly easy. When not in use, charcoal should be kept in something such as a small tin, because too much air exposure can render charcoal more brittle. Students should try to use charcoal in dust-free environments because dust also damages charcoal over time. Your students should be able to identify charcoal that has picked up dust by running a finger over it. Clean charcoal should be smooth; dusty charcoal will have bumps.

Lastly, it is critical to never get charcoal wet, as wet charcoal will damage the paper that it is used on. Wet charcoal makes darker colors than regular charcoal.

- **Pastels** are powdered dyes mixed with enough binder to form sticks or pencils. These dyes are the same types used in creating oil paints, but having minimal binder in the mixture allows for vibrant, textured-looking colors in a drawing. With the right care, drawings made with pastels last considerably longer than traditional oil paintings. Your students should avoid touching the surface of a pastel piece or the tip of a pastel marker because the oils from human fingers will mix with the pigment and deteriorate the paper.

- **Paints and brushes** are often used hand in hand, so your students will practice care for both materials at once. Paints come in two primary types: oil and acrylic. Oil paints have a tendency to diffuse when left still for long enough, with oil rising to the top of a paint tube, so your students should stand oil paint tubes upright with the cap downward when storing them. Acrylics can be stored on their side, but too much pressure will cause them to burst from their tube, so it is critical that your students do not stack anything on top of these tubes. Whether using oil or acrylic paints, students should avoid pushing more paint out of the tube than they need, as storing and using excess, unused paint is incredibly difficult, especially in a classroom setting.

  When caring for paintbrushes, it is important that your students mind how deeply they are immersing their brushes in the paint. They should never immerse a paintbrush all the way to the ferrule (the metal casing between the bristles and the rest of the brush), as the base of the bristles is the hardest place to clean and will often harden the bristles. Students should also avoid over-soaking their brushes in water, and oil paints should be cleaned in mineral spirits or baby oil. After students remove the excess water from rinsing their brush, they should store them upright on the handle, lest the bristles flatten.

Design

- **Color** is most simply explained as pigmentation, but older students should have a base understanding of the three qualities that comprise any given color.

  A color's **hue** is where it lands around the general circumference of a color wheel and is most often how we differentiate color, as it is the quality that differentiates red from blue from yellow and every pigment in between. When people question whether to use a shade of indigo with more or less violet in it, they are often discussing the color's hue.

  A color's **saturation** dictates how concentrated the color's hue is. Higher levels of saturation will have bright, vibrant colors, while lower levels of saturation will be duller and less defined. Colors with no saturation are on a grayscale.

  A color's **brightness** (also referred to as brilliance) represents its intensity and level of shading. Higher levels of brightness will turn red into pink, but lower levels of brightness will turn red into a brick or wine color, depending on the hue. Color brightness can also be manipulated with perspective. By putting a color of neutral brightness in front of a background with low brightness, the middle-brightness color will appear brighter than it otherwise would.

  Understanding what looks good when adjusting these three color levels is the basis to developing sound color theory.

- **Lines and shapes** are the foundations for the structure of art. A line is any mark with a length notably greater than its width. Lines can be literal or suggested through the alignment of shapes throughout a piece, and they serve well to lead a viewer's eye throughout a piece.

  Shapes are created when a series of lines closes into a two-dimensional form. Shapes create contrasting images that distinguish themselves from background colors in a piece and are, at their core, the foundation for all two-dimensional art that involves objects in space.

- **Balance and composition** concern the artistic harmony of a piece. A piece's composition is the way in which the artist combines different artistic elements, creating visually harmonious work that is greater than the sum of its parts. Balance specifically refers to how positive and negative spaces interact to evoke a sense of stability. Balance can exist in shape or color, and unless a student's artistic goal is to make one part of the piece visually overpower another, they should attempt to make balanced use of their visual space in both shapes and colors, thereby creating a sound composition.

Connections and Value

Art in Daily Life

Whether we are conscious of it or not, we are constantly surrounded by both the presence and practice of art. Even in our own homes, we are influenced by the pictures hanging on our walls, or the patterns in the quilt that rests on our sofa. Even a well-made desk is a display of art that we interact with on a regular basis.

People can consume art actively, which means they are paying attention to the process and what it evokes in them personally, or they can consume it passively, simply by noticing its presence while their minds are focused on other things. Passive consumption of art still influences people. Though one might not actively stare at and retain every art piece in their home on a consistent basis, it is the composition of every artistic expression in one's home that establishes the home's mood. If a home has many cool blue and gray tones with grayscale photographs hanging on the walls, that home is going to have a considerably different baseline "feel" than a home with warm browns and oranges with vibrant paintings and elaborate woodwork. When we exist in spaces where we passively consume art, we tend to take that "feel" into the world in a way that can influence our own neutral state. The home, however, is just one example of this. Passive consumption of art happens in classrooms, at work, and even on the road in transit; everything from the artistic design of a billboard to one's car can passively influence people.

Daily Life in Art

Just as art influences life, life in turn influences art. Artists can use their technical knowledge to bring daily events of the real world to a new type of light in visual art, displaying and spotlighting the artistry in things done from day to day. Take, for example, *The Milkmaid* by Johannes Vermeer, a painting that simply displays a Dutch milkmaid at work upon a dinner table.

There is nothing inherently fantastical or expressionistic about this piece, but due to the artist's knowledge of positioning, shading, and color/shape balance, we as an audience are given an aesthetically pleasing piece that communicates a soft peace and nobility to the grind of everyday work.

How this everyday work is displayed differs from culture to culture. While western Europe has historically placed much value on elaborate oil paintings, other cultures approach art differently. Note the Japanese piece below from the Shuntei Miyagawa print collection from the Ukiyo no Hana Group.

It also depicts women at work, but the technical artistry around it is represented very differently than in The Milkmaid. Rather than drawing a heavily detailed recreation of a traditional milkmaid at a dinner table, the artist for the Shuntei Miyagawa piece minimized any detail outside of the characters that did not serve to communicate the setting. The use of color further emphasizes that the women themselves are the focus of this piece, not the field that they are in or the work that they are doing. This genre of art is more common in Japanese and general East Asian art, and your students will have a stronger artistic eye if they can understand how different global cultures display everyday life.

Cultural Values

Because art is a universal language that can impact anyone emotionally, it is able to aid us in understanding cultures that might otherwise be difficult to relate to. As mentioned previously, art cannot exist without some level of influence, and this influence is often cultural. By understanding what different cultures value in their artwork, your students will gain a better understanding of those cultures' values in general. Cultural value consists of many potential smaller types of values, some of which are described below.

- **Aesthetic value**: The types of visual displays and patterns that soothe one's eyes. For example, Western visual art has historically preferred aesthetics with strong geometric balance and mathematically harmonious symmetry. Detailed realism is also a highly valued aesthetic. However, Eastern art is more focused on the representational essence of a matter than realism or mathematical perfection, so Eastern Asian art tends to have more permissions for abstraction and is still culturally considered aesthetically pleasing.

- **Social value**: Whereas aesthetic value stresses what a culture values in an image, social value stresses what a culture values in people. Art that makes a statement about the world surrounding the piece of artwork has some inherent kind of social value. An artist who exemplifies this change well is Claude Monet, who was famous for painting beautiful natural landscapes. In 1877, as the industrial revolution started to come around, Monet created *Arrival of the Normandy Train*, which displays a cramped-seeming, smoke-choked train station with people packed shoulder to shoulder in order to board.

Without saying anything in words, Monet is able to use imagery common in his social zeitgeist to present a suffocating, socially charged depiction of the changing world around him.

- **Spiritual value**: Religion has historically been inseparable from culture, and thus a majority of artists throughout history have shown noticeable religious influence in their work. We know this to be clear in Western art, with many of our classics being Christian-motivated pieces such as *The Creation of Adam* and *The Last Supper*, but this is true everywhere else in the world as well. Many African cultures have historically created religiously significant, ceremonial, and even usable pieces of art by way of sculptures, jewelry, and masks. Chinese artists famously create grand colorful murals and massive sculptures displaying deific figures.

When you show a new piece of cultural art to students, challenge them to explain what makes the piece distinct to that culture. How does it differ from art that they have grown up around? What might those differences imply about the culture this piece comes from?

Presentation and Preservation

Though we traditionally tend to consider art as something to be put on a wall and appreciated, there are plenty of other methods in which art can be presented and appreciated. Consider the difference between a painting kept in a museum and a sculpture erected in the center of a town's square, or in a school courtyard. What is happening socially when this distinction is made? What is the world telling people about who does and does not get to appreciate certain types of art? What does that say in turn about the culture that sets these standards? Consider cultures that use masks and regalia of religious significance—art pieces that are meant to be actively used in appropriate circumstances and seen on days of importance. Under what circumstances is this art to be enjoyed? How do they preserve their art? Whereas art in museums can be preserved with fierce protection and paint-friendly chemical layers and light treatment, how is something like a wooden mask preserved? How often are new ones made? Is there a cultural taboo around replacing ceremonial garb in such a way? Ensure that your students are asking these questions about the means of a piece's presentation and preservation when they are shown a new work of art.

286

Purposes

Art exists for many different purposes and, more often than not, artists will have a particular intent or function in mind for their piece when making it. Ensure that your students understand and are able to identify purposes of different pieces of art when observing them. Below are some primary examples of various art purposes, but it is fully possible for art to have other purposes beyond this list.

Note also that many forms of art hold more than one purpose. A ceremonial art piece can often also be narrative; a persuasive piece can also be educational, etc.

Ceremonial art is intended to be observed or even used in some degree of ritual or tradition. Examples of ceremonial art include masks, deific sculptures, adornments on books, bindings of books themselves, vessels, and incense burners. Often, ceremonial art will include imagery sacred to the culture utilizing it and can often act as a mental and emotional bridge for its people to feel closeness with a practice or faith of some kind.

Expressive art is often more about the artist themselves than anyone or anything else. Bright streaks of colors with no identifiable form attributed to them and general deconstruction of pointed purpose are good indicators of expressive art. Understanding basic artistic symbolism, such as jagged lines representing intensity, cool colors representing unhappy or muted emotions, or compositional imbalance representing skewed attention are especially helpful in analyzing expressive art and understanding what the artist wishes to express.

Narrative art tells a story. The story need not be as complicated as a full wall mural or a line of cave drawings; narrative art simply displays something taking place. *The Last Supper* or *Washington Crossing the Delaware* are primary examples of such pieces. Students should be able to observe the various individuals, objects, or points of focus in a narrative piece and identify not only what is happening in the art, but also how different parts of the art aid in giving the complete narrative.

Educational art can often go hand in hand with narrative art, as most stories are educational to some degree, but while narrative art exists only to tell a story, educational art specifically aims to transfer knowledge. Narrative educational art educates someone about an event, and possibly a moral lesson in said event, but examples of non-narrative educational art can be found in classrooms and doctors' offices around the world. Robert Plutchik's *Wheel of Emotions*, while not recognized as a traditional art piece, is a primary example of non-narrative educational art.

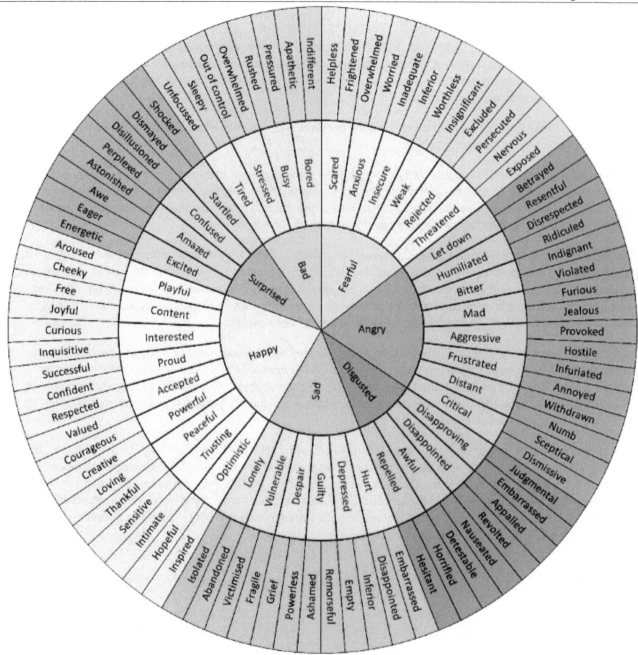

Plutchik uses colors and lines and shapes in an eye-pleasing way to differentiate sub-categories of emotions in a way that is easy to explain to people who are not psychology experts, proving the inherent educational value of basic art-theory knowledge.

Persuasive art intends to win over the minds or goodwill of an audience to a particular cause or way of thinking. Every single political cartoon ever made is, by definition, persuasive art. Persuasive art can be as empowering as Eugene Delacroix's *Liberty Leading the People* or as nefarious as Soviet propaganda posters of the 1950s and 60s.

When analyzing this work, your students should be less concerned with whether they agree with the persuader's stance and focus more on what artistic elements of the piece serve to emphasize the perspective being given.

Practice Quiz

1. Sandra is assessing her dance students and notices that one boy tends to lean his body somewhat backward when he dances. This would indicate a problem with what?
   a. Poise
   b. Posture
   c. Frame
   d. Balance

2. When analyzing music, students must learn to listen to all aspects of the music. One aspect of musical analysis includes evaluating the supporting notes that provide tonal depth to the song. What are these notes called?
   a. Melody
   b. Harmony
   c. Pitch
   d. Tonality

3. Which part of the technical crew would be best suited to control the portrayal of different times of day during a play?
   a. Lighting
   b. Set
   c. Sound
   d. Props

4. It is imperative that visual arts students understand how to properly use and store their materials lest they get wasted or ruined. Which material is best stored in an upright position?
   a. Charcoal
   b. Acrylic paints
   c. Oil paints
   d. Pastels

5. Students in an eighth-grade class are analyzing a painting. They are discussing the visual representation of the subject, the colors and patterns that the artist used, and the overall visual feel of the piece. What aspect of the art are the students considering here?
   a. Social value
   b. Aesthetic value
   c. Spiritual value
   d. Presentation value

See answers on the next page.

Answer Explanations

1. A: Poise refers to the body's directional weight placement in relation to the feet. The boy is demonstrating a backward-positioned poise, which could result in his falling backward rather than staying centered. Choice *B*, posture, refers to the body's structural alignment, or the position of the head, shoulders, ribs, and hips. Choice *C*, frame, is the position of the arms and torso while dancing, and Choice *D*, balance, is the symmetry of the body during movement.

2. B: The harmony of a song is the blending of notes and tones that support the melody and provide depth to a musical composition. The melody, Choice *A*, is the central focus of a song, its musical throughline. Pitch, Choice *C*, refers to the frequency of sound on a higher-to-lower scale. Tonality, Choice *D*, is the focal pitch of the song, also called the song's key.

3. A: The lighting design of a play can help indicate different times of day by using soft, warm lights to simulate a rising sun or cooler blue/white lighting to simulate twilight, for example. There can be some indication of time of day using the set and props, Choices *B* and *D*, such as changing the set to a bedroom scene or having characters preparing coffee, but changing these things is often more involved than using the more subtle lighting cues. Sound, Choice *C*, can also be used, but trying to make obvious nighttime noises, for example, can prove distracting for the audience and overwhelm the action of the play.

4. C: Oil paints tend to separate when they are stored for long periods of time. Thus, they should be stored in an upright position, cap downward. Charcoal, Choice *A*, should be stored in an airtight tin, while pastel sticks or pencils, Choice *D*, and acrylic paints, Choice *B*, are generally stored horizontally.

5. B: The aesthetic value of a painting refers to the visual display of subject, technique, color, and pattern that makes the painting pleasing to the eye. Social value, Choice *A*, is an assessment of the work as it relates to a specific locale, time period, or social subject matter. Choice *C*, spiritual value, generally refers to art with religious subject matter, such as deities, ceremonies, or religiously significant artifacts. Presentation in Choice *D* refers to how a piece of art is displayed, such as wall placement and lighting. Presentation value, however, is a made-up term.

Practice Test #1

Subtest I: Reading, Language, and Literature

1. What type of literary device gives human-like characteristics to animals or inanimate objects?
    a. Anthropomorphism
    b. Synecdoche
    c. Conceit
    d. Onomatopoeia

2. When teaching students how to read, what is the most complex type of activity a teacher can employ?
    a. Teaching students to hear individual phonemes in words
    b. Teaching students to hear onsets and rimes in words
    c. Teaching students to hear syllables in spoken words
    d. Teaching students to hear oral rhymes and alliteration

3. What is the term used to describe the ability to easily adapt different levels, styles, or kinds of languages to a particular context?
    a. Alliteration
    b. Objectivity
    c. Phoneme awareness
    d. Code switching

4. Of the following statements, which is most accurate about topic sentences?
    a. They are always first in a paragraph.
    b. They are always last in a paragraph.
    c. They are only found once in every essay.
    d. They may be explicit or implicit.

5. Being familiar with English words such as claustrophobia, photophobia, arachnophobia, hydrophobia, acrophobia, etc. could help a reader determine that the Greek word *phobos* means which of these?
    a. Love
    b. Fear
    c. Hate
    d. Know

6. Which of the following is a writing technique recommended for attaining sentence fluency?
    a. Varying the endings of sentences
    b. Making sentence lengths uniform
    c. Using consistent sentence rhythm
    d. Using various sentence structures

7. A *complex sentence* can be defined as which of the following?
    a. A sentence that contains no prepositional phrases
    b. A sentence that contains an indefinite pronoun
    c. A sentence that contains two independent clauses
    d. A sentence that contains at least one independent clause and at least one dependent clause

8. "I like writing, playing soccer, and eating" is an example of which grammatical convention?
   a. Appositive
   b. Complement
   c. Verbal
   d. Parallelism

9. Which of the following sources does NOT require a citation when writing?
   a. Summaries
   b. Paraphrases
   c. Common knowledge
   d. Direct quotations

10. A reader comes across a word they do not know in the book they are reading, and they need to find out what the word means in order to understand the context of the sentence. Where should the reader look?
    a. Table of contents
    b. Introduction
    c. Index
    d. Glossary

11. Which of the following is involved in prewriting?
    a. Drafting
    b. Revising
    c. Publishing
    d. Outlining

The next two questions are based on the following passage:

Rehabilitation, rather than punitive justice, is becoming much more popular in prisons around the world. Prisons in America, where the recidivism rate is 67%, would especially benefit from mimicking the prison tactics used in Norway, where the recidivism rate is only 20%. In Norway, the idea is that a rehabilitated prisoner is much less likely to offend than one who was harshly punished. Rehabilitation includes proper treatment for substance abuse, psychotherapy, healthcare and dental care, and education programs.

12. Which of the following best captures the author's purpose?
    a. To show the audience one of the effects of criminal rehabilitation by comparison
    b. To persuade the audience to donate to American prisons for education programs
    c. To convince the audience of the harsh conditions of American prisons
    d. To inform the audience of the incredibly lax system of Norwegian prisons

13. Which of the following describes the word *recidivism* as it is used in the passage?
    a. The lack of violence in the prison system
    b. The opportunity of inmates to receive therapy in prison
    c. The event of a prisoner escaping the compound
    d. The likelihood of a convicted criminal to reoffend

292

The next three questions are based on the following passage.

The old castle soon proved to be too small for the family, and in September 1853 the foundation-stone of a new house was laid. After the ceremony the workmen were entertained at dinner, which was followed by Highland games and dancing in the ballroom.

Two years later they entered the new castle, which the Queen described as "charming; the rooms delightful; the furniture, papers, everything perfection."

The Prince was untiring in planning improvements, and in 1856 the Queen wrote: "Every year my heart becomes more fixed in this dear Paradise, and so much more so now, that *all* has become my dearest Albert's *own* creation, own work, own building, own laying out as at Osborne; and his great taste, and the impress of his dear hand, have been stamped everywhere. He was very busy today, settling and arranging many things for next year."

Excerpt from the biography *Queen Victoria* by E. Gordon Browne, M.A.

14. Which of the following is this excerpt considered?
    a. Primary source
    b. Secondary source
    c. Tertiary source
    d. None of these

15. How many years did it take to build the new castle?
    a. One year
    b. Two years
    c. Three years
    d. Four years

16. What does the word *impress* mean in the above passage?
    a. To affect strongly in feeling
    b. To urge something to be done
    c. To impose a certain quality upon
    d. To press a thing onto something else

The next two questions are based on the following passage.

The play proceeded, although "Our American Cousin," without Mr. Sothern, has, since that gentleman's departure from this country, been justly esteemed a very dull affair. The audience at Ford's, including Mrs. Lincoln, seemed to enjoy it very much. The worthy wife of the President leaned forward, her hand upon her husband's knee, watching every scene in the drama with amused attention. Even across the President's face at intervals swept a smile, robbing it of its habitual sadness.

About the beginning of the second act, the mare, standing in the stable in the rear of the theater, was disturbed in the midst of her meal by the entrance of the young man who had quitted her in the afternoon. It is presumed that she was saddled and bridled with exquisite care.

Having completed these preparations, Mr. Booth entered the theater by the stage door; summoned one of the scene shifters, Mr. John Spangler, emerged through the same door with that individual, leaving the door open, and left the mare in his hands to be held until he (Booth) should return. Booth who was even more fashionably and richly dressed than usual, walked thence around to the front of the theater, and went in. Ascending to the dress circle, he stood for a little time gazing around upon

293

the audience and occasionally upon the stage in his usual graceful manner. He was subsequently observed by Mr. Ford, the proprietor of the theater, to be slowly elbowing his way through the crowd that packed the rear of the dress circle toward the right side, at the extremity of which was the box where Mr. and Mrs. Lincoln and their companions were seated. Mr. Ford casually noticed this as a slightly extraordinary symptom of interest on the part of an actor so familiar with the routine of the theater and the play.

Excerpt from *The Life, Crime, and Capture of John Wilkes Booth* by George Alfred Townsend

17. How is the above passage organized?
   a. Chronological
   b. Cause and effect
   c. Problem to solution
   d. Main idea with supporting details

18. Given the author's description of the play "Our American Cousin," which one of the following is most analogous to Mr. Sothern's departure from the theater?
   a. A ballet dancer who leaves the New York City Ballet just before they go on to their final performance
   b. A basketball player leaves an NBA team and the next year they make it to the championship but lose.
   c. A lead singer leaves their band to begin a solo career, and the band drops in sales by 50% on their next album.
   d. A movie actor who dies in the middle of making a movie and the movie is made anyway by actors who resemble the deceased.

The following four questions are based on the excerpt from Variation of Animals and Plants *by Charles Darwin.*

Peach (*Amygdalus persica*).—In the last chapter I gave two cases of a peach-almond and a double-flowered almond which suddenly produced fruit closely resembling true peaches. I have also given many cases of peach-trees producing buds, which, when developed into branches, have yielded nectarines. We have seen that no less than six named and several unnamed varieties of the peach have thus produced several varieties of nectarine. I have shown that it is highly improbable that all these peach-trees, some of which are old varieties, and have been propagated by the million, are hybrids from the peach and nectarine, and that it is opposed to all analogy to attribute the occasional production of nectarines on peach-trees to the direct action of pollen from some neighbouring nectarine-tree. Several of the cases are highly remarkable, because, firstly, the fruit thus produced has sometimes been in part a nectarine and in part a peach; secondly, because nectarines thus suddenly produced have reproduced themselves by seed; and thirdly, because nectarines are produced from peach-trees from seed as well as from buds. The seed of the nectarine, on the other hand, occasionally produces peaches; and we have seen in one instance that a nectarine-tree yielded peaches by bud-variation. As the peach is certainly the oldest or primary variety, the production of peaches from nectarines, either by seeds or buds, may perhaps be considered as a case of reversion. Certain trees have also been described as indifferently bearing peaches or nectarines, and this may be considered as bud-variation carried to an extreme degree.

The grosse mignonne peach at Montreuil produced "from a sporting branch" the grosse mignonne tardive, "a most excellent variety," which ripens its fruit a fortnight later than the parent tree, and is equally good. This same peach has likewise produced by bud-variation the early grosse mignonne.

Hunt's large tawny nectarine "originated from Hunt's small tawny nectarine, but not through seminal reproduction."

19. Which statement is not a detail from the passage?
    a. At least six named varieties of the peach have produced several varieties of nectarine.
    b. It is not probable that all of the peach trees mentioned are hybrids from the peach and nectarine.
    c. An unremarkable case is the fact that nectarines are produced from the seeds and buds of peach trees.
    d. The production of peaches from nectarines might be considered a case of reversion.

20. What is the meaning of the word "propagated" in the first paragraph of this passage?
    a. Multiplied
    b. Diminished
    c. Watered
    d. Uprooted

21. Which of the following most closely describes the author's tone in this passage?
    a. Enthusiastic
    b. Objective
    c. Critical
    d. Desperate

22. Which of the following is an accurate paraphrasing of the following phrase?

Certain trees have also been described as indifferently bearing peaches or nectarines, and this may be considered as bud-variation carried to an extreme degree.

    a. Some trees are described as bearing peaches and some trees have been described as bearing nectarines, but individually the buds are extreme examples of variation.
    b. One way in which bud-variation is said to be carried to an extreme degree is when specific trees have been shown to casually produce peaches or nectarines.
    c. Certain trees are indifferent to bud-variation, as recently shown in the trees that produce both peaches and nectarines in the same season.
    d. Nectarines and peaches are known to have cross-variation in their buds, which indifferently bears other sorts of fruit to an extreme degree.

Questions 23–26 are based on the following passage:

Nobody knew where she went. She wasn't in the living room, the dining room, or the kitchen. She wasn't underneath the staircase, and she certainly wasn't in her bedroom. The bathroom was thoroughly checked, and the closets were emptied. Where could she have possibly gone? Outside was dark, cold, and damp. Each person took a turn calling for her. "Eva! Eva!" (23) they'd each cry out, but not a sound was heard in return. The littlest sister in the house began to cry. "Where could my cat have gone?" Everyone just looked at each other (24) in utter silence. Lulu was only five years old and brought this kitten home only six weeks ago and she was so fond of her. (25) Every morning, Lulu would comb her fur, feed her, and play a cat-and-mouse game with her before she left for school. At night, Eva would curl up on the pillow next to Lulu and stay with her across the night (26). They were already becoming best friends. But this evening, right after dinner, Eva snuck outside when Lulu's brother came in from the yard. It was already dark out, and Eva ran so quickly that nobody could see where she went.

It was really starting to feel hopeless when all of a sudden Lulu had an idea. She remembered how much Eva loved the cat-and-mouse game, so she decided to go outside and pretend that she was playing with Eva. Out she went. She curled up on the grass and began to play cat and mouse. Within

295

seconds, Lulu could see shining eyes in the distance. The eyes got closer, and closer, and closer. Lulu continued to play so that she wouldn't scare the kitten away. In less than five minutes, her beautiful kitten had crawled right up to her lap as if asking to join in the game.

23. Choose the best replacement punctuation:

"Eva! Eva!" they'd each cry out,

a. No change
b. 'Eva! Eva!'
c. 'Eva, Eva'!
d. "Eva, Eva"!

24. Choose the best replacement word or phrase:

Everyone just looked at each other

a. No change
b. one another
c. themselves
d. each one

25. Choose the best replacement sentence:

Lulu was only five years old and brought this kitten home only six weeks ago and she was so fond of her.

a. No change
b. Lulu brought this kitten home only six weeks ago and she was so fond of her.
c. Lulu brought this kitten home only six weeks ago, and she was so fond of her.
d. Lulu was only five years old, and brought this kitten home only six weeks ago, and she was so fond of her.

26. Choose the best replacement phrase.

At night, Eva would curl up on the pillow next to Lulu and stay with her across the night.

a. No change
b. below the night
c. through the night
d. amidst the night

Constructed-Response #1

Use the information below to complete the exercise that follows.

A teacher tracks the following behaviors displayed by one English Language Learner (ELL) during math class:

Activity	Behavior
Math Reflection Journal	Refuses to write; talks to fellow ELLs instead
Numerical Computation	Completes tasks as assigned
Independent Work Activities (Summarizing Directions)	Puts head down; fails to complete assignment
Word Problems	Disengages; fidgets; appears distracted

Write a response in which you describe both the potential interlanguage effects and exceptional circumstances that may have motivated these behaviors. Make sure to cite specific evidence to support your conclusions.

Constructed-Response #2

Use the information below to complete the exercise that follows.

A school principal asks you to lead a workshop on reading development. Using your knowledge of the stages of reading development, prepare a brief outline in which you:

- Identify the five stages of reading development.
- Select three to discuss in detail, noting potential behaviors and proactive forms of instruction.
- Explain how each stage might be enhanced by an integration of Bloom's Taxonomy.

Subtest I: History and Social Science

1. Which South Carolinian politician led the charge in the nullification crisis?
   a. Henry Clay
   b. Andrew Jackson
   c. John C. Calhoun
   d. James K. Polk

2. When were the first two constitutional conventions in California?
   a. 1849 and 1879
   b. 1851 and 1861
   c. 1858 and 1868
   d. 1872 and 1892

3. Which ancient civilization emerged next to the Tigris and Euphrates rivers?
   a. Egypt
   b. China
   c. Hebrew
   d. Mesopotamia

4. What was the foremost point of disagreement between Thomas Jefferson and Alexander Hamilton?
   a. Slavery
   b. War of 1812
   c. Declaration of Independence
   d. National bank

5. What religion did most members of the early Jamestown colony follow?
   a. Anglican Church
   b. Dutch Reform Church
   c. Puritan Church
   d. Roman Catholic Church

6. Which Muslim group established itself in Spain, renaming it Al-Andalus in 732 AD?
   a. Umayyad Empire
   b. Mughal Empire
   c. Safavid Empire
   d. Ottoman Empire

7. Which Supreme Court case saw the Cherokee Nation sue a state over the forced removal of Native Americans?
   a. *Worcester v. Georgia*
   b. *McCulloch v. Maryland*
   c. *Loving v. Virginia*
   d. *Miranda v. Arizona*

8. Which famous document championed the basic political rights of all English citizens?
   a. Magna Carta
   b. Declaration of Sentiments
   c. Quartering Act
   d. *Common Sense*

9. What is the name of the famous dynasty that existed on the southern Nile River in 1000 BC?
   a. Hebrew
   b. Kush
   c. Umayyad
   d. Safavid

10. Why are there more representatives than senators in Congress?
    a. Senators are more prestigious than representatives, so fewer are needed.
    b. Voters decide how many representatives they want each year.
    c. The number of representatives is dictated by a state's population size.
    d. The number of representatives and senators was established by the Bill of Rights, which states that there should be 100 senators and 435 representatives.

11. When it was founded, what was the Republican Party's primary issue?
    a. States' rights
    b. Tax cuts
    c. Manifest Destiny
    d. Abolition of slavery

12. How did Jim Crow laws impact the American South?
  a. African American slaves could vote for the first time in American history.
  b. The South diversified from a one-crop economy.
  c. The South industrialized, following the Northern example.
  d. The Southern states contravened the Reconstruction Amendments.

The following document is an excerpt from Abraham Lincoln's "House Divided" speech, which was delivered to the Republican state convention on June 16, 1858.

> A house divided against itself cannot stand. I believe this government cannot endure, permanently, half slave and half free. I do not expect the Union to be dissolved—I do not expect the house to fall—but I do expect it will cease to be divided. It will become all one thing or all the other. Either the opponents of slavery will arrest the further spread of it, and place it where the public mind shall rest in the belief that it is in the course of ultimate extinction; or its advocates will push it forward, till it shall become lawful in all the States, old as well as new—North as well as South.

13. When President Lincoln uses the phrase a "house divided," what is he most likely referring to?
  a. Political conflicts in the White House
  b. Tensions between the North and South over slavery
  c. Dissolution of the Union
  d. Ideological differences in his family

14. Which of the following was the first European colony established in North America?
  a. St. Augustine
  b. Roanoke
  c. Jamestown
  d. Hudson's Bay

15. Which of the following best describes the 10th Amendment to the US Constitution?
  a. The 10th Amendment reserves all non-specific powers to the states and people.
  b. The 10th Amendment establishes the existence of rights not named in the document.
  c. The 10th Amendment protects the right to bear arms.
  d. The 10th Amendment protects a series of rights for people accused of crimes.

16. What was the primary cause of widespread urbanization in the United States?
  a. The First Industrial Revolution
  b. The Second Industrial Revolution
  c. The Great Migration
  d. Successive waves of immigration

17. What is the government's role in a centrally planned economic system?
  a. The government distributes resources based solely on merit.
  b. The government allows the private market to set all prices based on supply and demand.
  c. The government makes all decisions related to production, distribution, and price.
  d. The government balances the private and public sector to stabilize the economy.

18. What was NOT included in the Missouri Compromise of 1820?
  a. Slavery was banned in Washington, D.C.
  b. Missouri was admitted as a slave state.
  c. Slavery was prohibited in future northern territories.
  d. Maine was admitted as a free state.

19. What treaty ended the American Revolution?
    a. Treaty of Paris
    b. Treaty of Ghent
    c. Treaty of Alliance
    d. Treaty of Versailles

20. What was included in the Connecticut Compromise?
    a. Two legislative bodies with different methods of representation
    b. Two legislative bodies with the same method of representation
    c. One legislative body with representation based on population
    d. One legislative body with one vote per state

Electoral Results for the Presidential Election of 1876				
Candidate	Political Party	Popular Vote Count	Popular Vote Percentage	Electoral Vote
Samuel J. Tilden	Democratic	4,286,808	50.92%	184
Rutherford B. Hayes	Republican	4,034,142	47.92%	185
Peter Cooper	Greenback	83,726	0.99%	0
Green Clay Smith	Prohibition	6,945	0.08%	0

21. Which statement about the presidential election of 1876 is true, according to the table?
    a. The Democratic candidate won the presidential election of 1876.
    b. Rutherford B. Hayes won a higher percentage of the popular vote than Samuel J. Tilden.
    c. Green Clay Smith received more popular votes than Peter Cooper.
    d. No candidate received both the majority of the popular vote and the majority of electoral votes.

22. Which of the following powers is exclusive to the federal government in the United States?
    a. Regulate immigration
    b. Regulate local government
    c. Implement welfare and benefit programs
    d. Levy taxes

23. How did large-scale agriculture facilitate European colonization in the Americas?
    a. Large-scale agriculture increased American exports to Europe, and the colonies received military aid in return.
    b. Large-scale agriculture led to the development of new technologies that were applied to the military.
    c. Large-scale agriculture supported the development of major cities in the American South, and Native Americans couldn't pierce the city's defenses.
    d. Large-scale agriculture produced a food surplus that supported a larger population, permanent settlements, and a centralized government.

24. Which of the following laws was NOT a major cause of the American Revolution?
    a. Indian Removal Acts
    b. Proclamation of 1763
    c. Quebec Act
    d. Townshend Acts

300

25. What event exposed the Articles of Confederation as a deeply flawed system of government?
    a. Publication of The Federalist Papers
    b. John Brown's raid at Harper's Ferry
    c. Whiskey Rebellion
    d. Shays' Rebellion

The next question is based on the following passage from The Federalist No. 78 *by Alexander Hamilton.*

> According to the plan of the convention, all judges who may be appointed by the United States are to hold their offices *during good behavior*, which is conformable to the most approved of the State constitutions and among the rest, to that of this State. Its propriety having been drawn into question by the adversaries of that plan, is no light symptom of the rage for objection, which disorders their imaginations and judgments. The standard of good behavior for the continuance in office of the judicial magistracy, is certainly one of the most valuable of the modern improvements in the practice of government. In a monarchy it is an excellent barrier to the despotism of the prince; in a republic it is a no less excellent barrier to the encroachments and oppressions of the representative body. And it is the best expedient which can be devised in any government, to secure a steady, upright, and impartial administration of the laws.

26. What is Hamilton's point in this excerpt?
    a. To show the audience that despotism within a monarchy is no longer the standard practice in the states
    b. Hamilton is trying to convince the audience that judges holding their positions based on good behavior is a practical way to avoid corruption.
    c. To persuade the audience that having good behavior should be the primary characteristic of a person in a government body and their voting habits should reflect this
    d. To convey the position that judges who serve for a lifetime will not be perfect and, therefore, should be forgiven for their bad behavior when it arises

Constructed-Response #1

Use the information below to complete the exercise that follows.

Alexander Hamilton and Thomas Jefferson had diverging philosophical views about the nation's economic future. These differences led to larger political debates in the 1790s.

Using your knowledge of US history, prepare a response in which you:

- Identify two important philosophical differences that led to this debate;
- Identify the biggest cause for conflict; and
  - Explain why that cause was a decisive factor in bringing about the debates of the 1790s

Constructed-Response #2

Use the information below to complete the exercise that follows.

The Mexican-American War ended with a US victory against Mexico in 1848, forever changing the geographic landscape of North America.

Using your knowledge of US history, prepare a response in which you:

- Identify the factors leading to the war;
- Identify the ways in which the Bear Flag Revolt stemmed from the unrest of the Mexican-American War; and
- Explain the short-term and long-term consequences of the war.

Subtest II: Science

1. There are multiple steps that the gastrointestinal system performs. In which step do chemicals and enzymes break down complex food molecules into smaller molecules?
    a. Digestion
    b. Absorption
    c. Compaction
    d. Ingestion

2. How do neuroglia support neurons?
    a. They provide nutrition to neurons.
    b. They provide a framework around the neurons and protect them from the surrounding environment.
    c. They relay messages to neurons from the brain.
    d. They connect neurons to other surrounding cells.

3. In the periodic table, what similarity do the elements in columns have with each other?
    a. They have the same atomic number.
    b. They have similar chemical properties.
    c. They have similar electron valence configurations.
    d. They have the same density.

4. What number on the pH scale indicates a neutral solution?
    a. 13
    b. 8
    c. 7
    d. 0

5. Which molecule is the simplest form of sugar?
    a. Monosaccharide
    b. Fatty acid
    c. Polysaccharide
    d. Amino acid

6. Which type of macromolecule contains genetic information that can be passed to subsequent generations?
    a. Carbohydrates
    b. Lipids
    c. Proteins
    d. Nucleic acids

7. What is the primary unit of inheritance between generations of an organism?
    a. Chromosome
    b. Gene
    c. Gamete
    d. Atom

8. In which situation is an atom considered neutral?
    a. The number of protons and neutrons are equal.
    b. The number of neutrons and electrons are equal.
    c. The number of protons and electrons are equal.
    d. There are more electrons than protons.

9. Which is an example of a physical property of a substance?
   a. Odor
   b. Reactivity
   c. Flammability
   d. Toxicity

10. Which type of matter has molecules that cannot move within its substance and breaks evenly across a plane caused by the symmetry of its molecular arrangement?
   a. Gases
   b. Crystalline solids
   c. Liquids
   d. Amorphous solids

11. What type of reactions involve the breaking and re-forming of bonds between atoms?
   a. Chemical
   b. Physical
   c. Isotonic
   d. Electron

12. If a vehicle increases speed from 20 m/s to 40 m/s over a time period of 20 seconds, what is the vehicle's rate of acceleration?
   a. 2 m/s^2
   b. 1 m/s^2
   c. 10 m/s^2
   d. 20 m/s^2

13. Under which situation does an object have a negative acceleration?
   a. It is increasing velocity in a positive direction.
   b. It is at a complete stop.
   c. It is increasing velocity in a negative direction.
   d. It is moving at a constant velocity.

14. Which system consists of a group of organs that work together to transform food and liquids into fuel for the body?
   a. Respiratory system
   b. Immune system
   c. Genitourinary system
   d. Gastrointestinal system

Questions 15–18 are based on the following information:

Our solar system is made up of eight planets. In order from the Sun moving outward, they are Mercury, Venus, Earth, Mars, Jupiter, Saturn, Uranus, and Neptune. The first four planets are the smallest and have some similarities in characteristics, while the outer four planets are larger and also have some comparable traits. Kepler studied the movements of the planets and devised three laws for planetary motion. Some basic information regarding the planets is listed in the tables below:

Planet Name	Distance from Sun (km)	Mass (10^{24}kg)	Gravity (m/s^2)
Mercury	57.9 million	0.330	3.7
Venus	108.2 million	4.87	8.9
Earth	149.6 million	5.97	9.8
Mars	227.9 million	0.642	3.7
Jupiter	778.6 million	1,898	23.1
Saturn	1,433.5 million	568	9.0
Uranus	2,872.5 million	86.8	8.7
Neptune	4,495.1 million	102	11.0

Planet	Mercury	Venus	Earth	Mars	Jupiter	Saturn	Uranus	Neptune
Length of Orbit (Days)	88.0	224.7	365.2	687	4,331	10,747	30,589	59,800
Number of Moons	0	0	1	2	67	62	27	14

15. The mass of Venus is approximately what percentage of the Earth's mass?
    a. 8.16%
    b. 81.6%
    c. 1.22%
    d. 12.2%

16. What would NOT be a likely reason for the variations in gravity on each planet?
    a. The pull of the moons on a planet
    b. The speed of rotation of a planet
    c. The make-up of the core of a planet
    d. The mass of a planet

17. What is the average length of orbit, in days, of the planets listed?
    a. 365.2
    b. 13,354
    c. 29,944
    d. 59,800

18. Which distance is the shortest?
   a. Distance from Mercury to the Sun
   b. Distance from Mercury to Venus
   c. Distance from Venus to Earth
   d. Distance from Mars to Earth

19. Which two magnetic poles would attract each other?
   a. Two positive poles
   b. Two negative poles
   c. One positive pole and one negative pole
   d. Two circular positive magnets

20. Which of the following compounds is an example of a strong base?
   a. HCl
   b. HNO_3
   c. HBr
   d. NaOH

21. What is the primary difference between the Earth's inner core and outer core?
   a. The inner core is made of nickel, while the outer core is made of iron.
   b. The inner core is solid, while the outer core is molten.
   c. The inner core is inaccessible to people, while the outer core is accessible to people.
   d. The inner core is hot, while the outer core is cool.

22. Which of the following is an example of friction?
   a. A rubber band that is pulled taut then snapped
   b. Jumping on the end of a diving board
   c. Throwing a baseball at an angle
   d. Applying a car's brakes at a red light

23. The process in which a gas becomes a liquid is known as which of the following?
   a. Melting
   b. Sublimation
   c. Vaporization
   d. Condensation

24. Which of the following is an example of a homogenous mixture?
   a. Distilled water
   b. Sand
   c. Shallow tidal pools
   d. Deep ocean water

25. Which layer of the Earth is approximately 760 miles wide and comprised primarily of nickel and iron?
   a. The crust
   b. The atmosphere
   c. The mantle
   d. The inner core

26. Earthquakes and the formation of mountain ranges are two natural events influenced directly by which of the following geological processes?
   a. Underground sulfur springs
   b. Lunar cycles
   c. Plate tectonics
   d. Atmospheric pressure shifts

Constructed-Response #1

Use the information below to complete the exercise that follows.

A developing country has been focused on its economic output for the last fifty years, hoping to increase its status to a developed country. The country has focused on manufacturing, technology, and textiles. It has established a number of factories that run primarily off fossil fuels, and has employed thousands of workers in the nearby towns. Most of these workers are thrilled to have a relatively high-paying, stable job that allows them to support their families and have a personal vehicle for the commute. A visiting epidemiologist and environmental health specialist survey the town for approximately three months, in order to provide feedback to guide national occupational health and environmental regulations. While they notice many people have material belongings and bigger housing, they also notice that many marine organisms have depleted in count and the respiratory infection rate amongst citizens has dramatically increased.

Using your knowledge of the water and carbon cycles:

- Describe in detail the processes contributing to marine life depletion and the human respiratory problems;
- Describe conservation-oriented solutions that could be proposed within the regulatory feedback offered by the visiting scientists;
  - Explain one other potential health impact that the scientists should examine.

Constructed-Response #2

Use the information below to complete the exercise that follows.

A family is going on a beach vacation that has been planned for a year. The location is in the northern hemisphere. A week prior to the trip, they learn that there are some tropical disturbances near the body of water that they are visiting. They also hear in the news reports that the ocean water is about 10 degrees warmer than normal, and that the disturbances are expected to organize into a storm before reaching the warmer waters. When the family arrives at the ocean-front house they've rented for the vacation, they notice the water is a murky color and has an odd smell. Rows of dead fish are on the sand.

Using your knowledge of convection currents, climate and meteorological concepts, and disaster management:

- Describe the meteorological forces that will cause the tropical disturbance to develop into a storm, what physical changes might happen to the storm body as it moves into warmer waters, and what factors contribute to these changes;

- Describe the phenomenon that is occurring in front of the beach house, what contributed to this event, and how marine and coastal organisms are likely to be impacted;

- Develop a safety plan for the family to follow to prepare for a coastal natural disaster and list the technological tools that could be used by both the family and the beach town in this scenario.

Subtest II: Mathematics

1. What is the product of $\frac{5}{14}$ and $\frac{7}{20}$, in lowest possible terms?
    a. $\frac{1}{8}$
    b. $\frac{35}{280}$
    c. $\frac{12}{34}$
    d. $\frac{1}{2}$

2. What is the solution to the equation $3(x + 2) = 14x - 5$?
    a. $x = 1$
    b. No solution
    c. $x = 0$
    d. All real numbers

3. What is the result of dividing 24 by $\frac{8}{5}$, in lowest possible terms?
    a. $\frac{5}{3}$
    b. $\frac{3}{5}$
    c. $\frac{120}{8}$
    d. 15

4. Which of the following is the result when solving the equation $4(x + 5) + 6 = 2(2x + 3)$?
    a. Any real number is a solution.
    b. There is no solution.
    c. $x = 6$ is the solution.
    d. $x = 26$ is the solution.

5. Subtract $\frac{5}{14}$ from $\frac{5}{24}$. Which of the following is the correct result?
    a. $\frac{25}{168}$
    b. 0
    c. $-\frac{25}{168}$
    d. $\frac{1}{10}$

6. Which of the following is a correct mathematical statement?

    a. $\dfrac{1}{3} < -\dfrac{4}{3}$

    b. $-\dfrac{1}{3} > \dfrac{4}{3}$

    c. $\dfrac{1}{3} > -\dfrac{4}{3}$

    d. $-\dfrac{1}{3} \geq \dfrac{4}{3}$

7. What is the median for the times shown in the chart below?

100 m Dash Times	
Olivia	11 s
Noah	13 s
Amelia	15 s
Elijah	12 s
Luca	12 s
Chloe	16 s
Asher	19 s

    a.   11 s
    b.   14 s
    c.   12 s
    d.   13 s

8. A car manufacturer usually makes 15,412 SUVs, 25,815 station wagons, 50,412 sedans, 8,123 trucks, and 18,312 hybrids a month. About how many cars are manufactured each month?

    a.   120,000
    b.   200,000
    c.   300,000
    d.   12,000

9. A family goes to the grocery store every week and spends $105. About how much does the family spend annually on groceries?

    a. $10,000
    b. $50,000
    c. $500
    d. $5,000

10. Bindee is having a barbeque on Sunday and needs 12 packets of ketchup for every 5 guests. If 60 guests are coming, how many packets of ketchup should she buy?

    a.   100
    b.   12
    c.   144
    d.   60

11. A grocery store sold 48 bags of apples in one day. If 9 of the bags contained Granny Smith apples and the rest contained Red Delicious apples, what is the ratio of Granny Smith bags to Red Delicious bags that were sold?
   a. 48:9
   b. 39:9
   c. 9:48
   d. 9:39

12. If Oscar's bank account totaled $4,000 in March and $4,900 in June, what was the rate of change in his bank account total over those three months?
   a. $900 a month
   b. $300 a month
   c. $4,900 a month
   d. $100 a month

13. From the graph below, which two genres are preferred by more men than women?

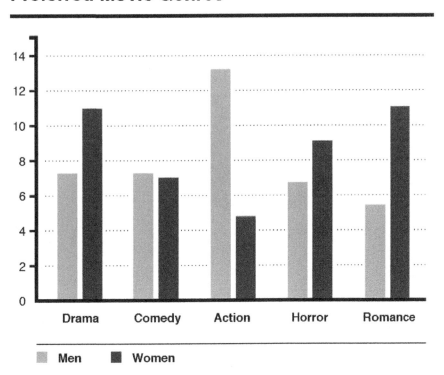

Preferred Movie Genres

   a. Drama and comedy
   b. Comedy and action
   c. Action and horror
   d. Horror and drama

14. Which type of graph best represents a continuous change over a period of time?
   a. Bar graph
   b. Line graph
   c. Pie graph
   d. Histogram

15. What is the area of the shaded region?

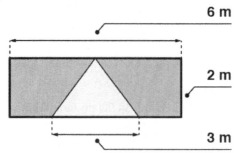

a. 9 m²
b. 12 m²
c. 6 m²
d. 8 m²

16. What is the volume of the cylinder below? Use 3.14 for π.

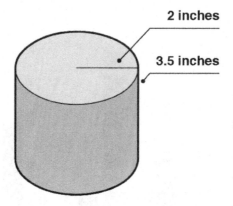

a. 18.84 in³
b. 45.00 in³
c. 70.43 in³
d. 43.96 in³

17. How many kiloliters are in 6 liters?
    a. 6,000
    b. 600
    c. 0.006
    d. 0.0006

18. What type of units are used to describe surface area?
    a. Square
    b. Cubic
    c. Single
    d. Quartic

19. Which of the following is the equation of a vertical line that runs through the point $(1, 4)$?
    a. $x = 1$
    b. $y = 1$
    c. $x = 4$
    d. $y = 4$

20. What is the area of the following figure?

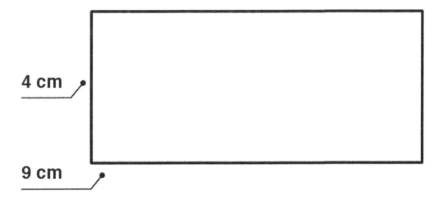

    a. 26 cm
    b. 36 cm
    c. 13 cm^2
    d. 36 cm^2

21. Approximately how many pounds are in 5 kilograms?
    a. 5 lbs
    b. 8 lbs
    c. 11 lbs
    d. 14 lbs

22. Use the graph below entitled "Projected Temperatures for Tomorrow's Winter Storm" to answer the question.

Projected Temperatures for Tomorrow's Winter Storm

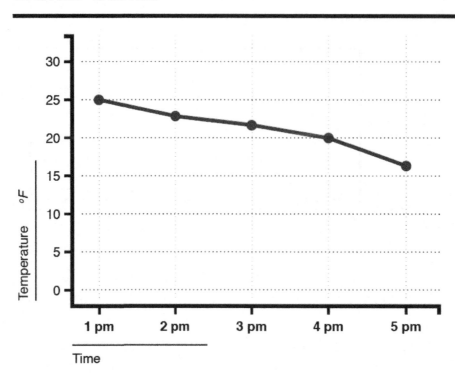

What is the expected temperature at 3:00 p.m.?
- a. 25 degrees
- b. 22 degrees
- c. 20 degrees
- d. 16 degrees

23. What is the missing length x?

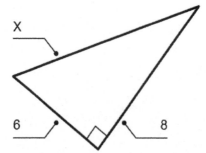

- a. 6
- b. 14
- c. 10
- d. 100

24. What is the solution to the following linear inequality?

$$7 - \frac{4}{5}x < \frac{3}{5}$$

a. $(-\infty, 8)$
b. $(8, \infty)$
c. $[8, \infty)$
d. $(-\infty, 8]$

25. What is the solution to the following system of linear equations?

$$2x + y = 14$$

$$4x + 2y = -28$$

a. $(0, 0)$
b. $(14, -28)$
c. All real numbers
d. There is no solution

26. What is the probability of rolling a number larger than 4 on a six-sided die?
a. $\frac{1}{6}$

b. $\frac{1}{3}$

c. $\frac{1}{2}$

d. $\frac{2}{3}$

Constructed-Response #1

Use the information below to complete the exercise that follows.

You have been asked to construct a garden at your grandmother's house. She wants to have three large flower beds, totaling 400 square feet. One flower bed needs to be built in the shape of a square, and the other two need to be triangular.

What is one scenario that will satisfy her request? Specifically, what is the measurement of the sides of the square bed, and what are the base and height dimensions of each of the triangular beds? The two triangles do not have to be equal in size. A drawing might be helpful in this problem. Finally, if you are going to close off the square flower bed with fencing, how many feet of fencing do you need?

Constructed-Response #2

Use the information below to complete the exercise that follows.

You have decided to add a recreation room onto the first floor of your house. It needs to be rectangular in shape, and in order to stick to your budget, its total area needs to be less than 400 square feet. However, you want it to be larger than 300 square feet to fit your new pool table and couch. This room will share one wall with your house.

Use the following grid to draw the room, making sure to label the dimensions of each side. Each square on the grid represents 1 square foot. Once the room is built, the floor will be tiled. If each tile costs $5.15 per square foot, what will the total cost be to tile the room? What is the perimeter of the room?

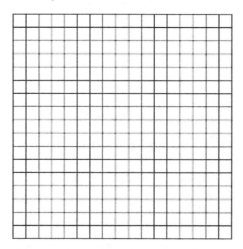

Subtest III: Physical Education

1. Which of the following is an appropriate use of frequency to help a 16-year-old female student achieve their goal of running a mile in under 8 minutes?
    a. Begin every PE class with 10 minutes of jogging.
    b. Encourage the student to sign up for the basketball team with her friends.
    c. Suggest that the student track how often she and her friends go running after school.
    d. Invite the student to jog for a longer period at the beginning of each PE class.

2. How might a unit on weightlifting in a high school PE class improve the students' positive self-image?
    a. Lifting weights increases the workout's intensity. Increased muscular strength improves a student's idea of their physical appearance.
    b. Learning proper weightlifting techniques encourages students to practice making and achieving personal goals.
    c. Weightlifting encourages adolescent competition, supporting those who perform well compared to their peers.
    d. Building muscular strength inspires students to continue exercising and reduces the likelihood of illness due to inactivity later in life.

3. Which component of physical fitness is improved by jogging for 10 minutes at the start of each high school physical education class?
    a. Cardiorespiratory endurance
    b. Muscular endurance
    c. Frequency
    d. Body composition

4. Which of the following is an example of anaerobic exercise?
    a. Playing basketball each Saturday morning with friends
    b. An hour of interval training, where the student sprints across the gym and completes a set of weightlifting exercises
    c. A cheerleader's daily after-school practice of dance rehearsal, gymnastics, and lifting teammates
    d. Completing five sets of 10 squats while holding a 50-pound weight, with a short rest in between

314

Practice Test #1

5. Which of the following is NOT a risk of living a sedentary lifestyle?
   a. Obesity
   b. Heart disease
   c. High blood pressure
   d. Type 1 diabetes

6. A 13-year-old girl working out for the fall season of cross country goes running for 20 minutes on Mondays, Wednesdays, and Fridays. The coach suggests she increase her running time to 25 minutes. Which principle of exercise does the coach's suggestion make use of?
   a. Intensity
   b. Time
   c. Frequency
   d. None—the coach's suggestion is intended to improve the girl's cardiorespiratory endurance.

7. Which of the following fitness regimes would best help an 11-year-old boy improve his body composition over a period of three months?
   a. Do light jogging every day, starting at 15 minutes and increasing by 5 minutes per week until the boy reaches 60 minutes each day.
   b. Focus on changing the child's diet, incorporating exercise naturally through sports and outdoor play as time allows.
   c. Play basketball for 30 minutes on Mondays, Wednesdays, and Fridays. On Tuesdays and Thursdays, play catch with a medicine ball, go rowing, or do another form of exercise that uses the upper body.
   d. Perform body weight exercises with parents every Monday and Friday evening, such as pushups, crunches, holding a plank position, and jumping jacks.

8. Ten children are spaced irregularly in a gymnasium for an activity in which they will stand still and throw a ball to one another in an attempt to keep the ball in the air as long as possible. Which category of physical skills does this activity demonstrate?
   a. Relationships
   b. Manipulative skills
   c. Non-locomotor skills
   d. Throwing and catching

9. Which of the following activities practices the movement concept of effort?
   a. Zigzagging between cones in a race between students
   b. Running and jumping to reach a basketball net
   c. Learning to swim
   d. Practicing a baseball swing over and over

10. Which of the following demonstrates a manipulative physical skill?
    a. Skipping 100 meters
    b. Avoiding a dodgeball
    c. Dribbling a basketball
    d. Climbing on a playground

11. Which of the following physical skills most often makes use of biomechanical momentum for optimal performance?
    a. Balancing on one foot
    b. Throwing a baseball
    c. Touching one's toes
    d. Catching a football

12. If a six-year-old boy struggles to master hopping on one foot, in later years he may have difficulty learning to:
    a. Kick a soccer ball.
    b. Perform a standing long jump.
    c. Dance a waltz.
    d. Make a basketball layup.

13. Which of the following is a traditional childhood game?
    a. Freeze tag
    b. Ultimate Frisbee
    c. Hiking
    d. 100-meter sprint

Constructed-Response #1

Design an activity for a fourth-grade physical education class.

How does the activity incorporate cooperative behavior? How does it incorporate competitive behavior?

Subtest III: Human Development

1. Which of the following statements demonstrates childhood egocentrism?
    a. "Give the toy back, it's mine."
    b. "Don't buy me those red shoes—I know everyone will make fun of me because they're ugly."
    c. "Can't you tell I need the blue pencil?"
    d. "We didn't eat lunch yet, so it can't be afternoon."

2. An 11-year-old girl says, "The election for class president was unfair because Timmy was absent and didn't vote for me." Does the student's statement reflect use of abstract concepts? Why or why not?
    a. Yes. Claiming the election was unfair indicates that the student is beginning to use ideas such as democracy or justice.
    b. Yes. Understanding that an absent peer may have voted for her demonstrates the student no longer requires concrete subjects of thought to be present.
    c. No. The student is not yet a teenager and therefore has not entered the stage of formal operations in her cognitive development.
    d. No. This statement reflects the student's perception of unfairness to herself, not participation in an abstract concept.

3. Which behavior in a seven-year-old boy best describes practicing classification?
    a. Collecting trading cards and sorting them alphabetically
    b. Assembling and deconstructing a LEGO® set until he can build it without reading the instructions
    c. Inventing rules for a make-believe game with his classmates
    d. Collecting rocks on a field trip for show and tell

4. A 10-year-old girl struggles to pay attention for longer than 30 minutes during classroom instruction and has difficulty remembering information on arithmetic and language arts tests. She is social with her classmates and enjoys participating in both structured and unstructured songs and games. With which of the multiple intelligences does this student seem strong and weak?
    a. Strong with creative; weak with analytic
    b. Strong with practical; weak with analytic
    c. Strong with creative; weak with practical
    d. Not enough information to say

5. Which of the following students best represents an individual who makes moral judgments using conventional morality?
   a. A clever six-year-old girl who struggles to share toys with classmates unless the teacher intervenes
   b. A punctual 14-year-old boy who doesn't want to waste his friends' time
   c. A quiet eight-year-old boy arguing that countries shouldn't go to war because then other countries will enter into war with them
   d. A studious 17-year-old girl scolding her friend after the friend was caught cheating

6. What is an appropriate first support to provide for a seven-year-old girl who still struggles to learn to read?
   a. Ask a counselor to evaluate the child for dyslexia.
   b. Encourage the parents to pay for private tutoring so she can catch up with her classmates.
   c. Use part of the student's allotted recess time to provide additional reading instruction.
   d. Advocate for transferring the student to a classroom with an emphasis on special education.

7. Which of the following is an accurate sign a teacher might notice which indicates that a 13-year-old girl is experiencing puberty?
   a. She grew three inches since the last school year.
   b. She has begun talking more about dating and romance.
   c. She has visible underarm hair.
   d. She has started wearing cosmetics.

8. A student who jumps when their name is called, looks tired or sleeps during class, and dislikes playing games involving physical contact (such as tag) may be experiencing:
   a. Sexual abuse
   b. Reactive attachment disorder
   c. Neglect
   d. Late nights using their phone

9. Which of the following is an element of the pragmatics of a language?
   a. Proximity to another speaker
   b. Using past, present, and future tense
   c. Speaking in full sentences
   d. Slang that expresses meaning quickly

10. How might a high school music teacher best motivate their students to engage in class material?
    a. Invite a local pianist to play live music for the class.
    b. Focus on the music of Bach, Mozart, and other composers with universal appeal.
    c. Provide simple percussive instruments so the students can experiment together with rhythm and melody.
    d. Listen to contemporary pop songs to provide music theory examples.

11. How might malnutrition during infancy and early childhood impact a child's physical development?
    a. Without sufficient nutrients, the child is at increased risk of developing autism spectrum disorder.
    b. The myelin coating on the child's nervous system may take longer to develop, impacting their physical growth and development of motor skills.
    c. The child will need to remain nursing longer, hindering their social independence.
    d. The child should start school earlier, taking advantage of free lunch programs in order to improve nutrition.

12. Which of the following examples describes a student struggling with practical intelligence?
    a. A seven-year-old girl who knows roads near her house but struggles with reading unfamiliar signs
    b. A 14-year-old boy with a history of emotional abuse who feels so anxious when called on to answer math problems that he has asked the teacher not to call on him
    c. A 12-year-old girl who refuses to use the library to study despite complaining about noise in the classroom
    d. An eight-year-old boy with good marks on spelling tests who struggles to use new vocabulary in composition essays

13. At what age should learning and social supports be implemented for a child diagnosed with autism spectrum disorder? Why?
    a. When entering school around age five because children with autism spectrum disorder only begin struggling with communication once in a social environment outside of the home
    b. When entering high school around age 14 because teenagers are more aware of difficulties socializing than younger children
    c. One year after the diagnosis to make sure the child really does have autism spectrum disorder
    d. As young as possible because early intervention generally improves outcomes

Constructed-Response #1

Summarize the cognitive developments that take place as a typical child moves from preschool to elementary school. Then describe how these changes in the child's thought process impact their development of emotion management and social skills.

Subtest III: Visual and Performing Arts

1. Which of the following CANNOT be used as inspiration for dances?
    a. Images
    b. Poems
    c. Tasks
    d. None of the above

2. What is the dance term used to describe your body's directional weight?
    a. Frame
    b. Balance
    c. Poise
    d. Posture

3. Which of the following is NOT a helpful question to ask when analyzing dances?
    a. Do I think the dance is good?
    b. What genre of dance is this?
    c. Do I like the dance?
    d. How is the dance structured?

4. What is the range of notes on a music staff?
    a. A to F
    b. A to H
    c. A to A
    d. A to G

5. What does the bottom number in a time signature indicate?
    a. How many beats comprise a single measure
    b. How many quarter notes should be in a measure
    c. How many measures are in a bar
    d. What kind of note is given a single beat

6. If a key signature has three sharps in it, what key is the music in?
    a. E major
    b. G major
    c. A major
    d. F# major

7. Which type of music is free from cultural influence?
    a. Narrative music
    b. Improvised music
    c. Educational music
    d. None of the above

8. Which of the following story beats should occur latest in a traditional plot?
    a. Exposition
    b. Falling action
    c. Climax
    d. Interlude

9. When improvising a story with another person, what is the most important rule to remember?
    a. Establish a framework story before the performance.
    b. Assign one scene partner to steer the story while the rest support their narrative.
    c. "Yes, and" your partner and contribute new details to the story that support what has already been established.
    d. Ensure that there are no inconsistencies in your story.

10. Which type of prop is ideal for most student theatre?
    a. Representational props
    b. Non-representational props
    c. Both are equally appropriate depending on the situation.
    d. Neither is appropriate.

11. Which of the following does NOT degrade the quality of charcoal sticks?
    a. Water
    b. Excessive pressure
    c. Air exposure
    d. Oil from your skin

12. Which of the following is NOT a quality that determines something's color?
    a. Saturation
    b. Sharpness
    c. Hue
    d. Brightness

13. Which of the following art categories are you least likely to see in a museum?
    a. Persuasive art
    b. Narrative art
    c. Educational art
    d. Expressive art

Constructed-Response #1

Use the information below to complete the exercise that follows.

A standard plot contains, in this order, an exposition, rising action, a climax, falling action, and a resolution. Using your knowledge of storytelling:

- Identify a plot in which these story elements are given differently or out of this established order.

- Explain what this intentional re-structuring of the plot says about the story's message, concept, or design on a technical level.

Answer Explanations #1

Subtest I: Reading, Language, and Literature

1. A: The answer is Choice *A*, anthropomorphism, because anthropomorphism gives human-like traits to non-human things. Choice *B*, synecdoche, is wrong because it is any figure of speech that is only presented as a part but is representative of a whole. Choice *C*, conceit, is wrong because a conceit is a comparison of two unlike things that extends throughout the entirety of a paragraph, chapter, stanza, set of stanzas, poem, or novel. This is sometimes referred to as a sustained metaphor. Choice *D*, onomatopoeia, is wrong because it is a word used to mimic a sound.

2. A: The answer is Choice *A*, teaching students to hear individual phonemes in words. This answer is right because research shows this is the last, and most complex, step for teaching students how to read. Choices *B-D* are listed in decreasing order of complexity.

3. D: The answer is Choice *D*, code switching, because this is the official term used to describe the act of changing levels, dialects, or types of language based on context. Choice *A*, alliteration, is a literary device that repeats word sounds within a sentence. Choice *B*, "objectivity," is a scientific, factual type of evidence. Choice *C*, phonemic awareness, is a reading strategy that helps students identify and understand phonemes in words.

4. D: The topic sentence in a paragraph may be stated explicitly, or it may only be implied, requiring the reader to infer what the topic is rather than identify it as an overt statement. Thus, Choice *D* is correct. The topic sentence of a paragraph is often at or near the beginning, but not always, so Choice *A* is incorrect. Some topic sentences are at the ends of paragraphs but not always. Therefore, Choice *B* is incorrect. There is more than one topic sentence in an essay, especially if the essay is built on multiple paragraphs, so Choice *C* is incorrect.

5. B: *Phobos* means "fear" in Greek. From it, English has derived the word *phobia*, meaning an abnormal or exaggerated fear, and a multitude of other words ending in *-phobia*. The beginnings of such words specify the object of the fear, as seen in the examples given. The Greek word for love, Choice A, is *phil*, found in English words such as *philosophy, hydrophilic, philanthropist,* and *philharmonic*. The Greek word for hate, Choice *C*, is *miseo*, found in English words like *misogyny* and *misanthrope*. The Greek word meaning wise or knowledge, Choice *D*, is *sophos*, found in English words such as *sophisticated* and *philosophy*.

6. D: Some writing techniques recommend varying sentence structures among simple, compound, complex, and compound-complex, making Choice *D* correct. Other techniques for attaining sentence fluency include varying the beginnings of sentences, making Choice *A* incorrect; varying sentence lengths rather than making them all uniform, making Choice *B* incorrect; and varying sentence rhythms rather than consistently using the same rhythm, making Choice *C* incorrect.

7. D: A complex sentence is one that contains at least one independent clause and at least one dependent clause. Choices *A* and *B* are incorrect because the number of prepositional phrases or indefinite pronouns has no bearing on whether a sentence is considered complex. Choice *C* is incorrect because a sentence with two independent clauses is a compound sentence.

8. D: Choice *D* is correct because parallelism refers to the state of being the same or congruent. The present participles *writing, playing,* and *eating* are congruent parts of speech within a list and are thus parallel. Choices *A*, *B*, and *C* are all unrelated.

9. C: Common knowledge is typically considered to be well-known facts that can be found undocumented in five or more scholarly sources. An example of common knowledge is the fact that the boiling point of water is 212 °F. Common knowledge does not need to be cited, so Choice *C* is correct. Summaries and paraphrases, Choices *A* and *B*, are a condensed version of another person's writing in one's own words. Even though the writer rephrases the original content in their own words, the ideas are not original and therefore require a citation to give credit to the original author. Direct quotations, Choice *D*, are completely borrowed from someone else and must be attributed to their original author or speaker.

10. D: A glossary is a section in a book that provides brief definitions or explanations for words that the reader may not know. Choice *A* is incorrect because a table of contents shows where each section of the book is located. Choice *B* is incorrect because the introduction is usually a chapter that introduces the book about to be read. Choice *C* is incorrect because an index is usually a list of alphabetical references at the end of a book that a reader can look up to get more information.

11. D: Prewriting involves the steps a writer completes before actually starting to write, such as researching, brainstorming, developing the thesis, outlining, etc. Choice *A* is incorrect because drafting is done after prewriting. Choice *B* is incorrect because revising cannot be accomplished until the writing has occurred. Choice *C* is incorrect because, if a piece or writing is going to be published, that would be the very final step in the process once all prewriting, writing, and revising/editing is finished.

12. A: The best answer that captures the author's purpose is Choice *A*, because the author compares Norwegian and American prison recidivism rates. Although it is obvious the author favors rehabilitation, Choice *B* is incorrect because the author never asks for donations from the audience. Choices *C* and *D* are also incorrect. We can infer from the passage that American prisons are probably harsher than Norwegian prisons as a result of the author's comparisons; it is not their purpose to inform or convince us.

13. D: The passage explains how Norway believes that prisoner rehabilitation reduces the likelihood of a prisoner to reoffend, as evidenced by their smaller rate of recidivism. Choices *A* and *B*, the lack of violence and the opportunity of inmates to receive therapy, are both positive attributes, so Norway would probably not have a lower rate of these two things. Choice *C* is possible, but it does not make sense in the context. The author does not talk about tactics to keep prisoners inside the compound but rather ways in which to rehabilitate criminals so that they can live as citizens when they get out of prison.

14. B: This excerpt is considered a secondary source because it actively interprets primary sources. We see direct quotes from the queen, which would be considered a primary source (Choice *A*). But since we see those quotes being interpreted and analyzed, the excerpt becomes a secondary source. Choice *C*, tertiary source, is an index of secondary and primary sources, like an encyclopedia or Wikipedia.

15. B: It took two years for the new castle to be built. The author states this in the first sentence of the second paragraph. In the third year, Choice *C*, we see the Prince planning improvements and arranging things for the fourth year.

16. C: Choice *C* is correct because the phrase in the passage is meant figuratively since the workmen did most of the physical labor, not the Prince. The sentence states that "the impress of his dear hand [has] been stamped everywhere." Choice *A* is one definition of *impress*, but this definition is used more as a verb than a noun: "She impressed us as a songwriter." Choice *B* is incorrect because it is also used as a verb: "He impressed the need for something to be done." Choice *D* is incorrect because it is part of a physical act: "The businessman impressed his mark upon the envelope."

17. A: The passage presents us with a sequence of events that happens in chronological order. Choice *B* is incorrect because cause and effect organization would explain why something happened or list the effects of something. Choice *C* is incorrect because problem and solution organization would detail a problem and then present a solution to the audience, and there is no solution presented here. Finally, Choice *D* is incorrect because we are entered directly into the narrative without any main idea or any kind of argument being delivered.

18. C: Choice C is the correct answer. The original source of the analogy displays someone significant to an event who leaves, and then the event becomes worse for it. We see Mr. Sothern leave the theater company, and then the play becomes a "very dull affair." Choice *A* depicts a dancer who backs out of an event before the final performance, so this is incorrect. Choice *B* shows a basketball player leaving an event, and then the team makes it to the championship but

322

then loses. This choice could be a contestant for the right answer; however, we don't know if the team has become worse for his departure or better for it. Choice *D* is incorrect; the actor departs an event, but there is no assessment of the quality of the movie. It simply states what actors filled in instead.

19. C: Choice *C* is the correct answer because the word "unremarkable" should be changed to "remarkable" in order for it to be consistent with the details of the passage. This question requires close attention to the passage. Choice *A* can be found where the passage says, "no less than six named and several unnamed varieties of the peach have thus produced several varieties of nectarine," so this choice is incorrect. Choice *B* can be found where the passage says "it is highly improbable that all these peach-trees ... are hybrids from the peach and nectarine." Choice *D* is incorrect because the passage says, "the production of peaches from nectarines, either by seeds or buds, may perhaps be considered as a case of reversion."

20. A: The word *multiplied* is synonymous with the word *propagated*, making Choice *A* correct. The context of the passage implies that the number of peach trees has increased. Choice *B* is incorrect because *diminished* means to decrease or recede and is the opposite of *propagated*. Choice *C* is incorrect; *watered* is closer, but it pertains to the growth of trees in development rather than in number. Finally, Choice *D* is incorrect; *uprooted* could also pertain to trees, but in the sense of moving or pulling out of the ground.

21. B: The author's tone in this passage can be considered objective. An objective tone means that the author is open-minded and detached about the subject. Most scientific articles are objective. Choices *A*, *C*, and *D* are incorrect. The author is not very enthusiastic on the paper; the author is not critical but rather interested in the topic. The author is not desperate in any way here.

22. B: Choice *B* is the correct answer because the meaning holds true even if the words have been switched out or rearranged some. Choice *A* is incorrect because it has trees either bearing peaches or nectarines, and the trees in the original phrase bear both. Choice *C* is incorrect because the statement does not say these trees are "indifferent to bud-variation," but that they "indifferently [bore] peaches or nectarines." Choice *D* is incorrect; the statement may use some of the same words, but the meaning is skewed in this sentence.

23. A: Choice *A* is the best answer. To write a direct quotation, double quotation marks are placed at the beginning and ending of the quoted words. All punctuation specifically related to the quoted phrase or sentence is kept inside the quotation marks. Single quotation marks, as those used in Choices *B* and *C*, are not used for dialogue in American English.

24. B: The best answer is Choice *B*. The reciprocal pronoun "one another" generally refers to more than two people. Choice *C* implies each person would look at themselves, while Choice *D* refers to individual objects.

25. C: The best answer is Choice *C*: "Lulu brought this kitten home only six weeks ago, and she was so fond of her." There are two independent clauses in one sentence, so separating the two clauses with a comma is the best option. The original line and Choice B do not separate the clauses with a comma. Additionally, the information that Lulu was only five years old is not necessary in this particular sentence; it is out of context, making Choice *D* incorrect.

26. C: Choice *C* is the best answer. We would use the preposition *through* when talking about staying with someone during the night. In the original line, *across* is a preposition that refers to objects in orientation to each other, e.g., "across the road." Choice *B* doesn't make sense in this context. *Amidst* refers to something in the middle of two objects, making Choice *D* incorrect.

Subtest I: History and Social Science

1. C: Calhoun led the state of South Carolina in the nullification crisis, which championed state rights over federal rights and almost led to secession. Choice *A*, Henry Clay, actually helped create a compromise between John C. Calhoun and US President Andrew Jackson. James K. Polk was the US president who led Americans into the Mexican-American War.

2. A: The original constitutional convention occurred in 1849, a year after the annexation of California. Revisions to the California Constitution occurred in 1879, thirty years after the original convention. These are the two major conventions. All other answer choices are simply false distractors.

3. D: The flooding of the Tigris and Euphrates rivers helped fertilize the Fertile Crescent of Mesopotamia, leading to the advancement of a civilization there. Egypt was established along the Nile River. China emerged near the Yellow River. The Hebrew civilization developed near the Mediterranean Sea.

4. D: Hamilton and Jefferson's biggest point of contention was the formation of a national bank. Hamilton staunchly supported a national bank while Jefferson fervently opposed it. Hamilton wanted to centralize the minting and banking of money. Both Jefferson and Hamilton, like many early leaders, supported slavery, making Choice *A* incorrect. There is no historical record of a debate over the Declaration of Independence between Jefferson and Hamilton. Political debate over the War of 1812 occurred later, after Hamilton's death.

5. A: Jamestown was mostly settled by people from the Anglican religion, also known as the Church of England, the official national church. The Dutch Reform Church (Choice *B*) was the major religion of New Amsterdam, the Dutch colony in modern-day New York. Puritans settled mostly in New England. Roman Catholics settled in small pockets, mostly Maryland and Georgia.

6. A: Islam first entered Europe when the Umayyad Dynasty established itself in Spain in the 700s, creating a strong Muslim state called Al-Andalus. The Mughal Empire, Choice *B*, was located in the Indian subcontinent between the 16th and 19th centuries. The Safavid Empire expanded from the Middle East to Central Asia throughout the 15th to 18th centuries, making Choice *C* incorrect. The Ottoman Empire expanded across North Africa, Europe, and the Middle East. It lasted from the 15th century to the 20th century, when it fell after World War I.

7. A: The Supreme Court case of *Worcester v. Georgia* saw the Cherokee Nation sue the state of Georgia for forcibly removing their people with its militia. The Supreme Court ruled that Georgia had no right to remove the Cherokee; only the federal government had that right. Georgia, however, ignored the decision and maintained its violent efforts. Choice *B*, *McCulloch v. Maryland*, ruled that the federal government had the power to establish a national bank. Choices *C* and *D* were landmark cases during the 20th century.

8. A: The Magna Carta (Great Charter) championed the basic political rights of all English citizens. The goal was to place more power in the hands of the nobles by limiting the king's powers. On June 15, 1215, King John reluctantly accepted the Magna Carta under the pressure of the nobles' resistance. Originally, the document only had clauses that extended rights to the nobles. However, in later years, the Magna Carta's democratic values evolved to include *all* citizens of England. These rights included such principles as: no taxation without representation, the right to a fair trial by jury, and protection of citizens by the law. The Declaration of Sentiments is an important women's suffrage document. The Quartering Act was a controversial English colonial act in the Thirteen Colonies that helped pave the way to the American Revolution. *Common Sense* was written by Thomas Paine in response to growing debates over whether the colonies should claim independence.

9. B: Choice *B*, the Nubian kingdom of Kush, resided just south of Egypt, along the upper Nile River. For centuries, the Kush kingdom had served as a sort of vassal state for Ancient Egypt. When Egypt's power declined in 1000 BC, however, Nubia established a Kushite dynasty on the Egyptian throne. The Hebrew civilization developed along the Mediterranean Sea, near modern-day Israel. The Umayyad Dynasty was concentrated in North Africa and Spain in the 700s. The Safavid Empire expanded from the Middle East to Central Asia prior to the 15th century.

10. C: The answer is Choice *C*; the number of representatives is dictated by a state's population size. Although being a senator is typically seen as prestigious (Choice *A*), prestige has no effect on the number of representatives and senators in office. Voters choose representatives in elections, but they do not choose how many representatives there are in office (Choice *B*). The Bill of Rights does not discuss the necessary number of congressmen (Choice *D*).

11. D: Northern Whigs and Free Soil Democrats created the Republican Party to advocate for the abolition of slavery, so Choice *D* is the correct answer. Abraham Lincoln was the first Republican to be elected president. The Republicans exposed the Southern theory of states' rights, and their pro-business agenda didn't develop until after the Civil War. Manifest Destiny also wasn't the Republicans primary issue.

12. D: Immediately after the federal government withdrew troops from the South, ending Reconstruction, the Southern states enacted Jim Crow laws. These laws contravened the Reconstruction Amendments by preventing African Americans from voting and enforcing segregation policies. Therefore, Choice *D* is the correct answer. African Americans voted for the first time during Reconstruction, but following the passage of Jim Crow laws, they couldn't vote until the 1960s civil rights movement. The South didn't diversify from a one-crop economy (cotton) or industrialize until the 20th century.

13. B: The speech was made before the Civil War, which began in 1861; it captures the rising tension over slavery between the North and the South. Choices *A* and *D* are incorrect because Lincoln is not talking about an actual house. Instead, he is talking about a nation divided over slavery by using the metaphor of a house. Choice *C* is incorrect because the speech was given in 1858 before the secession of South Carolina and the dissolution of the Union in 1861.

14. A: Spanish explorers established St. Augustine in 1565. All other colonies were founded at least a decade later, making Choice *A* the right answer. Sir Walter Raleigh founded Roanoke in 1585, making it the first British colony, but it was abandoned by 1590. Established in 1607, Jamestown was the first successful British colony, making Choice *C* incorrect. Choice *D* is incorrect because the British explorer Henry Hudson did not explore Hudson's Bay until the 1610s, with the French establishing trading outposts in the area during the 1670s.

15. A: The 10th Amendment reserves all non-specific powers to the states or people, establishing the principle of federalism; Choice *A* is the correct answer. The Ninth Amendment, Choice *B*, establishes the existence of unnamed rights. The Second Amendment protects the right to bear arms, making Choice *C* incorrect. The Fourth, Fifth, and Sixth Amendments include procedural protections for people accused of crimes.

16. B: Choice *B* is the correct answer. Widespread urbanization didn't occur until after the Civil War; it was caused by the technological innovations of the Second Industrial Revolution, like steel production, railways, and more sophisticated factory machinery. The United States first industrialized during the First Industrial Revolution to replace the decline in British imports caused by the War of 1812; however, this development was limited to towns in the Northeast. The Great Migration and successive waves of immigration, Choices *C* and *D*, increased the pace of urbanization, supplying labor to the urban boom. Yet, urbanization wouldn't have occurred without the Second Industrial Revolution transforming America from an agricultural to industrial economy.

17. C: The government makes all decisions related to production, distribution, and price in a centrally planned economic system; therefore, Choice *C* is the correct answer. This allows communist governments to oversee price control, and, as a result, the production and distribution of resources is less efficient but more equitable. If a government distributes resources solely based on merit and allows private markets to set prices, as in Choices *A* and *B*, then the economy is operating under a free-market system. A government that balances a private and public sector is characteristic of a mixed economic system, making Choice *D* incorrect.

18. A: The Missouri Compromise did not ban slavery in Washington, D.C.; therefore, Choice *A* is correct. The Compromise of 1850 banned slavery in Washington, D.C. The question is asking what was NOT included in the Missouri Compromise of 1820. The Missouri Compromise had three parts: Maine was admitted as a free state (Choice *D*); Missouri was admitted as a slave state (Choice *B*); and slavery was prohibited in new territories north of the 36°30' parallel (Choice *C*).

19. A: The Treaty of Paris concluded the American Revolution, securing American independence. Thus, Choice *A* is the correct answer. The Treaty of Ghent, Choice *B*, ended the War of 1812. The United States and France signed the Treaty of Alliance, Choice *C*, during the American Revolution, and French support turned the tides of war for the Americans. Choice *D* is incorrect because the Treaty of Versailles ended World War I.

20. A: Delegates at the American Constitutional Convention agreed on the Connecticut Compromise, establishing two legislative bodies. Representation in one house was based on population (House of Representatives), and the other granted each state two votes (Senate). As such, Choice *A* is the correct answer. The New Jersey Plan proposed a single legislative body with one vote per state, as per Choice *D*, but it was rejected in favor of the Connecticut Compromise.

21. D: None of the candidates received both the majority of the popular vote and the majority of electoral votes. Samuel J. Tilden received the majority of the popular vote, and Rutherford B. Hayes received the majority of electoral votes. Thus, Choice *D* is the correct answer. Rutherford B. Hayes received the majority of electoral votes, so the Republican candidate won the presidential election. Therefore, Choice *A* is incorrect. Samuel J. Tilden won the popular vote; therefore, Choice *B* is incorrect. Peter Cooper garnered significantly more votes than Green Clay Smith, so Choice *C* is incorrect.

22. A: The power to regulate immigration is exclusive to the federal government, so Choice *A* is the correct answer. The powers to regulate local government and implement welfare programs are reserved to the states, so Choices *B* and *C* are incorrect. Both the federal and state governments enjoy the power to levy taxes; therefore, Choice *D* is incorrect.

23. D: The European system's large-scale production of crops and livestock produced a food surplus that sustained permanent settlements and centralized government. So, Choice *D* is the correct answer. The European colonies didn't trade agriculture for military aid (Choice *A*); agriculture didn't lead to military technological advancements (Choice *B*); and the American South didn't urbanize for several centuries (Choice *C*).

24. A: The Indian Removal Acts weren't passed until the Andrew Jackson administration; so, Choice *A* is the correct answer. The question is asking what was NOT a major cause of the American Revolution. Choice *B*, the Proclamation of 1763, angered colonists by prohibiting colonial expansion west of the Appalachian Mountains. Likewise, the Quebec Act and Townshend Acts (Choices *C* and *D*) increased resentment. The Quebec Act granted rights to French Canadians. At the same time, Great Britain passed a series of laws known as the Townsend Acts to increase taxes in the Thirteen Colonies.

25. D: From 1786 to 1787, Revolutionary War veteran Daniel Shays led an armed insurrection in western Massachusetts, and the government's inability to quash the rebellion exposed the Articles of Confederation's flaws. Thus, Choice *D* is the correct answer. The Federalist Papers, Choice *A*, were published during the ratification process, and, at that time, the Articles of Confederation was widely considered to be untenable. The question was what form of government would replace it. John Brown's raid at Harper's Ferry increased regional tension before the Civil War, and President George Washington's suppression of the Whiskey Rebellion demonstrated the strength of the US Constitution, making both Choices *B* and *C* incorrect.

26. B: Hamilton is trying to convince the audience that having judges hold their positions based on good behavior is a practical way to avoid corruption. Choice *A* is incorrect because although he mentions the condition of good behavior as a barrier to despotism, he does not discuss it as a practice in the states. Choice *C* is incorrect because the author does not argue that the audience should vote based on judges' behavior, but rather that good behavior should be the condition for holding their office. Choice *D* is not represented in the passage, so it is incorrect.

Subtest II: Science

1. A: During digestion, complex food molecules are broken down into smaller molecules so that nutrients can be isolated and absorbed by the body. Absorption, Choice *B*, is when vitamins, electrolytes, organic molecules, and water are absorbed by the digestive epithelium. Compaction, Choice *C*, occurs when waste products are dehydrated and compacted. Ingestion, Choice *D*, is when food and liquids first enter the body through the mouth.

2. B: Neuroglia are cells that protect delicate neurons by making a frame around them. Neurons are responsible for transferring and processing information between the brain and other parts of the body; therefore, Choices *A* and *C* are incorrect. They also help to maintain a homeostatic environment around the neurons.

326

3. B: The elements are arranged such that the elements in columns have similar chemical properties, such as appearance and reactivity. Each element has a unique atomic number, not the same one, so Choice *A* is incorrect. Elements are arranged in rows, not columns, with similar electron valence configurations, so Choice *C* is incorrect. Density is a physical property, not a chemical one, so elements in columns do not necessarily have the same density. Furthermore, the density of an element depends on the state it is in.

4. C: The pH scale goes from 0 to 14. A neutral solution falls right in the middle of the scale at 7. Choice *A*, a value of 13, indicates a strong base. Choice *B*, a value of 8, indicates a solution that is weakly basic. Choice *D*, a value of 0, indicates a strong acid.

5. A: Monosaccharides are the simplest sugars that make up carbohydrates. They are important for cellular respiration. Fatty acids, Choice *B*, make up lipids. Polysaccharides, Choice *C*, are larger molecules with repeating monosaccharide units. Amino acids, Choice *D*, are the building blocks of proteins.

6. D: Nucleic acids include DNA and RNA, which are strands of nucleotides that contain genetic information. Carbohydrates, Choice *A*, are made up of sugars that provide energy to the body. Lipids, Choice *B*, are hydrocarbon chains that make up fats. Proteins, Choice *C*, are made up of amino acids that help with many functions for maintaining life.

7. B: Genes are the primary unit of inheritance between generations of an organism. Humans each have 23 pairs of chromosomes, Choice *A*, and each chromosome contains hundreds to thousands of genes. Genes each control a specific trait of the organism. Gametes, Choice *C*, are the reproductive cells that contain all of the genetic information of an individual. Atoms, Choice *D*, are the small units that make up all substances.

8. C: Atoms are considered neutral when the number of protons and electrons is equal; therefore, Choice *C* is correct. Protons carry a positive charge, and electrons carry a negative charge. When they are equal in number, their charges cancel out, and the atom is neutral. If there are more electrons than protons, or vice versa, the atom has an electric charge and is termed an ion. Neutrons do not have a charge and do not affect the electric charge of an atom.

9. A: Physical properties of substances are those that can be observed without changing the substances' chemical composition, such as odor, color, density, and hardness. Reactivity, flammability, and toxicity are all chemical properties of substances; therefore, Choices *B, C,* and *D* are all incorrect. They describe the way in which a substance may change into a different substance. They cannot be observed without chemically changing the substance.

10. B: Solids have molecules that are packed together tightly and cannot move within their substance. Crystalline solids have atoms or molecules that are arranged symmetrically, making all the bonds of even strength. When they are broken, they break along a plane of molecules, creating a straight edge, making Choice *B* correct. Amorphous solids do not have the symmetrical makeup of crystalline solids, so they do not break evenly; thus, Choice *D* is wrong. Gases and liquids both have molecules that move around freely.

11. A: Chemical reactions are processes that involve the changing of one set of substances to a different set of substances. In order to accomplish this, the bonds between the atoms in the molecules of the original substances need to be broken. The atoms are rearranged, and new bonds are formed to make the new set of substances. Combination reactions involve two or more reactants becoming one product. Decomposition reactions involve one reactant becoming two or more products. Combustion reactions involve the use of oxygen as a reactant and generally include the burning of a substance. Choices *B, C,* and *D* are not discussed as specific reaction types.

12. B: The equation for calculating acceleration is:

$$a = \frac{\Delta v}{\Delta t} = \frac{v_f - v_i}{\Delta t}$$

In this case, $V_f = 40$ m/s, $V_i = 20$ m/s, and $\Delta t = 20$ s. Plugging in the numbers gives an acceleration rate of 1 m/s^2, Choice *B*.

13. C: If an object is moving in a negative direction, it has a negative velocity. If the velocity is increasing in that negative direction, it is becoming increasingly more negative and would therefore have a negative acceleration. In Choice *A*, the object would have a positive acceleration. Acceleration is zero in both Choices *B* and *D* because the velocity of the object is not changing.

14. D: The gastrointestinal system consists of the stomach and intestines, which help process food and liquid so that the body can absorb nutrients for fuel. The respiratory system is involved with the exchange of oxygen and carbon dioxide between the air and blood, making Choice *A* incorrect. The immune system helps the body fight against pathogens and diseases, making Choice *B* incorrect. The genitourinary system helps the body to excrete waste.

15. B: Choice *B* correctly calculates the relative percentage of Venus' mass as compared to Earth's mass by utilizing the following:

$$mass\ of\ Venus = x\% \times Earth's\ mass$$

$$4.87 = x\% \times 5.97$$

$$x = 81.6\%$$

Choice *A* does not move the decimal correctly to convert to a percent; Choice *C* reverses the values for the mass of Venus and the mass of Earth in the calculations; and Choice *D* reverses the values for the mass of Venus and the mass of Earth in the calculations, and it also does not move the decimal correctly to convert to a percent.

16. A: Not all planets in the solar system have moons, so Choice *A* would not be a cause for variation in the gravity of a planet. Choices *B*, *C*, and *D* all have to do with characteristics that could potentially influence a gravitational pull on a planet.

17. B: Choice *B* is the only option that correctly calculates the average orbit, in days, using the following:

$$\frac{\Sigma\ orbits}{number\ of\ values} = \frac{106,831.9}{8} = 13,354\ days$$

Choice *A* is the orbit of Earth, Choice *C* is an incorrect calculation of the average, and Choice *D* is the orbit of Neptune.

18. C: Choice *C* is the closest at 41.4 million kilometers apart, while Choice *B* is next closest at 50.3 million kilometers apart. Next is Choice *A* at 57.9 million kilometers apart, and the furthest is Choice *D* at 78.3 million kilometers apart.

19. C: Magnets follow the same rules of charge as other items. Positive and negative poles attract each other. Two poles with the same charge, positive or negative, would repel each other; therefore, Choices *A* and *B* are incorrect. Although circular magnets do not have ends, they still have poles and follow the same rules of charge. So, circular positive magnets would repel each other, making Choice *D* incorrect.

20. D: A strong base dissociates completely and forms the anion OH^-. All bases include a hydroxide group (OH) in their formula, as in Choice *D*, but not all basic compounds will dissociate completely; only strong bases dissociate completely into ions. Choices *A*, *B*, and *C* all represent strong acids and have a hydrogen atom, which is always present in acidic compounds.

21. B: The inner core is solid, while the outer core is molten. The inner and outer core are both made up of the same elements (iron and nickel), both are extremely hot, and both are inaccessible to humans.

22. D: Friction refers to any force that works opposite to an initial force, typically to slow down or stop the initial force. In this example, the brakes are working in the opposite direction from the way the wheels are rolling. Pulling a rubber band, jumping, and throwing a ball are adding more force to an event rather than working in the opposite manner.

23. D: Condensation refers to the process of a gas becoming a liquid. For example, surface water on blades of grass evaporates when ground and surface temperatures are warmer in the daytime; as nighttime temperatures cool, the water vapor condenses into droplets. Melting is the process of turning a solid into a liquid. Vaporization is the process of turning a liquid into a gas. Sublimation is the process of turning a solid into a gas.

24. A: A homogenous mixture refers to any substance composed of two or more elements; distilled water is the purest type of water, consisting of just hydrogen and oxygen atoms. These elements can be metal or nonmetal in nature. Homogenous mixtures cannot be perceived to have various components within them with the five senses. Mixtures that can be perceived to have multiple components are known as heterogeneous mixtures. Other types of water, such as tidal pool water and deep ocean water, will contain compounds such as salt or sea debris. Sand is also made up of various materials, such as rocks and shells.

25. D: The inner core of the Earth is a solid sphere made of nickel and iron, and it is approximately 760 miles long. Scientists believe that while the Earth initially formed as a molten, gaseous ball, it cooled down and its four main layers were created. While the outer three layers are made of a variety of elements and consist of different forms of matter, the inner core is very hot, yet solid.

26. C: Plate tectonics refers to a scientific theory that describes the Earth's crust as consisting of numerous plates that shift against one another. The tremendous friction and pressure that consequently take place result in earthquakes (as plates violently slide against or away from one another) or contribute to the formation of mountain ranges (as plates push into one another and create elevation where they meet). Underground bodies of water, lunar cycles, and atmospheric changes do not directly influence earthquakes or mountain formation, making Choices *A*, *B*, and *D* incorrect.

Subtest II: Mathematics

1. A: A product is found by multiplication. Multiplying two fractions together is easier when common factors are canceled first to avoid working with larger numbers:

$$\frac{5}{14} \times \frac{7}{20} = \frac{5}{2 \times 7} \times \frac{7}{5 \times 4}$$

$$\frac{1}{2} \times \frac{1}{4} = \frac{1}{8}$$

2. A: First, the distributive property must be used on the left side. This results in:

$$3x + 6 = 14x - 5$$

The addition principle is then used to add 5 to both sides:

$$3x + 6 + 5 = 14x - 5 + 5$$

$$3x + 11 = 14x$$

Then, subtract $3x$ from both sides:

$$3x - 3x + 11 = 14x - 3x$$

$$11 = 11x$$

Finally, the multiplication principle is used to divide each side by 11:

$$\frac{11}{11} = \frac{11x}{11}$$

$$1 = x$$

3. D: Division is completed by multiplying by the reciprocal. Therefore:

$$24 \div \frac{8}{5} = \frac{24}{1} \times \frac{5}{8}$$

Multiplying two fractions together is easier when common factors are canceled first to avoid working with larger numbers:

$$\frac{3 \times 8}{1} \times \frac{5}{8} = \frac{3}{1} \times \frac{5}{1} = \frac{15}{1} = 15$$

4. B: The distributive property is used on both sides to obtain:

$$4x + 20 + 6 = 4x + 6$$

Then, like terms are collected on the left, resulting in:

$$4x + 26 = 4x + 6$$

Next, the addition principle is used to subtract $4x$ from both sides:

$$4x - 4x + 26 = 4x - 4x + 6$$

$$26 = 6$$

This results in the false statement $26 = 6$. Therefore, there is no solution.

5. C: Common denominators must be used to subtract fractions. Remember that in order to find the least common denominator, the least common multiple of both of the denominators must be determined. The smallest multiple that 24 and 14 share is 168, which is 24×7 and 14×12. This means that the LCD is 168, so each fraction must be converted to have 168 as the denominator.

$$\frac{5}{24} - \frac{5}{14} = \frac{5}{24} \times \frac{7}{7} - \frac{5}{14} \times \frac{12}{12}$$

$$\frac{35}{168} - \frac{60}{168} = -\frac{25}{168}$$

6. C: The correct mathematical statement is the one in which the smaller of the two numbers is on the "less than" side of the inequality symbol. The correct statement is Choice C, $\frac{1}{3} > -\frac{4}{3}$, which can also be written as $-\frac{4}{3} < \frac{1}{3}$.

7. D: The median is the value in the middle of a data set. In the set of 11, 12, 12, 13, 15, 16, and 19 seconds, the value in the middle is 13 seconds, making it the median. Twelve seconds represents the mode, as it is the value that occurs the most. Fourteen seconds represents the mean, as it is the sum of all seven listed times divided by seven.

8. A: Rounding can be used to find the best approximation. All of the values can be rounded to the nearest thousand. 15,412 SUVs can be rounded to 15,000. 25,815 station wagons can be rounded to 26,000. 50,412 sedans can be rounded to 50,000. 8,123 trucks can be rounded to 8,000. Finally, 18,312 hybrids can be rounded to 18,000. The sum of the rounded values is 117,000, which is closest to 120,000.

9. D: There are 52 weeks in a year, which can be rounded down to about 50 weeks. The family spends $105 on groceries each week, which can be rounded down to about $100. Therefore, the family's annual grocery bill is approximately $100 a week for 50 weeks, which is found through the product:

$$50 \times \$100 = \$5,000$$

10. C: This problem involves ratios and proportions. If 12 packets are needed for every 5 people, this statement is equivalent to the ratio $\frac{12}{5}$. The unknown amount x is the number of ketchup packets needed for 60 people. The proportion $\frac{12}{5} = \frac{x}{60}$ must be solved. Cross-multiply to obtain $12 \times 60 = 5x$. Therefore, $720 = 5x$. Divide each side by 5 to obtain $x = 144$.

11. D: There were 48 total bags of apples sold. If 9 bags were Granny Smith and the rest were Red Delicious, then $48 - 9 = 39$ bags were Red Delicious. Therefore, the ratio of Granny Smith to Red Delicious is 9:39.

12. B: The average rate of change is found by calculating the difference in dollars over the elapsed time. Therefore, the rate of change is equal to ($4,900 - $4,000) ÷ 3 months, which is equal to $900 ÷ 3, or $300 per month.

13. B: The bar graph shows how many men and women prefer each genre of movies. The dark gray bars represent the number of women, while the light gray bars represent the number of men. The light gray bars are higher and represent more men than women for the genres of comedy and action.

14. B: A line graph represents continuous change over time. The line on the graph is continuous and not broken, as on a scatter plot. A bar graph may show change, but it isn't necessarily continuous over time. A pie graph is better for representing percentages of a whole. Histograms are best used in grouping sets of data in bins to show the frequency of a certain variable.

15. A: The area of the shaded region is calculated in a few steps. First, the area of the rectangle is found using the formula:

$$A = length \times width = 6\,\text{m} \times 2\,\text{m} = 12\,\text{m}^2$$

Second, the area of the triangle is found using the formula:

$$A = \frac{1}{2} \times base \times height = \frac{1}{2} \times 3\,\text{m} \times 2\,\text{m} = 3\,\text{m}^2$$

The last step is to take the rectangle area and subtract the triangle area. The area of the shaded region is:

$$A = 12\,\text{m}^2 - 3\,\text{m}^2 = 9\,\text{m}^2$$

16. D: The volume for a cylinder is found by using the formula:

$$V = \pi r^2 h = \pi(2\,\text{in})^2 \times 3.5\,\text{in} = 43.96\,\text{in}^3$$

17. C: There are 0.006 kiloliters in 6 liters because 1 liter is 0.001 kiloliters. The conversion comes from the metric prefix, *kilo-*, which has a value of 1,000. Thus, 1 kiloliter is 1,000 liters, and 1 liter is 0.001 kiloliters.

18. A: Surface area is a type of area, which means it is measured in square units. Cubic units are used to describe volume, which has three dimensions multiplied by one another. Quartic units describe measurements multiplied in four dimensions.

19. A: A vertical line has the same x-value for any point on the line. Other points on the line would be $(1, 3)$, $(1, 5)$, $(1, 9)$, etc. Mathematically, this is written as $x = 1$. A vertical line is always of the form $x = a$ for some constant a.

20. D: The area for a rectangle is found by multiplying the length by the width. The area is also measured in square units, so the correct answer is Choice *D*. The number 26 in Choice *A* is incorrect because it is the perimeter. Choice *B* is incorrect because the answer must be in centimeters squared. The number 13 in Choice *C* is incorrect because it is the sum of the two dimensions rather than the product of them.

21. C: There are approximately 11 pounds in 5 kilograms because 1 kilogram is approximately 2.2 pounds (around 2.2046226). Multiplying 5 kilograms by 2.2 gives 11 pounds; while not exact, 11 pounds is the closest answer provided.

22. B: Look on the horizontal axis to find 3:00 p.m. Move up from 3:00 p.m. to reach the dot on the graph. Move horizontally to the left to the vertical axis to between 20 and 25; the best answer choice is 22. The answer of 25 is too high above the projected time on the graph, and the answers of 20 and 16 degrees are too low.

23. C: The Pythagorean theorem can be used to find the missing length x because it is a right triangle. The theorem states that $6^2 + 8^2 = x^2$, which simplifies into $100 = x^2$. Taking the positive square root of both sides results in the missing value $x = 10$.

24. B: The goal is to first isolate the variable. The fractions can easily be cleared by multiplying the entire inequality by 5:

$$(7 - \frac{4}{5x})(5) < \left(\frac{3}{5}\right)(5)$$

$$35 - 4x < 3$$

Then, subtract 35 from both sides and divide by -4:

$$35 - 35 - 4x < 3 - 35$$

$$\frac{-4x}{-4} < \frac{-32}{-4}$$

$$x > 8$$

Notice the inequality symbol has been flipped because both sides were divided by a negative number. The solution set, all real numbers greater than 8, is written in interval notation as $(8, \infty)$. A parenthesis shows that 8 is not included in the solution set.

25. D: This system can be solved using the method of substitution. Start by solving for y in the first equation:

$$2x + y = 14$$

$$2x - 2x + y = 14 - 2x$$

$$y = 14 - 2x$$

Next, plug this into the second equation and simplify:

$$4x + 2(14 - 2x) = -28$$

$$4x + 28 - 4x = -28$$

$$28 = -28$$

This is an untrue statement, so this system has no solution because no x-value will satisfy the system.

26. B: There are two dice rolls that are larger than 4 on a six-sided die: 5 and 6. There are six possible outcomes on a six-sided die. Therefore, the probability of rolling a 5 or a 6 is $\frac{2}{6} = \frac{1}{3}$.

Subtest III: Physical Education

1. C: Choice *C* is correct because it empowers the student to increase the frequency of her workouts independently. Choices *A* and *B* do not support the individual student's goal, while Choice *D* focuses on intensity, not frequency.

2. B: Choice *B* is correct because an adolescent's self-image is best improved through accomplishing personal goals. The most important development is in the student's mind, not their body. Choice *A* makes this mistake, while Choice *C* does not support the entire class of students. Choice *D* is an accurate statement, but it does not focus on the student's self-image.

3. A: Choice *A* is correct because a short, frequent period of jogging can improve cardiorespiratory endurance over time but will have little impact on muscular endurance (Choice *B*). While the exercise is frequent, Choice *C* is incorrect because the FITT principle helps implement exercises to improve the components of fitness. Daily jogging will contribute to improving body composition (Choice *D*) but does so as part of a holistic program of physical education.

4. D: Only Choice *D* describes a set of anaerobic exercises because the other choices include a significant cardiorespiratory element. Basketball, cheerleading, and sprint intervals are each aerobic forms of exercise in which frequent motion increases respiration, sending oxygen to the muscles to improve power generation and endurance.

5. D: Choice *D* is correct because type 1 diabetes is believed to develop primarily due to genetic factors, while type 2 diabetes is a risk factor for obesity. Living a sedentary lifestyle increases the individual's risk of obesity, which in turn increases their risk for various illnesses, such as heart disease and high blood pressure.

6. B: The coach is suggesting Choice *B*, running for a longer time each day, to improve the girl's cardiorespiratory endurance and muscular endurance over several weeks. Choices *A* and *C* each identify an incorrect portion of the FITT principle. In particular, intensity is incorrect because a longer workout isn't necessarily more difficult; if the coach had suggested the girl begin running a new route with more hills, that would increase the exercise's intensity. Choice *D* misidentifies the components of physical fitness with the principles for assigning appropriate exercises.

7. C: Choice *C* is the best fit because an 11-year-old boy will be most engaged in physical activity through age-appropriate games, sports, or other activities. The boy will have less motivation to do repetitive gym exercises. In addition, Choice *C* presents a more holistic approach by using activities that target multiple areas of the body, allowing others to rest. Choice *A* lacks appropriate rest time for a child beginning a physical fitness program. Changing one's diet (Choice *B*) is a helpful component, but a child who requires this program likely needs outside support to engage in sufficient physical activity. The activity in Choice *D* is not scheduled frequently enough (although incorporating parents will support the program's success).

8. B: Choice *B* is correct because practice throwing and catching a ball is one of several types of manipulative skills. Choice *A* is one of the concepts of movement, not a physical skill (an act a person can perform). Choices *C* mistakes standing still for practicing a specific skill, while Choice *D* correctly identifies the skill but not the skill's category.

9. A: In Choice *A*, the zigzagging motion practices changes in speed as the students go back and forth across the course. Choices *B* and *D* don't describe activities that involve the changes in motion, direction, or force that are typical of activities designed to practice controlling the student's effort. Learning to swim (Choice *C*) may well include elements of effort, but this statement in and of itself doesn't provide enough information about how the student is learning to swim to provide a clear answer.

10. C: Dribbling a basketball (Choice *C*) is correct because it requires manipulating an independent object. Choice *D* involves the use of an object (the playground) but does not require hand manipulation of that object. Choices *A* and *B* both describe locomotor skills, not manipulative skills.

11. B: Choice *B* is correct because the leg movements, torso twist, and follow-through motion of the arm all use the principles of biomechanics to improve the power and accuracy of a baseball throw. Choices *A* and *C* each describe a non-locomotor skill with little need for momentum. Choice *D,* catching a football, likewise does not typically incorporate additional movements that use momentum to improve catching performance.

12. D: Choice *D* is correct because a layup is an advanced composite of multiple basic movement skills. The final step requires hopping on one foot. Each other choice requires movement and balance, like hopping, but does not directly build upon the skill of hopping on one foot to complete the listed skill correctly.

13. A: Freeze tag (Choice *A*) is an example of a game that children often learn from other children without adult instruction. While Choice *B,* Ultimate Frisbee, is a game children may enjoy, they typically learn it through structured activities. Likewise, racing might be considered a traditional childhood activity, but Choice *D's* 100-meter sprint is a specific event devised for athletic purposes. Finally, Choice *C,* hiking, lacks the spontaneity and interpersonal elements required to be a childhood game.

Subtest III: Human Development

1. C: Choice *C* represents egocentrism because the child assumes their audience shares the same information and desires as they do. While Choice *B* also demonstrates egocentrism, this expression of the concept is typical of adolescence. Choices *A* and *D* are statements many children might make, but Choice *A* expresses selfishness and Choice *D* a flawed understanding of temporal causality.

2. D: Choice *D* is correct because the student claims the election was unfair to herself, not that it violated an abstract notion of fairness or justice. Choice *C* is in error because it assumes the student is incapable of abstract thought due to her age; the age at which an individual begins to use formal operations is variable, not static. Choice *A* doesn't pay enough attention to how the statement focuses on the speaker's election outcome. Meanwhile, Choice *B* misunderstands that children who use concrete operations do not require the person discussed to be present.

3. A: In Choice *A,* the child is sorting objects of his choice—in this case, trading cards—in a way that exercises the skill of alphabetization. Although Choice *D* exhibits the collecting practices typical of middle childhood, the child isn't organizing the objects according to similar or dissimilar properties. Choices *B* and *C* are both common behaviors at this age, but Choice *B* practices reversibility, while Choice *C* is more strongly connected to social development.

4. D: The described tests and behaviors illustrate qualities of the student's memory and preferences, but they do not provide sufficient diagnostic information for the teacher to draw conclusions. Choice *A* mistakes her preference for musical, creative activities for demonstrated competence. Likewise, Choice *B* suggests that her enjoyment of games correlates with effectively putting lessons to work in the social sphere (practical intelligence). Choice *C* misidentifies the student's poor test scores as a struggle with practical intelligence rather than difficulty with memory.

5. B: Choice *B* is correct because the boy's attitude reflects respect toward specific individuals in his life rather than a general principle of respectfulness to others. Choices *A* and *D* each demonstrate preconventional morality because the student is concerned with negative consequences rather than whether or not the choice was moral. This is also the flaw in Choice *C;* even though that student is considering objects beyond his social environment, his attitude still reflects a consequence-focused judgment process.

6. A: Teachers and social workers must diagnose the situation before engaging one or more systems of support, making Choice *A* the best option. Choice *D* may be an appropriate support after less intrusive measures have been employed. Choice *C* neglects the important work children do practicing social skills during recess. While Choice *B* may improve the student's reading skills with one-on-one attention, advocating financial expenditure neglects to consider potential socioeconomic causes for the student's academic difficulties.

7. C: The underarm hair in Choice *C* indicates physical changes in the student's body. Choices *B* and *D* are each social behaviors which may manifest alongside hormonal and physical changes associated with puberty. However, since

334

those behaviors are not universal to all adolescents going through puberty—and may appear prior to the physical change of puberty—they aren't good evidence for pubescence. The growth spurt in Choice *A* is a possible indicator of puberty, but without corroborating evidence, this sign isn't distinct enough to draw a conclusion.

8. A: Choice *A* is most likely due to the student's overly vigilant and anxious behavior and their aversion to touch. It is still important that the teacher acquires more information regarding this suspicion before reporting it. Choices *B* and *C* both reflect possible abuse, but in each case, the teacher would expect increased attention-seeking behavior rather than avoidance and anxiety. Choice *D* is also a valid possibility, but sleep deprivation doesn't adequately explain the aversion to physical touch.

9. A: Choice *A*, proximity to speaker, correctly identifies pragmatics as the nonverbal elements used when communicating with language. Choices *B* and *C* instead describe language development milestones. While Choice *D* does describe a pragmatic use of slang by the speaker, this distractor does not use the definition of pragmatics within the context of language development.

10. D: By focusing on contemporary musicians the students listen to (and likely idolize), the teacher makes effective use of the adolescent tendency to seek novel and individual interests that set them apart from adults in their life. Choice *B* overestimates the universality of musical heritage. Meanwhile, Choices *A* and *C* provide good techniques for motivating younger students, who are often inspired by direct experiences rather than recordings and other indirect experiences.

11. B: Severe malnutrition forces the child's body to focus nutrition on survival rather than physical development. Choice *B* correctly highlights one risk of delayed development due to malnutrition. Choices *A* and *C* are incorrect because malnutrition has little direct impact on the development of social disorders such as ASD. While improving nutrition as soon as possible is important for the child's developmental health, Choice *D* is incorrect because starting academic study is not an age-appropriate response.

12. C: The girl in Choice *C* fails to use practical intelligence effectively because she struggles to change behavior in response to her environment. The children in Choices *A* and *D* are experiencing learning difficulties. In Choice *A*, the girl seems to have memorized street names in her neighborhood rather than actually reading the signs. This is common when children are first learning to read. Likewise, the boy in Choice *D* displays effective memory, but struggles in a developmentally appropriate way to put his knowledge to use. The teenager in Choice *B* uses practical intelligence effectively; asking not to be called on due to struggles with anxiety and self-esteem concomitant with abuse is an appropriate support to help the student to feel comfortable in the classroom.

13. D: The earliest age at which a child can be diagnosed with ASD is generally around three years old. However, some research indicates that delayed language and communication development can provide warning signs to the parents at a younger age. Studies show that, like most communication or behavioral disorders, early diagnosis and support for children with ASD improves academic and vocational outcomes throughout the individual's life. Choices *A* and *B* are incorrect because they focus on the child's social life, which is an external symptom of their internal challenges with language and cognition. Choice *C* is incorrect because the longer that teachers and mental health professionals wait before implementing supports, the less likely it is that the supports will provide long-term benefits.

Subtest III: Visual and Performing Arts

1. D: Choice *D* is correct because dance inspiration can come from any source with any degree of structure. Choices *A*, *B*, and *C* are all valid inspiration sources.

2. C: Choice *C* is correct because the body's directional weight is the definition of poise. Choices *A*, *B*, and *D* can all contribute to poise, but they are not the same thing as poise.

3. A: Choice *A* is correct because it asks for a judgment, which is not the purpose of analyzing a dance. Choices *B* and *D* are helpful technical questions, and Choice *C*, while similar to Choice *A* at first sight, asks a less objective question that ultimately serves to help you better understand your own tastes.

4. D: Choice *D* is correct because music octaves repeat after the G note. Choices *A*, *B*, and *C* are incorrectly structured.

5. D: Choice *D* is correct because the bottom number on a time signature indicates what kind of note is given a single beat. Choice *A* is the top number on a time signature, which indicates how many beats are in a measure; Choices *B* and *C* have nothing to do with a time signature.

6. C: Choice *C* is correct because you can identify the key of a song as the note one degree above the final sharp in a key signature, and the third sharp in a key signature lands on a G space. Choices *A*, *B*, and *D* are the keys for four sharps, one sharp, and six sharps, respectively.

7. D: Choice *D* is correct because cultural influence is almost entirely inseparable from the artistic creative process. Choices *A*, *B*, and *C* are always incredibly likely to be influenced by the culture from which it was made.

8. B: Choice *B* is correct because falling action occurs in the latter half of a traditional plot, only followed by the ending itself. Choices *A* and *C* occur before falling action, and Choice *D* has nothing to do with written plot structure; it is simply a time for a break in the narrative.

9. C: Choice *C* is correct because the "yes, and" rule is the cornerstone of all partnered improvisation. Choices *A*, *B*, and *D* are all antithetical to the improvisational process.

10. B: Choice *B* is correct because non-representational props are more realistically possible for a student tech crew to create and are considerably less expensive for a student organization that likely puts on multiple different shows per year. Choice *A* is unrealistically expensive and potentially dangerous, depending on the prop. Choices *C* and *D* cannot be correct by virtue of Choice *B* being correct.

11. D: Choice *D* is correct because Choices *A*, *B*, and *C* all render charcoal more brittle and liable to break during use. Oil does not immediately degrade the quality of a piece of art charcoal, though it may impact the drawing surface.

12. B: Choice *B* is correct because sharpness pertains to line quality, not color. Choices *A*, *C*, and *D* are the three qualities that comprise a color.

13. C: Choice *C* is correct because, while educational art can also serve other purposes, purely educational art is often used for graphics and is featured in places such as classrooms and doctors' offices rather than in museums. Choices *A*, *B*, and *D* are all far more likely to be seen on the walls of a museum.

Practice Tests #2 and #3

The 2nd and 3rd practice tests are available as digital tests along with the first test. Go to the following URL or scan the code below.

apexprep.com/bonus/cset.

After you go to the website, you will have to create an account and register as a "new user" and verify your email address before you begin.

If you need any help, please contact us at info@apexprep.com.

Greetings!

First, we would like to give a huge "thank you" for choosing us and this study guide for your **CSET Multiple Subjects exam**. We hope that it will lead you to success on this exam and for your years to come.

Our team has tried to make your preparations as thorough as possible by covering all of the topics you should be expected to know. In addition, our writers attempted to create practice questions identical to what you will see on the day of your actual test. We have also included many test-taking strategies to help you learn the material, maintain the knowledge, and take the test with confidence.

We strive for excellence in our products, and if you have any comments or concerns over the quality of something in this study guide, please send us an email so that we may improve.

As you continue forward in life, we would like to remain alongside you with other books and study guides in our library. We are continually producing and updating study guides in several different subjects. If you are looking for something in particular, all of our products are available on Amazon. You may also send us an email!

Sincerely,
APEX Test Prep
info@apexprep.com

FREE

Free Study Tips Videos/DVD

In addition to this guide, we have created a FREE set of videos with helpful study tips. **These FREE videos provide you with top-notch tips to conquer your exam and reach your goals.**

Our simple request is that you give us feedback about the book in exchange for these strategy-packed videos. We would love to hear what you thought about the book, whether positive, negative, or neutral. It is our #1 goal to provide you with quality products and customer service.

To receive your **FREE Study Tips Videos**, scan the QR code or email freevideos@apexprep.com. Please put "FREE Videos" in the subject line and include the following in the email:

   a. The title of the book

   b. Your rating of the book on a scale of 1-5, with 5 being the highest score

   c. Any thoughts or feedback about the book

Thank you!

33588956R00190